Revolutionary England, c. 1630–c. 1660

Revolutionary England, c. 1630–c. 1660 presents a series of cutting-edge studies by established and rising authorities in the field, providing a powerful discourse on the events, crises and changes that electrified mid-seventeenth-century England.

The descent into civil war, killing of a king, creation of a republic, fits of military government, written constitutions, dominance of Oliver Cromwell, abolition of a state church, eruption into major European conflicts, conquest of Scotland and Ireland, and efflorescence of powerfully articulated political thinking dazzled, bewildered or appalled contemporaries, and has fascinated scholars ever since. Compiled in honour of one of the most respected scholars of early modern England, Clive Holmes, this volume considers themes that both reflect Clive's own concerns and stand at the centre of current approaches to seventeenth-century studies: the relations between language, ideas, and political actors; the limitations of central government; and the powerful role of religious belief in public affairs.

Centred chronologically on Clive Holmes' seventeenth-century heartland, this is a focused volume of essays produced by leading scholars inspired by his scholarship and teaching. Investigative and analytical, it is valuable reading for all scholars of England's revolutionary period.

George Southcombe is Director of the Sarah Lawrence Programme at Wadham College, Oxford, where he is also College Lecturer in History. His publications include *English Nonconformist Poetry, 1660–1700* (editor, 3 volumes, 2012) and *Restoration Politics, Religion and Culture: Britain and Ireland, 1660–1714* (2010, with Grant Tapsell).

Grant Tapsell is Fellow and Tutor in History, Lady Margaret Hall, Oxford. His publications include *The Nature of the English Revolution Revisited* (edited with Stephen Taylor, 2013); *The Later Stuart Church, 1660–1714* (editor, 2012) and *The Personal Rule of Charles II, 1681–85* (2007).

Figure 0.1 Clive Holmes.
Photograph by Felicity Heal.

Revolutionary England, c. 1630–c. 1660

Essays for Clive Holmes

Edited by George Southcombe and Grant Tapsell

LONDON AND NEW YORK

First published 2017
by Routledge
2 Park Square, Milton Park, Abingdon, Oxon OX14 4RN

and by Routledge
711 Third Avenue, New York, NY 10017

Routledge is an imprint of the Taylor & Francis Group, an informa business

© 2017 selection and editorial matter, George Southcombe and Grant Tapsell; individual chapters, the contributors

The right of the editors to be identified as the authors of the editorial material, and of the authors for their individual chapters, has been asserted in accordance with sections 77 and 78 of the Copyright, Designs and Patents Act 1988.

All rights reserved. No part of this book may be reprinted or reproduced or utilised in any form or by any electronic, mechanical, or other means, now known or hereafter invented, including photocopying and recording, or in any information storage or retrieval system, without permission in writing from the publishers.

Trademark notice: Product or corporate names may be trademarks or registered trademarks, and are used only for identification and explanation without intent to infringe.

British Library Cataloguing in Publication Data
A catalogue record for this book is available from the British Library

Library of Congress Cataloging in Publication Data
Names: Southcombe, George, 1978– editor, author. | Tapsell, Grant, editor, author. | Holmes, Clive, honoree.
Title: Revolutionary England, c.1630–c.1660 : essays for Clive Holmes / edited by George Southcombe and Grant Tapsell.
Description: Abingdon, Oxon : Routledge, 2016. | Includes bibliographical references and index.
Identifiers: LCCN 2016035288 | ISBN 9781472438379 (hardback : alk. paper) | ISBN 9781315606316 (ebook)
Subjects: LCSH: Great Britain—Politics and government—1603–1714. | Great Britain—History—Stuarts, 1603–1714.
Classification: LCC DA375 .R49 2016 | DDC 942.06/3—dc23
LC record available at https://lccn.loc.gov/2016035288

ISBN: 978-1-4724-3837-9 (hbk)
ISBN: 978-1-315-60631-6 (ebk)

Typeset in Bembo
by Apex CoVantage, LLC

Cover image: © The Trustees of the British Museum. All rights reserved.

Contents

List of figures   vii
Acknowledgements   viii
Abbreviations   ix
Notes on contributors   xi

1 Clive Holmes and the historiography of early modern England: The quiet revolution   1
GEORGE SOUTHCOMBE AND GRANT TAPSELL

2 Policy enforcement during the Personal Rule of Charles I: The Perfect Militia, Book of Orders, and Ship Money   9
HENRIK LANGELÜDDECKE

3 Party politics in the Long Parliament, 1640–8   32
DAVID SCOTT

4 Henry Ireton and the limits of radicalism, 1647–9   55
SARAH MORTIMER

5 'Parliament', 'liberty', 'taxation', and 'property': The civil war of words in the 1640s   73
GRANT TAPSELL

6 A trader of knowledge and government: Richard Houncell and the politics of enterprise, 1648–51   92
PERRY GAUCI

7 The uses of intelligence: The case of Lord Craven, 1650–60   106
MANFRED BROD

8	The definition of treason and the offer of the crown JONATHAN FITZGIBBONS	127
9	England's 'atheisticall generation': Orthodoxy and unbelief in the revolutionary period LEIF DIXON	146
10	Thomas Ady and the politics of scepticism in Cromwellian England GEORGE SOUTHCOMBE	163
11	The demand for a free parliament, 1659–60 BLAIR WORDEN	176
12	The revolution of memory: The monuments of Westminster Abbey PETER SHERLOCK	201
13	'A pair of *Garters*': Heralds and heraldry at the Restoration ADRIAN AILES	218
14	Remembering regicides in America, 1660–1800 MATTHEW JENKINSON	235

Bibliography of the writings of Clive Holmes, 1967–2016 251
Index 255

Figures

0.1	Clive Holmes	ii
12.1	Memorial at St Margaret's Westminster erected by the Cromwell Association	202
12.2	Monument of Dudley Carleton, Viscount Dorchester (d. 1632), Westminster Abbey	206
12.3	Monument of Grace Scot (d. 1645), Westminster Abbey	207
12.4	Monument of Richard Gouland (d. 1659), cloister, Westminster Abbey	210
12.5	Monument of Edward Popham (d. 1651), Westminster Abbey	214
13.1	Seal of the Protectorate	226

Cover image: Vera effigies Illustrissimi amplissimiq[ue] Herois Oliveri Cromwelli-© The Trustees of the British Museum. All rights reserved.

Acknowledgements

This book grew out of a conference held in honour of Clive Holmes in Lady Margaret Hall, Oxford, on 10 September 2011, and we would like to thank all of the participants, the College, and particularly its then Principal Frances Lannon for what was a memorable occasion. We are grateful to Tom Gray and his colleagues at Ashgate for their work on this book and their good-humoured approach. Our individual contributors will have benefitted from different scholarly interactions, but all will want to record their thanks to the many librarians and archivists who have made their work possible. Jennifer Southcombe and Catherine Wright have provided much needed respite and laughter at key moments, and Felicity Heal has been a constantly supportive presence. Catherine Wright heroically also produced the index, for which our gratitude is profound. Our sons, George and Samuel, make everything better, not least by showing a bracing, and happy, lack of interest in their fathers' scholarly activities.

Our greatest thanks are reserved for the book's dedicatee.

Abbreviations

A&O	C.H. Firth and R.S. Rait (eds.), *Acts and Ordinances of the Interregnum* (3 vols, 1911)
AHR	*American Historical Review*
APC	Acts of the Privy Council
BL	British Library, London
Bodl.	Bodleian Library, Oxford
Burton	*Diary of Thomas Burton, Esquire . . .*, ed. J.T. Rutt (4 vols, 1828)
CCC	Mary Anne Everett Green (comp.), *Calendar of the Proceedings of the Committee for Compounding, 1643–1660* (5 vols, 1889–92)
CCSP	*Calendar of the Clarendon State Papers*, ed. O. Ogle *et al.* (5 vols, Oxford, 1869–1970)
CJ	*Journals of the House of Commons*
CP	*The Clarke Papers*, ed. C.H. Firth (4 vols, Camden Society, 1891)
CSPD	*Calendar of State Papers Domestic*
CSPV	*Calendar of State Papers Venetian*
CTB	*Calendar of Treasury Books*
EcHR	*Economic History Review*
EHR	*English Historical Review*
HJ	*Historical Journal*
HLQ	*Huntington Library Quarterly*
HMC	Historical Manuscripts Commission
HOP 1660–1690	Basil D. Henning (ed.), *History of Parliament: The House of Commons, 1660–1690* (3 vols, 1983)
JBS	*Journal of British Studies*
JEH	*Journal of Ecclesiastical History*
JMH	*Journal of Modern History*
LJ	*Journals of the House of Lords*
NS	New Style
ODNB	*Oxford Dictionary of National Biography*
OED	*Oxford English Dictionary*
P&P	*Past & Present*
PCH	*The Parliamentary or Constitutional History of England* (24 vols, 1751–62)
RO	Record Office

SP	State Papers (Domestic)
SPC	*State Papers Collected by Edward, Earl of Clarendon*, ed. R. Scrope and T. Monkhouse (3 vols, Oxford, 1767–86)
TNA	The National Archives, Kew
TRHS	*Transactions of the Royal Historical Society*
TSP	*A Collection of State Papers of John Thurloe Esq* . . ., ed. T. Birch (7 vols, 1742)
VCH	*Victoria County History*
WMQ	*William and Mary Quarterly*

All works were printed in London unless otherwise noted.

Notes on contributors

Adrian Ailes is a Principal Records Specialist at The National Archives. His publications include *The Origins of the Royal Arms of England: Their Development to 1199* (1982); 'Le développement des 'visitations' de hérauts en angleterre et au Pays de Galles 1450–1600', *Revue du Nord*, 88 (2006); and 'Ancient Precedent or Tudor Fiction? Garter King of Arms and the Pronouncements of Thomas, Duke of Clarence', in Katie Stevenson (ed.), *The Herald in Late Medieval Europe* (2009). His Oxford DPhil thesis was supervised by Clive Holmes: 'Elias Ashmole's "Heraldicall Visitacion" of Berkshire 1665–66' (2008).

Manfred Brod is an independent scholar. His publications include *The Case of Reading: Urban Governance in Troubled Times, 1640–1690* (2006); *Abingdon in Context: Small-Town Politics in Early Modern England, 1547–1688* (2010); 'A Radical Network in the English Revolution: John Pordage and His Circle, 1646–54', *EHR*, 119 (2004); and 'A Prophetess from the Vale of White Horse: Joan Vokins of West Challow', *Southern History*, 26 (2004). His Oxford DPhil thesis was supervised by Clive Holmes: 'Dissent and Dissenters in Early Modern Berkshire' (2002).

Leif Dixon is Director of Studies for History and Lecturer in Early Modern History at Regent's Park College, Oxford. His publications include *Practical Predestinarians in England, c. 1590–1640* (2014); 'Calvinist Theology and Pastoral Reality in the Reign of King James I: The Perspective of Thomas Wilson', *The Seventeenth Century*, 23 (2008); 'Richard Greenham and the Calvinist Construction of God', *JEH*, 61 (2010); and 'William Perkins, "Atheisme," and the Crises of England's Long Reformation', *JBS*, 50 (2011). His Oxford DPhil thesis was supervised by Clive Holmes: 'Predestination and Pastoral Theology: The Communication of Calvinist Doctrine, c. 1590–1640' (2006, i.e. 2007).

Jonathan Fitzgibbons is A.H. Lloyd Junior Research Fellow at Christ's College, Cambridge. His publications include *Cromwell's Head* (2008); 'Not in Any Doubtfull Dispute? Reassessing the Nomination of Richard Cromwell', *Historical Research*, 83 (2010); and 'Hereditary Succession and the Cromwellian Protectorate: The Offer of the Crown Reconsidered', *EHR*,

128 (2013). His Oxford DPhil thesis was supervised by Clive Holmes: 'The Cromwellian "Other House" and the Search for a Settlement, 1656–1659' (2010, i.e. 2011).

Perry Gauci is V.H.H. Green Fellow, Tutor in History, Lincoln College, Oxford. His publications include *Politics and Society in Great Yarmouth, 1660–1722* (1996); *The Politics of Trade: The Overseas Merchant in State and Society, 1660–1720* (2001); *Emporium of the World: The Merchants of London, 1660–1800* (2007); *William Beckford: First Prime Minister of the London Empire* (2013); as editor (with José Ignacio Martínez Ruiz), *Mercaderes Ingleses en Alicante en el Siglo XVII: Estudio y Edición de la Correspondencia Comercial de Richard Houncell & Co.* (2008); as editor, *Regulating the British Economy, 1660–1850* (2011); '"For Want of Smooth Language": Parliament as a Point of Contact in the Augustan Age', *Parliamentary History*, 17 (1998); 'Informality and Influence: The Overseas Merchant and the Livery Companies, 1660–1720', in Ian Gadd and Patrick Wallis (eds), *Guilds, Society & Economy in London 1450–1800* (2002); and 'The Clash of Interests: Commerce and the Politics of Trade in the Age of Anne', *Parliamentary History*, 28 (2009). His Oxford DPhil thesis was supervised by Clive Holmes: 'The Corporation and the Country: Great Yarmouth, 1660–1722' (1991).

Matthew Jenkinson teaches at New College School, Oxford. His publications include *Culture and Politics at the Court of Charles II, 1660–1685* (2010); 'Nathanael Vincent and Confucius's "Great Learning" in Restoration England', *Notes and Records of the Royal Society (of London)*, 60 (2006); (with Nicholas Fisher), 'Rochester and the Specter of Libertinism', *HLQ*, 70 (2007); 'John Crowne, the Restoration Court, and the "Understanding" of *Calisto*', *Court Historian*, 15 (2010); 'Preaching at the Court of Charles II: Court Sermons and the Restoration Chapel Royal', in Peter McCullough *et al.* (eds), *The Oxford Handbook of the Early Modern Sermon* (2011); and 'Preaching at the Court of James II, 1685–1688', *Court Historian*, 17 (2012). His Oxford DPhil thesis was supervised by Clive Holmes: 'The Politics of Court Culture in the Reign of Charles II, 1660–1685' (2007, i.e. 2008).

Henrik Langelüddecke teaches at Frankfurt International School. His publications include 'Law and Order in Seventeenth-Century England: The Organization of Local Administration during the Personal Rule of Charles I', *Law and History Review*, 15 (1997); '"Patchy and Spasmodic"? The Response of Justices of the Peace to Charles I's Book of Orders', *EHR*, 113 (1998); '"The Chiefest Strength and Glory of this Kingdom"': Arming and Training the "Perfect Militia" in the 1630s', *EHR*, 118 (2003); '"The Pooreste and Symplest Sorte of People"? The Selection of Parish Officers during the Personal Rule of Charles I', *Historical Research*, 80 (2002); and '"I Finde All Men & My Officers All Soe Unwilling": The Collection of Ship Money, 1635–1640', *JBS*, 46 (2007). His Oxford DPhil thesis was supervised by

Clive Holmes: 'Secular Policy Enforcement during the Personal Rule of Charles I: The Administrative Work of Parish Officers in the 1630s' (1995).

Sarah Mortimer is Student and Tutor in Modern History, Christ Church, Oxford. Her publications include *Reason and Religion in the English Revolution: The Challenge of Socinianism* (2010); as editor (with John Robertson), *The Intellectual Consequences of Religious Heterodoxy in Europe* (2012); 'Human Liberty and Human Freedom in Faustus Socinus and His Readers', *Journal of the History of Ideas*, 70 (2009); 'Exile, Apostasy and Anglicanism in the English Revolution', in Philip Major (ed.), *Literatures of Exile in the English Revolution and Its Aftermath, 1640–1690* (2010); 'Natural Law and Holy War in the English Revolution', in Charles C.W. Prior and Glenn Burgess (eds), *England's Wars of Religion, Revised* (2011); and 'Freedom, Virtue and Socinian Heterodoxy', in Quentin Skinner and Martin Van Gelderen (eds), *Freedom and the Construction of Europe* (2013). Her Oxford DPhil thesis was co-supervised by Clive Holmes: 'The Challenge of Socinianism in Mid Seventeenth-Century England' (2007).

David Scott is Senior Research Fellow at the History of Parliament Trust and Senior Research Fellow in Early Modern History at the University of Buckingham. His publications include *Leviathan: The Rise of Britain as a World Power* (2013); *Politics and War in the Three Stuart Kingdoms, 1637–49* (2004); as editor (with Keith Lindley), *The Journal of Thomas Juxon, 1644–1647* (1999); '"Hannibal at Our Gates": Loyalists and Fifth-Columnists during the Bishops' Wars – The Case of Yorkshire', *Historical Research*, 70 (1997); 'The "Northern Gentlemen", the Parliamentary Independents, and Anglo-Scottish Relations in the Long Parliament', *HJ*, 42 (1999); 'The Barwis Affair: Political Allegiance and the Scots during the British Civil Wars', *EHR*, 115 (2000); 'Motives for King-Killing', in Jason Peacey (ed.), *The Regicides and the Execution of Charles I* (2001); 'Counsel and Cabal in the King's Party, 1642–1646', in Jason McElligott and David L. Smith (eds), *Royalists and Royalism during the English Civil Wars* (2007); and 'Rethinking Royalist Politics, 1642–9', in John Adamson (ed.), *The English Civil War: Conflict and Contexts 1640–1649* (2009).

Peter Sherlock is Vice-Chancellor of the University of Divinity, Melbourne. His publications include *Monuments and Memory in Early Modern England* (2008); as editor (with Megan Cassidy-Welch), *Practices of Gender in Late Medieval and Early Modern Europe* (2008); 'Monuments, Reputation and Clerical Marriage in Reformation England: Bishop Barlow's Daughters', *Gender and History*, 16 (2004); 'Episcopal Tombs in Early Modern England', *JEH*, 55 (2004); and 'Henry VII's "Miraculum Orbis": Royal Commemoration at Westminster Abbey 1500–1700', in F.W. Kent and Charles Zika (eds), *Rituals, Images and Words. Varieties of Cultural Expression in Late Medieval and Early Modern Europe* (2005); 'The Monuments of Elizabeth Tudor and Mary

Stuart: King James and the Manipulation of Memory', *JBS*, 46 (2007); 'The Reformation of Memory in Early Modern Europe', in S. Radstone and B. Schwarz (eds.), *Memory: History, Theories, Debates* (2010). His Oxford DPhil thesis was supervised by Clive Holmes: 'Funeral Monuments: Piety, Honour and Memory in Early Modern England' (2000).

George Southcombe is Director of the Sarah Lawrence Programme at Wadham College, Oxford, where he is also College Lecturer in History. His publications include as editor, *English Nonconformist Poetry, 1660–1700* (3 vols, 2012); (with Grant Tapsell), *Restoration Politics, Religion and Culture: Britain and Ireland, 1660–1714* (2010); '"A Prophet and a Poet Both!": Nonconformist Culture and the Literary Afterlives of Robert Wild', *HLQ*, 73 (2010); 'Reading Early Modern Literature Historically', *Literature Compass*, 7 (2010); (with Anna Bayman), 'Shrews in Pamphlets and Plays', in David Wootton and Graham Holderness (eds), *Gender and Power in Shrew-Taming Narratives, 1500–1700* (2010); 'Dissent and the Restoration Church of England', in Grant Tapsell (ed.), *The Later Stuart Church, 1660–1714* (2012); and 'The Polemics of Moderation in Late Seventeenth-Century England', in Almut Suerbaum *et al.* (eds.), *Polemic: Language as Violence in Medieval and Early Modern Discourse* (2015). His Oxford DPhil thesis was supervised by Clive Holmes: 'The Responses of Nonconformists to the Restoration in England' (2005).

Grant Tapsell is Fellow and Tutor in History, Lady Margaret Hall, Oxford. His publications include *The Personal Rule of Charles II, 1681–85* (2007); (with George Southcombe), *Restoration Politics, Religion and Culture: Britain and Ireland, 1660–1714* (2010); as editor, *The Later Stuart Church, 1660–1714* (2012); as editor (with Stephen Taylor), *The Nature of the English Revolution Revisited* (2013); 'Parliament and Political Division in the Last Years of Charles II, 1681–5', *Parliamentary History*, 22 (2003); 'Laurence Hyde and the Politics of Religion in Later Stuart England', *EHR*, 125 (2010); and 'The Reluctant Chaplain: William Sancroft and the Later Stuart Church', in H. Adlington *et al.* (eds.), *Chaplains in Early Modern England: Patronage, Literature, and Religion* (2013).

Blair Worden, FBA, is Emeritus Fellow of St Edmund Hall, Oxford. His publications include *The Rump Parliament, 1648–53* (1974); as editor, Edmund Ludlow, *A Voyce from the Watch Tower, 5: 1660–1662* (1978); as editor (with Hugh Lloyd-Jones and Valerie Pearl), *History and Imagination: Essays in Honour of H.R. Trevor-Roper* (1981); as editor, *Stuart England* (1986); *The Sound of Virtue: Philip Sidney's 'Arcadia' and Elizabethan Politics* (1996); as editor (with Ian Gentles and John Morrill), *Soldiers, Writers and Statesmen of the English Revolution* (1998); *Roundhead Reputations: The English Civil Wars and the Passions of Posterity* (2001); *Literature and Politics in Cromwellian England* (2007); *The English Civil Wars 1640–1660* (2009); as editor, Marchamont Nedham, *The Excellencie of a Free State: Or, the Right Constitution of a Commonwealth* (2012); and *God's Instruments: Political Conduct in the England of Oliver Cromwell* (2012).

1 Clive Holmes and the historiography of early modern England

The quiet revolution

George Southcombe and Grant Tapsell

Clive Holmes, it has been noted on more than one occasion, asks clever questions.[1] He also asks a lot of questions. At conferences and in seminars, Clive is always among the first to interrogate the paper-giver. At the conference held in his honour, from which this collection of essays grew, he was a key participant. He has never, however, fallen into the modern academic vice of asking questions that are thinly disguised exercises in self-promotion. As many will attest, this does not necessarily mean that answering Clive's questions – acute, probing, pertinent – is a comfortable experience. Clive is himself a fluent and engaging speaker. His papers and lectures are driven by argument and, while carefully prepared, are developed orally in interaction with his audience. If he does not quite engage in the passionate extemporizing of Oliver Cromwell, his style is closer to the Lord Protector's than to the dryasdust, solemn, scripted performances that can characterize academic discourse. There is therefore ostensibly little that is quiet about Clive Holmes.

Clive as a historian, however, has not been given to making grand, iconoclastic statements. As many intelligent young men and women, let loose as graduates in the county archives in the late 1960s and early 1970s, started to invert the propositions on which the Whig historical interpretation of the seventeenth century had been based and to forge a new and vigorous 'revisionist' picture, Clive remained, in most respects, unmoved. The article for which he perhaps remains best known, 'The County Community in Stuart Historiography', launched a powerful attack on accounts that stressed the localist and particularist mentalities of the seventeenth-century political nation and provided the basis for an account in which national concerns and ideological conflict could continue to play a role in explaining the outbreak of the civil war. His later article on early Stuart parliaments, directly contrasting with the influential account provided by Conrad Russell, identified the different ideological understandings – particularly surrounding the property rights of the subject – displayed by MPs and the crown that had the potential to combust in the volatile context provided by the rule of Charles I. More recently, an implicit critique of the new British history has been offered in his resolutely Anglo-centric *Why Was Charles I Executed?*, the first chapter of which offers a tour de force of argument tracing the reasons for the collapse of Charles I's government back to Tudor processes of state development. Finally, he has resoundingly restated older accounts of the trial of Charles I, just when undergraduate essays were succumbing *en masse* to fashionable siren voices.[2] In all of these important contributions to the debates, part of Clive's work has been to remind his readers of the potency of some older accounts. In this way he has effected a quiet revolution in the historiography in a sense that was still common in the seventeenth century. He has returned the debates to something like their starting position. Lawrence Stone once called Clive and himself 'the last of the Whig historians'. It is a label Clive has accepted with some pride. One index of his success, and it is one to which he likes to point, is the tendency of others to claim that they have agreed with him all along.[3]

It is a mistake, however, simply to stress the ways in which Clive has challenged what he sees as unnecessary innovation. Both of Clive's first two monographs did much more than critique previous writings. *The Eastern Association in the English Civil War* displaced misguided religious or socio-economic explanations for the unique success of that body with one that captures 'the complex and tension-ridden dialogue' between three layers of political action: the national, the regional, and the local.[4] *Seventeenth-Century Lincolnshire* displayed a powerful awareness of the key intellectual currents in the writing of empirically grounded local history, notably evolving understandings of 'community'. Nevertheless, it was written in two parts – 'structure' and 'narrative' – with the specific intention of marrying sensitivity to local circumstances with a sense of the shaping force of national developments. Here a particular focus was kept on the lawyers, clerics, and gentry who acted as '"brokers", channelling the products of the national culture into the localities'.[5] This emphasis on brokers points in microcosm to what has perhaps been the energizing conceptual force behind Clive's most constructive contributions to historiography: the emphasis on dialogue. One of the most fruitful outcomes of this has been his reconstruction of the role played by those below the level of the gentry in shaping political developments, and his demonstration of the depth of their political acumen and understanding.[6]

Clive's work has therefore been wide-ranging, powerfully argued, and professedly unfashionable. How are these scholarly predilections to be explained? Here it is necessary to examine the interplay between Clive's role as a tutor and the different geographical contexts in which he has played that role and in which his intellect was forged.

For Clive, it is axiomatic that teaching is the bedrock of intellectual life, and it is in his teaching that many of his modes of working can be seen to have developed. Clive's students – whether they knew it or not – were inoculated against current fashions at an early age by an insistent emphasis on what was good, rather than on what was merely hot off the press. Incisive historiographical judgments and the phrases used to articulate them were honed in teaching and repeated in print or at scholarly gatherings. 'The paladins of modern revisionism' received short shrift from him.[7] Indeed, revisionists were almost invariably '*soi disant*', though that was at least preferable to being 'anaemic'. A.G.

Dickens was described in tutorials during the 1990s as a much more insightful historian than most of the angry young men who had built careers trashing his *oeuvre*. Christopher Hill captured the 'passion' of the period with greater acuity than any other historian. Lawrence Stone was praised at a symposium in 2008 for his imaginative use of legal records when most participants were taking it in turns to shoot Stone's corpse. Conrad Russell was 'simply brilliant', but nevertheless often wrong.[8] Others were just wrong. Students had to think for themselves rather than following superficially authoritative voices. And time and again this was all brought back to the handling of evidence. When Clive wrote of another scholar's 'selective and insufficiently critical reading of the sources', he was again committing to print something of the credo he always articulated whilst teaching.[9]

The forensic criticism of modern scholarship that was foundational to many of his publications was thus forged through teaching, but so, more importantly, was his constructive contribution. As one eminent reviewer sagely noted of a book co-authored with Felicity Heal, 'Its clarity and consistent good sense represent powerful arguments for the complementary disciplines of teaching and research to remain fully integrated in the historical profession'.[10] Weekly essays, or draft chapters of theses, would always feature encouraging written comments, or gentle suggestions for reshaping, before substantive criticism, primarily intended to sharpen the argumentative points at issue or else to add lustre to the prose in which those found expression. The necessity of entering into a dialogue with a new generation of undergraduates each year, however much they were dependent on his learning, also meant that he never stopped engaging afresh with big questions (even if he did not find many of the new answers to them compelling).

The process of revisiting big questions through teaching helps explain why he has at key points in his career focused upon them. Explaining quite why Clive is so good at addressing these big questions is not so easy. He has never been associated with a particular intellectual school possessing a readily identifiable scholarly toolkit. Nor has he confined himself to a single, manageable sphere of enquiry. Quite the reverse. The variety of Clive's interests are, perhaps, inherently intellectually fruitful; they have provided him with multiple perspectives, points of comparison, and a deep distrust of sectional or professional special pleading. This is most obvious in his writings on legal history. Few would have the confidence to criticise the pre-eminent modern historian of English law for offering a 'largely internalist' reading of legal change, one indicative of the extent to which he has 'internalized' the 'professional complacency' of early modern legal writers.[11] Sheer intellectual breadth has led Clive to invoke fourteenth-century legal examples when investigating statutory interpretation in the seventeenth century, and to quote Julian Pitt-Rivers' discussion of honour when writing about the later Stuart gentry.[12] Few historians would have thought to deploy Marx's *Eighteenth Brumaire* whilst discussing early modern Lincolnshire, or Mozart's *Marriage of Figaro* whilst evoking a clerical vendetta during the 1630s.[13] All who have been taught by Clive can testify to his enviable capacity to cite biblical texts, a useful legacy of a Calvinist upbringing.

Nevertheless, to ascribe Clive's scholarly achievements to a fine brain and wide reading deployed as a tutor will not quite do. The sharpness of his work also reflects the extent to which he has been influenced by different academic environments. Although he was a student at Gonville and Caius College, Cambridge, and benefitted from the panoramic vision of the great medievalist Philip Grierson, Clive was particularly inspired outside his college by the intellectually liberating tutorial example of the classicist Sir Moses Finley. Having Sir Jack Plumb as a doctoral supervisor placed a premium on intellectual self-reliance, and also further embedded a concern with clarity of argument and expression. But it was the experience of two decades of teaching at Cornell University in upstate New York that proved decisive in several ways. At one level, it was thanks to an unusually fine collection of early modern witchcraft pamphlets that Clive first began to develop what would become one of his core scholarly interests.[14] More profoundly, teaching big survey courses, and developing the skills to inspire vast lecture audiences, bred confidence within a previously rather uncertain personality. Cornell was the making of Clive, a fact witnessed not least by his receipt of that university's Clark Distinguished Teaching Award. Robert Ashton need not have been 'a trifle puzzled by the prevalence of spelling [in *The Eastern Association*] which would suggest Cambridge, Mass. rather than Cambridge, England': Clive might be taken out of America, but the positive experience of America has never been taken out of Clive.[15] Much as he has enriched scholarly life in Oxford, and contributed to the workings of both Lady Margaret Hall and the History Faculty, Clive retains an intellectual eclecticism and cosmopolitan outlook that reflects the importance of working for a quarter of a century in other places.

I

What makes Clive such an extraordinary teacher? According to many rather 'mechanical' modern benchmarks, Clive would struggle to pass muster: his written comments on essays are not usually voluminous; he rarely provides students with detailed reading lists; relatively little emphasis is placed on exams. Clive's pithy critiques of the work of modern historians, and his suspicion of the latest interpretations, mean that he does not waste much time in detailed discussion of historiography, and may spend the majority of a tutorial discussing in detail *what actually happened* in, as it may be, the English parliaments of the 1620s, or the machinery of Tudor government, or colonial American administration. This would be a recipe for disaster, or at least tedium, in other, lesser hands. Yet the lived experience of Clive's undergraduate tutorials and classes is thrilling. Clive's theatrical inclinations are given full rein, and rather than a dull recounting of events students are thrust into the turmoil of the past. 'You've got to be there. You've got to feel it', he shouts at classes of jaded Oxford finalists.

A key element in his performance is simply one of physical posture: Clive invariably sits poised on the front edge of an armchair, leaning forwards, exuding energy and engagement. Banal student comments tend to be instantly rephrased, significantly deepened, complimented, and then turned into a powerful question initiating the next round of discussion. If Clive's precarious position on the edge of his seat remains a dominant visual signal of tutorial intent, the sound of his teaching is invariably accompanied with laughter. Warmth and good humour are critical in encouraging students: risks can be taken because they are never punished, never subjected to ridicule. (Clive's deepest disdain – verging on loathing – has always been reserved for intellectual bullies.) That this intense sense of optimism is so successfully manufactured is all the more remarkable since Clive is, in fact, a self-confessed 'congenital pessimist'.[16] Students are made to feel that History is something they can do themselves. 'I suspect your reading of Shakespeare would be considerably more subtle than Professor X's' might with the benefit of hindsight appear a double-edged compliment to write in the margin of a tutorial essay, but it proved intensely liberating when laid before a nineteen-year-old. 'Be bold!' has always been his advice before exams.

Clive's career as a graduate supervisor gathered speed after his return to England. He has since 1988 seen thirteen doctoral students through to the completion of their theses, and he has supervised on a wide variety of subjects (from Restoration Great Yarmouth through colonial Virginia to Socinianism and the Cromwellian 'Other House'). It is easy for his students to develop a kind of heretical understanding of him, as he demonstrates in supervisions an apparent omniscience (though this impression is perhaps helped by the fact that most supervisions are viewed through an alcoholic haze over lunch). In both conversation and in written commentary on work, he corrects erroneous understandings of legal history, obscure biblical passages, and, perhaps more surprisingly, poetic scansion. His aim is always to allow others to develop their own voices and arguments. This can sometimes have the disconcerting effect of his then announcing – months after he has approvingly discussed a piece of work – 'of course, I've always thought you were wrong about that', but in fact his own charismatic authority ensures that his students' voices, at points, echo his own. Certain adjectives – 'oleaginous', 'serpentine', 'fissiparous' – and certain nouns – 'integument', 'tergiversation', 'skeins' – some of which, at least, sent his students hurrying to the dictionary on first hearing, have become more common as a result of Clive. There is, however, no Holmesian school – and, given the diverse interests of students, how could there be? Clive is at the forefront of those who think that this is A Good Thing.

II

This volume is an affectionate tribute to Clive from some of his students, friends, and colleagues. What it cannot be is a comprehensive reflection of

Clive's interests. As the introductory discussion makes clear, and as the bibliography of his work offered at the end of the book confirms, they are too various to be readily contained between a single set of book covers. The decision has therefore been taken to concentrate on the central period of Clive's interests, and the one to which he has always returned: the revolutionary decades of the mid-seventeenth century. All of the essays are also animated by a consideration of one or more of the relationships that have been important to Clive's work: between centre and locality, popular and elite, politics and language, law and its implementation, and ideology and action.

In Chapter 2, Henrik Langelüddecke, in a profoundly researched account, does much to support the dismantling of the revisionist case concerning the 1630s that was pioneered by Clive. While the Caroline reforms achieved a degree of success in some areas, notably in relation to the Perfect Militia, Langelüddecke's demonstration of the depth of resistance to Ship Money – and the ideological basis for it – means that it will be increasingly hard to sustain accounts asserting the success of the levy. The next three chapters turn to the 1640s, the period that first concerned Clive as a scholar. David Scott's careful reconstruction of party manoeuvres in the Long Parliament provides the most precise account available of key shifts in position in that turbulent period and illuminates the origins of modern party politics. Sarah Mortimer analyses the thought of a key individual, Henry Ireton, and shows the remarkable consistency with which he sought to strike a balance between the demands of *salus populi* and the limits set by the constitution (particularly parliament's role within it). Ireton's thought, while it shaped his critical response to more radical understandings of natural law, allowed him to defend the trial of Charles I and ultimately regicide. Grant Tapsell examines a satirical dictionary prepared by the royalist John Warner, bishop of Rochester. In a context where contemporaries thought that words had been wrested from their meanings in the unstable circumstances of civil war, Warner sought to attack the parliamentarian cause by exposing the new – often *paradiastolic* – meanings for previously innocent words that had been created by England's new masters. The next two chapters are in different ways indebted to the Clive's work on the means by which people sought to communicate with and harness central government. Perry Gauci uses the remarkable surviving cache of letters of the merchant Richard Houncell to show the ways in which he used local and metropolitan networks, and engaged with central government, in order to advance his trade. Manfred Brod's close examination of the case of William, Lord Craven – concerning the protracted controversy over the expropriation of his lands – casts light on the tensions running through the government of the Commonwealth and Protectorate and the mechanisms – not least print – that could be used by groups outside government to present their case. In Chapter 8, Jonathan Fitzgibbons, through a reading of treason trials during the Protectorate, provides an important new context for understanding one of the most important central political events: the offer of the crown. The change in thinking about kingship – the divorcing of the body politic and the body personal, and the assumption that the king was simply the chief magistrate whose powers came from the people – underlying the judges' conduct in treason trials was key to the attempts to make Oliver Cromwell king. Leif Dixon and George Southcombe both seek to examine changes and developments in religious thought. Dixon shows that, as the charge of atheism was used in the 1640s to assert the necessity of intolerance, radicals could redeploy the very languages and behaviours that were condemned to show up the contradictions of orthodoxy. Southcombe – concentrating on witchcraft, one of Clive's core interests – provides a reading of an important sceptical text produced by Thomas Ady in 1655, and demonstrates how Ady sought to make a radical case against witch beliefs in way that was palatable to a godly audience, perhaps an audience that included those at the very centre. In Chapter 11, Blair Worden explores the widespread campaign for a 'free parliament' that played a significant role in bringing about the peaceful end of the republic. This campaign saw the cooperation of those with divergent political opinions and, while it was expressed through county declarations, took on the character of a national movement. The next two chapters are both concerned with the intriguing continuity of a culture of honour in a time of change. Peter Sherlock's investigation of the monuments of Westminster Abbey shows both the ways in which the process of commemoration sustained many of its pre–civil war aspects and, at points, reflected the new order. Adrian Ailes highlights the tensions wrought by the 1640s and 1650s among the heralds of the College of Arms and their continuation into the Restoration. An analysis of a satirical broadsheet of 1660 concerning the heralds points to the way in which the trustworthiness of some of those who had served during the Interregnum was questioned when the king returned. In the final chapter, Matthew Jenkinson considers the regicides who fled to America, the ways in which attempts to find them were impeded, and the ways in which they were later remembered (particularly by those who were thinking about America's own revolution). In crossing the Atlantic at the end, this book also pays tribute to Clive's expertise in colonial America, which has been expressed through teaching and supervision for many years.

As is appropriate in a work of this kind, there is no party line. However, taken together, the essays make a powerful case for retaining the nomenclature used in the book's title. Certainly a number of the authors here identify some of the continuities that run through the early and mid-seventeenth century, but the changes that are mapped – in the conduct of politics, in the media used to disseminate messages, in religious thinking, in attitudes towards witchcraft and, perhaps most importantly, towards kingship – mean that it remains apt to refer to the 1640s and 1650s as England's *revolutionary* period. It is also apt that a volume for Clive Holmes should vindicate the use of an old-fashioned terminology. Clive has been a great force for good, and this collection of essays is offered to him with thanks, respect, and love.

Notes

1 It is no coincidence that his most accessible interpretation of the seventeenth century is found in a collection of essays that provide answers to titular questions: Clive Holmes, *Why Was Charles I Executed?* (2006).
2 Clive Holmes, 'The County Community in Stuart Historiography', *JBS*, 19 (1980), 54–73; idem, 'Parliament, Liberty, Taxation, and Property', in J.H. Hexter (ed.), *Parliament and Liberty from the Reign of Elizabeth to the English Civil War* (Stanford, CA, 1992), pp. 122–54; idem, *Why Was Charles I Executed?* (2006); idem, 'The Trial and Execution of Charles I', *HJ*, 53 (2010), 289–316. In 1997 it was striking to receive an undergraduate reading list on Anglo-Scottish and Anglo-Irish relations headed 'The Celtic Fringe'.
3 Clive Holmes, 'Centre and Locality in Civil-War England', in John Adamson (ed.), *The English Civil War: Conflict and Contexts, 1640–49* (Basingstoke, 2009), p. 154. An early example of a historian seeking to downplay the difference between Clive's arguments and those at which he took aim is found in Kevin Sharpe, 'Crown, Parliament and Locality: Government and Communication in Early Stuart England', *EHR*, 101 (1986), p. 335 n. 4. For the impact of the recent work on the trial, see e.g. Nicholas McDowell, 'The 1649 Writings', in *The Complete Works of John Milton Volume VI: Vernacular Regicide and Republican Writings*, ed. N.H. Keeble and Nicholas McDowell (Oxford, 2013), pp. 17–19.
4 Clive Holmes, *The Eastern Association in the English Civil War* (Cambridge, 1974), pp. 1–4.
5 Clive Holmes, *Seventeenth-Century Lincolnshire* (Lincoln, 1980), p. 5.
6 See e.g. Clive Holmes, 'Drainers and Fenmen: The Problem of Popular Political Consciousness in the Seventeenth Century', in Anthony Fletcher and John Stevenson (eds.), *Order and Disorder in Early Modern England* (Cambridge, 1985), pp. 166–95. For more on the dialogic in Clive's work, and in particular its importance in his work on witchcraft, see Chapter 10 of this volume.
7 Something of a favourite phrase: Review of G.E. Aylmer, *Rebellion of Revolution? England 1640–1660* (Oxford, 1986), in *AHR*, 92 (1987), 656; review of Mark Kishlansky, *A Monarchy Transformed: Britain 1603–1714* (1996), in *EHR*, 113 (1998), 120.
8 *Why Was Charles I Executed?*, p. 225.
9 Review article, Clive Holmes, 'New Light on the New Model', *HJ*, 24 (1981), 506. He was here referring to Mark Kishlansky's *The Rise of the New Model Army* (Cambridge, 1980).
10 Peter Marshall, review of Felicity Heal and Clive Holmes, *The Gentry in England and Wales 1500–1700* (1994), in *Sixteenth Century Journal*, 27 (1996), 262.
11 Review of J.H. Baker, *The Law's Two Bodies*, in *EHR*, 118 (2003), 206–7.
12 Clive Holmes, 'Statutory Interpretation in the Early Seventeenth Century: The Courts, the Council, and the Commissioners of Sewers', in J.A. Guy and H.G. Beale (eds.), *Law and Social Change in British History: Papers Presented to the Bristol Legal History Conference, 14–17 July 1981* (1984), p. 109; idem, 'The Strange Case of a Misplaced Tomb: Family Honour and the Law in Late Seventeenth-Century England', *Midland History*, 31 (2006), 22.
13 Clive Holmes, *Seventeenth-Century Lincolnshire*, p. 29; idem, 'Law and Politics in the Reign of Charles I: The Case of John Prigeon', *Journal of Legal History*, 28 (2007), 168.
14 See further the discussion in Chapter 10 of this volume.
15 Robert Ashton, review of *The Eastern Association in the English Civil War* (Cambridge, 1974), in *EHR*, 90 (1975), 853.
16 Holmes, *The Eastern Association*, p. viii.

2 Policy enforcement during the Personal Rule of Charles I

The Perfect Militia, Book of Orders, and Ship Money

Henrik Langelüddecke

The Personal Rule of Charles I (1629–40) is a crucial period that helps to explain why, by November 1640, there was a broad alliance of subjects who felt that the king's reign had gone wrong and needed to be put right. In *Why Was Charles I Executed?* Clive Holmes argues that the king's policies in the 1630s demonstrated a "fundamental failure to observe or even understand the structures of society, of government, and of ideology that circumscribed royal authority in England".[1] This view runs counter to some recent interpretations. These claim that the Personal Rule, after witnessing serious political clashes between the king and his Parliaments in the 1620s, saw harmony restored to the political nation by peaceful reform and cooperation between central government and local elites. Charles's experiment of ruling without Parliament was prevented from running its full course only because it was interrupted by the First Scots' War. Any ideological and constitutional conflicts before the Long Parliament were figments of Whig historians' imaginations.[2]

Charles abandoned Parliament in 1629 so that the people 'shall see more clearly into our intents and actions'.[3] Consequently, the policies he pursued for the next eleven years during his Personal Rule give us an idea of what Charles considered good government. As there was no obvious arena in which to voice views on the government in a period without Parliament, the response to Charles's policies is far more difficult to gauge. Hence, if we want to assess the success of the policies of the Personal Rule, we must focus on how thoroughly they were enforced by government officials in the counties and how ordinary people across the country reacted to them.

The scope and intensity of the key projects of the Personal Rule were unprecedented. The Perfect Militia tried to create an effective army out of an assortment of county militias of varying strength and quality. The Book of Orders addressed the acute economic crisis in the realm and aimed at implementing the existing poor laws that had been neglected by local officials. Ship Money raised the funds to build a powerful standing navy in order to provide English foreign policy with the necessary teeth in the Thirty Years' War. The success or failure of these projects rested not only on effective management by the privy council and supervision by the county administrators, the justices of the peace (JPs), sheriffs, and deputy lieutenants, but, above all, on the cooperation of the local officials in the divisions and parishes. These were the men who not only maintained the equipment and organized the training of the militia, provided for the poor and hunted down vagrants, and assessed and collected Ship Money, but who dealt with the king's subjects every day and faced – and responded to – the mood in the country.

Local studies on aspects of the Personal Rule have in the past come to conflicting conclusions for the rest of the country. Thomas Barnes's negative evaluation of the Somerset militia, for example, is at odds with Anthony Fletcher's more benevolent impressions mainly from Norfolk, Suffolk, and Essex and with D.P. Carter's study of the Lancashire militia.[4] The idea that the Book of Orders galvanized poor relief was rejected by Brian Quintrell and John Morrill in their studies of Essex and Cheshire respectively, while Clive Holmes and Thomas Barnes came to more favourable conclusions in Lincolnshire and Somerset respectively.[5] In the case of Ship Money, Morrill noted its smooth collection in Cheshire, as did Patricia Haskell in Hampshire, while Quintrell observed its early collapse in Essex, just as Holmes did in Lincolnshire.[6]

This essay explores the enforcement of the Perfect Militia, the Book of Orders, and Ship Money across the whole country in order to gain a more differentiated picture. Two types of sources are the key to this study. The first is the rich correspondence between the privy council and the JPs, sheriffs, and deputy lieutenants who reported their progress to Westminster – a total of about ten thousand documents.[7] The second are the account books of over five hundred parishes in thirty-five counties, which survived for this period. While the survival of these local records is far from comprehensive, its randomness ensures a degree of representation across the country, which a county study cannot provide. These account books, kept by petty constables, churchwardens, overseers of the poor, and other parish officers, are crucial for two reasons. First, as mentioned already, the officers who kept them were primarily in charge of enforcing the Perfect Militia, Book of Orders, and Ship Money. Secondly, since most of the activities related to this enforcement entailed expenses, the account books illustrate quite accurately to what extent parish officers implemented or did not implement these three projects.

I

Charles I's decision in 1625 to create a 'Perfect Militia' was a consequence of the poor performance of English expeditionary forces against Cadiz and the Isle of Rhé and of the realization that the English militia based on counties and comprising elements of conscription and voluntary service was probably no match for the mercenary armies of the Thirty Years' War. A flurry of instructions from the privy council were aimed at the modernization, uniformity, and training of the militia according to continental standards. The initial zeal in the localities for improving the county-based militias, however, soon waned because there was no central funding, and schemes to keep large numbers of troops on permanent alert were unrealistic. Nevertheless, not since 1588 had the training of the militia reached such a high standard.[8] Scholars are divided, however, as to what happened after the peace with France and Spain in 1629–30. Some insist that the militia utterly deteriorated during the eleven years of Personal Rule; more recent studies claim that the Perfect Militia was not a total failure.[9]

It has been recognised for some time that service in the militia had shifted from an individual duty based on wealth and status to a communal obligation by which, certainly in the case of the foot regiments, parishes had to forward a quota of soldiers.[10] In fact, the military duties of petty constables (in some parishes taken on by the churchwardens) were far-reaching.[11] If the assumption of a slumbering militia during the 1630s were true, parish accounts would contain no or very few references to military matters. Yet almost all constables' accounts from forty-four parishes surviving for this period, and the churchwardens' accounts from sixty-four more parishes, refer to military expenses. The vast majority of these accounts indicate that the English militias were in a state equivalent, if not superior, to that of the 1620s.[12] Many refer to the storage or regular cleaning of arms and equipment. In 1631 and 1632, for instance, the churchwardens of Charlton Marshall (Dorset) who spent 6d and 12d respectively for 'our tything armour', and the constables of Stathern (Leicestershire) who paid 4s for 'arms dressing' in 1634.[13] More importantly, they regularly refer to the repair and replacement of faulty equipment, which suggests that arms were inspected by the deputy lieutenants or frequently used. In 1635–6, one of the churchwardens of Mendlesham (Suffolk) paid 3s 6d 'for a newe stocke & tricker for the Towne Musket', a replacement undoubtedly caused by excessive use. The constable of Croft (Lincolnshire) in 1635 realised that he needed 'ii baggs to putt the bullets in'. In 1637–8, the sidemen of Dartington (Devon) expended 6s 9d 'for mending of two muskits and making cleane of an head peece' and for reparing 'A coslet and belt'.[14] A synopsis of the available data suggests that in most counties the equipment was monitored by the deputy lieutenants and actually used in training.[15]

With only a few exceptions, the accounts also mention the attendance of parish soldiers at annual musters. The soldiers of Pattingham (Staffordshire), Gislingham, Horham (Suffolk), and Fillongley (Warwickshire), for example, were inspected once a year, while their comrades from Nether Whitacre (Warwickshire) trained twice or three times in 1632, once in 1633 and 1635, and three times in 1637.[16] References to several musters suggest that deputy lieutenants resummoned soldiers who had shown faulty equipment the first time or that one meeting was dedicated to roll calls and inspections, while the others involved practising in company or regiment formation. In 1633, the constables of Egloskerry (Cornwall), for example, sent John Roger and Richard Dewning to the general muster at Launceston but Gregory Congdon 'to a privite muster' at Lewannick, while the churchwardens of Halberton (Devon) usually referred to one general muster and one 'petty muster'.[17] The durations of musters varied. The constables of Marston Trussell entered musters on 13 July 1633 and 4 July 1635, but on 19 January 1637, Edward Peerson of Cratfield (Suffolk) was paid for three days' training, and in 1632, the soldiers of High Bray (Devon) exercised at Melton from 17 to 19 June.[18] Richard Bower of Shelton (Norfolk) received pay for two days in 1633, three in 1634, five in 1635, and two in 1636.[19] The average militiaman, consequently, served between two and seven days a year in their arms.

While it is impossible to assess the fighting capacity and training standards of individual companies and regiments of the English militia, the value of musters in the 1630s can be deduced from the amount of firing practice musketeers received. This can be established by correlating their number in a parish with the amount of gunpowder and shot purchased. With an average of about 1s 6d per pound of gunpowder, according to the account books, the knowledge that a musket could fire about twelve bullets with one pound of powder and the fact that at most half the soldiers were musketeers rather than pikemen, the seven pounds procured by the churchwardens of East Budleigh (Devon) for each musketeer amounted to eighty-four rounds per man, and the per capita amount of ammunition in High Bray (Devon) varied between seventeen and fifty-five rounds.[20] Assuming that at most fifteen of the twenty-two soldiers of Exeter (Heavitree) had been musketeers, the 50s worth of powder bought in 1636 would have supplied each of them with about four pounds, or three hundred and twenty rounds.[21] This must be considered a generous amount, particularly if there were only a couple of days of annual firing practice. The majority of parishes also referred to wages for muster masters – expert instructors with plenty of combat experience – with only the exception of the surviving accounts from Leicestershire, Northamptonshire, and Somerset. This – along with the fact that the amounts paid were quite insignificant and rarely exceeded 4s per parish per annum, even in large parishes like Exeter (Heavitree), Dartington, and High Bray raising up to sixteen soldiers – shows that muster masters met less resistance for financial or political reasons than Barnes and Boynton have suggested.[22]

During the Scots' Wars, maintenance and practice significantly increased. Those parishes that had looked after their equipment in the early 1630s did not need to increase their expenses significantly for maintenance and purchase after 1638.[23] The constables' accounts particularly indicate a considerable surge of training days. In 1638, the men of Burton Latimer and Marston Trussell (Northamptonshire) practised seven times, as opposed to the one annual muster in previous years, and the soldiers of Stockton in Shropshire practised on fifteen days. In 1640, those of East Harling in Norfolk were summoned on fifty-two days.[24] Men selected for the expeditionary force often received a separate and even more rigorous training than the regular bandsmen. Parishes also kept stocking up on ammunition and provided generous combat supplies for the selected men. Shelton's churchwardens, for example, raised only one soldier but purchased powder, bullets, and match worth £4 in 1639. Crediton probably called up more than twenty soldiers (militiamen and selected men), but bought three hundredweight of gunpowder in 1638 and twenty-one pounds of match in 1640.[25]

These efforts during the Scots' Wars show that the militia could still be improved beyond the standards of the early 1630s. Yet it is obvious that they were dictated by the impending threat to the realm and could not be sustained over a longer period of time, inasmuch as the energies and time commitments of part-time officials and part-time soldiers were stretched to the limit. Of course, it is questionable whether the Perfect Militia would have been able to repel an invading force of Spanish *tercios*, and it is a fact that the English expeditionary force disintegrated in the face of the Covenanters. Yet it can be argued that this happened precisely because this force contained not regular regiments but mostly pressed and unfit substitutes. Unfortunately, the flawed legal and organizational framework of the English militia, which considered itself not a national army but a defence force of the counties, meant that the regular men refused to serve against Scotland and were replaced by largely untrained men.[26] The fact that more than 80 per cent of the Lincolnshire men selected for the campaign against Scotland were also willing to pay extortionate bribes not to be included in the expeditionary force shows that the Perfect Militia was not an army fit to fight an unpopular war.[27]

II

A series of harvest failures and slumps in the manufacturing trades necessitated crisis management and a reminder to local governors of their statutory duties to implement the Elizabethan poor laws. To experienced and conscientious JPs, the proclamation of a Book of Orders in 1631 merely restated existing legislation.[28] Poverty was to be relieved, labour to be provided, vagrants relentlessly punished, alehouses shut, grain markets regulated, highways and bridges repaired, and houses of correction built. While traditional in form and content, the operational procedures this Book of Orders prescribed were innovative and aimed at an unprecedented formalization of the mechanisms of local government. All active JPs were to be split into small groups and were to divide their county into divisions. In order to supervise the enforcement of the Book, they were directed to meet once a month together with all local officers of their division, thus establishing permanent petty sessions. In addition, quarterly reports were to be directed to the sheriff or the judges of assize, who forwarded them to the privy council. This bureaucratic approach of the Personal Rule to social policies seemed to change the liberal *ad hoc* enforcement of the Elizabethan poor laws radically. Apparently, the king and his advisers not only planned to establish a coherent and working social policy, but aimed at the reform of local government *per se*. Divisions and petty sessions were to become an additional, ubiquitous, and permanent tier in the organizational structure of local government. By making local officers part of a hierarchy and accountable for their performance, the crown attempted to bind them more closely to its orders and to convert them into a class of national officers. About one thousand four hundred certificates under the Book of Orders have survived in the State Papers Domestic and allow us to judge the JPs' effectiveness in supervising its enforcement. In addition, the surviving parish officers' account books are invaluable in assessing the enforcement of the Book of Orders, as they detail the expenses parish officers incurred in order to, for example, attend petty sessions, apprehend and punish vagrants, identify paupers, meet to set the poor rate, pay individual paupers, carry out employment measures, or apprentice poor children.[29]

Frederic Youngs and Thomas Barnes were convinced that the Book of Orders had led to the establishment of manageable divisions of counties and petty sessions as subsidiary administrative meetings to quarter sessions.[30] However, as the surviving JPs' certificates show, some counties kept their territorial organization as it had been before the Book of Orders, some subdivided oversized hundreds, while others combined several hundreds to a division. During the 1630s, only in Cambridgeshire, Hampshire, and Sussex did the configurations of divisions not change. In some counties, such as Northamptonshire, Hertfordshire, and Norfolk, for example, hundreds, which at the start of the Book of Orders had merged to divisions, suddenly split up; others, originally unconnected, as in Essex, after some time, formed a division.[31] Frequently, divisions were formed *ad hoc*, with one or two hundreds constituting the core. Of the surviving certificates from Ermington hundred in Devon, for example, two of its JPs reported with the hundreds of Lifton, Tavistock, Roborough, and Plympton, once with Stanborough, Coleridge, and Plympton, once with Plympton alone, and once on their own.[32] Obviously, many counties were stimulated by the Book of Orders to reconsider and reconfigure their territorial organization, while others decided to keep their traditional subdivisions. The Book of Orders may have initiated but it did not concretise or even finalize the establishment of petty session districts.[33]

Considering the large number of tasks the Book of Orders had set, its success or failure depended on the regular observance of petty sessions by all local officers in the division. Many JPs referred to monthly petty sessions, others only to 'diverse meetings' or meeting 'from time to time'.[34] Most, however, do not mention them at all.[35] While JPs decided to cancel petty sessions for practical reasons during outbreaks of the plague, in months when quarter sessions or musters were held, or during the harvesting period,[36] the prevalent mood may have been best reflected by some Oxfordshire JPs who met 'as often as was needful for the business and convenient for the country'.[37] The numbers of JPs' signatures – often only two – suggest that divisions often struggled to find a *quorum*.[38] Several JPs complained about absenteeism and the laziness of colleagues.[39] Hence, it appears that monthly petty sessions were not uniformly established but were prevented by undermanned divisions, practical considerations, and personal convenience.[40]

The requirement of the Book of Orders that the high constables and all parish officers had to attend petty sessions followed the logic that the Book could succeed only if JPs monitored local officers and coerced them into action. However, with the exception of Leicestershire, Northamptonshire, and Sussex, only one in three certificates referred to attending local officers at all and then mostly in vague terms.[41] Churchwardens' and overseers' accounts also mostly do not mention meetings with their JPs. None of the surviving churchwardens' accounts from Berkshire, Dorset, Essex, Hampshire, Lincolnshire, and Oxfordshire and only a small minority from Cheshire, Devon, Derbyshire, and Hertfordshire refer to petty sessions. Altogether, fewer overseers' accounts have survived for this period, but the reference pattern is very similar. Of the fifty-nine parishes whose accounts refer to monthly meetings, only a handful indicate that their churchwardens or overseers attended between four and ten petty sessions annually. Most of them, however, refer to a couple, often only one meeting a year, suggesting that they had been especially summoned by the JPs, usually to be sworn in to their offices or to submit their annual accounts. Constables' accounts, on the other hand, offer a different picture and indicate that petty sessions had become the administrative forum of divisions.[42] Some constables, such as in Branston (Leicestershire), Marston Trussell (Northamptonshire), and Stockton (Shropshire), attended up to twelve annual meetings. In most other parishes, constables met with their JPs between three and seven times, although in some that number dropped from the mid-1630s. Yet, in Cornwall, Lincolnshire, Somerset, and Suffolk, not even the surviving constables' accounts refer to petty sessions. Frequent references to 'presentments' suggest that constables were not invited to attend because the high constables collected written data from each parish and presented them to the JPs on their behalf.[43] Travel distances may have been one reason to limit the attendance of parish officers. The constables of Bishop's Tawton in Devon had to travel either to Chulmleigh (twelve miles) or South Molton (eight miles) to meet their JPs, and the meeting places for the constables of Croft in Lincolnshire were Partney (seven miles) Spilsby (eight miles), or Hagworthingham (thirteen miles).[44] Another reason may have been that, if all officers had assembled, the one day scheduled for petty sessions (as opposed to the two to three days for quarter sessions) would not have been sufficient for JPs to examine them. While some divisions, such as the West hundred of Cornwall consisted only of nine parishes, the average in a division ranged between fifteen and twenty-five and up to forty-eight, as in Hinckford in Essex.[45] Gathering all officers would have resulted in assemblies of thirty to forty constables or three to four hundred parish officers. Once again, common sense and the convenience of JPs and parish officers prevented the intervals and attendance at petty sessions that the Book of Orders had prescribed and limited the utility of these meetings to control local government at the grass-roots level.

Historians have been divided about the impact the Book of Orders made on its key target – poor relief. Some have acknowledged that it was an important impulse that reinforced the policies of previous decades and provided the foundation for the expanding poor relief during the civil war and Interregnum.[46] Others have denied any long-term impact on provision for the poor.[47] Poor relief was often mentioned in the JPs' certificates, but the assessment of poverty and description of relief measures were usually vague and amounted to statements of *omnia bene*. The assurance of Essex JPs in February 1637 that 'some care' had been taken in relieving the poor was more typical than the conscientious approach of their colleagues in the hundreds of North and South Clay and Bassetlaw (Nottinghamshire) who returned the names of all the paupers in their division and listed their doles.[48] After 1634, the number of references dropped significantly, with the exception of only a few counties. While this could have been due to the improving economic situation in the mid-1630s, which no longer warranted tight crisis management, stock references could also prove that the initial enthusiasm for the Book of Orders amongst JPs had worn off as time went by. Yet generalizations are misleading. The persistent lack of references to the poor from Kent, for example, is matched with continuously numerous, detailed, and compassionate certificates from Norfolk throughout the 1630s.[49]

When it came to poor relief, many JPs preferred 'other convenient wayes' to regular poor rates and limited taxation to a certain period.[50] Instead, they suggested the use of fines, shutting down alehouses, fasting, or charity.[51] Surprisingly, however, charitable bequests played only a minor role in the churchwardens' and overseers' accounts, while most of these refer to poor rates. This and the fact that nearly all surviving parish officers' lists mentioned overseers of the poor — the office created exclusively to administer the Elizabethan poor rate — indicate that taxation had probably become the predominant relief measure in the 1630s.[52] Indeed, some historians suggest that it was the Book of Orders that provided the breakthrough for the nationwide establishment of the poor rate.[53] Overseers' accounts show that the weekly collection interval the Elizabethan legislation prescribed was unrealistic and that some assiduous parishes raised the poor rate monthly, but most only twice or three times a year.[54] The accounts show that overseers continuously adapted assessments according to the actual need. They increased or decreased either the total amount of rates and doles, or the number of recipients or taxpayers, or the individual amounts of the doles or the rates, extremely flexibly.[55] While taxation prevailed, overseers sought to minimize its impact. The surviving data show that the sums spent on poor relief in the 1630s did not increase.[56] The Book of Orders did not mark a transition towards a publicly funded welfare state, but parishes maintained a rather conservative spending policy providing only a minimum of relief for a selected few.

Turning to vagrancy, JPs' certificates and parish accounts show that the watches prescribed by the Book of Orders for each parish were not uniformly kept, but parishes decided whether their benefits outweighed the burden they involved.[57] As in the case of resident paupers, all JPs were able to do was to assure the privy council that vagrants were 'taken care' of, but the quantities they quoted were often limited to 'some', 'few', or 'many', or the figures are suspiciously rounded.[58] Divisions consisting of dozens of parishes claimed only a handful of vagrants.[59] In 1637, the JPs of Bassetlaw hundred in Nottinghamshire reported no vagrants for twenty-nine out of their fifty-eight parishes.[60] The tired expressions we find in these reports and their noticeable attempts at keeping figures as vague as possible indicate that most JPs did not have the faintest idea about the extent of vagrancy in their division, not to mention the measures applied by parish officers.[61]

In contrast, parish accounts recorded dozens or hundreds of vagrants each year. The churchwardens of Woodbury (Devon) recorded forty-eight in 1631, eight in 1635 and thirty-three in 1637, and the constables of East Harling (Norfolk) entered twenty-four in 1633, sixty-seven in 1635 and eighty in 1638.[62] This discrepancy to the data of the JPs' certificates may be explained by the terminology used by parish officers. In East Harling, the differentiation between 'passengers' and 'vagrants' could suggest that passengers had carried valid passports before entering the parish, while vagrants had been apprehended and possibly punished according to the law. Who, however, were the 'poor' and 'travellers' and, above all, the large numbers of people of whom only their names were recorded in the accounts? The constables' accounts from Stathern and Waltham in Leicestershire and Croft in Lincolnshire, which spell out more clearly how many were whipped or were issued passports (presumably because they had none when they entered the parish), suggest that the travelers labelled as 'bedlam', 'Irish', 'cripples', 'soldier', or 'poor' – the vast majority – received no punishment.[63] Obviously, parish officers dealt resolutely with travelers whose origins and intentions were suspicious or who were considered criminal or a potential liability. In 1633, for example, the sidemen of Dartington (Devon) paid money 'for the watching of the cripple and A leamen [lame] Irish people at the Church howse and for the sending them from tithing to tithing'. In 1638, the Constable of Burton Latimer made 'foure hue and cryes to send east west north and south after a rogue one Giles Tompson who was whipped in o[u]r towne for taking widow Toothills pettiecoate off of the hedge, and was sent with a passe to Rothwell where he said he last dwelled. And in o[u]r field gave Whetbarke o[u]r be[a]dle a box on the Eare and ran away from him'.[64]

Yet, most parish accounts are testimonies to the extraordinary degree of compassion and hospitality local officers offered to travelers. In Algarkirk and Croft (both Lincolnshire), travelers were usually treated with supper, bed, and breakfast, and, in 1638, the constables of Burton Latimer paid 1s to 'Shrive and Arch o[u]r two Alehousekeepers for theire straw which have been used for this ye[a]re past about lodging of cripples and other *vagrants* whom wee have brought into them'.[65] Generosity extended also to genuine vagrants. In 1631, the churchwardens of Melksham (Wiltshire) reimbursed 'Henry Kyneton, for victuals to vagrants yt were corrected' and the constables of Worfield (Shropshire) gave 6d 'to 4 poore people that we punished'.[66] It is also important to recognize that nearly all parish accounts dealing with travelers recorded sums paid *to* them rather than accounting for payments *concerning* them (for example for their punishment or conduct). This implies that most vagrants not only escaped proper punishment, but also received some pocket money. We do not know whether these payments were a reflection of the officers' compassion, or constituted bribes. Most payments ranged from 2d to 6d, but some parishes were extraordinarily generous. Individual travelers received between 6d and 8d in Ilminster (Somerset), between 9d and 10d in Thaxted (Essex), 1s in Bristol, All Saints and Wimborne (Dorset), and up to 2s in Biddenden (Kent).[67] Details of vagrants' curricula vitae in parish accounts suggest that the more exotic and pitiful their story was, the more likely they were to be given credit and some money. Preferred beneficiaries were veterans from the Continent, Protestant refugees, and victims of piracy.[68] The numbers of discharged soldiers and people kidnapped by North African pirates in parish accounts raise suspicions as to their *bona fides*, but it becomes clear that a good story both prevented travelers from receiving the harsh treatment of vagrants and served parish officers as justification for their generosity when they had to account for their expenses.

It appears that parish officers did not enforce the harsh laws concerning migration and settlement. In their eyes, only a minority of migrants were vagrants and qualified for the punishment set down by the law. Only the rogues amongst vagrants who overtly offended popular sentiment or abused hospitality made acquaintance with the constable's whip. This highly pragmatic approach is reflected in the semantics of the constable of Long Melford in Suffolk who recorded payments 'for the relief of *diverse* vagrants, for whipping *some*, for carrying *some* to the Justice, and sending *all* out of the town'.[69]

III

One of the most controversial schemes of the Personal Rule was Ship Money. Charles I argued that England's safety was threatened by foreign powers and her trade and coastlines harassed by pirates, which required emergency funding for a standing navy based on his prerogative.[70] While many contemporaries questioned the government's claim that England was in imminent danger of war or even invasion, the Caroline Ship Money caused controversy primarily because it breached precedent in four respects. First, the king asked for money to build a fleet and did not, as in the past, lease ships from coastal towns. Secondly, after a trial period in 1634 in which only coastal counties were charged, Ship Money was extended to all counties in 1635. In the past, only maritime places had paid for the naval defence of the realm. Thirdly, unlike the traditional one-shot levy, Ship Money was raised year after year and seemed to turn into a permanent national tax that lacked any parliamentary approval. Fourthly, costing about £200,000 per annum (except for the 1638 levy, which was reduced because of the extra funding the counties were to bear for the war with Scotland), Ship Money was an unprecedented financial burden amounting to several subsidies.

Local studies are divided on how this levy proceeded and what response it met with in the country. Some have come to the conclusion that the collection of Ship Money did not meet significant resistance before the Scots' War or Hampden's Case and that opposition was grounded on fiscal objections.[71] Others have stressed the pressure Ship Money put on local government and the extent to which political objections were disguised with fiscal arguments.[72] A more recent view argues that Ship Money was one of the most successful taxes in early modern history. Over 90 per cent of it was collected, so people shut up and paid. Objections existed but focused on the inequitable quotas on counties and their subdivisions and on their mismanagement by individual sheriffs. Ship Money only collapsed when the government was preoccupied with the First Scots' War.[73]

A comprehensive analysis of the surviving five thousand letters between the privy council, sheriffs, and local officers draws a much bleaker picture.[74] The overall payment record was unimpressive insofar as the collection was never completed by the time set by the privy council, but only after two years – an unusual period for arrears. The relatively speedy payment under the first writ of 1635 suggests that people accepted a one-shot levy. Payment slowed down as early as 1636 and continued to slow down in all subsequent years.[75] While, under the writ of 1635, 75.1 per cent had been collected after six months, this dropped under the next writ to 34.5 per cent in the same period. Twelve to fifteen months after the issuing, 92.5 per cent had been collected under the 1635 writ, 94 per cent under the 1636 writ, 67.4 per cent under the 1637 writ, 73.7 per cent under the (much reduced) 1638 writ, and 21.3 per cent under the 1639 writ. In most counties, it took much longer to collect smaller percentages already under the 1636 writ, certainly under the 1637 writ – long before the Scots' Wars or even Hampden's Case. Under the first three writs from 1635 to 1637, after twelve months, the collection dropped in Bedfordshire from 95.8 per cent and 70 per cent to 63.3 per cent. In Wiltshire, the figures were 98.6, 59, and 48.7 per cent respectively, in Nottinghamshire 100, 96.8, and 54 per cent, and in Worcestershire 95.7, 72.6, and 24 per cent. Coastal counties were generally more forward in their payment, suggesting that inland counties were much more reluctant to pay for a navy. Yet even here payment slowed down twelve months after the writs of 1635, 1636, and 1637 from 99.5 and 96.2 to 50 per cent in Suffolk, and 100 and 95.5 to 78.4 per cent in Devon, to quote just two examples. Arrears after a twelve-month collection period had jumped up between the 1635 and 1637 writs in Shropshire from zero to 21 and 52 per cent, in Buckinghamshire from 30 to 66 and 56 per cent, in Northamptonshire from 35 to 30 and 72 per cent, and in Derbyshire from zero and zero to 36 per cent. While these figures clearly suggest a progressive deterioration and eventual collapse in the collection of Ship Money by 1639, its mere payment did not, of course, indicate support for this levy. Even without the detailed figures provided here, Esther Cope made the valid point that the significant amounts of Ship Money that were paid were no reflection of its inherent popularity.[76]

The sheriffs explained this slack payment with the strong opposition Ship Money met. While accounts of serious resistance were ubiquitous in the reports of the sheriffs in charge of the 1638 and 1639 Ship Monies, most counties related serious difficulties already under the writs of 1636 and 1637. Sheriff Russell of Cambridgeshire admitted that 'little or noe monies can be gotten but by ... forcible meanes', and sheriff Coningsby of Hertfordshire stated the arrears of each hundred, which in some parishes exceeded the 30 per cent mark.[77] Sheriff Littleton, in charge of the 1636 Ship Money of Staffordshire, stated that he had been 'very rough' with many but had only collected a quarter and that 'weare I to suffer death for my neglect I weare not able to doe more'. His colleague in Rutland declared that 'the trouble I have been put to has been such that were it not the king's command, no profit or reward could draw me to adventure upon the like business again'.[78] Yet, already under the first writ of 1635, reports from Bedfordshire, Devon, Dorset, Essex, Gloucestershire, Hampshire, Herefordshire, Kent, Northamptonshire, Oxfordshire, Shropshire, Suffolk, Surrey, Warwickshire, Wiltshire, and Worcestershire related resistance considered significant enough to inform the privy council.[79]

These reports show that opposition to Ship Money was real and widespread and that this levy was the most unpopular money raising measure since the Amicable Grant of 1524–5 and the Forced Loan of 1626–8. Opposition was expressed in acts of passive and active resistance. The most straightforward tactic was not to pay Ship Money to the local collectors – usually the parish officers – and see what happened. Remarkably, many members of the gentry or aristocracy – who could clearly afford to pay their assessments – took a leading part in this opposition and set a bad example to all the other taxpayers in their counties.[80] As early as November 1636, directions from the privy council to discharge from their commissions refractory lord and deputy lieutenants and JPs indicate the nervousness at Westminster about the success of this levy, as well as early signs of prominent resistance.[81] But even ordinary taxpayers did not mince their words when they expressed their views on Ship Money to the local assessors or collectors.[82] If people did not pay Ship Money, the prescribed procedure was for the sheriff to send bailiffs to distrain household goods – usually cattle. The overall number of reports referring to distraints as a matter of course is staggering, but, again, particularly remarkable is the extent to which sheriffs resorted to distraint under the first two writs. In September 1636, sheriff Russell of Worcestershire reported that he 'receaved little or none but by distresses taken'; in March 1637, sheriff Bassett of Somerset stated that 'most men force me to subscribe warrants to distress them', and in the same month sheriff Littleton of Staffordshire referred to 'hundreds' of orders to distrain.[83] Distraining – and this was the next step towards resistance – was ineffective, though, when tax refusers simply did not reclaim the impounded cattle against payment of Ship Money. Neighbours who were approached by the officials to buy the impounded goods questioned the authority of the sheriff to sell them under the Ship Money writ or refused for fear of being sued by the owners.[84] More often, however, as countless examples show, tax refusers refused to hand over distrained cattle, had their servants beat the bailiffs up, or threatened to sue them should they commence to impound. Essex bailiffs were lucky, when Sir Thomas Latham's 'sonnes and clarkes did resiste & stood in the gate & woulde not suffer his Cowes to be driven awaye'.[85] More common were reports such as from sheriff Thornhaugh of Nottinghamshire, who, in 1637, repeatedly entreated the privy council for assistance, since he and his officers were assaulted for impounding for Ship Money.[86] It was not unusual that distraining operations resulted in veritable riots, as in January 1638, when Northamptonshire bailiffs faced massive resistance in Long Buckby where 'the people did rise in Rebellion w[i]th forkes & staves ... sayeinge knock them dowen beat out theer braynes hange them Roages'.[87] A synopsis of the vast documentation in the *State Papers* and *Acts of the Privy Council* on Ship Money shows that verbal and physical abuses were far more common than the few examples quoted here might suggest. One of the most powerful strategies tax refusers used to derail Ship Money was threatening collecting or impounding officers with lawsuits, and over the course of the years, more and more irate taxpayers sued local officers. In October 1638, two Northamptonshire bailiffs who had distrained a horse from the earl of Peterborough were pursued by a hue and cry, 'apprehended and taken in our bedes by on[e] of the Cunstables of Woodford', and later bound to appear at the next Assize.[88] In many places, even sheriffs and head officers of corporate towns were threatened with suits.[89]

Why did people refuse to pay Ship Money? Much has been made of assessment disputes, and it is true that the quotas assigned by the privy council or modified by the sheriffs were often inequitable and that local assessors dealt poorly with individual assessments or assessed partially.[90] Yet there is reason to believe that many localities and individuals used disputes as a smokescreen to boycott Ship Money on principle.[91] When William Painter of Maldon declared that 'if he had any leisure he would pay £100 before he would pay Ship Money', did he merely express his unhappiness with his personal assessment?[92] Do the recurrent incidents of resistance and violence not indicate that people opposed Ship Money for more than fiscal reasons, particularly if having cattle impounded incurred much higher charges than paying Ship Money? Why was it that men did not flinch from paying bribes of £5 or £6 to get off the expeditionary force against Scotland but refused to pay 5s towards Ship Money?[93] Did people threaten or commence lawsuits against bailiffs really only because they disagreed with the process or with technicalities? Do the numerous attempts by prominent tax refusers to challenge Ship Money at quarter sessions, assizes, or the King's Bench not indicate that its legality was questioned in the country?[94] Did not people across the country attempt to bring test cases against Ship Money?[95] And is it not true that refusals to pay – legitimate and legal – parliamentary taxes were virtually unknown?[96]

Most remarkably, however, people did not pay Ship Money because they got away with it. Despite the – quite limited – threat of summonses to the privy council, refusers soon realized that the sheriffs and privy council lacked the resources to enforce the collection of Ship Money in every corner of the realm.[97] Above all, their refusal put enormous pressure on their neighbours who acted as assessors or collectors. Some of these collectors challenged the legality of Ship Money themselves, such as the constables of South Newington (Oxfordshire) who, in June 1637, told sheriff Wentworth that they would not collect Ship Money 'till you shall make knowne to us a lawe or Statute Bindinge'.[98] Others refused to carry out distraints, and this was often accepted by the sheriffs who hired bailiffs instead.[99] This reluctance to distrain, of course, jeopardised the success of a levy whose collection largely depended on distraint. Local officers also refused to assist bailiffs in distraining or absented themselves when bailiffs entered the village.[100] In most places, parish officers simply did not collect at all because they would 'rather fall into the hand of his Majesty than into the hands of resolute men', as the sheriff of Somerset put it fittingly.[101] Again, in many counties, this was the case from the very beginning of Ship Money. In January 1636, sheriff Stephens of Gloucestershire, for example, named eleven constables of Kiftsgate hundred who ignored his warrants for collection. A few months later, the sheriff of Sussex and Surrey concluded, 'I much feare it must be my owne worke to doe it', since his subordinates did not collect the levy.[102] A plethora of local examples, however, show that often even the assessment failed because parishioners refused to cooperate with parish officers to assess their community, or the officers declined to hand over the data to the sheriff. Under the first writ of 1635, officers who refused to assess were reported in Essex, Gloucestershire, Oxfordshire, Warwickshire, and Wiltshire.[103] In October 1635, according to the chief constables of Bloxham hundred (Oxfordshire), their subordinate officers 'thinke they have noe Authority to Assese or taxe any man neither do they conceive the warratt giveth them any power soe to doe'.[104] In February 1637, the petty constables of Cheshire sabotaged Ship Money by denying sheriff Delves any data on the previous assessment.[105] The collapse of the machinery was, of course, complete when officers did not answer the sheriffs' letters, ignored appointments for meetings, or absented themselves when the sheriffs visited them. In December 1636, the sheriff of Hertfordshire harshly reprimanded all high constables for having 'neither agreed to my rate nor made any returns'. In May 1638, sheriff Boteler of Bedfordshire was perplexed because he had sent warrants to the parish officers of Tilsworth '& appointed them severall daies of appearance & sent two particular messingers to them & yet could never have any answer'.[106] In June 1636, sheriff Wentworth of Oxfordshire went out to challenge negligent officers but was reduced to making 'some threatening speeches at the Constable's house'.[107] Since it was counterproductive to sack parish officers, and the privy council could summon only a small number of offenders, sheriffs soon hired (often desperate and incompetent) volunteers or employed their own servants or family to collect or distrain.[108] The extent to which sheriffs employed their own men because they could no longer rely on local officers has not been fully appreciated and is one of the clearest indications of the collapse of local government under Ship Money. It never seemed to occur to the privy council that they were admitting administrative and political defeat when they encouraged, for example, in January 1636, the Gloucestershire sheriff 'to make choyce of others' if officers refused or delayed the collection.[109] Once again confirming the early difficulties Ship Money ran into, the dates of these references show that in many counties sheriffs relied on private officers from as early as 1636.[110] In some counties, a whole echelon of privatised local government emerged.[111]

It cannot be stressed enough that most of these developments occurred in the early years of Ship Money, long before the disruption of the First Scots' War and even Hampden's Case. This suggests that Ship Money did not fail because the Scots' Wars disrupted the privy council's supervision and tied up the administrative resources of the country or because Hampden's Case turned out to be an eye-opener for the country, but because Ship Money was resented from the very beginning, and taxpayers as well as local officers plucked up degrees of courage and employed a variety of strategies to thwart its collection. By insisting, for entirely political reasons, on a quota levy raised by sheriffs and parish officers rather than a subsidy-based tax assessed by commissioners and approved by Parliament, Charles himself had provided the nails and hammer for the coffin of Ship Money.[112]

IV

Four factors determined the qualified success of the Perfect Militia, the moderate outcome of the Book of Orders, and the failure of Ship Money: legality, common sense, financial implications, and convenience. The Perfect Militia worked, despite its lacking legal foundation, because it made common sense for the county to have a capable defence force, because only a handful of parishioners were affected its financial implications were minimal, and because the work it entailed for parish officers was negligible. The Book of Orders was not opposed because it was based on statutes; it made common sense to care for the poor and shoo away vagrants, and its financial implications were bearable. Yet attitudes towards the poor and local relief practices did not change. The convenience of both JPs and local officers and their scepticism towards bureaucratic approaches and accountability prevented the establishment of a hierarchical chain of command via divisions and petty sessions. For its part, Ship Money failed because people were never convinced of its legality, they questioned the value of a standing fleet, and they distrusted the proper disposition of the money collected. While its financial implications were more significant, they were not severe enough to explain the extent of its opposition, which had political roots. As a consequence, its assessment and collection were not only inconvenient, but odious, and forced local officers – in their own interest – to terminate its enforcement.

Central policies were merely dead letters without the consent and cooperation of parish officers. Any scheme originating in Westminster was scrutinized by them as to its compatibility with local values and practices and then adapted to accommodate their part-time work as crown officers and the ever growing workload during the Personal Rule. If parish officers were the opinion leaders in their communities, they assessed the value of central directives themselves. If not, their social superiors put the necessary pressure on them to ensure that central policies were enforced according to local sentiment. This often resulted in conflicting loyalties and a highly selective enforcement of policies. The dependency of JPs, sheriffs, and deputy lieutenants on the cooperation of parish officers to carry out orders, as well as on information only they could provide, prevented their effective supervision. Yet the 1630s did not experience recruiting problems or a decline in the status of parish officers because the office enabled them to influence national policies and stay in the driver's seat.[113]

While there were clearly national trends in responding to central policies (and only a nationwide study can show this), local reactions varied, were determined by each individual community, and cannot be delineated by county boundaries, as local historians have claimed in the past. The formidable decentralization of local government in early modern England and the concentration of actual power at the lowest administrative level determined the fate of Charles's attempts at reform and prevented their uniform enforcement across the country.

Notes

1 Clive Holmes, *Why Was Charles I Executed?* (2006), p. 9.
2 Kevin Sharpe, *The Personal Rule of Charles I* (New Haven, CT, and London, 1992); Mark Kishlansky, *A Monarchy Transformed: Britain 1603–1714* (1996). See also Ronald Hutton, *Debates in Stuart History* (2004), Chapter 1, particularly pp. 17–18 and 28–9.
3 Cf. Norah Carlin, *The Causes of the English Civil War* (Oxford, 1999), p. 139.
4 Thomas Barnes, *Somerset 1625–1640: A County's Government During the 'Personal Rule'* (Cambridge, MA, 1961), pp. 244–80; Anthony Fletcher, *Reform in the Provinces: The Government of Stuart England* (New Haven, CT, and London, 1986), pp. 286–316; D.P. Carter, 'The "Exact Militia" in Lancashire, 1625–1640', *Northern History*, 11 (1975), 87–106.
5 Brian Quintrell, 'The Making of Charles I's Book of Orders', *EHR*, 95 (1980), 553–72; John Morrill, *Cheshire 1630–1660: County Government and Society during the English Revolution* (Oxford, 1974).
6 Clive Holmes, *Seventeenth-Century Lincolnshire* (Lincoln, 1980); Barnes, *Somerset*.
7 TNA, SP Charles I, Great Britain, series II, 1625–1702, and TNA, APC, new series, 2, vols. 40–52.
8 On the history of the English militia: Lyndsey Boynton, *The Elizabethan Militia, 1558–1638* (London and Toronto, 1967), esp. pp. 3–125; Barnes, *Somerset*, pp. 68–123. On the militia during the Thirty Years' War: Barnes, *Somerset*, pp. 254–5, 272; Mark Fissel, *The Bishops' Wars: Charles I's Campaigns against Scotland 1638–1640* (Cambridge, 1994), pp. 215–63; Carter, 'Exact Militia'; Sharpe, *Personal Rule*, pp. 487–506, 792–812.
9 Boynton and Barnes stress the deterioration, while Fissel, Carter, Fletcher, and Sharpe highlight the achievements of the Perfect Militia.
10 For a discussion of this shift towards a communal defence obligation, see Barnes, *Somerset*, pp. 114–16 and Joan Kent, *The English Village Constable 1580–1642: A Social and Administrative Study* (Oxford, 1986), pp. 175, 178.
11 Barnes, *Somerset*, pp. 121–2, is very critical of the constables' military work, while Kent, *Village Constable*, pp. 40, 175–85, is, overall, more positive.
12 This part of the chapter is based on my article '"The Chiefest Strength and Glory of This Kingdom": Arming and Training the "Perfect Militia" in the 1630s', *EHR*, 118 (2003), 1264–1303.
13 Dorset RO: PE/CHM CW 1/1; Leicestershire RO: DE 1605/56; Charlton Marshall usually sent one soldier to the musters. The Stathern accounts provide no evidence, but the expenses suggest two to three militiamen.
14 Suffolk RO: FB 159/65; Lincolnshire Archives: Croft 12/1; East Devon RO: Dartington PW2, fol. 475
15 For more details, see Langelüddecke, '"Perfect Militia"', 1272–8 and 1282–91.
16 Staffordshire RO: D 3451/2/2; Suffolk RO: FB 130/I2/3–10; FC 85/I2, 8, 9, 13; Warwickshire RO: DR 404/85 and DRB 27/9.
17 Cornwall RO: DDP 53/9/2; East Devon RO: Halberton PW 1+2.
18 Northamptonshire RO: 206p/102; Suffolk RO: FC 62 A6/171; East Devon RO: 815 A/PW 1. All my references to dates are NS, the year beginning on 1 January.
19 Norfolk RO: PD 358/33.

20 Regarding the bullet-to-gunpowder ratio and ratio of musketeers, see John Tincey and Richard Hook, *The Armada Campaign 1588*, Osprey Military Elite Series 15, p. 32; Stuart Reid and Graham Turner, *Scots Armies of the English Civil Wars*, Osprey Military Men-at-Arms Series 331, p. 19. During the 1588 Armada threat, the London militia was the most modern force with a ratio of 1:1: Tincey and Hook, *The Armada Campaign*, p. 48; in 1644, the Earl Marischal's and Lord Gordon's regiments of the Scottish levies had advanced to a ratio of two musketeers to one pikeman, which was considered a very uncommon concentration of firepower: Reid and Turner, *Scots Armies*, p. 19. For East Budleigh, see East Devon RO: 1180 A add 2/PW 15, fol. 41; High Bray: North Devon RO: 815 A/PW 1, 1637: 10 lb of powder; 1635: 25 lb; 1634: 32 lb; in 1631 and 1635, the accounts suggest that seven of the on average thirteen soldiers were musketeers, since, in 1635, there was a separate practice of seven men at Bratton, referred to as the 'shoate men'.

21 East Devon RO: 3004 A/PW 4/1, fols 155, 161. For a more detailed discussion, see Langelüddecke, '"Perfect Militia"', 1292–4.

22 See Boynton, *Militia*, pp. 271–2; Barnes, *Somerset*, pp. 119, 249, 263–5. For a detailed discussion, see Langelüddecke, '"Perfect Militia"', 1294–5.

23 See Langelüddecke, '"Perfect Militia"', 1296–7.

24 Northamptonshire RO: 55p/504; 206p/102; Shropshire RO: 3076/3/1; Norfolk RO: PD 219/126.

25 Norfolk RO: PD 358/33; North Devon RO: 815 A/PW 1.

26 Fissel, *Bishops' Wars*, pp. 195–9, 207–13.

27 See my article '"Or Else I Could Not Have Gott Of": Recruitment for Service in the First Scots' War in Lincolnshire', *Midland History*, 38 (2013), 152–68. It is based on the investigation by the Lincolnshire Deputy Lieutenants into bribery to evade conscription for the expeditionary force in 1639: Bodl., MS Top. Linc. c. 3, fols 68–299 (Hussey Letters and Military Papers).

28 TNA, APC 2/40, 214–15, or BL, Add. MS 12496, fols 263–91; in print: John Rushworth (ed.), *Historical Collections* (8 vols, 1659–1680), II, Part 2, Appendix, 82–9, or Frederic Eden, *The State of the Poor* (2nd edn., 1965), pp. 156–60.

29 For interpretations as to the number and content of the JPs certificates, see my article, '"Patchy and Spasmodic?" The Response of Justices of the Peace to Charles I's Book of Orders', *EHR*, 113 (1998), 1231–48.

30 Frederic Youngs, 'Towards Petty Sessions: Tudor JPs and Divisions of Counties', in DeLloyd Guth and John McKenna (eds.), *Tudor Rule and Revolution: Essays for G.R. Elton from His American Friends* (Cambridge, 1982), pp. 201–16; and Barnes, *Somerset*, p. 200.

31 Splits, e.g. Northamptonshire, TNA, SP 16/193/24, 220/18 and 194/9, 220/17 vs. 301/47, 328/72, 348/17, 348/28; Hertfordshire: 198/11, 247/47, 266/4 vs. 329/56, 383/57, 427/3; Norfolk: 190/20, 192/70 vs. 272/44, 301/104, 329/24, 364/27. Mergers: e.g. Essex: 190/70, 244/38 vs. 329/48, 426/67.

32 TNA, SP 16/184/60, 193/25, 203/67, 258/35, 377/182.

33 For a more detailed discussion, see my article, 'Law and Order in Seventeenth-Century England: The Organization of Local Administration during the Personal Rule of Charles I', *Law and History Review*, 15 (1997), 49–76.

34 Phrases that suggest monthly meetings in divisions of e.g. Cambridgeshire: TNA, SP 16/270/12; Devon: 252/23; Dorset: 262/64; Hampshire, 185/70, 250/11i, 400/57; Huntingdonshire: 237/70, 237/71, 237/72, 273/24; Lincolnshire: 189/58; Norfolk: 329/13, 349/47, 395/32, 415/121; Nottinghamshire: 329/57; Oxfordshire: 293/10; Sussex: 348/43; Worcestershire: 215/27. Vague references in divisions of Berkshire: 206/33, 225/8, 267/37, 314/79, 314/133, 347/50, 367/3; Buckinghamshire: 201/52, 269/40, 281/85, 281/86; Cambridgeshire: 189/75, 216/45, 269/64, 271/41, 273/4, 274/45, 275/53, 277/90, 285/99, 328/67, 364/26, 395/11; Derbyshire: 316/23; Dorset: 203/76, 233/44, 250/38, 260/111; Essex: 363/60; Flintshire: 185/75; Glamorganshire: 193/64; Hampshire: 185/70, 188/19, 188/101, 248/69, 250/11iii; Hertfordshire:

182/40, 185/27; 211/26, 215/88, 257/97; Kent: 203/91; Lincolnshire: 220/58, 281/82; 294/31; Monmouthshire: 270/17, 329/86; Norfolk: 310/104, 329/12; Northamptonshire: 192/84i, 194/9, 220/17, 220/18, 224/3, 271/26; Oxfordshire: 291/81; Rutlandshire: 186/69; Somerset: 176/18, 193/35, 219/46, 230/55, 262/70, 273/5; Staffordshire: 342/104; Surrey: 268/15, 272/22; Sussex: 363/130, 426/19; Wiltshire: 218/41, 220/29, 247/25, 289/19; Yorkshire: 189/8x, 206/94, 250/47, 293/129, 293/130, 294/6, 317/11.
35 Only 418 out of 1,376; see Langelüddecke, 'Law and Order', 58–9.
36 Cambridgeshire: TNA, SP 16/271/85; Hampshire: 288/94; Hertfordshire: 364/73; Huntingdonshire: 201/19, 201/20, 201/21; Lancashire: 273/55; Leicestershire 201/26, 201/27; Lincolnshire: 220/58; 223/54; Nottinghamshire: 193/78; Sussex: 351/106; Warwickshire: 200/40.
37 TNA, SP 16/293/9.
38 Langelüddecke, 'Law and Order', 60–1.
39 Berkshire: TNA, 16/176/35; Derbyshire: 188/94, 192/96; Hampshire: 250/11iii; Shropshire: 197/47.
40 Concerning absenteeism and cross-divisional activities of JPs, see Langelüddecke, 'Law and Order', 62–4.
41 For data and a discussion of the difficulties identifying what local officers attended, according to these certificates, see Langelüddecke, 'Law and Order', 65–8.
42 *Ibid.*, 69–71.
43 JPs' certificates and some parish accounts containing phrases that might suggest this: TNA, SP 16/194/9, 196/90, 197/52, 198/51, 268/14, 382/71; Leicestershire RO: DE 720/30 (1634 and 1637), DE 1605/56 (1632), DE 625/60 (1637).
44 North Devon RO: 1469 A/PC 6 (1631); Lincolnshire Archives: Croft 12/1 (1632, 1635, 1637).
45 TNA, SP 16/198/33 and 269/109; for further examples, see Langelüddecke, 'Law and Order', 72–3.
46 Julian Hill, 'A Study of Poverty and Poor Relief in Shropshire 1550–1640' (unpublished MA thesis, University of Liverpool, 1973), p. 267; Alison Hems, 'Aspects of Poverty and the Poor Laws in Early Modern England' (unpublished PhD thesis, University of Liverpool, 1985), p. 314; Gordon Forster, 'The East Riding Justices of the Peace in the Seventeenth Century', *East Yorkshire Local History Society*, 30 (1973), 46; and A.L. Beier, 'Poor Relief in Warwickshire 1630–1660', *P&P*, 35 (1966), 77–100.
47 John Walter and Keith Wrightson, 'Dearth and Social Order in Early Modern England', *P&P*, 71 (1976), 41; Paul Slack, *Poverty and Policy in Tudor and Stuart England* (1988), p. 207; Peter Clark, *English Provincial Society from the Reformation to the Revolution: Religion, Politics and Society in Kent 1500–1640* (Hemel Hempstead, 1977), p. 353; Barnes, *Somerset*, p. 189; Hems, 'Aspects of Poverty', p. 289; G.P. Higgins, 'County Government and Society in Cheshire c. 1590–1640' (unpublished MA thesis, University of Liverpool, 1973), pp. 241, 250; more recently, Steve Hindle, *The State and Social Change in Early Modern England, 1550–1640* (Basingstoke, 2002), pp. 146–75.
48 Essex: Hundreds of Harlow, Ongar, and Waltham: TNA, SP 16/347/73; Nottinghamshire: 329/63
49 Examples: Kent: TNA, SP 16/186/6, 203/91, 246/34, 312/83, 347/68, 382/52, 425/93; Norfolk: 190/20, 191/78, 192/79, 193/74, 193/88, 328/79, 349/46, 364/50, 385/27. For a more detailed discussion of the JPs' approach to poor relief, see Henrik Langelüddecke, 'Secular Policy Enforcement during the Personal Rule of Charles I: The Administrative Work of Parish Officers in the 1630s' (unpublished DPhil thesis, University of Oxford, 1995), pp. 81–4.
50 Quoted from the certificate of JPs from Agbrigg and Morley (Yorkshire): TNA, SP 16/317–11. For a discussion of a variety of poor relief measures, see also Steve Hindle, *On the Parish: The Micro-Politics of Poor Relief in Rural England c. 1550–1750* (Oxford, 2005), pp. 262–71.

51 Fasting: New Forest division (Hampshire): TNA, SP 16/190/38; Wells (Somerset): 194/19; exclusive shopping hours for the poor: Somerset: TNA, SP 16/192/49; Southwark: 190/66; Surrey: 185/6; Sussex: 177/61; Yorkshire: 189/8ix, 190/58; lifting the ban on buying corn straight from the producer: Cambridgeshire: 194/65; Hertfordshire: 193/2, 198/39; Lincolnshire: 192/40; Norfolk: 210/61; Surrey: 192/66; Sussex: 190/51; buying corn to establish grain stocks for the poor: Bedford: 189/7ii; Derby: 193/5; Hertfordshire: 206/73; Leicester: 191/69; Norfolk: 191/79; Norwich: 186/26; lowering the corn prices for the poor: Abingdon: 195/7; Cambridgeshire: 189/75; Essex: 187/10; Norfolk: 195/47; Sussex: 192/99; punishment of middlemen: Doncaster: 189/8iv; giving bread not conforming to the assize or meat slaughtered at Lent to the poor: St. Albans: 16/262/29; hundreds of Edwinstree and Odsey (Hertfordshire): 193/3; Bramber rape (Sussex): 239/4.

52 Eighty-nine parish officers' lists have survived for the period of operation for the Book of Orders – and seventy-eight mention overseers. As these officers' lists originate from parishes scattered across the country, ranging from Pulloxhill (Bedfordshire) to Alderley (Cheshire), Modbury (Devon), Swanage (Dorset), Finchingfield (Essex), Weyhill (Hampshire), Cranbrook (Kent), Horbling (Lincolnshire), Benhall (Suffolk), and Ashton Steeple (Wiltshire), to name only a few, they provide a fairly representative statistical sample of all the officers' lists that once existed. Hence, the mentioning of overseers in seventy-eight out of eighty-nine parish officers' lists implies that poor rates were levied in nine out of ten communities.

53 Slack and Hindle seem to disagree over my suggestion that poor rates were widely used by local officers in the 1630s. Slack is not persuaded that annual rating was practised in the majority of country parishes before 1650: Paul Slack, *From Reformation to Improvement: Public Welfare in Early Modern England* (Oxford, 1999), p. 67 n. 55. Hindle, on the other hand, has found a number of local examples, which seem to support my suggestion: Hindle, *On the Parish*, pp. 245–51.

54 On the intricacies of establishing rating intervals from overseers' accounts, see Langelüddecke, 'Secular Policy Enforcement', pp. 92–3.

55 For detailed data and local examples, see *ibid.*, pp. 92–102.

56 Poor rate data are near complete for the 1630s in St. Werburgh: Bristol RO: P/St.W./ChW/3(b); Amersham: Centre for Buckinghamshire Studies: PR 4/12/2; Ashburton: East Devon RO: 2660 A/PW 2; Bere Ferrers: 1237 A/PO 20; Chudleigh: East Devon RO Chudleigh PO 1; Churston Ferrers: 1235 A/PO 2; Dean Prior: East Devon RO Dean Prior PO 1; Frithelstock: North Devon RO: 3788 A/PW 1; Northam: 1843 A/PW 2; Parkham: 1892 A add 3/PO 1; Beaminster: Dorset History Centre: PE BE OV 1/1; Swyre: PE/SWY OV 1/1; Finchingfield: Essex RO: D/P 14/8/1A; Roydon: D/P 60/8/1; Waltham: D/P 75/5/1; Slimbridge: Gloucestershire RO: P 298 A OV 2/1; Chawton: Hampshire RO: 1 M 70/PO 1; Totteridge: Hertfordshire Archives and Local Studies: Mf 1120; Bredgar: Centre for Kentish Studies: P 43/12/2; Buckland St. Mary: Somerset Archives: D/P/b.my.13/2/1; Burrington: D/P/bur.13/2/1; Ilminster: D/P/ilm.13/2/1; Pitminster: DD/SAS/CH 20; Trull: D/P/tru.13/2/1; Checkley: Staffordshire RO: D 113/1/PC/1; Cratfield: Suffolk RO: FC 62 A2/1; Mellis: FB 123 E1/2; Rickinghall Superior: FB 121 E1/1; Devizes (St. John): Wiltshire and Swindon RO: 632/107.

57 For a detailed discussion of watches and wards, as well as provost marshals, see Langelüddecke, 'Secular Policy Enforcement', pp. 110–15.

58 Vague and evasive comments, e.g. Derbyshire: TNA, SP 16/293/113, 293/114, 293/115, 316/23; Leicestershire: 193/69, 191/69, 216/103, 190/3, 200/24, 219/49, 222/51; Oxfordshire: 191/19, 274/65, 275/48, 291/81, 293/10; Staffordshire: 294/36, 294/37, 329/44, 330/7, 342/104; Warwickshire: 293/44, 293/65, 314/116. Vague numbers: 'Diverse': Buckinghamshire: TNA, SP 16/269/40; Dorset: 233/44; Hampshire: 285/70; Hertfordshire: 203/103. 'Some': Berkshire: 314/132; Suffolk: 187/92. 'Few': Berkshire:

390/131; Northamptonshire: 191/67; Wiltshire: 262/33. 'Less': Hampshire: 250/11iv; 188/101. 'Many': Buckinghamshire: 281/85; Cambridgeshire: 364/26; Herefordshire: 330/98; Shropshire: 263/47; Staffordshire: 330/7. Rounded numbers: Lincolnshire: 342/107 (twenty), 349/115 (one hundred); Nottinghamshire: 349/85 ('about sixty'); Suffolk: 329/31 (fifty); 349/12 (fifty); 395/63 (forty).

59 In the Petty Session minutes of the Purbeck division (Dorset), only one out of the nine parishes reported any vagrants in 1638: Dorset History Centre: D/PLR D 320/X 4. In May 1635, the list of a Devon division showed blank columns for fifteen out of thirty-seven parishes; seven recorded only one vagrant: TNA, SP 16/289/43; in December 1636, twenty-six out of thirty-four parishes of Barkston wapentake (Yorkshire) denied the existence of vagrants: 304/100.

60 TNA, SP 16/351/115.

61 Consequently, I do not share Hindle's assessment that the JPs' reports are invaluable evidence of the successful prosecution of vagrants in the 1630s. He makes the important point, however, that JPs were unable to prove their subordinates' negligence: Hindle, *State and Social Change*, pp. 168–9.

62 East Devon RO: Woodbury PW 1; Norfolk RO: 219/126.

63 Leicestershire RO: DE 625/60; DE 1605/56; Lincolnshire Archives: Croft 12/1.

64 East Devon RO: Dartington PW 2; Northamptonshire RO: 55p/504.

65 Lincolnshire Archives: Algarkirk 12; Croft 12/1; Northamptonshire RO, 55p/504 (my italics); similar in Cransley: *ibid.*, 89p/100; and Elstree (Hertfordshire): TNA, SP 16/347/67.

66 Wiltshire and Swindon RO: 1368/55; Shropshire Archives: 1374/295. Other examples: North Devon RO: High Bray, 815 A/PW 1 (1633); Leicestershire RO: Branston, DE 720/30 (1632).

67 Somerset Archives: D/P/ilm.4/1/2; Essex RO: T/P 99/3; Bristol RO: P/AS/ChW5; Dorset History Centre: PE/WM CW 1/41; CKS: P 26/5/1. Other generous parishes: Cambridgeshire RO: Cambridge/Holy Trinity, P 22/5/2+3; Gloucestershire RO: Twyning, P 343 VE 2/1; East Sussex RO: Lewes/St. Michael, PAR 414/9/1/1c. In contrast, recipients of parish doles received between 4d and 6d per week: Hindle, *On the Parish*, pp. 274–5.

68 Soldiers, e.g.: East Devon RO: Exeter/Heavitree, 3004 A/PW 4/1/(1640); Herefordshire RO: Madley, MX 806 (1632); Centre for Kentish Studies: Tenterden, P 364/5/14 91633); Loose, P 233/5/1 (1635); Leicestershire RO: Waltham, DE 625/60 (1632); Suffolk RO: Cratfield, FC 62 A/165 (1633); Framlingham, FC 101 E2/22 (1632); Mendlesham, FB 159/66 (1636); Warwickshire RO: Nether Whitace, DRB 27/9 (1632). Yarmouth magistrates expressed their worries about large numbers of disembarking veterans in 1636 and 1637: TNA, SP 16/328/79 (thirty), 364/37 (sixty-five). JPs of Arundel rape (Sussex) reported numerous forged discharge papers in 1636: TNA, SP 16/314/115. Regarding the ingenuity of vagrants, see also A.L. Beier, *Masterless Men: The Vagrancy Problem in England 1560–1640* (1985), pp. 37, 42–3, 45, 70–1; Paul Slack, 'Vagrants and Vagrancy in England 1598–1664', *Economic History Review*, 2nd series, 27 (1974), 361–2, 368–76. Forged passports: Northamptonshire RO: Burton Latimer, 55p/504 (1635); Warwickshire RO: Nether Whitacre, DRB 27/9 (1632). Beier, *Masterless Men*, p. 143, points out that it was easier to forge a passport than a 'brief of calamity', a begging license.

69 Suffolk RO: FL 509/5/1/69 (my italics).

70 TNA, APC 2/45, 71–80, 85, dated 12 August 1635; APC 2/46, 378–83, 394–402, dated 9 October 1636; APC 2/48, 236–42, 255–64, dated 2 October 1637; APC 2/49, 449–54, 466–73, dated 9 November 1638; APC 2/51, 121–5, 135–44, dated 1 December 1639.

71 Morrill, *Cheshire 1630–1660*, p. 28, and *Revolt in the Provinces: The People of England and the Tragedies of War, 1630–48* (2nd edn., 1999), pp. 238–48; Anthony Fletcher, *A County Community in Peace and War: Sussex 1600–1660* (1975), pp. 202–8; Peter Lake, 'The Collection of Ship Money in Cheshire during the Sixteen-Thirties: A Case Study of Relations between Central and Local Government', *Northern History* 17 (1981), 44–71; M. Faraday, 'Ship Money in Herefordshire', *Transactions of the Woolhope Naturalists' Field Club*,

Herefordshire 41 (1974), 210–29; Patricia Haskell, 'Ship Money in Hampshire', in John Webb *et al.* (eds.), *Hampshire Studies, Presented to Dorothy Dymond* (Portsmouth City RO, 1981), pp. 73–106; C. Clifford, 'Ship Money in Hampshire: Collection and Collapse', *Southern History*, 4 (1982), 91–106; Jill Dias, 'Politics and Administration in Nottinghamshire and Derbyshire 1590–1640' (unpublished DPhil thesis, University of Oxford, 1973), pp. 381–90, 433–40.

72 Holmes, *Lincolnshire*, pp. 131–4; Brian Quintrell, 'The Government of the County of Essex, 1603–1642' (unpublished PhD thesis, University of London, 1965), Chapter 9. They are supported by Derek Hirst, *Authority and Conflict; England 1603–1658* (1986), pp. 178–9. Lake, 'Cheshire', 68 and 71, expresses serious reservations about the success of Ship Money.

73 Sharpe, *Personal Rule*, pp. 545–95, 717–23, cf. 585; and earlier in *idem*, 'The Personal Rule of Charles I', in Howard Tomlinson (ed.), *Before the English Civil War: Essays on Early Stuart Politics and Government* (1983), pp. 69–74 (here Sharpe calls Ship Money a 'great success story'). Recent support has been offered by Kishlansky, *A Monarchy Transformed*, p. 122, who states that Ship Money was paid 'punctually'. Sharpe has based his conclusions on the pioneering study by M.D. Gordon, 'The Collection of Ship-Money in the Reign of Charles I', *TRHS*, 3rd series, 4 (1910), 141–62. Despite identifying its political costs, an unpublished doctoral thesis by Alison Gill has claimed that Ship Money was a fiscal success and not seriously challenged before Hampden's Case and that widespread dissatisfaction with the levy did not occur until its later years: 'Ship Money during the Personal Rule of Charles I: Politics, Ideology and the Law 1634 to 1640' (unpublished PhD thesis, University of Sheffield, 1990).

74 See n. 7. The following section of this chapter is based on my article, '"I Finde All Men & My Officers All Soe Unwilling": The Collection of Ship Money, 1635–1640', *JBS*, 46 (2007), 509–42.

75 Payment figures, for example, regarding the 1635 writ: TNA, SP 16/318/4 (1 April 1636), 330/55 (20 August 1636), and 344/48 (20 January 1637); 1636 writ: 351/55 (31 March 1637), 369/36 (7 October 1637), and 378/22 (6 January 1638); 1637 writ: 387/37 (7 April 1638), 399/33 (29 September 1638), and 418/77 (27 April 1639).

76 Esther Cope, *Politics without Parliament 1629–1640* (1987), p. 115.

77 TNA, SP 16/395/92, 408/149; both sheriffs were in charge of the 1637 Ship Money.

78 TNA, SP 16/346/108, 349/2.

79 For more details, see Langelüddecke, 'Secular Policy Enforcement', p. 188.

80 Some examples: Derbyshire: TNA, SP 16/399/16; Dorset: 367/2; Essex: 335/67i, TNA, APC 2/48, 297; Gloucestershire: APC 2/47, 178 and 181; Herefordshire: SP 16/464/98; Hertfordshire: APC 2/50, 663; Lincolnshire: SP 16/315/121, 318/51, 352/67; Shropshire: 303/71; Somerset: 327/66; Warwickshire: 336/4; Wiltshire: 448/63.

81 TNA, APC 2/46, 443 and 448–9; locally specific orders: 2/46, 447; 2/50, 256.

82 See the more detailed cases of Roger Harmans, George Plowright, Thomas Mace, and Edward Boys, described in Langelüddecke, 'Ship Money', 517–18.

83 TNA, SP 16/331/12, 350/39 and 349/88. For more examples, see Langelüddecke, 'Ship Money', 519–20.

84 Neighbours not daring to buy distrained goods, e.g.: Bedfordshire: TNA, SP 16/463/86ii; Bristol: 460/34; Cardiganshire: 376/141; Hampshire: 427/47; Middlesex: 333/22; Monmouthshire: 467/57; Oxfordshire: 327/126; Norfolk: 450/1, 455/36; Suffolk: 464/12; Surrey: 379/131; Worcestershire: 467/133.

85 TNA, SP 16/337/27; continuing in 337/32, 337/41; TNA, APC 2/47, 37; SP 16/337/66, 337/67; APC 2/47, 76–7. A selection of incidents involving preventing distraining or 'rescuing' distrained cattle: Bedford: APC 2/45, 447–8; Bedfordshire: 2/46, 359–60; Derbyshire: 2/45, 279; Dorset: SP 16/433/2; Herefordshire: 447/8; Lincolnshire: 399/13; Merionethshire: APC 2/46, 24; Monmouthshire: SP 16/467/57; Northamptonshire: 333/2, 349/17, 352/19i, 367/33; 401/13; Nottinghamshire: 420/133; Oxfordshire: 438/100; 467/80, 468/31; Shropshire: APC 2/52, 592; Somerset: SP 16/379/29, 389/124, 464/23; Staffordshire: 452/10; Warwickshire: 468/49; Worcestershire: 457/58; APC 2/46, 462–3.

86 TNA, SP 16/352/18, 362/83, 367/46.
87 TNA, SP 16/379/132.
88 TNA, SP 16/400/27; see also e.g. Derbyshire: 341/56; Devon: 376/138, 432/78; Durham: 398/18; Essex: 361/18; Gloucestershire: APC 2/50, 633; Lincolnshire: SP 16/399/83, 457/92; Monmouthshire: 459/39; Northamptonshire: 333/2ii; 398/116; Oxfordshire: 467/80; APC 2/46, 419; Somerset: SP 16/363/11ii, 464/23; Surrey: 389/132; Suffolk: 451/18i; APC 2/46, 177; Wiltshire: SP 407/41.
89 E.g. Cheshire: TNA, SP 16/460/35; Barnstaple: 376/138; Lincolnshire: 352/67; Banbury: 537/47; Shrewsbury: 400/22; Worcester: 467/133.
90 Descriptions of local assessment disputes in Barnes, *Somerset*, pp. 213–21; Elaine Marcotte, 'Shrieval Administration in Cheshire, 1637: Limitations of Early Stuart Governance', *Bulletin of the John Rylands University Library of Manchester*, 58 (1975), 150–7, and Lake, 'Ship Money in Cheshire', 45–53. For a detailed analysis of all prominent Ship Money assessment disputes, see Langelüddecke, 'Secular Policy Enforcement', pp. 143–80.
91 Suggested by Hirst, *Authority and Conflict*, pp. 178–9 and, again, *England in Conflict 1603–1660: Kingdom, Community*, Commonwealth (1999), p. 148. See also Holmes, *Lincolnshire*, pp. 132–3; Langelüddecke, 'Ship Money', 522–4.
92 TNA, SP 16/302/29.
93 See n. 27.
94 E.g. Lord Saye and Sele: Maidstone, Centre for Kentish Studies: Twysden MSS, U 47/47 O1, p.191; TNA, SP 16/362/76, f.2; 357/96vii; see also *The Earl of Strafforde's Letters and Dispatches*, ed. William Knowler (2 vols, Dublin, 1740), II, 86, and Nelson Bard, 'The Ship Money Case and William Fiennes, Viscount Saye and Sele', *Bulletin of the Institute of Historical Research*, 50 (1977), 230–7; William Strode: TNA, SP 16/336/29, 345/33; APC 2/47, 104–5, 110.
95 Mentioned in, e.g. Banbury: TNA, SP 16/361/25; Cornwall: 346/88; Derbyshire: 535/124; Devon: 351/20; Herefordshire: 464/98; Hertfordshire: HMC, *Fourth Report*, p. 292; Lincolnshire: TNA, SP 16/333/23ii, 345/18i; Oxfordshire: 327/126, 366/19; Somerset: 341/44, 363/11i, 389/71, 392/1; Suffolk: APC 2/46, 177; Yorkshire: SP 16/438/105. Petitions by grand juries against Ship Money in 1640: Northamptonshire: SP 16/441/63, 447/46, 447/47, 450/25; Berkshire: *Diary of John Rous, incumbent of Santon Downham, Suffolk, from 1625 to 1642*, ed. Mary A. Green (Camden Society, 66, 1856), 91.
96 Michael J. Braddick, *Parliamentary Taxation in Seventeenth-Century England* (Woodbridge, 1994), pp. 39–54, 117–25.
97 For details about the sheriffs' approaches and Privy Council's responses, including summonses of tax refusers, see Langelüddecke, 'Ship Money', 523–4.
98 TNA, SP 16/327/126.
99 The situation of local officers was best summed up in 1637 by one of the Middlesex sheriffs who reassured the collectors of Pinner 'that he thought it not fit that your pet[itioner]s should distrayne themselves because they would gett the ill will of their Neighbours': TNA, SP 16/376/124.
100 TNA, Dorset: SP 16/464–23; Lincolnshire: 333/23i, 345/18i, 357/96i-1, 357/96iii-1, 357/96vi, 357/124, 399/13, 404/120; Middlesex: 398/122; Norfolk: 385/1, 397/46i; Northamptonshire: 349/74, 351/65; Oxfordshire: 366/19, 468/80, 468/123, 537/47; Somerset: 336/29, 363/11ii; Worcestershire: 467/58i. In some counties, particularly Berkshire, Essex, and Northamptonshire, hundredal bailiffs ignored the sheriffs' orders as their appointment had been granted out to local magnates. The fact that none of the patentees made the slightest effort to support the sheriffs is yet another indication of the deep-rooted unpopularity of Ship Money: TNA, SP 16/367/9, 395/59, 433/22, 463/66, 464/24, 465/13, 468/79; APC 2/46, 269–70, 2/50, 596–8, 2/51, 109–10.
101 TNA, SP 16/464/23.

102 TNA, SP 16/311/78, 329/37. Examples of other pre-1640 incidents: Bedfordshire: 390/62; Devon: APC 2/48, 206; Essex: 2/47, 18–19; Gloucestershire: 2/49, 395; Hampshire: SPD 16/319/76, 380/71, 388/40; Hertfordshire: 381/71; Huntingdonshire: 389/133; Lancashire: 304/34; Leicestershire 385/2; Lincolnshire: 345/18i, 376/121, 427/106; Merionethshire: 313/76; Middlesex: 398/29; 433/9; Norfolk: 389/9; Northamptonshire: 349/74; Nottinghamshire: 352/18; Somerset: 388/69, 389/71, 433/10; Staffordshire: 346/108, 349/88, 371/78; Surrey: 346/106; Worcestershire: APC 2/46, 462–3; 2/50, 365.
103 E.g. Essex: TNA, APC 2/45, 305; Gloucestershire: 2/46, 154–5; Oxfordshire: 2/45, 353; SP 16/313/93, 315/123; Warwickshire: 322/8; Wiltshire: 302/18.
104 TNA, SP 16/302/90i.
105 TNA, SP 16/348/35. Other references to difficulties under the 1636 writ: Essex: 335/67; Gloucestershire: 347/51; Hertfordshire: BL, Add. MS 61681, fol. 14; Leicestershire: TNA, SP 16/346/109, 351/91; Northamptonshire: 348/64, 348/64i-vii; APC 2/47, 222; SP 16/350/47, 354/72; Oxfordshire: 349/92; Somerset: 347/23; Staffordshire: 346/108, 349/88.
106 BL, Add. MS 61681, fol. 14; TNA, SP 16/390/62.
107 TNA, SP 16/327/126.
108 On privy council advice and prosecution of refractory local officers, see Langelüddecke, 'Ship Money', 528–9.
109 TNA, APC 2/45, 387–8. Similar recommendations: Berkshire: 2/49, 344–5; Essex: 2/47, 134; Oxfordshire: 2/50, 66; Staffordshire: 2/50, 624–5.
110 E.g. Cheshire: TNA, SP 16/460/35 (July 1640); Cornwall: 463/53 (August 1640), but already 424/43 (June 1639); Devon: 303/127 (December 1635), 372/3 (November 1637); Gloucestershire: 331/39 (October 1637), 464/64 (August 1640); Lincolnshire: 357/96 (May 1637), 464/5 (August 1640); Northamptonshire: 333/2 (September 1636), 465/13 (August 1640); Oxfordshire: 367/53 (September 1637); Somerset: 369/86 (October 1637).
111 The most remarkable piece of evidence of this privatised local government is a report from sheriff Freke of Dorset, who, in charge of the 1635 Ship Money, in December 1636, announced that 'ye bailiffs w[hi]ch were my servants fittest to act by distress ar now ye next Sherife servants': TNA, SP 16/337/36. See also the references in the notebook of Cheshire sheriff Cholmondeley: John Rylands Library, Manchester, English MS 1091, e.g. fols 25v, 26.
112 In this context, it is disappointing to read Professor Kishlansky's claim, 'By every account, including that of Henrik Langelüddecke, it was a remarkably successful fiscal expedient and roused far less overt resistance than had the 1627 loan', when, in the article he refers to, I state precisely the opposite: Mark Kishlansky, 'Charles I: A Case of Mistaken Identity – Reply', *P&P*, 205 (2009), 220.
113 For a discussion of who served as parish officers in the 1630s, see my article, '"The Pooreste and Sympleste Sorte of People"? The Selection of Parish Officers during the Personal Rule of Charles I', *Bulletin of the Institute of Historical Research*, 80 (2007), 225–60.

3 Party politics in the Long Parliament, 1640–8[1]

David Scott

Clive Holmes is first and foremost a historian of the English Revolution, for all his subsequent forays into witchcraft and gentry and legal culture in early modern England. As a good Commonwealthsman, he has looked more to the 'country' for inspiration than to the court or its 1640s parliamentary rival. Nevertheless, in his groundbreaking book *The Eastern Association in the English Civil War* (1974), he was always sensitive to the role of factional manoeuvrings at Westminster in shaping the pattern and structures of regional politics.[2] Our perception of the political forces operating in and upon the Long Parliament has changed considerably in the intervening four decades, of course, thanks in particular to the work of Michael Mahony and John Adamson.[3] What follows is an attempt to integrate their findings with the wealth of new and as yet unpublished material generated by the 1640–60 section of the History of Parliament.[4] The coverage here will be broad in the sense that it will span the years between the assembling of the Long Parliament and Pride's Purge – a period too often broken up by obfuscating chronological divides. But the spotlight will not be upon the majority of Parliament-men who avoided any consistent alignment with the Westminster parties, but upon the 'grandees': the politicians in both Houses with a programme as to how and on what terms to achieve a settlement with Charles and who expected to dominate his court and counsels once peace had been restored.

I

It is impossible to understand the British civil wars of the 1640s without first taking full account of the ambitions and rivalries of Westminster's grandee politicians – groups that I have labelled parties or factions. Much of the basic narrative of events in the Long Parliament, its great debates and legislative initiatives, was shaped by what the MP Sir Simonds D'Ewes referred to in 1643 as the 'secrett workings & machinations of each partie'.[5] The creation of a parliamentarian army under the Earl of Essex in the summer of 1642, the new modelling of that and Parliament's other field forces in 1644–5, and the assault on the New Model that began in 1646 and ended with it seizing the king and marching on London in 1647 – to name but three major developments of the period – were largely instigated and driven on by the grandees. A number of the Long Parliament's most powerful executive committees – in effect, organs of national government – were set up to address not simply the administrative requirements of the moment but also the partisan agendas of particular parties.[6] Parliament's various sets of peace proposals to the king were, to a greater or lesser extent, party manifestos for settlement that reflected their promoters' aspirations as a court-in-waiting. The Newcastle Propositions that were presented to the king in 1646, for example, were rightly perceived as a design by which the Independent grandees and their Anglo-Irish allies sought to destroy the Covenanting interest in post-war England and Ireland and advance their own bid for supremacy in Charles's restored government.[7] Party politics in the Long Parliament was fundamentally 'restoration politics'.[8]

The parties provided much of the political infrastructure through which Parliament conducted relations with the Covenanting Scots and the French crown – the Continental power most deeply involved in the affairs of civil-war Britain and Ireland. In a formal and diplomatic sense, the Covenanters allied with the English Parliament in 1643. But in fact their intervention in the civil war was masterminded by the war-party grandees in the face of concerted resistance from their peace party rivals.[9] Similarly, French diplomats, though accredited by Parliament, pursued their key objectives in collaboration with party politicians associated with the Earl of Essex and the Anglo-Scottish Presbyterian alliance of 1644.[10] Royalist factions, too, owed much of their influence in post-war British politics to their secretive but sometimes close relations with the parliamentary grandees.[11]

The entrenchment of party politics at Westminster and the massive growth of state power that accompanied it completely transformed the English people's perception of Parliament and its workings.[12] A great deal of radical as well as royalist commentary by the later 1640s sought to expose the tyranny of England's new parliamentary state and its unaccountable grandee masters.[13] 'Did you ever dream', asked the Leveller writer William Walwyn in 1648:

> that the oppressions of Committees would have exceeded those of the [Privy] Councel-table; or that in the place of Pattents and Projects, you should have seen an Excise established, ten fold surpassing all those, and Shipmoney together? . . . all the quarrell we have at this day in the Kingdome, is no other then a quarrel of Interests, and Partyes, a pulling down of one Tyrant, to set up another, and instead of Liberty, heaping upon our selves a greater slavery then that we fought against.[14]

The political groups referred to in this chapter as parties were not, of course, the durable, nationwide entities of the eighteenth century. Even so, the longest surviving of the parties in the Long Parliament, the Independents, retained its core membership and basic agenda for almost five years – which, amid the turmoil of politics in the 1640s, showed an impressive degree of unity and strength of purpose.[15]

Cohesiveness and longevity were not the only defining features of parliamentary parties in the 1640s. The Independent grandees can be identified as serious party animals by their possession of a powerbase in both Houses, for, of course, neither House could implement policy without the approval of the other. Without such a bicameral presence, no parliamentary grouping could operate effectively as a force for national settlement.[16] The same applied to any party that did not have an army or other military resources at its disposal, whether it be to underwrite a treaty with the king or, if necessary, to coerce its parliamentary rivals.

No party in the Long Parliament could function without a life beyond the confines of the Palace of Westminster. Parliaments before the 1640s had often been fractious affairs, vulnerable to competing interests and ideologies.[17] But the 'disjointing' at Westminster as a result of the civil war was of a more profound order.[18] Steering even minor initiatives, let alone major policies, through the two Houses in this highly charged political atmosphere required an unprecedented degree of pre-planning and coordination. The grandees must necessarily hold 'private meetings and councils' to devise strategy and to refine their managerial tactics in Parliament.[19] Such meetings were invariably held *in camera*. But the impact of these 'Councells without the walles' on the Houses' proceedings was often clear enough to observers.[20] It required no great political insight for the Scots commissioners to work out that the reports flooding Westminster from mid-1645 concerning their army's 'abuses' in northern England were part of a highly orchestrated attack by the Independents upon the entire Presbyterian programme for settlement.[21]

Good management alone could not build and sustain working majorities in both Houses, however. Party leaders must appeal to public interest, to issues of principle in settling church and state, in order to rally their political forces. It was therefore not enough to have capable managers on the floor of the Commons, or well placed committeemen dispensing patronage behind the scenes (more of which later); a successful party also required skilled orators and spokesmen of acknowledged influence in affairs of state. The grandees could not lead where they could not persuade and convince the non-engaged majority of Parliament-men to follow. John Pym's ability to stir the Houses and the public in the fight against 'popery' and to appropriate that cause for highly partisan ends was at least as important as his exalted aristocratic connections in propelling him to the forefront of party politics in the Long Parliament.[22]

II

Surveying the political scene at Westminster in 1640–1, there is only one faction that possessed the essential features of a party as outlined above – and that is the so-called 'junto' that Edward Hyde identified as the core of the parliamentary leadership from the opening of the Long Parliament. This group consisted of the earls of Essex and Warwick, Viscount Saye and Sele, and a few other peers, along with their closest allies in the Commons – most notably, Pym, John

Hampden, and Oliver St. John.[23] The junto was held together, in part, by the bonds of fellowship engendered by its treasonous assault on royal government in England during the summer of 1640. With the help of the Scottish Covenanters, the junto had staged a coup against Charles that had brought down the Personal Rule and forced him to call the Long Parliament. The manner of Charles's defeat in 1640 and the fact that he knew who had plotted treason against him to a great extent dictated the kind of settlement that the junto-men sought with the king. Besides their ideological preference for imposing severe restrictions upon the exercise of personal monarchy, they needed a settlement that reduced the king to little more than a cipher – a 'Duke of Venice' as he angrily put it – in order to protect themselves against royal vengeance.[24]

Essex, Pym, and other adherents to the principle of a Venetian-style monarchy were joined during 1641 by another influential bloc of parliamentary politicians headed by the earls of Northumberland, Pembroke, Holland, and their associates in the Commons. How closely these two groups integrated is not certain, but there is evidence that they were concerting strategy and attempting to orchestrate the two Houses' proceedings – in other words, acting together as a party – by the summer of 1642 at the very latest.[25] Working closely with the junto was a powerful group of godly London citizens headed by one of their MPs – and, from August 1642, lord mayor – Isaac Penington. There was more than a little truth in D'Ewes's assertion that 'these fierie spirited citizens . . . weere [sic] the maine instruments w[hi]ch Hampden & the other violent men of the Howse of Commons [used] to blow upp the flame of our present civill warrs'.[26] It was probably no accident that Penington and the junto-man Oliver St. John sat next to each other in the Commons.[27]

Having failed either to overawe Charles or to gain his trust, as was clearly the case by mid-1642, the junto promoted two policies designed to enforce a settlement. The first of these was the raising of a parliamentary army under the Earl of Essex. The second was the activation of the Anglo-Scottish treaty of 1641 by which the Covenanters had agreed to send an army to assist Parliament against popish aggression. Because these two policies were highly controversial and likely to meet with stiff opposition in both Houses, the junto moved much of their planning and implementation to a new bicameral executive, the Committee of Safety. Established on 4 July 1642, this committee assumed the formidable task of raising, equipping, and supplying Essex's army.[28] It initially comprised five peers – the earls of Northumberland, Essex, Pembroke, Holland, and Viscount Saye and Sele – and ten members of the Commons and was dominated by junto-men and MPs with close connections to Parliament's new 'generalissimo'.

The drafting (usually by Pym) of parliamentary declarations and petitions to the king was an important part of this committee's work during the summer and autumn of 1642. In July and August alone, it produced at least ten of what were essentially policy statements, including Essex's commission as lord general. Some of this material was printed and was undoubtedly vital in shaping opinion at Westminster and in reconciling Parliament and London to the necessity of military defiance of the king. D'Ewes was almost certainly not alone in regarding the committee's declarations as an important part of the parliamentary leadership's 'fierce and hot preparations for a civil war'.[29]

Concurrent with its work to put Essex's army into the field, the Committee of Safety strove to implement the junto's strategy of forging a military alliance with the Scots and a dictated settlement once the king had been defeated. The most influential of the declarations drawn up by the committee was that of 2 August 1642, 'expressing the Reasons and Grounds that force the Parliament to raise Arms'.[30] Replete with what D'Ewes termed 'virulent expressions against the king', this declaration contained a thinly veiled call for military assistance from the Covenanters.[31] The junto made its point more explicitly on 22 October – the day before the battle of Edgehill – when Pym reported from the committee a declaration calling for a Scottish-style 'solemn Oath and Covenant' to 'defend this Cause, with the Hazard of our Lives, against the King's Army'. The declaration concluded by stating Parliament's expectation that 'our Brethren of Scotland ... will help and assist us in Defence of this Cause'.[32]

The junto of 1642 can be considered the prototype of what a party in the Long Parliament looked like and how it functioned. It was typical, firstly, in that its core membership was small – its cabinet counsels probably shared by no more than twenty members of both Houses. At various stages of remove from this inner circle were those Parliament-men to whom the junto turned for support in the Houses at critical moments. Oliver Cromwell can probably be numbered among that group of MPs who, in Hyde's words, 'observed and pursued the dictates and directions' of the junto 'according to the parts which were assigned to them, upon emergent occasions'.[33] But the vast majority of Parliament-men, even after the exodus of royalist members during the spring and summer of 1642, were excluded from the junto's private counsels and could not be relied upon to back its policies in the absence of careful management and skillful persuasion. Secondly, the junto, like most of its successors, used its control of at least one bicameral executive committee – in the junto's case, the Committee of Safety – to manipulate the content and flow of information to the Houses. D'Ewes would complain early in October 1642 that the members of the Committee of Safety 'dispatched all the great business of the kingdome w[hi]ch concerned that wofull and fated civill warre into w[hi]ch we weere unfortunatelie fallen, so as the Howse had little or nothing to do till they came amongst us and communicated as much as they thought it fitting for us to know and then commonlie they had power to carrie by voices whatsoever they pleased'.[34]

To the many Parliament-men who were not privy to the junto's counsels or the deliberations of the Committee of Safety, the proceedings of the two Houses could appear both sinister and bewildering by the summer of 1642. D'Ewes inclined to the conspiracy theory view. Everywhere in the Commons, he could see evidence of partisan politicking, but, being largely ignorant of its origins, he applied the factional label of 'fiery' or 'violent spirit' to a diverse range of speakers: from those who were indeed members of the junto (Pym and Denzell Holles, for example) to Alexander Rigby, John Gurdon, and other Commons-men who were on its outer fringes at best, though they shared its primary objectives of military victory and a dictated settlement.[35] Bulstrode Whitelocke, another party outsider like D'Ewes, inclined more towards bewilderment than anger at evidence of a militant spirit prevailing at Westminster against the wishes of many members, himself included, who had yet to abandon hope of an accommodation. He thought it strange that Parliament had 'insensibly slid into this beginning of a civil war by one unexpected accident after another, as waves of the sea, which have brought us thus far; and we scarce know how'.[36] But what seemed to Whitelocke like a mysterious tide in the affairs of Parliament-men may well have appeared rather more premeditated to Pym and his confederates.

III

For much of 1642, the junto reigned supreme at Westminster. The fallout from the king's attempted arrest of Pym and five other junto-men in January 1642 effectively destroyed the fledgling royalist party in the two Houses. For the next eight months or so, neither the dwindling royalist presence in the Houses nor peace-minded parliamentarians such as D'Ewes constituted a genuine party capable of challenging the junto. It was not until after the battle of Edgehill in October that an organised challenge to the junto's leadership took shape at Westminster in the form of a bicameral peace party.

The first signs that autumn of a formed opposition to the junto emerged on 29 October, with a motion in the Lords 'to consider of some Means to beget a Peace'.[37] A similar motion was made by Edmund Waller in the Commons on 31 October, which the junto-men on the Committee of Safety attempted to head off but without success.[38] On 2 November, the two Houses ordered the Committee of Safety to prepare a petition to the king, requesting peace talks. That same day, Pym reported a declaration that he had penned in the committee, requesting 'the speedy and powerful assistance of our Brethren of Scotland . . . and a more strict Conjunction of the Counsels, Designs, and Endeavours of both Nations'. The Commons passed this declaration only after a series of divisions, however, and on reaching the Lords it was laid aside altogether.[39] On 3 November, the draft of Parliament's petition to the king 'for settling the Peace of the Kingdom' was reported in the Lords by the Earl of Northumberland – the peer who had hosted an important meeting of the junto just five months earlier to finalise plans for raising a parliamentary army.[40]

After Edgehill, the Houses were faced with the prospect of a protracted civil war that would encourage foreign intervention and revolutionary upheaval, and to junto-men like Northumberland and William Pierrepont, this was unacceptable.[41] They had supported the raising of a parliamentary army largely, it seems, on the assumption that royal resistance would be crushed in a single battle and that Charles would be forced to accede to Parliament's terms. With the king undefeated and advancing on London, they decided to cut their losses and to distance themselves from their more deeply compromised confederates (the conspirators of 1640). In the weeks after Edgehill, therefore, the junto divided to form rival war and peace parties – and as it did so the Committee of Safety's role as a political executive contracted markedly. From November 1642, its leading members were too divided over the crucial issues of fighting for absolute victory or seeking a negotiated settlement to cooperate in pursuit of either objective.

None of the peace-party grandees had figured prominently in the struggle against personal monarchy before 1641, and therefore they had no qualms about pushing for a swift, negotiated settlement that would leave Charles with the prerogative powers he had enjoyed at the end of that year. The peace party was headed in the Lords by the earls of Holland, Northumberland, Pembroke, and Salisbury and in the Commons by Holles, Sir John Evelyn of Wiltshire, John Maynard, William Pierrepont, and Edmund Waller.[42] Rivalry within the junto may have hastened the peace party's formation. Its leaders, claimed Hyde, 'thought themselves as much overshadowed by the greatness of the earl of Essex and the chief officers of the army as they could be by the glory of any favourite or power of any [royal] counsellors, [and] were resolved to merit as much as they could of the King by advancing an honourable peace'.[43] On returning to the House on 19 November, after a month's absence, D'Ewes quickly noted the realignment that had occurred, commenting that Holles, Pierrepont, and other MPs who had 'formerlie been verie opposite against an accomodation . . . did now speake earnestlie for it'.[44]

The war party that emerged from the break-up of the junto in the autumn of 1642 was dominated by the architects of Charles's ruin in 1640. In the Lords, it was headed by the earls of Warwick and Manchester, Viscount Saye, and lords Wharton and Brooke, and in the Commons by Pym, St. John, and Sir Henry Vane junior. The Earl of Essex was also part of this new war party, as were his leading staff officers John Hampden and Sir Philip Stapilton.[45] With so many of the 1640 conspirators in its ranks, the war party's objectives were identical to those of the old junto: to push for absolute victory and a dictated settlement that would leave Charles little better than a puppet monarch. It therefore persisted with the junto's policy of maintaining Essex and his army, although it also backed the creation of new armies where practical. Above all, however, it continued the junto's efforts to forge a military alliance with the Scots.

Although the existence of rival war and peace parties at Westminster was well attested by contemporaries, the secret deliberations of these groups were – unsurprisingly – rarely committed to paper. Nevertheless, their impact at Westminster is detectable. In July 1643, for example, with the peace party looking to build a majority in the Commons for reopening negotiations with the king, D'Ewes urged the House to appoint a committee to prepare 'proposic[i]ons for a treaty of peace to bee sent to his Ma[jes]ty, not doubting but a blessed issue may ensue on it'. At this point he expected the peace-party grandees Holles, Pierrepont, and Sir John Evelyn of Wiltshire to have seconded him – 'especiallie', he added, 'Mr Perepont, who had promised me to speake'. D'Ewes, who was on the peace party's fringes, later learned 'that these men [Holles, Pierrepont, and Evelyn] expected that the Lords . . . would have voted the sending of propositions to the King & soe reserved themselves to speake to the whole matter when that vote should come downe'.[46]

IV

The bipartite model of factional politics presented here challenges J. H. Hexter's influential analysis of the Long Parliament in the year after Edgehill, for he discerned not only war and peace parties, but also a third force, which he labelled the 'middle group'. Supposedly led by Pym, this small but influential group of swing voters, 'hybrid MPs', tried to hold the ring between the advocates of all-out war and a sell-out peace.[47] Hexter's tripartite model of politics in the Commons in 1642–3 – he virtually ignored the Lords – has been chipped away at in recent years. Yet it lingers on in even in the most sophisticated accounts of the civil war period.[48]

Hexter left the peace party more or less where S. R. Gardiner had found it in the late nineteenth century. But the Hexterian war party, like his middle group, is something new – a faction that was republican in sympathy, opposed to peace almost on principle, and determined to replace Essex with commanders willing to fight for outright victory. Its leading members were identified by Hexter as Henry Marten, Sir Henry Vane junior, Sir Peter Wentworth, and Alexander Rigby.[49] That this highly unpromising material for the leadership of a party is made to look even remotely credible by Hexter is because he cloaked it in borrowed garments. In effect, he robbed the war-party grandees of their vision for total victory and a dictated settlement and bestowed it instead upon Marten and his fellow Commons' militants. There is overwhelming evidence, however, that it was Pym and his fellow war-party grandees who were the architects of what was undoubtedly the most militant and far-reaching policy pursued at Westminster during the first year of the civil war: the forging of a military alliance with the Scots. Bringing the Covenanters into the English civil war was devised as a means of crushing royalist resistance and then imposing a settlement on Charles that respected the Scots' confederal ambitions in the three kingdoms and that left him with as little power in each as he enjoyed in the now *de facto* republic of Scotland. If the supposedly 'moderate' Pym was obsessed with any policy during the first year of the civil war, this was it.

This objective of securing a Scottish alliance was certainly shared by Henry Marten and other so-called extremists. Where these fiery spirits and the war-party grandees differed was not over strategy but tactics, over means rather than ends. Until the autumn of 1643, Pym, Vane, and St. John thought it expedient to court Essex and his powerful military following and keep them committed to the principle of securing an outright victory. Essex's dilatory generalship, however, and evidence of a martial spirit in London and the Eastern Association that could be tapped either to supplement or supplant his army, persuaded the fiery spirits that the earl was dispensable – indeed, that he was an obstacle to securing victory. What Marten, Rigby, Wentworth, and a few other Commons-men also objected to was the grandees' use of the Committee of Safety to apportion Parliament's military resources – which the militants thought gave too much power to Essex and pro-peace elements in the Lords. These two objectives – removing Essex and abolishing the Committee of Safety – were the only two that distinguished and were exclusive to the war party as Hexter defined it. Yet they were hardly constructive policies and certainly not condu-cive to the exercise of party influence. Moreover, the idea that other supposed members of Hexter's war party shared the presumed desire of its leader and 'typical member', Marten, to abolish monarchy or the House of Lords has no basis in the evidence. Vane junior and Rigby, for example, were no more – or rather, no less – republican in their thinking at this stage in the war than were Pym and St. John. Marten and his colleagues were not, as Hexter would have it, the leaders of a party. They were merely the most prominent members of a group of militant MPs that shared the war-party grandees' strategy but disagreed over the necessity of sticking with Essex as its principal military component.

Hexter's middle group, like his war party, was a figment of his own imagina-tion. The existence of such a group, he argued, could be deduced largely from Pym's contribution to the parliamentary debates over the winter of 1642–3 about whether to seek an accommodation with the king.[50] Ignoring the fact that his hero's very life might depend on securing a peace that preserved the 1640 conspirators from royal vengeance, Hexter claimed that Pym and his middle-group associates were either 'merely inert' to the idea of a treaty or took a position of 'benevolent rather than impartial neutrality'.[51] Yet when we follow Gardiner and turn to the parliamentary diaries of D'Ewes and Walter Yonge, they are full of references to speeches and initiatives by Pym and his closest collaborators that would render Parliament's terms severe or impractical to the point where they were sure that the king would reject them.[52] In Novem-ber 1642, for example, far from sitting silent as Hexter claimed, Pym joined Vane junior and Stapilton in urging that, as part of any peace talks, the king should return to Westminster and deliver up to justice his leading counsellors and adherents.[53] Obviously, Charles – as they well knew – would never accede to such terms.

By February 1643, the debate on the peace and its implications had shifted to the question of whether king and Parliament should disband their armies before a treaty or after it. The argument here was not over mere technicalities, as Hexter implied,[54] but a bitter dispute between those Commons-men genuinely committed to seeking a negotiated settlement and the war-party grandees, their Commons' allies, and the Earl of Essex and his circle,[55] who were determined to undermine the treaty before it had even begun. Pym stated his position clearly on 11 February: 'yf the kinge yelde not to a disbanding [before a treaty] wee shall haue no hope of peace'.[56] D'Ewes, Sir Thomas Roe, and a variety of com-mentators were adamant, however, that disbandment before a treaty – as Pym, Hampden, and other war-party grandees were urging – was 'preposterous …

of hard digestion at Court' and 'to propose an impossibilitie against the making of peace'.[57]

V

The Earl of Essex's role in the factional reconfigurations at Westminster during the second half of 1643 exposed the intimate connection that now existed between political and military power. Parliament's inability to keep the lord general's army adequately paid and provisioned led to a marked deterioration in his relations with his fellow war-party grandees during the summer of 1643. On 9 July, Essex sent Stapilton and Arthur Goodwin to Westminster with a letter in which he suggested that in light of his army's weaknesses, the two Houses sue for peace.[58] The lord general's 'cold affections' encouraged his critics in the Commons and among London's militant parliamentarians to press ahead with a scheme for channelling the City's resources into a new army under Sir William Waller that would fight wholeheartedly for victory. Anxious not to offend the City, the war-party grandees supported this initiative but at the cost of further alienating Essex, who saw Waller's command as an affront to his honour and authority.[59]

Neglected by his supposed friends at Westminster, Essex lent a favourable ear to the peace-party grandees, who were keen to detach him from their rivals and to use his army to compel Parliament into accepting an exclusively English peace settlement before it could conclude an alliance with the Scots. Seemingly assured of the lord general's support, Northumberland and his allies in the Lords drew up the softest of peace terms, prompting a dramatic realignment of political forces in the Commons, where the lord general's officers, headed by Stapilton, now made common cause with the peace-party grandees. In several divisions on 5 August, Holles, Stapilton, and another Essexian, Sir Henry Cholmley, were tellers in favour of the propositions.[60] Outvoted in the Commons, the war-party grandees and the City militants roused the London mob against its enemies, and on 7 August the Commons duly rejected the proposed treaty, citing among its reasons that Parliament had agreed not to conclude a peace without the consent of the Scots.[61] After this demonstration that the war party still controlled London, Essex contented himself with assurances concerning his authority as commander-in-chief and that his army would have first claim upon the City's resources. Abandoned by Essex, the Earl of Holland and four other peace party peers made their way to Oxford, while the earls of Northumberland and Pembroke waited to see how they were received before deciding whether to follow them. Many of the more peace-minded Commons-men likewise withdrew from the House, handing undisputed control of Parliament to the war party.[62]

The Solemn League and Covenant of September 1643 and the king's cessation with the Irish rebels that same month broke and recast the political mould at Westminster. The implications of Charles's *de facto* alliance with Irish Catholics so appalled the peace-party grandee the Earl of Northumberland that he came to accept Scottish intervention as a necessary evil to secure the king's utter defeat and a dictated settlement that would strip him of power. By December 1643, therefore, he had thrown in his lot with Vane junior, St. John, and other architects of the Scottish alliance.[63] Moving in the opposite direction late in 1643 were the Earl of Essex and most of his officers, who disliked the Covenanters' religious demands and resented having to share military honours and Parliament's resources with the Scottish Army. Essex now began to push for a swift, negotiated settlement that would restore the king to something like his former glory and Essex himself to his father's role as England's greatest Protestant champion. The goal of a moderate and exclusively English settlement was shared by the peace party, and by early 1644 the two groups – Essex's and the peace-party grandees (minus Northumberland) – had converged in common opposition to the new Anglo-Scottish war party. Joining this reconfigured peace interest were two of the Commons' leading managers of Irish affairs, Sir John Clotworthy and Robert Reynolds, who were angered that the war-party grandees had conceded supreme command of the British forces in Ireland to the Scots.[64] It was here, in the second half of 1643, in reaction to the Covenant and cessation, that the future leaderships of the Independent and Presbyterian factions coalesced.

These changes in party formation elicited new patterns of political behaviour at Westminster. D'Ewes and other peace-minded Commons-men, for example, having formerly questioned all military expenditure, now tended to support the upkeep of Essex's army as the best means to 'command a peace' against the warmongers at Westminster or Oxford.[65] The heirs of the war party, by contrast, having supported Essex's army in the past, were now prepared to join the City militants in clipping its wings. Distrusting Essex's political ambitions and new-found eirenicism, they strove to redirect Parliament's resources to the armies of Sir William Waller, the Earl of Manchester, and the Scots and to commit the whole conduct of the war to their new Anglo-Scottish executive, the Committee of Both Kingdoms.[66]

VI

In the six months or so following Essex's disastrous campaign in the West Country during the summer of 1644, the Essexian peace party and the pro-Scots war party assumed new guises and, in time, acquired new names: the Presbyterians and the Independents.[67] The changes in grandee alignment that attended this development were few but significant. Abandoning the Essexian camp in favour of the pro–New Model, Independent interest were the earls of Pembroke and Salisbury, and the influential Commons-men William Pierrepont and Sir John Evelyn of Wiltshire. Their change of political course was probably linked to disillusionment with Essex and his officers – who by late 1644 were widely regarded as incompetent or worse – and to hostility towards a Covenanted settlement.[68] The Presbyterian grandees would come to include those godly stalwarts and former darlings of the war party, the earls of Manchester and

Warwick, and Sir William Waller, but they were, for the most part, merely the leaders of Essex's party by another name.[69]

Underlying and contributing to this factional reshuffle was a major shift in the two parties' relations with the Scots. The war-party grandees had acquiesced in Scottish plans for a clericalist Presbyterian church settlement only on sufferance, as the purchase price of total victory. Once it became clear, as it had by September 1644, that Scottish intervention would not win the war, they switched their support from the Scots to the most resolute of English fighters, such as Cromwell, many of whom were hostile to 'rigid' Presbyterianism. Consequently, Vane, St. John, and their friends were obliged to defend the idea of liberty for tender puritan consciences against the Scots' demands for a 'covenanted uniformity'.[70] In dismay at this betrayal by their erstwhile allies, the Scots made overtures to Essex's party, and by November 1644 the two groups had joined political forces. Alarmed by the spread of radical ideas, particularly among Parliament's soldiers, the Essexians were now willing to back Scottish demands for the establishment of a coercive Presbyterian church in England. The Scots, for their part, were now prepared to support the Essexians' desire for a negotiated settlement that would restore Charles with most of his prerogative powers – except, of course, the royal supremacy in religion. Like their Independent rivals, the Presbyterian grandees expected to occupy the principal offices of state once the king had resumed the throne, but they relied on his gratitude, not coercion, to secure them power. Central to their plans was that Charles should be allowed to return to London 'in honour and safety' to conclude a personal treaty.[71]

In entering into this Presbyterian alliance, the Essexians gained new strength. Besides the lord general's army, they could now count on the Scots' army in northern England and, in time, the powerful 'Covenant-engaged' faction among London's municipal and clerical leadership. To some extent, therefore, the Independent grandees' championing of the causes of self-denying and new modelling over the winter of 1644–5 was deeply reactive, for as matters stood in November 1644, they had all but lost the considerable military power they had enjoyed since the autumn of 1643. Essex had long since deserted their ranks. The Earl of Manchester, who commanded the Eastern Association Army, was moving towards Essex in common hostility to Cromwell and other religious radicals. And now Scottish leaders and therefore their army were aligned with the Essexians.[72] The Independents responded to this military crisis by using their dominance of the Committee of Both Kingdoms and by exploiting discontent at Westminster with the conduct of the war in order to create the New Model Army.[73]

VII

The names Presbyterian and Independent that attached to the parties after 1644 often conveyed only a partial – indeed, at times, downright misleading – sense of the ideas that animated them. Despite acquiring these religious labels, both parties were dominated by men who would have settled for an erastian Presbyterian church.[74] Among the Independents grandees only the radical anti-formalist Sir Henry Vane junior was willing to dispense with a national, state-sponsored church. Yet whatever their individual ecclesiological preferences, the Independent grandees supported, at the very least, limited toleration for 'orthodox' Congregationalists. This was partly a matter of principle and partly to retain the support of Cromwell and other godly swordsmen.[75] The Presbyterian grandees' backing for Scottish-style Presbyterianism was no less politically motivated. They supported 'rigid' Presbyterianism firstly as a bulwark against the rising tide of radicalism, and secondly as the necessary price of Scottish cooperation in negotiating with the king.[76]

The core of every parliamentary party during the period 1640–8 coalesced around the primarily secular goal of seizing the political and military power necessary to impose a settlement upon the king and his war-torn kingdoms. Attaining power was the grandees' primary objective, the basis of their party unity. At no time during the 1640s did establishing Presbyterianism or any other form of church government become their overriding concern. Instead it remained a secondary issue within the larger struggle for power to impose a general settlement.[77] Thus the allies of the Independent grandees included Commons-men who combined a sincere reverence for Presbyterianism and for Presbyterian clerics with consistent support for the New Model Army and a dictated settlement with the king. Sir William Armyne, Samuel Browne, William Ellys, John Gurdon, Sir William Masham, Gilbert Millington (chairman of the Committee for Plundered Ministers from 1645), John Moore, Isaac Penington, Edmund Prideaux, William Purefoy, and Humphrey Salwey all fell into this category. Indeed, Browne and Prideaux can be regarded as Independent grandees in their own right, and Millington, Moore, and Purefoy would sign the king's death warrant. The Presbyterian church interest they occasionally sided with in the House during the later 1640s was not a formed party; it was a single-issue pressure group and as such lacked either the intent or means to pursue peace with the king.[78]

Much the same could be said of the loosely organised bicameral groups that agitated at Westminster on behalf of their particular region in England or province in Ireland. These regional interest groups occasionally exerted a major influence on parliamentary politics – as in late 1643, when the 'northern gentlemen' and the 'western men' battled with the Earl of Essex's supporters for military funding.[79] More often than not, however, the regional and the Irish lobbies and their respective standing committees at Westminster were themselves divided and hamstrung by national party rivalries. This was particularly true of the various committees for Irish affairs and the Committee of the West. The Committee of the Eastern Association at Westminster, on the other hand, generally seems to have aligned with the association's war-party backers and, subsequently, the Independents.[80] Likewise, the eagerness of the northern gentlemen for a Scottish alliance in 1643 – partly as an expeditious means of freeing the north from royalist control – and then for a swift withdrawal of Scottish forces from the region once the war had been won, ensured that Parliament's standing committees for northern affairs generally operated as regional auxilliaries to the war-party and Independent grandees.[81] Equally, the Presbyterian grandees' endorsement of a Covenanted settlement secured them the considerable political and military resources of London's Covenant-engaged interest.[82]

VIII

Control of the Long Parliament's standing bicameral committees enabled the grandees to punch well above their weight in terms of their numbers in each House.[83] These committees possessed wide-ranging executive powers and in some cases their own revenue sources and nationwide administrative networks. The Independent grandees or their allies dominated most of them – notably, the Committee for the Army (to which the county assessment committees were answerable), the Committee for the Revenue, and the Committee for Advance of Money. The Presbyterian grandees were a powerful presence on the Committee of Both Kingdoms by 1645, on the Admiralty Committee under its chairman the Earl of Warwick, and on Parliament's principal executive during the first half of 1647, the Committee for Irish Affairs at Derby House.

As already noted in the case of the Committee of Safety and the Committee of Both Kingdoms, the grandees were adept at using Parliament's executive to implement policies of a highly partisan nature. Perhaps the most aggressive and potentially sanguinary deployment of an executive committee for overtly factional ends during the 1640s occurred in the spring of 1646 in response to the king's flight to the Scottish Army. So fearful were the Independent grandees that the Presbyterians were preparing to restore Charles by force that they used the Committee for the Army to intimidate the City and to mobilise the New Model for military confrontation with the Scots. The situation grew so fraught that the 'weightiest heads' in the Commons believed 'the civill warr of the civill war is within a few days of begining'.[84]

Under cover of Parliament's executive committees, the grandees could convert state revenues into what amounted to party slush funds. The Scots were probably thinking first and foremost of the Committee for the Revenue – chaired by Northumberland's close friend Sir Henry Vane senior – when they indignantly noted the Independents' success in colonising Parliament's 'Money committees'. 'All this while', wrote the Scottish polemicist David Buchanan in 1645–6:

> the Independents are getting themselves in all Committees and Counsells, namely where money is a handling: So by degrees they get benefit and power into their hands, and then pleasure some whom they do affect, and put back others whom they do dislike. By this means, divers of all ranks, to get their desires either of benefit or employment, do side with them; or to have their turn served for the present, do cog in with them for a time ... They [the Independents] have gotten the fingring of the moneys of State by gathering it, and they distribute it for the most part among themselves.[85]

Denzell Holles was even more specific on this last point, insisting that the revenue committeemen 'shar'd and divided amongst themselves all the Fat of the Land ... and we [the Presbyterians], not one of us had any thing to do in all this ... And did not they make use of the price in their hands? And did they not like charitable persons begin at home, give Gifts and Offices to all their own Party ... ?'[86] That this was more than merely Presbyterian mud-slinging is amply demonstrated by the committee's own records, in which it is clear that the hundreds of thousands of pounds that passed through its hands, and the multitude of offices, pensions, and perquisites in its gift, found their way in disproportionate quantity to the committeemen themselves and their political allies.

The grandees' control of Parliament's executive and purse strings was seen by the MP Clement Walker, and doubtless by others, as a design to 'draw a generall dependency after them, for he that commands the money, commands the men: These Committee-men are so powerfull that they overawe and overpower their fellow members, contrary to the nature of a free Parliament'.[87] The massive parliamentary state that emerged during the 1640s thus gave those who managed it unprecedented political influence. Moreover, the machinery needed to put that influence to practical effect was apparently in place by the mid-1640s, for in addition to their 'Teazers'[88] (provocateurs) and 'Beagles', their 'Sticklers' and 'dividers' (division lobby managers), the grandees used 'Vote-drivers', the forerunners of today's Whips, to help construct majorities in the Commons.[89] Holles further alleged that the Independents 'took notice' of how MPs voted and bestowed or withheld their patronage accordingly.[90] Little wonder that Sir Arthur Hesilrige and Oliver Cromwell (both prominent Independents) opposed a Presbyterian-backed proposal in September 1646 to introduce a ballot box for Commons' votes relating to grants of money or office.[91]

But it was not only the two Houses that the grandees sought to manipulate by means of their money committees. The luxury accessories, horses, and clothing that the Committee for the Revenue lavished upon the king during the second half of 1647 – largely without the knowledge or approval of most Parliament-men – represented perhaps the most scandalous use of public money for party ends during the entire seventeenth century. In authorising this expenditure, as in negotiating with the king over the Heads of Proposals, the Independent grandees were collaborating with the Army to act the part of a loyal and generous court-in-waiting. Their largesse at the public's expense was intended to convince Charles not simply of their intent and power to effect a settlement but also to assure themselves of royal favour in the event of what they anticipated that summer and autumn would be his imminent restoration.

IX

The winding down of the civil war in the year or so after Naseby and the withdrawal of the Scottish Army from England early in 1647 brought about another shift in the pattern of party politics. With the New Model no longer needed as a bulwark against royalist and Scottish revanchism, some Parliament-men who had supported new modelling and a dictated settlement moved towards the Presbyterian grandees, who were headed after Essex's death in September 1646 by the earls of Manchester and Warwick, and Holles and Stapilton. Most of those who fell away from the Independents after 1645 were attracted by the prospect of creating a strong Presbyterian church once the war had been won. This was especially the case with the 'Scottified' Presbyterian Zouche Tate – who had abandoned the Independents by early 1646 – and also applies in varying degree to the Earl of Pembroke, William Ashhurst, John Boys, Edward Bayntun, Sir Anthony Irby, and John Swynfen.[92]

The failure of the Holles-Stapilton counter-revolution in July 1647 and the Army's triumphant march into London in August destroyed the Presbyterian grandees as a political force. They were either imprisoned, forced into exile, or frightened into political quiescence. Yet the army and Independent grandees' repeated attempts to reach a settlement with the king during the summer and autumn of 1647 would prove almost as damaging to their own support base at Westminster. In September 1647, a group of radical Commons-men led by Thomas Chaloner, Lord Grey of Groby, Henry Marten, Thomas Rainborowe, Major Thomas Scot, and Sir Peter Wentworth emerged to challenge the Independent grandees' policy of trying to negotiate with Charles.[93] Whether this grouping was a party as previously defined is open to question. It certainly lacked support in the Lords, and it is not clear that it possessed an agreed programme for settlement.[94] Its emergence represented the falling away of the Independent grandees' radical allies in the Commons and the army rather than any fracturing within the core of the party itself.

The distinction that David Underdown and other historians have drawn between the 'radical' Independent grandees – notably Hesilrige, Prideaux, and Vane junior – and their supposedly more conservative, 'middle group' associates – for example, Evelyn of Wiltshire, St. John, and Nathaniel Fiennes – is anachronistic in the context of the mid-1640s, resting largely on awareness of these men's divergent careers after Pride's Purge.[95] In fact, Evelyn of Wiltshire and Fiennes expressed views that were more fraught with revolutionary implications than anything in surviving contemporary statements by Hesilrige, Prideaux, and Vane.[96] A strong case has been made that Cromwell and Henry Ireton were contemplating radical constitutional change from November 1647.[97] But then the same may have been true of their leading civilian allies. Only the Earl of Northumberland among the Independent grandees is known to have opposed the Vote of No Addresses – the parliamentary resolution of mid-January 1648 prohibiting further negotiations with Charles.[98] Ireton undoubtedly exaggerated in claiming that 'all men' understood the Vote to 'imply some further intentions of proceeding in Justice against him [the king] and settling the Kingdome without him'.[99] Nevertheless, it is worth noting that the chief contrivers of what looks very much like a plan – concocted soon after the Vote – to depose Charles and to establish a puppet monarchy under the Prince of Wales were reportedly Cromwell and the 'middle group' Independent, Oliver St. John.[100]

X

The prospect of a Scottish invasion of England in 1648 would transform party politics at Westminster, just as the withdrawal of a Scottish Army had the previous year. In desperate need of allies to help keep City and Parliament firm against a sell-out peace, the Independent grandees courted the Earl of Manchester, William Ashhurst, Sir Gilbert Gerard, John Swynfen, and other 'rigid' Presbyterians during the early months of 1648. To this end, leading Independents in the Commons voted with the Presbyterians on 28 April in favour of reopening parliamentary negotiations with the king.[101] Underdown has referred to these votes as 'a great turning-point' – the moment when the so-called 'moderates' and the 'radicals' in the Independent party finally parted company and the Independent–army alliance collapsed.[102] The divisions on 28 April certainly suggest an increase in the number of radical Independents – that is, the group that had emerged in opposition to the grandees in September 1647 and that was defined by its bitter opposition to any compromise with Charles. Yet whatever falling away there may have been at the margins, it is clear that the 28 April votes did not produce any major division within the core of the party's civilian leadership: even the 'radical' Vane junior was willing to vote with the pro-negotiations majority.[103] Furthermore, Cromwell and Sir Thomas Fairfax would remain on friendly terms with Hesilrige, Pierrepont, Vane junior, and other Independent grandees for months to come.

What the 28 April votes – and the informal alliance they reveal between the Independent grandees and 'rigid' Presbyterians[104] – do point to is a split within the ranks of those Parliament-men who had lined up behind Holles and Stapilton in the spring and summer of 1647. Manchester, Gerard, Swynfen, and other religious Presbyterians would not accept a settlement with the king unless it established a robust Presbyterian church, and on this score they found the assurances of the Independent grandees more credible than those of the Scottish Engagers. At the same time, however, there were political Presbyterians whose hatred of the grandees and the army outweighed their misgivings about the Engagers and their royalist allies.[105] Few of them went as far as Waller and Edward Massie in recruiting reformadoes to resist the army.[106] But given their willingness to sanction the king's return to London for treaty negotiations without any preconditions, many of these anti-army Presbyterians were prepared to accept a peace at almost any price.[107] Prominent in this category were the six peers who had been imprisoned for their part in the Presbyterian counter-revolution of July 1647.[108] Readmitted to the Lords in June, these peers were so eager for Charles's restoration that they refused to declare the Duke of Hamilton and his invading army enemies of the kingdom.[109] It is this split within the Presbyterian interest of 1647 that is the most significant political realignment of 1648, for it allowed the Independent grandees, after some judicious trimming, to retain control in the Commons and at Derby House during the Second Civil War.

Party politics in the Long Parliament 49

The unity of the Independent grandees, the most durable of all the parties in the Long Parliament, did not finally crumble until late in 1648. The majority of the party's civilian leaders were apparently willing to accept the king's answers at the treaty of Newport as an acceptable basis for settlement or at least for continuing to negotiate with him. Only Vane junior, Prideaux, and possibly Vane senior seem to have thought otherwise, and of these, only Prideaux – the most zealously Presbyterian of the Independent grandees – supported Pride's Purge.

Although the established party structure of rival courts-in-waiting was swept away by the revolutionary events of 1648–9, the political arts that had sustained this system would have a long future ahead of them. The pioneers of the parliamentary 'machine of management' and therefore of modern party politics were not – as has variously been claimed – Lord Clifford in the 1660s or the Earl of Danby in the 1670s, but the grandees in the Long Parliament.[110]

Notes

1 This chapter is based closely on my personal reading of unpublished articles filed for the 1640–60 section of the History of Parliament by John Adamson, Andrew Barclay, Dorothy Gardiner, Sarah Jones, Vivienne Larminie, Patrick Little, Jason Peacey, Stephen Roberts, Roland Thorne, and myself. However, the views represented in it are my own, and not those of the History of Parliament or any other Research Fellow at the History of Parliament Trust. I am grateful to my colleagues and to the Editorial Board and Trustees of the History of Parliament for permission to review this material in advance of publication and to use it in this chapter. I would like to thank John Adamson, Andrew Barclay, Vivienne Larminie, Patrick Little, Sarah Mortimer, Jason Peacey, Stephen Roberts, and Elliot Vernon for reading and commenting on earlier drafts of this chapter.
2 C. Holmes, *The Eastern Association in the English Civil War* (Cambridge, 1974).
3 M.P. Mahony, 'The Presbyterian Party in the Long Parliament, 2 July 1644–3 June 1647' (unpublished DPhil thesis, University of Oxford, 1973); 'Presbyterianism in the City of London, 1645–7', *HJ*, 22 (1979), 93–114; 'The Savile Affair and the Politics of the Long Parliament', *Parliamentary History*, 7 (1988), 212–27; J.S.A. Adamson, 'The Peerage in Politics 1645–49' (unpublished PhD thesis, University of Cambridge, 1986); 'Parliamentary Management, Men-of-Business and the House of Lords, 1640–9', in C. Jones (ed.), *A Pillar of the Constitution: The House of Lords in British Politics, 1640–1784* (1989), pp. 21–50; 'Politics and the Nobility in the Civil-War England', *HJ*, 34 (1991), 231–55; 'Of Armies and Architecture: the Employments of Robert Scawen', in I. Gentles et al. (eds.), *Soldiers, Writers, and Statesmen of the English Revolution* (Cambridge, 1998), pp. 36–67; 'The Triumph of Oligarchy: the Management of War and the Committee of Both Kingdoms, 1644–1645', in C. Kyle and J. Peacey (eds.), *Parliament at Work: Parliamentary Committees, Political Power and Public Access in Early Modern England* (Woodbridge, 2002), pp. 101–27; *The Noble Revolt: the Overthrow of Charles I* (2007).
4 Where reference is made in this chapter to named MPs and committees in the Long Parliament, it should be assumed that the author is drawing on the relevant biographies and committee articles filed for the 1640–60 section of the History of Parliament.
5 He further claimed that parliamentary affairs were 'cheifelie ledd & guided by some few members of either Howse': BL, Harleian MS [Harl.], fol. 93.
6 This was particularly true in the case of the Committee of Safety, the Committee of Both Kingdoms, and the Committee for the Army. See Adamson, 'The Triumph of Oligarchy', pp. 101–27.

7 D. Scott, 'The "Northern Gentlemen", the parliamentary Independents, and Anglo-Scottish relations in the Long Parliament', *HJ*, 42 (1999), 365–70.
8 John Adamson has employed this phrase in his forthcoming history of the English Civil War (Weidenfeld & Nicolson). I am grateful to him for allowing me to read draft chapters of this work prior to publication.
9 See page 35–6, 37, 41, and Holmes, *Eastern Association*, p. 208.
10 BL, Harl. 165, fols 256r-v; W.A. Day (ed.), *The Pythouse Papers* (1879), pp. 2–3; Mahony, 'The Presbyterian Party', pp. 60–1, 233, 239–40, 255–6; L. Bienassis, 'Jean de Montreuil [*known as* Montereul]', *ODNB*.
11 D. Scott, 'Rethinking Royalist Politics, 1642–9', in John Adamson (ed.), *The English Civil War: Conflicts and Contexts, 1640–49* (Basingstoke, 2009), pp. 52, 54–7.
12 J. Peacey, *Print and Public Politics in the English Revolution* (Cambridge, 2013), Chapter 4.
13 For one royalist response to this development, see Chapter 5, by Grant Tapsell, in this volume.
14 J.R. McMichael and B. Taft (eds.), *The Writings of William Walwyn* (Athens, GA, 1989), pp. 299, 301.
15 David Underdown has questioned the existence of coherent parties in the Long Parliament: *Pride's Purge: Politics in the Puritan Revolution* (Oxford, 1971), pp. 45–6. In his earlier work, however, he noted 'groups recognisable as parties', with 'a recognisable outlook on national issues': 'Party Management in the Recruiter Elections, 1645–1648', *EHR*, 83 (1968), 237–8.
16 Adamson, 'Politics and the Nobility in Civil-War England', *HJ*, 34 (1991), 232.
17 C. Roberts, *Schemes and Undertakings: A Study of English Politics in the Seventeenth Century* (Columbus, OH, 1985), pp. 14–15; see also the chapters by Clive Holmes and Johann P. Sommerville in J.H. Hexter (ed.), *Parliament and Liberty, from the Reign of Elizabeth to the English Civil War* (Stanford, CA, 1992).
18 A point made by Sir Henry Vane junior: *The Tryal of Sir Henry Vane, Kt* (1662), p. 40.
19 B. Whitelocke, *Memorials of the English Affairs* (4 vols, Oxford, 1853), I, 100, 151; Peacey, *Print and Public Politics*, pp. 146, 149–50; Mahony, 'The Presbyterian Party', pp. 477–8; Adamson, 'Parliamentary Management', p. 21 and *passim*; P. Seaward, 'Divisions, Tellers, and Management in the 17th-Century House of Commons', *Parliamentary History*, 32 (2013), 81–2.
20 BL, Add. MS 18779, fol. 61.
21 Scott, 'Northern Gentlemen', 354–65.
22 J. Morrill, 'The Unweariableness of Mr Pym: Influence and Eloquence in the Long Parliament', in S.D. Amussen and M.A. Kishlansky (eds.), *Political Culture and Cultural Politics in Early Modern England* (Manchester, 1995), pp. 19–44.
23 Edward, Earl of Clarendon, *The History of the Great Rebellion*, ed. W.D. Macray (6 vols, Oxford, 1888), I, 241–50; Adamson, *Noble Revolt*, pp. 138–9.
24 Adamson, *Noble Revolt*, Chapters 1 and 2 and p. 194.
25 Adamson, 'Parliamentary Management', p. 30.
26 BL, Harl. 164, fol. 327v.
27 *Ibid.*, fol. 266.
28 *CJ*, II, 651.
29 V.F. Snow and A.S. Young (eds.), *The Private Journals of the Long Parliament: 2 June to 17 September 1642* (New Haven, CT, and London, 1992), pp. 256–7, 284.
30 *CJ*, II, 694.
31 Snow and Young (eds.), *Private Journals of the Long Parliament*, p. 270; *LJ*, V, 257–9; C. Russell, *The Fall of the British Monarchies 1637–1642* (Oxford, 1991), p. 519.
32 BL, Harl. 164, fol. 40; *LJ*, V, 417–19.
33 Clarendon, *History of the Rebellion*, I, 250; J.S.A. Adamson, 'Oliver Cromwell and the Long Parliament', in J. Morrill (ed.), *Oliver Cromwell and the English Revolution* (1990), pp. 50–4; Adamson, *Noble Revolt*, pp. 329, 427. For a glimpse at how this process worked, see BL, Add. MS 70003, fol. 232.
34 BL, Harl. 164, fol. 9v.

35 Snow and Young (eds.), *Private Journals of the Long Parliament*, pp. viii, xiv.
36 Whitelocke, *Memorials*, I, 176.
37 *LJ*, V, 424.
38 BL, Add. MS 31116, p. 9.
39 *CJ*, II, 832; *LJ*, V, 430–1.
40 *LJ*, V, 431; Adamson, 'Parliamentary Management', p. 30.
41 BL, Harl. 164, fol. 272v; HMC, *Portland*, I, 87; Adamson, 'Of Armies and Architecture', pp. 43–4.
42 For the peace party and its main protagonists, see *CJ*, II, 858, 905–6, 907, 911, 928, 959, 960, 961, 962, 969, 970, 983, 985, 999; III, 17, 27, 28, 33; BL, Harl. 164, fols 99, 210v, 275, 294, 295v, 302, 304v, 306, 334, 341v, 345, 352, 359v, 361, 364, 391v; Harl. 165, fols 97, 98, 125, 134v, 142v-143, 145v, 152v, 156v; Harl. 1901, fol. 58v; Bodl., MS Tanner 60, fol. 182; *Mercurius Aulicus*, no. 3 (15–21 January 1643), pp. 27–8; no. 6 (5–11 February 1643), p. 77; no. 33 (13–19 August 1643), p. 442; *An Honest Letter to a Doubtfull Friend* (1643), sig. A2v; J.B. Crummett, 'The Lay Peers in Parliament 1640–1644' (unpublished PhD thesis, University of Manchester, 1972), pp. 298–9, 367, 381–2.
43 Clarendon, *History of the Rebellion*, II, 393–4.
44 BL, Harl. 164, fol. 99.
45 For the war party and its leaders, see *CJ* references in note 41; BL, Harl. 164, fols 248, 264, 270v, 271, 275, 277v, 296v, 301v-303, 318v, 323, 324, 334, 341v, 345v, 346, 348, 350, 359v, 383, 397; *Sober Sadnes: or Historicall Observations upon the Proceedings, Pretences, & Designs of a Prevailing Party in Both Houses of Parliament* (1643), pp. 15, 16–17, 18, 22; *An Honest Letter*, sig. A2v; Crummett, 'The Lay Peers in Parliament', pp. 298–9, 367.
46 BL, Harl. 165, fol. 125.
47 J.H. Hexter, *The Reign of King Pym* (Cambridge, MA, 1941), pp. 8–10 and *passim*.
48 See, for example, Snow and Young (eds.), *Private Journals of the Long Parliament*, p. xviii; A. Woolrych, *Britain in Revolution 1625–1660* (Oxford, 2002), p. 275.
49 Hexter, *King Pym*, pp. 9, 49, 59, 67, 70, and *passim*.
50 *Ibid.*, pp. 48–51.
51 *Ibid.*, pp. 50, 57.
52 BL, Harl. 164, fols 270v, 271, 275, 291v, 301v, 302, 308, 318v, 324r-v, 334, 341v, 345v, 363; Add. MS 18777, fols 64–5v, 66–7, 101, 104, 119v, 146–7, 147v–8, 149v, 151–3, 157–8, 158v, 160v–1, 169v, 173r–v; S.R. Gardiner, *History of the Great Civil War 1642–1649* (4 vols, 1905 edn.), I, 62–3.
53 BL, Add. MS 18777, fols 66v, 67; Hexter, *King Pym*, p. 51.
54 Hexter, *King Pym*, p. 69.
55 For example, Sir Gilbert Gerard, John Hampden, and Sir Philip Stapilton. For Essex and his circle's opposition to the treaty, see BL, Harl. 164, fols 270v, 277v, 303v–304, 318r, 318v, 322–3, 324v, 334, 348.
56 BL, Add. MS 18777, fol. 153.
57 BL, Harl. 164, fols 295, 296v, 300, 301v, 302, 308; Harl. 1901, fol. 58v; Add. MS 18777, fols 65, 67, 148, 151–3, 158, 158v; *Mercurius Aulicus*, no. 7 (12–18 February 1643), pp. 85–7; no. 8 (19–25 February 1643), p. 95; *Sober Sadnes*, pp. 16–17; *CSPV 1642–3*, p. 215.
58 *CJ*, III, 160; *LJ*, VI, 127.
59 BL, Harl. 165, fols 128r-v, 130v, 131v, 134v–135, 149, 157v, 179; *Mercurius Aulicus*, no. 28 (9–15 July 1643), pp. 368–9, 370; no. 29 (16–22 July 1643), pp. 376–7; no. 30 (23–9 July 1643), pp. 397–8; D. Scott, *Politics and War in the Three Stuart Kingdoms* (Basingstoke, 2004), p. 63.
60 *CJ*, III, 196; BL, Harl. 165, fols 141v–143; Bodl., MS Tanner 62, fol. 262.
61 *CJ*, III, 197; BL, Harl. 165, fols 145–148v; Add. MS 18778, fols 9v–10; *Mercurius Aulicus*, no. 32 (6–12 August 1643), pp. 431–2, 434, 437.
62 Scott, *Politics and War*, pp. 64–5.
63 *The Letters and Journals of Robert Baillie*, ed. D. Laing (3 vols, Edinburgh, 1841–2), II, 107, 141; T. Carte (ed.), *The Life of James Duke of Ormond* (6 vols, Oxford, 1851), VI, 206; *Mercurius Aulicus*, no. 12 (17–23 March 1644), p. 892; Clarendon, *History of the Rebellion*, III,

495; Mahony, 'The Presbyterian Party', pp. 47–8; Adamson, 'Of Armies and Architecture', pp. 44–6. Two of the earl's main parliamentary clients, Robert Scawen and Sir Thomas Widdrington, would shift, like him, over the course of 1643–5 from favouring a swift, negotiated settlement to support for the New Model Army.

64 BL, Harl. 165, fols 254r-v; Longleat House, Whitelocke Papers IX, fol. 27; *Letters and Journals of Robert Baillie*, ed. Laing, II, 141, 155; Clarendon, *History of the Rebellion*, III, 303; Mahony, 'The Presbyterian Party', pp. 7, 40, 45, 51–2, 57, 61; Scott, *Politics and War*, p. 69; R. Armstrong, 'Ireland at Westminster: the Long Parliament's Irish committees, 1641–1647', in Kyle and Peacey (eds.), *Parliament at Work*, pp. 88–9, 93.

65 Laing, *Letters and Journals of Robert Baillie*, II, 118–19; Mahony, 'The Presbyterian Party', pp. 31–3, 39–40, 45, 50–2. Thus we find D'Ewes praising Essex and his 'gallant' officers from early in 1644 – a turnaround from his attitude towards them a year earlier – and describing attempts to frustrate the ordinance for recruiting Essex's army as 'impertinent' and likely to bring about Parliament's ruin: BL, Harl. 165, fol. 266v; Harl. 166, fols 3, 7, 10, 14v, 36, 37, 41, 55v–56, 62, 73, 79v, 86, 124.

66 *Mercurius Aulicus*, no. 12 (17–23 March 1644), p. 888; Clarendon, *History of the Rebellion*, III, 340; Mahony, 'The Presbyterian Party', pp. 50, 52–4, 56–7, 64–79, 80–1, 95; Adamson, 'Of Armies and Architecture', pp. 45–6; 'The Triumph of Oligarchy', pp. 104–12.

67 For the religious origins of these labels and how they came to be affixed to the Westminster parties, see L. Kaplan, 'Presbyterians and Independents in 1643', *EHR*, 84 (1969), 244–56; Mahony, 'The Presbyterian Party', pp. 8–11, 104–6.

68 Adamson, 'The Triumph of Oligarchy', pp. 115–16, 119–21, 123. Heading the Independent party were the earls of Northumberland, Viscount Saye and Sele, Philip Lord Wharton, William Pierrepont, Nathaniel Fiennes, Sir Henry Vane senior and junior, Oliver St. John, Sir John Evelyn of Wiltshire, Sir Arthur Hesilrige, Samuel Browne, and Edmund Prideaux.

69 Manchester and Waller were admirers of Scottish Presbyterianism, but it is unlikely that Warwick would have favoured a strongly clericalist church, particularly one that challenged his extensive rights of clerical patronage. (I am grateful to Christopher Thompson for discussion on this point.) The Presbyterian party was dominated by the earls of Essex, Warwick, Manchester, and Holland, Denzell Holles, Sir Philip Stapilton, Sir William Lewis, Sir John Clotworthy, and John Glynne.

70 Scott, *Politics and War*, pp. 83–5.

71 For the Presbyterian alliance of late 1644, see K. Lindley and D. Scott (eds.), *The Journal of Thomas Juxon, 1644–1647* (Camden Society, 5th series, 13, 1999), pp. 35, 68, 76, 79, 83; Mahony, 'The Presbyterian Party', pp. 14–15, 106–12, 121–2, 129–30, 133–4, 140–1, 144–5, 182–4; Adamson, 'The Triumph of Oligarchy', pp. 118–19.

72 Mahony, 'The Presbyterian Party', pp. 113–15, 121, 123–7, 151.

73 Adamson, 'The Triumph of Oligarchy', pp. 115–22.

74 Mahony, 'The Presbyterian Party', p. 22. For the position of the majority of Commons-men on church government by 1646, see *CJ*, IV, 513.

75 Scott, *Politics and War*, pp. 84–5.

76 Adamson, 'The Peerage in Politics', pp. 123–5. Of the Scots' leading allies at Westminster, by mid-1645 none were convinced religious Presbyterians except the Earl of Manchester, Sir Gilbert Gerard, and Sir William Waller: Mahony, 'The Presbyterian Party', pp. 15–16, 129–30, 184, 482; Adamson, 'The Peerage in Politics', pp. 150–1.

77 The Independent grandees Viscount Saye and Sele and his son Nathaniel Fiennes were explicit on this point: *A Declaration of the Lords and Commons Assembled in Parliament, Concerning the Papers of the Scots Commissioners* (1648), p. 30; V. Pearl, 'The "Royal Independents" in the English Civil War', *TRHS*, 5th series, 18 (1968), 95. See also V. Rowe, *Sir Henry Vane the Younger: a Study in Political and Administrative History* (1970), pp. 61–3.

78 See J.T. Cliffe, *Puritans in Conflict: the Puritan Gentry During and after the Civil Wars* (1988), pp. 154–5.

79 BL, Harl. 165, fol. 233.
80 Holmes, *Eastern Association*, pp. 186, 220–1.
81 Scott, 'Northern Gentlemen', pp. 347–75.
82 Mahony, 'Presbyterianism in the City of London', pp. 93–114; Lindley and Scott (eds.), *The Journal of Thomas Juxon*, pp. 17–21; E. Vernon, *The London Presbyterian Movement and the Politics of Religion in the British Revolution, c. 1638–1662* (forthcoming). I am grateful to Elliot Vernon for allowing me to read draft chapters of his book prior to publication.
83 Mahony, 'The Presbyterian Party', pp. 4–5; Adamson, 'Parliamentary Management', pp. 33, 37–8, 49.
84 Bodl., MS Clarendon 28, fol. 5; BL, Add. MS 78223, fol. 29.
85 D. Buchanan, *An Explanation of Some Truths* (1646), pp. 53, 56.
86 D. Holles, *Memoirs of Denzil Lord Holles* (1699), p. 132.
87 Walker, *Mysterie of the Two Iuntos*, p. 7.
88 'Teazer' was a hunting term and referred to one who rouses the game: *OED*.
89 Bodl., MS Eng. hist. b.205, fol. 86 (I would like to thank Grant Tapsell for this reference); *Mercurius Pragmaticus*, no. 18 (25 July–1 August 1648), sigs. S4, S6; no. 21 (15–22 August 1648), sigs. Aa4, Bb2; [W. Prynne], *A Brief Iustification of the XI. Accused Members* (1647), p. 10; J. Chestlin, *Persecutio Undecima. The Churches Eleventh Persecution* (1648), p. 60; Clarendon, *History of the Rebellion*, II, 181; Holles, *Memoirs*, pp. 60, 65; *PCH*, XVI, 91, 156; Mahony, 'The Presbyterian Party', p. 182; Seaward, 'Divisions, Tellers, and Management', pp. 81–2; Peacey, *Print and Public Politics*, pp. 142–3, 147.
90 Holles, *Memoirs*, pp. 137–8; Adamson, 'Parliamentary Management', pp. 37–8.
91 *CJ*, IV, 690a.
92 Scott, *Politics and War*, pp. 132–3; Adamson, 'The Peerage in Politics', pp. 152–3.
93 *CJ*, V, 312, 314; Bodl., MS Clarendon 30, fols 60, 73r–v, 76v, 171, 181v, 189; BL, Verney corresp. M636/8: Denton to Verney, 6 October 1647; same to same, 18 November 1647.
94 There may well have been disagreement within this group between Commons supremacists and those such as the 'Leveller' Major Thomas Scot – and possibly Marten and Grey of Groby – who favoured the introduction of a 'law paramount' that would circumscribe parliamentary authority. See E. Vernon and P. Baker, 'What Was the First Agreement of the People?', *HJ*, 53 (2010), 39–59.
95 Underdown, *Pride's Purge*, pp. 61, 71–2, 83–4, 88; A. Woolrych, *Soldiers and Statesmen: The General Council of the Army and Its Debates 1647–1648* (Oxford, 1987), p. 7; Pearl, 'Royal Independents', 73, 74.
96 In November 1646, Fiennes told the Scots commissioners that having 'conquered' the king 'they [Parliament] might dispose of the kingdome and affaires as they pleased'; and Evelyn of Wiltshire reminded the commissioners that 'this was not the first tyme they [the English] had a kinge of Scottl [and] prisoner, And they might remember they had not longe agoe cutt of their Queenes head': National Library of Wales, Aberystwyth, Wynnstay manuscripts, 90/16. I am grateful to Lloyd Bowen for this reference.
97 J. Morrill and P. Baker, 'Oliver Cromwell, the Regicide and the Sons of Zeruiah', in J. Peacey (ed.), *The Regicides and the Execution of Charles I* (Basingstoke, 2001), pp. 17–21.
98 A rift that would be healed in April when the Houses overturned the Vote: Adamson, 'The Peerage in Politics', pp. 223–5, 235–7, 241.
99 *A Remonstrance of His Excellency Thomas Lord Fairfax* (1648), p. 8.
100 Gardiner, *Great Civil War*, IV, 56–8; Morrill and Baker, 'Sons of Zeruiah', p. 24.
101 *CJ*, V, 547; S.R. Gardiner (ed.), *The Hamilton Papers* (Camden Society, 2nd series, 27, 1880), p. 191.
102 Underdown, *Pride's Purge*, pp. 96–7.
103 *CP*, III, 17.
104 For evidence of this alliance, see Bodl., MS Clarendon 31, fols 67v, 72, 82v, 85; National Archives of Scotland, Hamilton Manuscripts, GD 406/1/2372, 2398; *Mercurius Pragmaticus*, no. 7 (9–16 May 1648), sig. G3v; Gardiner (ed.), *The Hamilton Papers*,

pp. 191–2, 202–3, 205; *CP*, III, 6–7; M.J. Braddick and M. Greengrass (eds.), 'The Letters of Sir Cheney Culpeper, 1641–1657', in *Seventeenth-Century Political and Financial Papers* (Camden Society, 5th series, 7, 1996), p. 339; Adamson, 'The Peerage in Politics', pp. 237–8, 241–2.

105 For example, Sir Walter Erle, Thomas Gewen, Edward Massie, Sir John Maynard, and Clement Walker.

106 I. Gentles, 'The Struggle for London in the Second Civil War', *HJ*, 26 (1983), 293.

107 *CJ*, II, 622, 650; Adamson, 'The Peerage in Politics', p. 236. The tellers both for and against an unconditional treaty held in or near London included the former Holles–Stapilton group Presbyterians Sir Thomas Dacres (for), Francis Drake (for), Sir Walter Erle (for), Sir John Evelyn of Surrey (for), John Swynfen (against), and Sir John Trevor (against).

108 The earls of Lincoln, Suffolk, and Middlesex, and lords Berkeley, Hunsdon, and Maynard.

109 *LJ*, X, 384; Adamson, 'The Peerage in Politics', pp. 232–3, 236–7, 246–9.

110 G. Holmes, *The Making of a Great Power: Late Stuart and Early Georgian Britain 1660–1722* (1993), p. 112; A. Marshall, *The Age of Faction: Court Politics, 1660–1702* (Manchester, 1999), p. 110.

4 Henry Ireton and the limits of radicalism, 1647–9[1]

Sarah Mortimer

> *Salus populi suprema Lex*, is of all others most apt to be abused, or mis-applyed, and yet none more surely true.[2]

Few politicians of the 1640s comprehended the political and conceptual problems of the civil war era more clearly than Henry Ireton. A soldier and an MP, with a powerful intellect and even more powerful connections, he recognised both the strength and the fragility of the parliamentarian case; his efforts to justify his own actions and those of his allies reveal his intense concern to prove their legitimacy and necessity. A man of action, Ireton was Commissary General in the New Model Army from 1645, but he was also the Army's chief 'penman', fascinated by constitutional principles and political theory. In his writing and his speeches, there was a sustained attempt to uncover the core principles of an English constitution which, for Ireton, was ultimately grounded in the human need for peace and security. Parliament's actions must be directed towards this end, and if they were not, then force might be necessary to bring Parliament back to its true course. As Clive Holmes has commented, Ireton set out the Army's position in June 1647, and his words remained the basis for the Army's actions and principles until at least the end of 1648; indeed, his significance in national politics at this time was immense.[3] And yet the coherence and consistency of Ireton's own thought have not often been appreciated.

Ireton was concerned to establish a settlement based on Parliament and the existing constitution, insofar as these were compatible with the law of nature and the safety of the people. The preservation and safety of the community were the central ideals of Ireton's political thought, and he believed that these could best be ensured by vesting supreme power in Parliament, as the representative of the people. Indeed, he was convinced that Parliament had taken up arms against the king upon this very ground, and the same principle of *salus populi* would be used again by the Army in 1648 against the members of Parliament themselves. But Ireton recognised that it was such a powerful principle, with the potential to dissolve all existing constitutional arrangements, that it needed to be used with extreme caution. At the same time, he was aware of the need to defend parliamentary authority and to explain its relationship to that core parliamentarian principle, the safety of the people. How he sought to do this, in the shifting and complex circumstances of 1647 and 1649, will be the subject of this chapter.

Although historians have recognised the political importance of Henry Ireton, their interpretations of his place within seventeenth-century intellectual culture have diverged widely. To Austin Woolrych, at Putney Ireton offered an 'impromptu expression of ideas that were widely and deeply held', articulating the concerns of landed gentlemen fearful of the soldiers' proposals. Richard Tuck saw Ireton very differently, suggesting that his contributions at Putney and beyond showed that he was a devotee of the new theory of rights developed by the lawyer and MP John Selden, at the cutting edge of political philosophy. Dissatisfied with both these accounts, Ireton's most recent biographer, David Farr, argued that we should instead see Ireton as 'a Biblical republican'.[4] Mark Kishlansky has commented on Ireton in the context of his survey of the army's political agenda, and Ireton's attitude towards Leveller principles has been sketched by Barbara Taft.[5] Here, however, I will suggest that Ireton's thinking can best be appreciated by recognising his commitment to the 'safety of the people' as this was understood in the 1640s and to Parliament as the chief instrument through which this objective could be achieved. Greater attention to Ireton's position will help to make sense not only of the apparent inconsistencies within his own thought but also of the broader agenda of the Army and their parliamentary allies in the crucial years before the execution of Charles.

I

Ireton's career as an Army writer began in earnest in the early summer of 1647, when hostility between the Presbyterians in Parliament and the New Model Army had flared into the open. The immediate cause of this conflict was the Presbyterians' plan to disband part of the Army and send the rest to Ireland. However, the central, unresolved issue that divided the parliamentarian cause at this point was the nature of settlement with the king. On 14 June, the Army published a sweeping statement of their principles and their grievances in a *Humble Representation* addressed to Parliament.[6] Almost certainly written by Ireton, this document played an important role not only in shaping the Army's agenda but in providing some of the key concepts and phrases for the soldiers' understanding of their own mission. The importance of the *Representation* has long been recognised, and yet historians have tended not to analyse it in much detail or to examine how it might relate to later statements by Ireton or the Army. But to understand the events and the ideas of 1647, it is necessary first to look more closely at the Army's statement of 14 June.

At the heart of the *Representation* is the claim that the Army had been called by Parliament to the defence of the people's just rights and liberties and that it could not abandon this task. The Army needed to explain why it was unwilling to follow parliamentary orders concerning disbandment, while continuing to regard itself as a loyal servant of Parliament whose current course was in no way mutinous or disobedient. In drafting this document, Ireton needed to justify the

Army's actions and to show that he and his comrades-in-arms were following the true interests and principles of Parliament itself. He began, therefore, by insisting that the Army was 'called forth and conjured by the several declarations of Parliament to the defence of our own and the people's just rights and liberties'. The Army has a cause to fight, which has been endorsed by Parliament itself, and they could not forsake this cause while Parliament was dominated by corrupt members intent on destroying such loyal soldiers. Moreover, Ireton defended the Army's reluctance to obey Parliament as itself consistent with Parliament's views. As the *Representation* argued, 'Parliament hath declared it no resistance of magistracy to side with the just principles of law, nature, and nations', and these principles encouraged self-defence when destruction was threatened.[7] In other words, Ireton accepted that the principles of natural law and self-defence could be invoked, *in extremis*, to challenge the authority of Parliament. The implications of this line of argument were not spelled out in June 1647, but they would be fully explored over the next eighteen months.

Although the Army was troubled by the recent actions of some MPs and peers, the *Representation* envisaged a positive role for Parliament itself. The tract argued that freedom must come from Parliament, which is the foundation of 'common and equal right and freedom to ourselves and all the free-born people of this land'. Without successive Parliaments, England (and it was England alone that concerned Ireton in this document) could not be described as free. Ireton still saw a place for a king within England but one with little independent authority whose primary role would be in assenting to legislation proposed to him. This was clear from Ireton's proposal that these 'things we desire may be provided for by bill or ordinance of Parliament, to which the Royal Assent may be desired'. The authority of Parliament was not to be limited by the monarch; indeed, the only check on the power of Parliament was the fact that MPs did not sit perpetually but were to be elected at regular intervals. As Ireton made clear, the power of Parliament is 'in its own nature so arbitrary, and in a manner unlimited unless in point of time', by the prospect of dissolution every two years. Ireton had no wish to imply that the Army's actions were designed to limit the authority and supremacy of Parliament, merely to recall the MPs to their duty.[8]

There were two strands to the *Representation*, strands that pointed in different directions. Ireton believed that rights and liberties could be established only through a Parliament with supreme authority, but he also recognised that the 'just principles of law, nature and nations' provided the ultimate sanction for any system of government. To Ireton, these strands were not incompatible; after all, Parliament had itself appealed to 'just principles' to vindicate its actions, and both had formed part of parliamentarian rhetoric from at least 1642. But Ireton was aware that the concept of natural law could be used against Parliament; indeed, the Army's actions in this instance were based upon their claim to a more authoritative (and parliamentary) interpretation of natural law than that offered by the current, corrupt MPs. In the *Representation* Ireton sought to resolve this tension by pointing to Parliament's commission to the Army, which provided the Army with the legitimacy it might otherwise lack. Even at this early stage, then, there was a necessary ambiguity in Ireton's thought, occasioned by his intense commitment to Parliament as an institution and by his hostility towards the policies being pursued by his enemies at Westminster. Only a natural-law principle authorising the defence of community could justify the Army's action, he believed, but the legitimate defence of the people could be exercised only through Parliament or its agents. Ireton would soon find that the appeal to natural law, which he had placed at the heart of the *Representation*, was a powerful hostage to fortune.

The *Representation* needs to be set within the context of earlier parliamentarian statements, for it highlighted the tension already inherent within the line of argument associated with the leading parliamentarian propagandist, Henry Parker. Back in 1642, when defending the Militia Ordinance, Parker had famously described 'the paramount law that shall give law to all human laws whatsoever, and that is *Salus Populi*', claiming that this law justified Parliament's unprecedented rejection of positive law in its resort to an Ordinance that lacked Royal Assent. Furthermore, Parker added, '[T]he Charter of nature intitles all Subjects of all Countries vvhatsoever to safetie by its supreame Law'. When outlining the cases in which it was legitimate to invoke the principle of *salus populi*, he referred to the example of a general who turns his cannon on the soldiers – an example that would be repeated in the *Representation*.[9] Parker had strongly aligned *salus populi*, self-defence, and the law of nature, insisting that because a people could not consent to its own destruction, Parliament was right to take up arms against Charles. But his was always a high-risk strategy. As the royalist bishop John Bramhall commented, picking up on Parker's language, 'the charter of nature entitles mankind indefinitely to the whole earth; – will the Observer [that is, Parker] therefore give his neighbour leave to enter as a coparcener into [i.e. to share] his freehold?'[10] In Bramhall's view, it was impossible to circumscribe and contain this kind of appeal to nature and to natural rights, for it would quickly prove a powerful solvent, not only to all established laws but even to property itself. Parker sidestepped this challenge by insisting that it was Parliament that interpreted and imposed the law of nature. But in 1647 this could not be stated so straightforwardly. By this time, the potential difficulties in the parliamentarian argument were coming into the open, and the relationship between Parliament and the principles of natural law needed to be assessed more carefully.

Perhaps the fullest attempt to explain the position of the Army and its allies at this time came from the pen of the lawyer John Cook. In his *Redintegratio Amoris*, published at the end of August 1647, Cook offered a lengthy defence of the recent actions of the Army – and the £15 he received for 'extraordinary service' as part of the disbursements authorised by Lord General Fairfax in July 1647 may have been related to this publication.[11] Cook and Ireton must have been moving in similar circles, and by the time of Ireton's death in 1651 they would be close friends. About their personal relationship in the summer of 1647 we know little, but it is striking that their views on parliamentary power were similar and suggest that Ireton's views were not unique. Central to Cook's argument was the claim that the 'artificial body' of the kingdom was convened together in Parliament and that Parliament could therefore determine 'the arduous and most difficult affairs of the Kingdom, both for titles of land when they please, and all the great turnings and windings of state', and from the decisions of Parliament there could be no appeal.[12] He was well aware that the decisions of Parliament would not always be perfect, and there were plenty of disgruntled royalists who objected to Parliament's determinations in matters of land and property, but he was adamant that there must be some final court of appeal in any nation. In England, it was to the Parliament that 'I must submit my Interest, though my judgement is not enthralled; the ultimate resolution of all things not against the laws of God and Nature (which only interpret themselves) is in Parliament'.[13]

Although Cook believed that Parliament must be able to decide all questions of civil right and justice, he was anxious to justify the Army's stance and its refusal to acquiesce in Parliament's efforts to disband it. Echoing the logic of the *Representation*, he argued that the Army had been raised by Parliament for a purpose and that they continued steadfast in that purpose – 'all was done by the Parliament, for the publike good'. For him, the continuance of the Army was absolutely necessary, for 'without the intervention and intercession of this Army, this Parliament, as things stand, can never be able to settle the publike Liberties and happiness of this Kingdom'.[14] The Army was not a rival to Parliament but its agent, enabling the MPs and peers to complete the work for which they had begun the war in the first place. At the same time, he was as keen as Ireton had been to insist that no civil or positive laws should be obeyed that contravened the clear laws of God and of nature and that these laws commanded self-preservation and self-defence. No one could be bound to obey a law that threatened him with imminent destruction, and insofar as the Army seemed to be disobeying Parliament, they were, in fact, simply deferring to the higher laws of God and nature. Cook and Ireton did not want to restrict the power of Parliament but rather to ensure that it was used correctly and to show that it remained, in the final analysis, bounded by the clear laws of God and nature.

By the end of 1646, however, it was not only royalists who questioned the scope of these ideas but also men sympathetic to the Army and its friends within the parliamentarian coalition. These civilian radicals were becoming increasingly concerned about the arbitrary power they saw concentrated in the hands of MPs and peers, and they drew on an alternative but similar concept of the laws and rights of nature in order to counter this pernicious development. In *An Arrow against all Tyrants*, written by Richard Overton in October 1646, we can see this process at work. Overton had been supportive of the parliamentarian cause from the start, writing pamphlets from 1640 against Laudian tyranny, and by 1646 his opposition to clerisy and to arbitrary government had broadened into a far-reaching political programme, at the heart of which was a claim about natural rights. To Overton, because all men are born with liberty, freedom, and ownership of themselves, no one could claim authority over other men unless those men consented. All legitimate power was a trust, granted by individuals for their own benefit and the benefit of society. In Overton's view, 'by naturall birth, all men are equally and alike borne to like propriety, liberty and freedome' and should therefore be able 'every one equally and alike to enjoy his Birthright and priviledge; even all whereof God by nature hath made him free'.[15] Here was a claim about the natural birthright of individual men, and Overton was suggesting that the fundamental principles of nature were directed towards the preservation not of the community but of the individual.

Men as Overton described them were abstract individuals, free from all ties and obligations except those to which they have consented. Overton's men are not bound by the agreements of their ancestors, and there is no sense of a historic community in which the acts of one generation can and should shape those of their successors. Society existed to guarantee individual liberty, freedom, and 'propriety', and any government should be tested by its ability to safeguard and even improve these fundamental and individual natural rights and privileges. Whereas in the writing of Ireton, Parker, and Cook, the law of nature and the fundamental principles of communal defence were channelled through Parliament, as the representative of the community and the repository of historic agreements, in Overton's pamphlet Parliament no longer had that special place. Every man had a right to what nature had given him, and a government that did not respect these individual rights was not legitimate. As Rachel Foxley has recently shown, the concept of an appeal to the people – now understood in abstract terms – became increasingly important within Leveller thinking at this time, and Overton was its key proponent.[16]

In the summer of 1647, Overton began to make overtures to the soldiers for he, like them, had incurred the wrath of Parliament for his petitioning campaigns. His *An Appeal to the Degenerate Representative*, published in July of that year, was clearly designed to align his own ideas with the declarations of the Army. The central theme of this pamphlet was the need for all laws to be based upon right reason, equity, and the spirit of God – all principles that, he believed, Parliament was currently violating. Most importantly for our purposes, Overton drew on the language of the Army's *Representation* in order to strengthen his case. He quoted the Army's claim, 'That the Parliament hath declared it no resistance of Magistracie to side with the just principles and law of nature and nations' and repeated their distinction between the office of Parliament and the individual MPs.[17] From this, however, Overton drew the conclusion that when the parliament betrayed its trust, the power it once held reverted to the people, understood here as discrete individuals. The 'appeal' of the title was meant literally – an appeal to the common people and to the soldiers to whom, in accordance with what Overton described as 'the just principles' of nature, sovereign power had now reverted in light of Parliament's inability to govern for their benefit.

In the writing of Overton, at least, 'nature' and individual natural rights could be used against the current constitution, to call for fundamental change in the existing political arrangements. The prediction of men like John Bramhall had come true: the 'charter of nature' was now being invoked against Parliament and against existing laws. Overton had shown how the language of the *Representation* could be taken in a very different direction to that intended by Ireton and how an appeal to the soldiers could be made that might align their cause with the more radical programme now being canvassed by Overton and his friends.

II

These rival interpretations of the Army's cause would not have mattered very much if the grandees had been able to reach a settlement with the king. But Charles had no wish to compromise, and, as negotiations with him dragged on through the autumn, many of the soldiers and civilians grew increasingly resentful. They refused to accept that the king should have a stake in the new regime, preferring instead to cry up popular sovereignty and to push for a settlement based on the fundamental rights and liberties of the English people (or at least freeborn English men). The radical ideas circulating at this time have been the subject of much scholarly attention, and several recent studies have offered exciting new interpretations.[18] It is clear that many of these ideas had their roots in Parliament's own publications, but what I want to emphasise here is their connection to the Army's rhetoric. Indeed, what made these radical proposals so divisive and so problematic for Ireton and the grandees was that they could be portrayed as the culmination of the ideas of the June *Representation*, ideas to which the Army leaders were already publicly committed. By the autumn of 1647, with the prospect of an imminent settlement receding, the inherent tensions within the Parkerian position became clearer – and no one was more aware of these tensions than Henry Ireton.

Ireton's attention was initially directed to a pamphlet entitled *The Case of the Army Truly Stated*, a fierce and bitter critique of the Army grandees for failing to make good their earlier promises. The *Case* also bears the marks of some kind of collaboration between the Levellers, as the leading civilian radicals came to be called, and the Army, although the exact nature of that collaboration remains unclear.[19] Certainly, the concept of 'rights' that are independent of Parliament and of civil laws is important to the argument of the *Case* – and the authors claim that the Army's declarations already acknowledge these rights. Whether the authors were civilians or soldiers, they had begun to interpret the Army declarations through the lens provided by London pamphleteers like Overton. In the *Case*, the Army's own ideas were being developed in new and dangerous directions.

The authors of the *Case* claimed that in the *Representation*, the Army committed itself to preserving the rights of the people, rights that came from nature and from birth and not, or at least not necessarily, from Parliament. The authors reminded their readers that the Army took up arms 'for the people's just rights and liberties, and not as mercenary Souldiers', and that they proceeded 'upon the principles of right and freedom, and upon the law of nature and Nations'.

What that entailed, according to the authors of the *Case*, was that the soldiers must 'as free Commons claime their right and freedome as due to them'.[20] The role of Parliament, so central in Ireton's thought and in the original *Representation*, had now been downplayed in favour of the abstract, inherent rights of the people as individuals. On 14 June, claimed the authors, the Army had engaged to protect the people's rights as individual soldiers and Englishmen, though now some of the grandees were refusing to accept this. The first section of the *Case* cited the 14 June *Representation* explicitly and repeatedly echoed its language, but Ireton's words have been re-interpreted to suggest that the Army had pledged itself to enact far-reaching reform in the name of the people's rights.

The *Case* was not only a reworking of the Army's political principles; it was also a serious challenge to the grandees' policy of settlement with the king and with Parliament. It was published at the end of October, when Cromwell and Ireton were continuing to push for settlement with Charles but with seemingly little effect. The authors of the *Case* argued that a settlement should begin, not by establishing the powers of Parliament but with the people and the people's rights. The *Case* does assume parliamentary supremacy in practice, but the authors stress that power is originally in the people, that they must consent to government through their represetors, and that the reason why people choose governors was the 'apprehension of safety and good by them'. What was needed was a powerful Parliament, elected by all the freeborn and with a strong mandate for reform.[21] The *Case* suggested that it was time to start afresh, with a settlement based upon the timeless principles of reason and equity.

The criticisms of the 'Heads of the Proposals' – the grandees' effort to forge a settlement with the king in the summer of 1647[22] – and the interpretation of Army commitments that we see in the *Case* were repeated in another tract, *Putney Projects*, which came out in December 1647. It was written by John Wildman, one of the civilian radicals working with the Army adjutators in the autumn of 1647 and possibly one of the authors of the *Case*. In *Putney Projects*, Wildman appealed to 'the purest, most exact principles of freedome and righteousness, professed by these [i.e. the Army] to be the only grounds whereupon they thus ingaged even against the Parliament,' adding that 'the undefiled law of nature, was declared to be the rule of their proceedings, in their Declaration of Jun. 14'. Having made these engagements, Wildman claimed, the Army grandees could not in conscience go on to agree a personal treaty with the king. Instead, they must press for the establishment of liberty and freedom here in England.[23]

The discontent and disappointment that these tracts exuded must have alarmed the Army grandees, but the situation was made much worse by some of the more radical officer MPs who were increasingly intent on wrecking any treaty with the king.[24] According to one account, Cromwell and Ireton attributed the delay in settlement to 'the commotions of Colonel Martin and Colonel Rainsborough, with their adherents', for these troublesome officers had been trying to rouse the Army into mutiny.[25] Certainly Henry Marten had long been critical of the efforts to conciliate the king, and by the autumn of 1647 Colonel Thomas Rainborowe was also seriously frustrated with Cromwell's policies.[26] Rainborowe had been elected to the House of Commons for Droitwich in January 1647, and as commander of the garrison there he cannot have found it difficult to ensure that the handful of voters in this borough chose him.[27] In an important division in the Commons on 22 September, he and the radical Independent Sir Peter Wentworth were minority tellers against making any further addresses to the king. One of the winning tellers was Cromwell himself.[28] This was a clear attempt to scupper the Army grandees' ongoing talks with Charles and can hardly have improved relations between Rainborowe and Cromwell, who had already clashed over Rainborowe's efforts to become vice admiral. By early October, however, Rainborowe had achieved that ambition and was urged by the House of Lords to make haste to sea; perhaps they hoped that he would be less disruptive once distanced from the soldiers.[29] If so, they were mistaken, as the events a few weeks later would show.

Political and intellectual uncertainty continued through the autumn of 1647, and it was in this atmosphere of suspicion and recrimination that the famous Putney debates were called. Here, Ireton and Cromwell hoped to defend their continuing negotiations with the king and to reunite the Army around their interpretation of its engagements that summer. Ireton's intense involvement in the debates was surely due, at least in part, to the way in which his own words in the *Representation* had been deployed and distorted by soldiers and civilians alike. The *Case*, with its authors' move towards a much more radical understanding of the Army's programme, was present in the background from the start of the debates, but it was soon set to one side when a new document, the *Agreement of the People*, was read out. The novelty of the *Agreement* has been much commented upon, ever since Cromwell first described it as 'new to us'.[30] But it was the clear connections between the *Agreement* and the Army's earlier programme, at least in the minds of Wildman and some of the soldiers, that provoked Ireton to such a lengthy and heated riposte.

The *Agreement* was offered, or so it was claimed in the first printed edition, 'in order to the fulfilling of our Declaration of Iune the 14. wherein we promised to the people, that we would with our lives vindicate and cleare their right and power in their Parliaments'.[31] For all the impressive scholarship on the *Agreement* itself, this explanatory gloss has rarely been discussed by historians.[32] Yet much of the heated argument that passed between Ireton and his opponents concerned their different interpretations of the *Representation* of 14 June.[33] The *Representation* was central to the ensuing debates because Ireton's aim throughout was to show that his words and his appeal to the 'laws of nature and nations' in that work did not justify all the claims that the radicals were making. Insofar as men had rights by nature, Ireton insisted, these were not political rights, as the supporters of the *Agreement* were so keen to claim, but simply the right to life itself. Those born in England could claim a right to live here but not a share in the government of the land unless they enjoyed a fixed, local interest. As Ireton saw it, the law of nature did not provide the blueprint for any particular constitutional arrangement; it authorised nothing more than self-defence when it was absolutely necessary.[34]

The *Agreement* found its most vocal supporter in Thomas Rainborowe, who saw it as a promising alternative to current official plans for settlement. Certainly, he feared that the current negotiations were dangerous and that they were liable to destroy all chance of establishing the kind of constitution that he desired.[35] Rainborowe's intention seems to have been to detach the Army from a commitment to the Heads and to persuade the soldiers to call for a settlement that guaranteed true 'freedom' rather than one based upon the existing constitution. With unmistakeable disdain for current political arrangements or for conservative principles of reform, he announced that nothing would deter him from 'indeavouring by all meanes to gaine any thinge that might bee of more advantage to them [the people] then the Governement under which they live'.[36] This was a far-reaching call for change, for a new constitution based upon abstract principles of justice and equity. Rainborowe was suggesting that the Army discard the ancient constitution entirely, cease their negotiations with both king and Parliament, and create a new constitution based primarily on popular consent. It is hardly surprising that Ireton was deeply disturbed by his comments and anxious to provide a coherent response to them.

Whereas Rainborowe and the authors of the Agreement appealed to rights in the abstract, rights that belonged to all men, Ireton insisted that political and civil rights could be understood only in relation to particular communities, whose agreements over time had generated laws and customs. Rainborowe's attempts to abandon centuries of precedent and agreement could only lead to anarchy, Ireton thought, and his response was to insist instead that political and civil rights had to be understood within the context of the existing constitution. The one unshakeable principle of human social life was that men should keep the covenants they made with each other and that the ultimate purpose of these covenants was peace and security. It was the legal system founded upon these covenants that enabled men to hold property and to enjoy political rights and privileges; by the law of nature, a man had nothing except his own person. Any constitution that was based upon historic agreements was therefore just because the foundation of justice was the contracts and covenants that men made with each other.[37]

Ireton's views on property flowed from this position and were intimately connected to his view of parliamentary authority. Like many landed gentlemen who had studied at the Inns of Court, Ireton held that property rights were based upon custom and consent, and for him it followed that the holding of property necessarily placed men within specific communities located in both time and space. A property holder had what Ireton famously called a 'fix't or permanent interest' in the kingdom; he had literally bought in to the customs and laws that governed a particular community at a particular moment in time. When a person bought land by purchase or inherited it from his ancestors, he implicitly accepted that 'hee shall enjoy, hee shall have the property of [it] . . . with submission to that generall aucthoritie which is agreed uppon amongst us for the preserving of peace, and for the supporting of this law'. 'Constitution founds propertie', Ireton later said, for the system of property was underpinned by centuries of agreements, freely made, over a defined area of land. By the same token, the election of parliamentary representatives belonged to those men who, by virtue of their property, had a share in the constitution and a stake in the decisions made by that representative body.[38]

The property holders could choose who represented them, but they could not determine or restrict the power of the representative body, for that must be supreme – as Ireton had already made clear in the *Representation*.[39] As Cook had done before him, he insisted that there were no property rights that are independent of the constitution or that could be legitimately held against the express wish of Parliament. For Ireton, therefore, the only safeguard for current property arrangements was the interest that the current representatives had in maintaining it. Property was not sacrosanct; it was of human constitution, and humans could destroy as well as create it. It was for that reason that Ireton wanted the law to be made by those people that had 'a fixt property' in the land, insisting that 'the most fundamentall Constitution in this Kingedome, that is, that noe person that hath nott a locall and permanent interest in the Kingedome should have an equall dependance in Elections'. Only the propertied could elect parliamentary representatives, and only the threat of imminent destruction could legitimise any attempt to take that power back.[40]

As these comments suggest, Ireton believed that the war had been fought to eliminate personal monarchy and validate the supremacy of Parliament. Responding to Sexby, he insisted that the purpose of the parliamentarian cause had been to ensure that 'the law of this Kingedome should bee by a choice of persons to represent', in other words that laws for the people should be made by Parliament. He and his allies had sought to defend the constitution that currently existed and to prevent Charles from making laws according to his own will – that was the way to defend both liberty and property.[41] In his eyes, defending these axioms required no fundamental change to the constitution. Nevertheless, his sweeping claims for parliamentary power, limited only by a very thin notion of natural law and by the representative quality of the institution, opened up the possibility of change and reform within the existing system. And Ireton was no enemy to such reform, as he was keen to point out in the debate over the franchise.[42]

Rainborowe mounted a forceful attack on Ireton's argument, but support for his extreme view of natural right was actually quite limited. Foxley and Baker have, in different ways, shown that the Levellers' appeal to nature and natural rights tended to be combined with reference to existing law, and in this the soldiers were no different. Even Sexby, the soldier most critical of Ireton's position, emphasized the rights of Englishmen and the rights of soldiers, referring to the claims made on 14 June, as well making more vague comments about 'right' and 'birthright'.[43] Indeed, Ireton's insistence that reform must be based upon the rights that English men had under the constitution, and not upon natural right, may not have alienated everyone. Moreover, when it came to the crucial question of settlement, Ireton's position that settlement must start with the English Parliament, and not with natural right, was surely the prevailing view at Putney. And it was this view that would dominate political thinking, at least until April 1653.

III

Throughout 1647 and 1648, the central concern of Ireton and the other grandees was to forge a lasting settlement with the king. On this issue, Ireton's position was underpinned by his commitment to *salus populi*, the safety of the people, within the existing constitution as far as possible. As he said at Putney, 'I wish butt this, that wee may have a regard to safetie ... Lett's have that as the law paramount, and then lett us regard positive constitution as farre as itt can stand with safetie to these'.[44] This intellectual position did not change over the next eighteen months, although the dramatic events around him ensured that the implications of it became more radical, leading him eventually to support the execution of Charles.

In 1647, Ireton believed that the existing constitution gave rights and privileges to the king and the House of Lords, which ought to be honoured as far as possible, though he objected, of course, to the kind of 'free monarchy' so dear to James I and his son. Ireton wanted, therefore, to secure the agreement of the king to a new settlement, and this was clear from his part in the negotiations surrounding the Heads. As he explained at Putney, the constitution as it stood provided for the king's confirmation of laws, and so Charles's consent was needed if the new agreement were to be binding upon him. Indeed, Ireton's commitment to the principle of consent led him to argue that the king must accept the new settlement if he were to be bound by it in matters concerning his rights and privileges. But that did not mean that the king or the House of Lords was exempt from laws made by the Commons for the people of England, nor that they could break English laws with impunity. He even tried to reassure Wildman that '[t]he King and Lords are suable, impleadable in any Court. The Kinge may bee sued and tryed by a Jury'.[45] The officers and soldiers were not convinced of the value of continuing to treat with the king, however, and the Putney debates broke up as the animus against Charles grew ever more divisive.[46]

By the end of January 1648, Charles had escaped from the Army's custody and was preparing to wage war on his enemies once more, this time with the help of a Scottish Army. On 3 January, having learned of Charles's engagement with the Scots, Parliament passed the Vote of No Addresses, resolving to negotiate with him no longer. The Army committed itself to this policy, publishing a declaration in which they called for the 'setling and securing of the Parliament and the Kingdom without the King and against him'. If the historic rights of the king threatened to undermine the safety of the people, then there was no question as to which must yield. Although there is no concrete evidence of the authorship of this declaration, it has plausibly been suggested that it was the work of Ireton, at least in part, and certainly it fits with what we know of his views, including his prominent support for the Vote itself.[47] And from this point on, the emphasis in Ireton's argument would be upon the supremacy of Parliament over and – if necessary – against a king who could no longer be trusted.

The defeat of Charles in the ensuing Second Civil War strengthened a resolve within the Army to bring him to some kind of formal reckoning. But in the short term, the renewal of war improved the king's position as his pleas for a personal treaty found an increasingly sympathetic reception, even among MPs and peers. By November 1648, it looked like Parliament might be willing to allow Charles to London to put the finishing touches to the treaty talks at Newport that autumn – a development that would, in the eyes of the Army, betray the people's trust.[48] This turn of events clearly troubled Ireton, for although he remained committed to the principle that Parliament was supreme, he could not allow Parliament to endanger the safety of the people – as it would if MPs and peers placed their trust in a king who still seemed bent upon enslaving the people to his own will. In the *Remonstrance* that Ireton would draft in late November, these ideas are clearly expressed. Although the ideas articulated in the *Remonstrance* could be used to justify the king's trial and even his execution, it is important to appreciate how the logic of the argument in this work built upon the views that Ireton had articulated in the Army debates of 1647.

To Ireton, Parliament's willingness to make a treaty with the king was clear evidence that it was abandoning its role as the people's representative and ushering in the destruction of the kingdom. Ireton was resolutely opposed to Parliament's stance towards Charles, but to oppose it he had to show that it was contrary to Parliament's own principles and undermined its position as the guarantor of the people's safety. Resistance to Parliament could be justified only on these two, related but distinct grounds, both of which had first been articulated in the *Representation*. Ireton's message was not simply a negative one, however, for he was keen to demonstrate that settlement could be reached as long as the supremacy of Parliament was accepted and acknowledged by everyone, especially the king. Only on that basis would the laws and liberties of the land be secure. The *Remonstrance* was, therefore, the fullest statement by Ireton of his commitment to parliamentary supremacy – and his belief that resistance to Parliament could be justified if the people were in serious danger of destruction. His argument was thus consistent with his position in 1647, except that now the stakes were even higher.

Ireton's position was summed up in some of the opening lines of the *Remonstrance*: '*Salus populi suprema Lex*, is of all others most apt to be abused, or misapplied, and yet none more surely true'. Some people, Ireton argued, appeal to this principle to 'break those bonds of Law and Magistracie which they find to restraine them' but prudent, godly men could employ this maxim with 'very happy effects'.[49] What distinguished the two approaches was, for Ireton, the limited way in which the latter group used the principle – and here his experiences at Putney almost certainly shaped his reasoning. He wanted to show that it could be legitimate – in the eyes of God and according to the natural law – to break the letter of positive law and even to resist authority, if this was absolutely necessary to preserve the people. Central to the *Remonstrance* was Ireton's belief that constitutions and positive law are essential for human social and political life but that in exceptional circumstances they must be superseded in the name of *salus populi*. And late November 1648 was one such occasion.

Running through the *Remonstrance*, then, was a commitment to Parliament as the highest judge and arbiter of law within the land, a principle that he felt was threatened by the MPs' willingness to treat with the king as a special person, exempt from the normal course of law and subjection. Instead, Ireton insisted that Charles must be brought to trial, to make clear that he was not above the laws of England and that, in the final analysis, he must be answerable to the people in Parliament. He was extremely concerned that if the king were not proceeded against in justice, then this would demonstrate that he was above the law and above the reach of Parliament's power. It would give weight to the principle that kings could do no wrong, and it would imply that monarchs have their power from a source external to Parliament, namely God or their ancestors' conquests. For this reason, the king could not be readmitted to the political scene unless he agreed to a trial and to the surrender of his negative voice. At that trial, it must be up to Parliament to determine the guilt of the king and his chief accomplices, and if any mercy were to be exercised, it must be at the discretion of Parliament.[50] By 1648, Ireton refused to allow any grounds for exemption from the mighty power of Parliament; the limited concessions to royal and aristocratic rights he had made at Putney were now discarded.

The vehement opposition to a personal treaty between Charles and Parliament expressed in the *Remonstrance* was based upon the same principles as Ireton's critique of the *Agreement* at Putney. Charles could not use divine right to exempt himself from Parliament, Ireton thought, just as neither Rainborowe nor the Levellers could appeal to natural right for the same ends. The basic consistency of Ireton's position can also be seen at the Whitehall debates in December 1648, debates called to discuss a new version of the *Agreement of the People*. Here Ireton countered the call for a broad toleration of religious beliefs on the, by now familiar, grounds that individuals should not be allowed to use 'religion' to evade Parliament's jurisdiction or to make special space for themselves in the political sphere.[51] As we have seen, the realm of public life, as Ireton saw it, was guarded by contracts and covenants, built on the most minimal foundations of natural law and *salus populi*, then refined and adapted through time. Those who wanted a share in these political rights must place themselves within that community, most obviously through the purchase of property. No one within the kingdom could be allowed to appeal beyond this political sphere, to divine or natural right, or to anything that they claimed their conscience dictated. The political, civil sphere had evolved with its own logic, and those who objected to it could either share in the making of new laws if they owned property or quit the kingdom if they did not. Parliament must be the guardians of this political sphere – and thus it must have the power to determine life and death and to punish even when no law has been transgressed. Its power rested upon and was anchored in the historic consent of the community (of property owners), but it existed for a purpose: common safety. Parliament could therefore legitimately do whatever was required to ensure public defence and preservation. In late 1648, the most obvious task for Parliament was to bring the king to justice.

Ireton's belief in the supremacy of Parliament did not blind him to its faults, however, and the *Remonstrance* suggests that he was continuing to work out how to make Parliament more legitimate and representative. In the *Remonstrance*, he even called for an *Agreement of the People*, but one implemented by and through Parliament rather than one that arose directly from the consent of the people themselves. And he continued to seek reform of the franchise, to ensure that Parliament represented the property owners of the kingdom as consistently and as fairly as possible.[52]

In the short term, the *Remonstrance* did not dissuade Parliament from pursuing a treaty with Charles, prompting the Army to purge the Commons on the morning of 6 December. Two months later, Charles was dead, and then later, in May, a commonwealth was declared; in February 1649, Ireton was involved with another declaration in which the authority of the Parliament was staunchly asserted and the trial of the king defended. In this tract, commissioned by the Rump and entrusted to Ireton and Marten, the Parliament's 'Intrinsicall Power and Trust' was invoked to legitimise its 'course of Justice against that Man of bloud' – a course that would, the tract explained, bring upon England the blessing of God. The tract also justified the Army's actions on the grounds that it was 'raised by full authority of Parliament, for the defence of the Liberties of the Kingdom', liberties that were threatened by the Parliament's willingness to treat with a king who sought only 'his and his families Interest, to the publique prejudice of the several Kingdoms, or at least of this'.[53] It was Ireton who reported on this Declaration to the House – and the biblical references and the echoes of the *Remonstrance* suggest his authorship and his continuing commitment to the ideas first set out in June 1647.[54] But this was the last declaration that Ireton would write in England, for in August 1649 he was sent to Ireland to assist in its reconquest and would die there of a fever, late in 1651.

IV

Edward Hyde, earl of Clarendon, would later describe Ireton as a man 'so radically averse to monarchy and so fixed to a republican government' that he would never have allowed Cromwell to indulge in his 'tyrannical excesses'.[55] Hyde may have exaggerated the potential for disagreement between Cromwell and his son-in-law, but it is clear that Ireton was uncomfortable with the erection of any power independent of or superior to Parliament that could impose its will upon the people without their consent. To that extent, Ireton might well have been critical of the rationale behind the Protectoral regime, in which Parliament's power was balanced by the Protector and his Council. But Ireton was a man whose views were formed in the 1640s, not the 1650s, who wrestled with the tensions and problems inherent within the parliamentarian cause as it developed through that decade. He hoped to alleviate the potential for parliamentarian tyranny through regular elections, a fairer franchise system and, perhaps, through an *Agreement of the People* sponsored by Parliament itself. Ireton's republicanism grew out of the parliamentarian arguments of the 1640s, in which Stuart personal monarchy was the main target; it was the arbitrary power and private interest of Charles that concerned him and that he tried to counter through an appeal to parliament and to the crucial principle of *salus populi*.

More than any of his contemporaries, Ireton realised the possibility of tension between these fundamental parliamentarian principles. He saw the need to strike a balance between natural and positive law, between the demands of *salus populi* and the constraints of the existing constitution, between necessity and the need for agreements. Ireton sought to steer a course through the dramatic events of the late 1640s and to bring order and coherence to the rhetoric of the Army and its parliamentarian allies. But the parliamentary supremacy he desired would prove even more unpopular than Charles's rule, and the restoration or recreation of a 'monarchical principle' was being canvassed by Cromwell and his other wartime colleagues only a few years after his death.

Notes

1. I would like to thank Phil Baker and David Scott for their comments on a draft of this article.
2. Thomas Fairfax, *A Remonstrance of his Excellency, Thomas Lord Fairfax* (1648), p. 4.
3. C. Holmes, *Why Was Charles I Executed?* (2006), p. 112.
4. A. Woolrych, *Soldiers and Statesmen: The General Council of the Army and Its Debates, 1647–1648* (Oxford, 1987) quotation from p. 236; R. Tuck, 'The Ancient Law of Freedom: John Selden and the Civil War', in John Morrill (ed.), *Reactions to the English Civil War 1642–49* (1982), p. 147; D. Farr, *Henry Ireton and the English Revolution* (Woodbridge, 2006), p. 154.
5. M. Kishlansky, 'Ideology and Politics in the Parliamentary Armies, 1645–9, in Morrill (ed.) *Reactions*, pp. 163–84; B. Taft, 'From Reading to Whitehall: Henry Ireton's Journey', in M. Mendle (ed.), *The Putney Debates of 1647: The Army, the Levellers and the English State* (Cambridge, 2001), pp. 175–93.
6. For the background to the document, see David Scott, *Politics and War in the Three Stuart Kingdoms, 1637–49* (Basingstoke, 2004), pp. 144–6; A. Woolrych, *Britain in Revolution 1625–1660* (Oxford, 2002), pp. 371–2; for Ireton's military career, see I. Gentles, 'Henry Ireton', *ODNB*.
7. A.S.P. Woodhouse, *Puritanism and Liberty: Being the Army Debates (1647–9) from the Clarke Manuscripts with Supplementary Documents* (2nd edn., 1974), quotations from p. 404.
8. *Ibid.*, quotations from pp. 407, 408, 406.
9. H. Parker, *Observations Upon Some of His Majesties Late Answers and Expresses* (1642), pp. 3–4. On Parker's tract, see also M, Mendle, *Henry Parker and the English Civil War: The Political Thought of the Public's 'Privado'* (Cambridge, 1995) pp. 70–89. Woodhouse, *Puritanism and Liberty*, p. 404.
10. J. Bramhall, *Serpent Salve* (1643) p. 47.
11. J.S.A. Adamson, 'The English Nobility and the Projected Settlement of 1647', *HJ*, 30 (1989), 589.
12. J. Cook, *Redintegratio Amoris* (1647) p. 23.

13 *Ibid.*, pp. 74–5.
14 *Ibid.*, quotations from pp. 69, 80.
15 R. Overton, *An Arrow Against all Tyrants* (1646), quotation from p. 3.
16 R. Foxley, *The Levellers: Radical Political Thought in the English Revolution* (Manchester, 2013), Chapter 2.
17 R. Overton, *An Appeale from the Degenerate Representative Body the Commons of England* (1647), pp. 4, 6.
18 Philip Baker and Elliot Vernon (eds.), *The Agreements of the People, the Levellers, and the Constitutional Crisis of the English Revolution* (Basingstoke, 2012); idem, 'What Was the First Agreement of the People?', *HJ*, 53 (2010), 39–59; Foxley, *Levellers*; Mendle (ed.) *Putney Debates* (2001).
19 Although this has been traditionally seen as the work of John Wildman, Morrill and Baker have recently argued for the role of Edward Sexby in its authorship: 'The Case of the Armie Truly Restated', in Mendle (ed.), *Putney Debates*, pp. 103–24.
20 The *Case* is printed in D.M. Wolfe (ed.), *Leveller Manifestos of the Puritan Revolution* (New York, 1944), pp. 198–222, quotations from p. 202.
21 *Ibid.*, p. 212.
22 For the text of this, see S.R. Gardiner (ed.), *The Constitutional Documents of the Puritan Revolution 1625–1660* (3rd edn., Oxford, 1906), pp. 316–26.
23 J. Wildman, *Putney Projects* (1647), quotations from p. 3.
24 See also Scott, 'Party Politics in the Long Parliament, 1640–8', Chapter 3 in this volume.
25 This account comes from Major Robert Huntington, *LJ*, X, 410.
26 History of Parliament Trust [HOPT], unpublished biography of Henry Marten for the 1640–60 section, by D. Scott; unpublished biography of Thomas Rainborowe for the 1640–60 section, by S.K. Roberts. I am grateful to the HOPT for allowing me to see these articles and the articles cited hereafter, in draft.
27 HOPT, unpublished constituency article of Droitwich for the 1640–60 section, by S.K. Roberts.
28 *CJ*, V, 312.
29 HOPT, unpublished biography of Thomas Rainborowe for the 1640–60 section, by S.K. Roberts.
30 *CP*, I, 236.
31 *An Agreement of the People* (1647), p. 14.
32 One exception is Baker and Vernon, 'What was the First Agreement of the People?', esp. p. 54.
33 A point I have also argued in 'What Was at Stake in the Putney Debates?', *History Today* (January 2015), 40–5.
34 *CP*, I, 302–3.
35 See Rainborowe's comments in *CP*, I, 273.
36 *Ibid.*, 247.
37 *Ibid.*, 262–4, see also his comments on p. 404.
38 Quotes from *ibid.*, pp. 314, 263, 322. This side to Ireton's thought is also briefly discussed in J.G.A. Pocock, *The Machiavellian Moment: Florentine Political Thought and the Atlantic Republican Tradition* (Princeton, NJ, rev. edn. 2003), pp. 375–7.
39 See also *CP*, II, 79.
40 *CP*, I, 319, 314.
41 *Ibid.*, 326–7.
42 *Ibid.*, 333.
43 Foxley, *Levellers*, Chapter 3; P. Baker, 'The Franchise Debate Revisited: The Levellers and the Army', in S. Taylor and G. Tapsell (eds.), *The Nature of the English Revolution Revisited: Essays in Honour of John Morrill* (Woodbridge, 2013), pp. 103–22; *CP*, I, 323.
44 *CP*, I, 403.
45 *Ibid.*, 405.

46 Woolrych, *Soldiers and Statesmen*, pp. 262–5.
47 Farr, *Henry Ireton*, pp. 122–3; HOPT, unpublished biography of Henry Ireton for the 1640–60 section, by D. Scott.
48 For these events, see D. Underdown, *Pride's Purge: Politics in the Puritan Revolution* (Oxford, 1971), esp. pp. 122–3.
49 *A Remonstrance*, pp. 4–5.
50 *Ibid.*, pp. 47–8, 51, 62–3.
51 *CP*, II, 114–15, 122–3; see also the comments on Ireton's thinking in G. Burgess, *British Political Thought, 1500–1660: The Politics of the Post-Reformation* (Basingstoke, 2009), p. 267.
52 *A Remonstrance*, p. 66; for the influence of the Levellers on the *Remonstrance*, see Holmes, *Why Was Charles I Executed?*, pp. 116–17.
53 *A Declaration of the Parliament of England, in Answer to the Late Letters Sent to Them from the Commissioners of Scotland* (22 February 1649), pp. 36–7, 13, 10.
54 *CJ*, VI, 131, 145; HOPT, unpublished biography of Henry Ireton for the 1640–60 section, by D. Scott.
55 E. Hyde, Earl of Clarendon, *History of the Rebellion and Civil Wars in England* (3 vols, 1707), III, 468.

5 'Parliament', 'liberty', 'taxation', and 'property'

The civil war of words in the 1640s[1]

Grant Tapsell

words, which are but wind ...[2]

One of Clive Holmes's most gleeful moments amidst the pugilistic politics so often practised in Oxford came when he was described during a meeting as a 'mere rhetorician' by an outraged and outmanoeuvred colleague. Although not intended to be complimentary, the comment did inadvertently point to an important theme: the interplay of language and politics that has often been the focus of Clive's scholarly work. In the 1974 monograph that made his name, for instance, the reader is exposed to Sir John Holland's linguistic wrigglings about his allegiances in 1642, and John Pym's vigorous efforts in the same year to create a national association whose written terms would be 'not subject to equivocation'.[3] Clive's concern for the language of politics has since permeated his work on both social elites and 'popular' groups. His brilliant 1980 critique of the 'county community' thesis of locally bounded political horizons in England emphasized that a 'common educational pattern' at Oxbridge and the Inns of Court 'produced a common language of intellectual discourse' amongst the gentry.[4] In 1985, he subjected the documents illustrating conflicts over the draining of the East Anglian fens in the first half of the seventeenth century to searching analysis, stressing that those produced by local fenmen displayed in language and 'tone' an 'acute sensitivity to the assumptions and concerns of their rulers' that indicated their 'sophisticated understanding of central politics'.[5] Most significantly for present purposes, the conclusion to a neglected 1992 essay (from which I derive the title for this chapter) took its central point from Francis Bacon's warning to the House of Commons in 1610: 'questions which concern the power of the king and the liberties of the subject should not be textual, positive and scholastical, but slide in practice silently and not be brought into position and order'. This warning came during the fractious debates over the 'Great Contract', a plan to remedy chronic deficiencies in crown finance, and, as Clive noted, was 'sound advice, but too late'.

[I]nchoate ideas of law and prerogative, of power and liberty, interwoven in the *mores majorum*, had already been the subject of dissection and exegesis;

74   Grant Tapsell

the tensions among elements that had previously coexisted had been noted and explored. The result was a constitutional crisis.[6]

Grey areas of commonly accepted but unexplored political norms and pieties could rapidly become dangerously polarised into black-and-white disputes when pressure was applied precisely to define them.

'Mere rhetoricians' were a much criticised breed in early modern England. Most famously, Hobbes viewed the rhetorical skills politicians had learned from reading the textual records of classical antiquity as a profoundly dangerous and destabilising force.[7] There was a growing cacophony of calls for the employment of 'plain English', whether in parliament, press, or pulpit.[8] Leading politicians sought to emphasize their sincerity through self-conscious linguistic simplicity. Lord Protector Cromwell began a very long speech at the opening of his second parliament in September 1656 with the injunction: 'let us be brief; not studying the Art of Rhetoricians. Rhetoricians, whom I do not pretend to much concern with; neither with them, nor with what they are used to deal in: Words! Truly our business is to speak Things!' And the following year, he expostulated that 'I am not a man scrupulous about words, or names, or such things. I have not hitherto clear direction – but as I have the Word of God'.[9] Such an anti-rhetorical stance was, of course, a kind of rhetoric in itself. Perhaps the most famous example is Shakespeare's Mark Antony rousing the mob against Caesar's murderers with a brilliantly constructed speech, whilst claiming, 'I am no orator, as Brutus is, / But, as you know me all, a plain blunt man'.[10] Charles I was well known to have read Shakespeare during his final captivity, as Milton would cruelly sneer in 1649 when quoting from *Richard III* as an archetype of a king who used pious words to a deceitful purpose.[11] Milton was particularly exercised by the use of 'demagogue' in an English context by Charles I (or his ghostwriter) in *Eikon Basilike* (1649): 'the affrightment of this Goblin word; for the King by his leave cannot coine English as he could Money, to be current'.[12]

Coining and redefining words were evidently matters of profound importance in early modern England.[13] They reached crisis point during the civil wars of the 1640s, and the broad contexts for the politics of language during that critical decade will form the first main section of this chapter, before attention is focused on a particular textual example: a satirical dictionary of 1648–9, written by a disgruntled royalist cleric, John Warner, bishop of Rochester, to explain the all too successful trickery employed by the new parliamentarian elite. Efforts at political lexicography will in conclusion be shown to reflect the rhetorical technique of *paradiastole*, of inverting linguistic meanings, and may have contributed to reactionary attempts to empty key words of their meaning to help a stalled process of 'healing and settling' in the 1650s. Overall, Warner's work is interesting both as a specific example of the politics of language during the English Revolution, and as part of a wider evaluation of the modes of activity open to defeated royalists. Dictionaries may be added to the literary arsenal that the Stuarts' supporters deployed against a militarily triumphant

Parliament alongside better known newsbooks, 'characters', poetry, prayers, and meditations.

I

Contemporaries of all political stripes saw linguistic instability as a means of explaining the dire disturbance of political and religious affairs during the 1640s.[14] The parliamentarian peer Philip Lord Wharton, for instance, reacted with horrified bemusement to the onset of the English Civil War in August 1642:

> The fate of a kingdome divided agaynst itself is notorious, especyally when the cure is made the disease. Yett itt seems a riddle, those about the king, and those in the parliament speake all one language; for religion, the king, the law, liberty, and priviledge of parliament. One of the two must bee in the right.[15]

For their part, those who decided the king was in the right would over time generate a literary milieu of striking variety and cumulative potency.[16] No sexual slander was too shocking to be hurled at rebellious Roundheads by some royalists; no prayer for divine intercession too fervent to be offered up to the Almighty by others.[17] The king himself claimed that he would be indefatigable when it came to undeceiving his people through authorship: 'this labour of Our Pen'.[18] And as the royalist cause declined, the theme of deception would be emphasized more and more, not least by preachers. Standing before the royalist Parliament at Oxford, one offered a rhetorical 'Looking-glasse of Rebellion', through which the king's rebellious subjects would finally be able to perceive how close their actions were to the sin of witchcraft.[19] Once the war had been lost, the royalist tone naturally became more bitter. As Jasper Mayne explained to the inhabitants of the subjugated royalist capital in 1646:

> [S]ome men, like the *Fish* which blacks the *streame* in which it swimmes, and casts an *Inke* from its bowels to hide it selfe from being seene, make *Words*, which were ordained to reveale their *Thoughts*, disguise them: And so like the *Father* of *lyes*, deale with their hearers, as he dealt with our first *Parents*, appeare to them, not in their owne, but in a false, and borrowed *Shape*; And thereby make them imbrace an *Imposture* and *Falshood*, in the *figure*, and *Apparence* of a *Reality* and *Truth*.[20]

Warner's dictionary may have been unusual in form, but it emerged from a wider world of clerical preaching and publishing that was nevertheless haunted by the fear of other more persuasive wordsmiths' success in manipulating the fickle common people.

Although the rival camps of parliamentarians and royalists were much given to reflect on the corrupting power of language during the civil wars, such concerns reached their apogee during the unstable peace that followed. The writings of radical authors displayed a horror that, for all the recent expenditure of blood and treasure by the English people, retrograde political and social assumptions had survived the military defeat of the king. For many Levellers, in particular, although the civil war had been fought by common soldiers intent on freedom and liberty, all that it had accomplished was to entrench an even more repressive and exploitative elite in power.[21] Such criticisms reached a crescendo between the outbreak of the Second Civil War in spring 1648 and the constitutional fallout from the execution of the king during the first half of 1649. In his *The Bloody Project*, William Walwyn called 1648 'this Yeare of dissembling'. He was savagely critical of the gullibility of his countrymen:

> Was it sufficient thinke you now, that the Parliament invited you at first upon generall termes, to fight for the maintenance of the true Protestant Religion, the Libertyes of the People, and Priviledges of Parliament; when neither themselves knew, for ought is yet seen, nor you, nor anybody else, what they meant by the true Protestant Religion, or what the Liberties of the People were, or what those Priviledges of Parliament were, for which nevertheless thousands of men have been slain, and thousands of Familyes destroyed?[22]

Removing the king did not make things better. In the wake of the regicide and abolition of the House of Lords, Leveller authors expressed abhorrence that the new unicameral parliament showed every sign of being worse than what had preceded it: the Rump was 'a more absolute arbitrary Monarchy than before. We have not the change of a Kingdom to a Common wealth; we are onely under the old cheat, the transmutation of Names, but with the addition of New Tyrannies to the old'.[23] Here we find the constitutional corollary of Milton's grim line that 'new *Presbyter* is but old *Priest* writ large'.[24]

Two fast-flowing streams merged to create the mighty torrent of linguistic chaos in the 1640s. As Francis Bacon had noted, attempts more precisely to define legal–constitutional positions were extremely dangerous. Efforts to trumpet the significance of English common law and to bolster the position of parliament vis-à-vis the crown, often turned on the close definition of terms. In the fractious debates prompted by the Earl of Salisbury's fiscal proposals for a 'Great Contract' in 1610, MPs fell upon *The Interpreter* (1607), a dictionary of legal terms, compiled by Dr John Cowell, the Regius Professor of Civil Law at Cambridge. Cowell's definitions of terms like '*subsidium*', '*rex*', '*praerogativa regis*',[25] and '*parlamentum*' were all viewed through the lens of increasingly fraught disagreements between crown and parliament over how to reconcile the rights of the crown and the liberties of the subject.[26] It was Cowell's misfortune to be taken by MPs as an apologist for crown prerogative power, not least because of his closeness, as vicar general, to the authoritarian archbishop of Canterbury, Richard Bancroft. Desperate to conciliate MPs in order to rescue the 'Great Contract', James I's tactical response was to argue that Cowell's work was 'in some points very derogatory to the supreme power of this crowne', ban *The Interpreter* by proclamation, and then have Cowell briefly detained.[27]

Cowell died in 1611, but definitional debates over key terms like 'franchise', 'time of war', and 'prerogative' would remain provocative during the parliaments of the 1620s and beyond.[28]

The second stream that fed into the wider linguistic instability of the 1640s was that of religious phrases, labels, and slogans in post-Reformation England. Central to this theme was the problem of puritanism. Polemical exchanges between different sections of the Church were immensely important in creating a polarised language of politics. The Martin Marprelate Tracts demonstrated the potential linguistic ingenuity – and offensiveness – of puritan authors, whilst puritans in the pulpit developed styles of communication that to an admirer like Philip Nye meant they 'have made a new language as it were, using new Termes et a new phraseology et therefore it were requisite one should make a new Lexicon for it'.[29] For their part, anti-puritan writers laid great emphasis on the hypocrisy and dissimulation of puritans, ridiculing their gestures in the pulpit, or lambasting in print their concealed immorality, notably in 'character' literature, definitional word games, and 'pseudo-academic' exercises.[30] Those fighting to retain episcopacy and the liturgy against later demands for 'root and branch' reform were understandably horrified by the linguistic pretensions of their critics. According to a preacher at St Paul's in October 1641, 'There goeth a *Jesuit, a Baal's priest, an Abbey-lubber,* one of *Canterburies whelpes*' had become 'the ordinary language as we walke the streets' of London.[31]

The explosive combination of religious and constitutional fears that destroyed Charles I's monarchy would lead many contemporaries to fear that the English language would be so destabilised that the English as a people would never be able to extricate themselves from cycles of deceit and violence. For Hobbes – never one to advocate half-measures – the sovereign should be a 'lexarch' overseeing language through law, 'that special class of language that determines "the distinction of right and wrong"', as he put it in *De Corpore*.[32] In the real world of the 1640s, Charles I had proved quite unable to exercise such power in a widely accepted way. Indeed, during the First Civil War, the parliamentarian newsbook *Mercurius Britanicus* criticized the word 'sanguine' as 'a new coyned expression at Court' – replete with overtones of blood, as well as merriment – after it was found to have been used by the king in one of the letters captured after the battle of Naseby.[33] In the absence of a 'lexarch', ridiculing their enemies was a more practicable option for individual royalists and was rendered pressing by the sheer scale and rapidity of political change. As Blair Worden has noted, for royalists 'the conversion of England in 1649 into a "Commonwealth and Free State" was a symptom of the debasement of language by the Roundheads and of their capacity to make words say the opposite of what they mean'.[34] There was an urgent need for royalists to respond.

II

The 'Parliament Dictionary' was one such response to a world gone mad.[35] By examining the definitions of 35 key words in contemporary political and religious discourse,[36] its author promised in his introduction to help every reader 'learne how by ... new coyn'd words' he 'hath been cheated, & undone' (85). Although the Scots had invaded England on several occasions, he was quick to emphasize that the real conquest was the result of a malign faction of Englishmen within both houses of Parliament acting 'instrumentally by a barbarous, rebellious, schismaticall Army' (85). Thereafter, in a text of almost sixty-five hundred words, the definitions provide a mix of learned etymological remarks in English, Greek, Latin, and French, and vigorous ridicule of the new civilian and military rulers of England. In an important sense, however, the 'Parliament Dictionary' failed at the first hurdle as a polemical exercise: it was not published, nor is there evidence of scribal circulation. Whether this was due to authorial anxiety or the forces of censorship is not clear.[37] Nevertheless, the careful presentation of the surviving text is suggestive of something that could have been designed for manuscript distribution, and its wording persistently presupposes a readership other than the author himself.

What of that author, and when was he writing? Although John Warner does not explicitly claim authorship of the piece, and although it is mainly written in the hand of his nephew and regular amanuensis, John Lee, it is clearly the bishop of Rochester's work: it survives in his family's papers amidst his other writings; it is annotated and corrected in his hand; the distinctive paper on which it is written is identical in style to that frequently used by Warner, and it reflects many of his particular concerns, as will become clear. Furthermore, drafts of some of the words in the 'Parliament Dictionary' can be found elsewhere in Warner's own hand.[38] Precisely dating the text is difficult. The combination of several internal references to events in 1648 and the absence of clear reference to the regicide suggest a dating of late 1648 or the opening weeks of 1649. The text probably remained a work in progress. It has been possible to locate elsewhere in Warner's papers several drafts of words not in the 'Parliament Dictionary'.[39] Most notable is 'court of Justice', which may refer to the High Court of Justice established to try Charles I, though the tenses are complicated and no outright mention of the final sentence occurs, as it surely would if Warner was writing after it was handed down.

Warner's work merits serious attention as an example of a genre that often falls between two scholarly stools. Sociolinguists have devoted considerable attention to early dictionaries but have naturally focused on what they reveal about developments within the English language and contemporary interactions with the scholarship of continental Europe, rather than their political or polemical significance.[40] Students of English literature have not been slow to perceive royalist concern about linguistic instability but have tended to focus either on the pamphlet 'characters' made famous by John Cleveland, or the bitterly didactic poetry of royalist poets like Abraham Cowley who argued that 'the *War* of the *Pen* is allowed to accompany that of the *Sword*'.[41] Warner's 'Parliament Dictionary' offers a vivid example of a satirical dictionary long before they became commonplace. Before turning to the detailed content of Warner's work, though, it is necessary to place his piece of royalist lexicography within a developing culture of published reflections on language and within his career as a whole.

Three interlocking trends may be identified as significant for Warner's choice of a satirical 'dictionary' form for his discontents. The first was a lexicographical impulse of a very wide-ranging kind. Bi- and trilingual dictionaries involving English had emerged from 1547, and Robert Cawdrey's *A Table Alphabeticall* (1604) provided the first explanation of 'hard usuall English wordes' in 'plaine English words'.[42] By the time that Warner wrote the 'Parliament Dictionary' in the late 1640s, there were at least fourteen editions of three general English only dictionaries, as well as a number of more specialised scientific and technical dictionaries.[43] A second trend emerged from an ever clearer sense of the close connection between language and power. The political integration – however partial – of all parts of the British Isles into a composite monarchy increasingly centred on London complemented the efforts of English-speaking Lowland writers and clerics to 'civilise' the 'barbarous' Highland regions, many of which remained stubbornly Catholic.[44] Here lessons could be drawn from the power of Latin as the language of Roman conquest and – even more controversially – from the impact of the Normans after 1066, not least via a vocabulary of *feudum*.[45] By the time that Warner wrote in the 1640s, such connections between language shifts and changing patterns of political dominance were starkly evident to defeated royalists confronting new vocabularies of power from the mouths of their parliamentarian puritan enemies. The third trend promoting Warner's choice of genre was that of making fun of the first two. 'Mocke-words' were being specifically defined in print as early as 1623, a move that paralleled efforts to shine light into the dark corners of England's criminal underworld via dissections of 'cant', the secret language of thieves, tricksters, and murderers.[46]

Couching his critique of parliamentarian politics in the form of a 'dictionary' was thus an understandable step for Warner to take, one conditioned by his intellectual development in a world increasingly self-conscious about the power and problems of language. In particular, it seems unlikely that Warner, as a fellow of Magdalen College, Oxford, from 1604 to 1610, would have been unaware of the efforts of teams of academics in Oxford and Cambridge over the years leading up to the publication of a new version of the Bible sanctioned by royal authority in 1611. These worked according to strict *Rules to be observed in the Translation of the Bible* drawn up by Archbishop Bancroft.[47] As an Oxford don, Warner was rated 'a good scholar, an able linguist, a deep divine, and one well read in the Fathers'[48] – all of which is evident to anyone with the determination necessary to plough through his substantial surviving manuscripts, written in a distinctively appalling cramped hand.[49] Here the intellectual habits of a scholarly seventeenth-century churchman are clear: time and again, Warner can be found exploring the Bible through detailed study of the 'significatons or sences' of individual Greek words.[50] Warner's interests included the cultural heritage of pre-Conquest England: he was a patron of William Somner's groundbreaking

Dictionarum Saxonico-Latino-Anglicum (1659).[51] Further evidence of Warner's intellectual range can be found in the sale catalogue of his books published in 1685. This listed a total of nearly twenty-four hundred items, with lexicons and texts in foreign languages very well represented.[52] How did Warner choose to deploy his scholarly concern with language against the parliamentarian victors of the 1640s?

Warner's tone throughout the 'Parliament Dictionary' occupies a fairly narrow spectrum of outrage, oscillating only between bitter reflection and splenetic rage. Like Roger L'Estrange's polemical writings later in the century, such a consistently angry tone carries with it a sense of preaching to the choir, of an intention to bolster the prejudices of any readers rather than of persuading the undecided. Warner certainly had a lot to be angry about by the late 1640s, in terms of both his personal circumstances and his public affairs. Thanks to very substantial inheritances from both his godmother and his father, Warner was one of the wealthiest men to sit on the episcopal bench in the early modern period.[53] Despite receiving early patronage from Archbishop George Abbot, he was also subsequently shrewd enough to jump onto Laud's coat-tails.[54] Dean of Lichfield from 1633, Warner was elevated to the bishopric of Rochester in 1637, an office he would hold through to his death in 1666 – a source of chagrin thanks to the poverty of the see and a rich sense of his own sacrifices for the royalist cause.[55] An aggressive patron of the 'beauty of holiness' in churches,[56] Warner was also unafraid of emphasizing his regard for royal authority by decrying from the pulpit any parliamentary resistance to Charles I's policies.[57]

Such positions perforce left him extremely vulnerable in the 1640s. Warner was chosen by his brethren to organise the defence of the thirteen bishops impeached in August 1641 for passing the 1640 canons, answered objections to the *et cetera* oath, and was one of the last bishops publicly to defend the right of his order to sit in the House of Lords in February 1642.[58] He would also publish, at the behest of Charles I, an eighty-one page defence of the church's right to hold lands against the sin of sacrilegious appropriation by laymen.[59] Even if he never penetrated into 'the inner circle of Caroline ecclesiastical power', Warner was deeply implicated in Laud's policies. Obnoxious politics and very considerable private wealth combined to ensure that he was aggressively pursued as a 'malignant' for large sums of money by parliamentary committees.[60] By May 1646, he was desperate enough to make a formal statement that 'I protest that for 5 years past, I have not contributed to the King by advice, action, money, horses, arms, or any other way'.[61] Although he was evidently not one of the handful of bishops known to have remained active as an ordainer of priests in the 1640s and 1650s, in his claims to parliament, Warner nevertheless exaggerated his neutralism: he was probably the largest financial supporter of ejected clergy during the period of disestablishment and was also a significant donor to the exiled court.[62] The 'Parliament Dictionary' thus offered Warner the opportunity to vent his spleen as a complementary activity to financial patronage of individual royalists.

III

Several core themes will be identified as running through Warner's superficially fissiparous work — the necessity of obedience to the king; of protecting the structures, wealth, and fabric of the Church of England; and of defending the integrity of the English nation vis-à-vis the Scots — before attention is turned to analysing his overall understanding of the recent violent upheavals.

Obedience to the king as God's anointed was a foundational part of the Church of England's identity, one cemented by a developing theory of the royal supremacy.[63] Warner's commitment to monarchical authority is evident from his strident hostility towards puritan and parliamentarian resistance to royal powers, a position no doubt further entrenched by his appointment as a royal chaplain in 1633. Defining 'priviledge' leads Warner to note the extension of a long recognised grant outside the common law to 'over-growen transcendent things', even to the extent that 'they exceed Gods power. . . . O ye height, ye depth, or rather ye bottomlesse pit of this infernall thing called priviledge!' (86v). For its part, 'property', which originated in the crown and used to be a 'hedge, or wall' against unjust encroachments, is in Warner's view 'broaken downe' and 'devoured by ye base multitude' in a terrifying example of democratic greed (86v).[64] Whereas an 'oath' used to indicate pledging to 'defend ye King', it was now inappropriately used in a negative sense: 'not to assist, or defend him; but to fight against, & destroy him' (87v). Such denigrating of the king was inevitable because his military power had been overborne: the 'militia' had 'ye originall power from ye King, who alone beares ye swo[rd]', but in the strange new post-war world 'it is an usurped power, forcibly taken, & tyranically exercised' in such a way as to deliver the people up to the 'custody of wolves' (87v).[65] Clearly for Warner, the loss of the king's pre-eminent role in the body politic had led to the overthrow of his subjects' true rights and liberties — an argument that would reach its classic encapsulation in Charles I's reasons for rejecting the authority of the High Court of Justice.[66]

Warner's second core gripe was the degradations suffered by the Church of England. Predictably, he focused considerable scorn on parliament's chosen instrument to re(-)form the church, the Westminster Assembly — or 'dissembly'.[67] Corruptly reliant on patron MPs, the members of the Assembly 'for their paines . . . shall have in surplusage, ye choicest, & fattest benefices in ye land yea 3 or 4 a peece, though those be (most uniustly) taken from ye true owners' (85v). Warner's defence of episcopacy is also unsurprisingly brisk: bishops were an apostolically sanctioned order, validated by the use of 'all Christian Churches, through all times successively, even to this last Centurie'. Root and branch abolition of the order was being pursued by evil-intentioned men 'to their own gainefull ends'.[68] (84) Thanks to disagreements within the victorious puritan coalition, Warner was able to mock the inability of the king's conquerors to create a structure for a new church: the full definition of 'elder' was impossible 'till ye Jewish Presbyterian, & ye Atheisticall Independent, can agree upon ye point' (87). Where God's priests once deployed the 'gospell' to speak 'ye glad tydings of peace', puritan preachers were like Mars' priests, inciting men to fight and kill, acting as 'firebrands of hell' (87). Nothing could be hoped for the future when the training grounds of clerics, the universities, were changed into 'academies' whose only fruits would be 'ye most accursed blades of schisme, heresy, faction, rebellion' (85). The Church of England was being stripped of its resources, ecclesiologically re(-)formed out of all recognition, and perverted in its teachings.

The third thread running through Warner's work is hatred and suspicion of the Scots.[69] It seems likely that this concern was first triggered by the experience of travelling to Scotland with Charles I as his chaplain during the disastrous coronation visit of 1633. Thereafter, his Scotophobia is clear, not least in a diary of parliamentary proceedings that he kept in 1641.[70] Within the 'Parliament Dictionary', Warner's English chauvinism requires him to emphasize that the degradation of England has been primarily achieved by the English themselves, but, as his prologue notes, it was invasion by the Scots that 'gave an onset to ye worke' (85). The 'classes' designed to supplant the traditional hierarchy of the Church of England were 'Scotized' and represented nothing better than 'a monstrous copulation of an Oxe & an asse, ye Spirituall & lay Elder' (84). At a broader level, Scotland was the nearest and most potent part of a larger ecclesiological Reformed axis of evil with significant centres in Europe and across the Atlantic. Warner blamed the degradation of English religion on the 'new invented doctrines of Devills ... brought over from Geneva; Amsterdam; New England, or Scotland' (85v). Such xenophobic spleen readily spread into other areas. The excise was 'invented by ye lower house in Hell' having first been levied in the Low Countries (87),[71] while 'plunder' could be blamed on 'ye base, bloody theeving souldiers' in the Holy Roman Empire during the Thirty Years War (86).[72]

Above and beyond the core themes of the 'Parliament Dictionary', how did Warner conceptualise the dynamics of change that had animated recent political and religious events? At a superficial level, misfortune could be described in a mocking language of the unnatural, hence the reference to a 'monstrous copulation' producing modern 'classes' (84). Indeed, Warner introduced his text as one that would be organised into two parts, with the definitions to be followed by a second section detailing in more general terms 'ye monstrous change of Religion, Lawes, men, & manners in this kingdome, since ye yeare of non-grace 1640' (85). Either this latter section does not survive, or else it was in practice subsumed into the definitions themselves. Such references fit with a broader theme in civil war writing, that of nature itself being out of frame, its disjointed state reflecting and reinforcing England's political chaos.[73] In more mundane terms, Warner also deployed the language of financial fraud. Twice in his introduction, he invoked the concept of false money, informing the reader that he would focus on 'ye strange sense, & use, of new & old words; lately coyned, & stamped by ye authority of ye 2 Houses in Parliam[en]t' (85).

When closely fitted together, monstrous events and varieties of fraud provided the horrific background to social upheaval. For Warner, maturity and rank had given way to an infantilised world in which the baseborn held sway over their natural superiors. Thus the divines sanctioned by Parliament to sit as the Westminster Assembly were 'iourneymen in Divinity', mere 'Apprentices' (85v) – one fraction of a broader discourse in which university-educated orthodox clerics decried the ignorance of 'mechanic' preachers.[74] Warner sneered that 'of all ye Parliamentary words' the one that had most retained its meaning was 'commons', because in the lower house of Parliament 'Knights, Esqu[ires] or Gent[lemen]' were no longer to be found: 'now it is hard to find one true antient Gent[leman] of them, but as for their understandings, endowments, & estats, they are but common men: so for faith, truth, & honesty, they are not so good as ye most common Porters, Carmen, & Dung<hill>-rakers' (84v). At the same time, the upper house was comprised of men 'so degennerate, & brought under, yt they are made subiect by their weaknes, & will, to ye meanest, & basest of all subiects, who in ye lower house, often doe rule, command, & cheate them aboue' (86). Small wonder that in such a world property had been overthrown by 'ye rampant begger ye Leueller, or ye wild boare ye souldier', and 'diuided betwixt Mephibosheth & sheba, ye poor tame owner, & ye base sycophant traytor' (86v). The end result of the civil wars was that a corrupt clique and a standing army had successfully conquered England in their own selfish interests.

For a highly educated cleric like Warner, it was easy to operate within a syncretic mindset that melded classical and Christian ideas of human weakness based on uncontrollable passions and original sin. Tellingly, Warner began his text by explicitly invoking the opening of Ovid's *Metamorphoses* (85).[75] He even offered 'a metamorphosis' as the subtitle for his work. The mutability of Warner's world was, of course, not the product of capricious pagan gods but of ongoing conflict between God and the Devil. Repeatedly he offers a sense of how the English were overturning aspects of the divine order according to a devilish plan. Thus, a covenant used to be 'an agreem[en]t, bargain, or contract, to pay, or performe some iust, & honest thing' but was now 'a scandall to yo[u]r conscience, a snare to yo[u]r liberty, & a net to yo[u]r estate, it is a siboleth, to difference men in religion, & faction', a change predicted in Isaiah 28:18,[76] shortened by Warner to 'A Couenant w[i]th death, & an agreem[en]t w[i]th hell' (84v). Because 'gospel' no longer referred to 'ye glad tydings of peace', having become 'an alarme all to warr', 'gospellers' were now 'fire-brands of hell, & not preachers of ye Gospell' (87). The multiplication and expansion of the concept of parliamentary 'privileges' meant that 'we call them by ye Deuills name in ye Gospell, which is Legion, for they are many, & too many for ye subiects ease, or good' (86v). Most pointedly of all, 'committee-men' had become so powerful that they could 'committ any, & all kind of iniustice, <yea> & to committ ye King & his Sauiour to death, if either seeme bu[t] to crosse his diuelish designes' (84v).[77] All this was inevitable since 'almighty' no longer meant God: apostates 'blasphemously hath made ye Parliament, such an other Almighty in England' (84). Such sentiments mirror those expressed in a sermon Warner preached on the first Sunday after the regicide. Taking Luke 18:31–3, 'The Son of man shall be delivered unto the Gentiles, and shall be mocked, and spitefully entreated, and spit on: And they shall put him to death', as his text, Warner offered a series of parallels between the death of Christ and the execution of the king. This was quickly printed as *The Devilish Conspiracy, Hellish Treason, Heathenish Condemnation, and Damnable Murder, Committed, and Executed by the Jewes, against the Anointed of the Lord, Christ their King*.[78] The devil's timeless use of force and fraud to accomplish his goals had reduced Warner's world to a perverted dumbshow of its former glory.

IV

The 'Parliament Dictionary' set out a clear and savage indictment of the state of England after the conclusion of the Second Civil War. Greed, ambition, violence, and impiety had laid both church and king in the dust. But the immediate means by which so much evil had been achieved in the world was a deliberate manipulation of language.[79] The whole piece is a vigorous example of early modern English suspicion about the impact of rhetorical acts of redescription, specifically the technique of *paradiastole*: 'to show that any given action can always be redescribed in such a way as to suggest that its moral character may be open to some measure of doubt'.[80] Although the technique could function as one amongst many in any rhetorician's armoury, by the 1590s it had come to be seen as peculiarly malignant and morally corrosive.[81] The Catiline conspiracy provided a strong instance of it in practice, but the paradigmatic example of *paradiastole* was provided by Thucydides in book three of the *History of the Peloponnesian War* when analysing the 'revolutions' that overtook many Greek cities in 427 B.C.E.: 'To fit in with the change of events, words, too, had to change their usual meanings'. For instance, 'what used to be described as a thoughtless act of aggression was now regarded as the courage one would expect to find in a party member'.[82]

Hobbes' translation of Thucydides' *History* was first published in 1629, and reprinted in 1634 and 1648, when it spoke to a new world of civil war and rapid linguistic change.[83] Although there is no direct reference either to Thucydides or Hobbes' recent translation in the 'Parliament Dictionary', Warner's definitions consistently aim to show how once 'good' words and phrases have been inverted and used in a corrosive fashion by ruthless parliamentarians.[84] Repeatedly he demonstrated the extent to which words had recently been given 'a quite contrary sense' (85, 87v). 'Obstruction', for instance, no longer connoted something positive: 'a let or stopp, whether in body naturall or ciuill, of any passage, course, or proceeding w[hi]ch might tend to ye helpe, <benefit, or> furtherance of ye same body'. Parliament had changed this to mean 'when conscience, iustice, or o[u]r law, hinders ye imposing any taxes, on our meates, drinkes, or goods'. As Warner fumed, 'this hypocrisy, disguise or cheating, is used in their mysticall language, therby to blind so much as they can, ye eyes of ye simple people, yt they might not see, & understand ye grosse fraud, vilany, & robbing ye King, & Subiects' (87v).[85]

At root, what the persecuted bishop wished to make clear was the extent to which a sacrilegious mindset had overwhelmed his countrymen. Such a reading of the 1640s is best known in Clarendon's writings, where the 'leprosy' of sacrilege is presented as having provoked God's wrath against the English.[86] James Loxley has also examined the use of *paradiastole* within a 'rhetoric of false prophets' during the civil wars, when royalist clergy like Jasper Mayne lambasted puritan ministers for deceiving the people.[87] There is clearly some interpretative overlap between Mayne's views and those of Warner. Indeed it is not impossible that Warner was directly aware of them: the published version of one of Mayne's Oxford sermons already quoted in this chapter attracted published criticism.[88] Mayne noted that '*Conspiracies*, and *Insurrections*, drest in these colours, have been called holy *Associations and Leagues*'.[89] Warner described the shift in meaning of 'associate' from 'an holy league, for ye defence of religion, law, libertie, & propertie, & all by ye assent, & authority of the supreme Councell', to an act of 'mallice, reuenge, faction, sedition, & contempt of authority' in which men joined 'hearts & hands, purses, & forces togither ... to roote out ye Israelits' and to 'destroy ye Prophets yt they be no more' (84). This was the ultimate evil. Social upheavals, the displacement of the king, and the tyrannical usurpations of the ignorant and the low-born all finally rested on the sacrilegious appropriation of the lands and goods of the established church. Echoing his own tract against the widespread misuse of church lands, Warner railed against the 'robbing of ye Church' by parliamentarians for 'their owne covetous interests'. Such men covenanted together 'to take ye houses of God in possession', depriving the king of his 'Inheritance of gouerning [the] Church' (84v). Small wonder that God had been provoked to the extent that He had embroiled England in vicious and debilitating civil wars.

V

Warner's preoccupation with the power of words would remain relevant in the decade that followed the writing of the 'Parliament Dictionary' as the English polity was bedevilled by fundamental problems that participants repeatedly boiled down to contested definitions. Most significantly, when offered the kingship in 1657, for instance, Oliver Cromwell's convoluted responses gave the lie to his pose as a simple man unused to weighing his words with care:

> Truly though Kingship be not a mere Title, but a Name of Office that runs through the whole of the Law; yet it is not so *ratione nominis*, from the reason of the name, but from what is signified. ... That signification goes to the *things*, certainly it does; and not to the name. Why, then, there can no more be said but this: As such a Title hath been fixed, so it may be unfixed.[90]

In the face of such apparent vacillation, tempers in Parliament frayed. As a supporter of the kingship, Major-General Jephson, sarcastically noted, 'There are some so out of love with those four letters [i.e. king], that we must, I think, have an Act to expunge them out of the alphabet, and that is my humble motion'.[91] Cromwell's eventual efforts to empty meaning from the title of king and make it a mere 'feather in a hat' were supremely unconvincing and contributed to his fundamental failure to pass a stable nation to his successors despite claiming that 'I am hugely taken with the word *Settlement*'.[92] As Clive Holmes has so convincingly argued, the appeals of the godly to Cromwell not to take the kingship were 'couched in rhetoric that resonated with his own earlier charismatic experiences' and proved 'irresistible'. For all his sympathy with their socially conservative ends, 'Cromwell could not entirely close with the "kinglings" because he could not reject the language and sentiments of his old comrades'.[93] Although Warner had lamented the extent to which perversions of language had helped to destroy the monarchical state and royal church he loved, he would live long enough to see a recovered rhetoric of Cavalier loyalism and divine-right episcopacy triumph after the return of the Stuarts brought revolutionary England to an end.

Notes

1 I am grateful to seminar audiences in Oxford, St Andrews, and Bangor for opportunities to try out versions of this chapter, and in particular to Tom Corns, Ken Fincham, Jason McElligott, David Scott, and George Southcombe for their comments.
2 Sir Edward Coke, 4 Co. Rep. 20b, quoted in Clive Holmes, 'The Strange Case of a Misplaced Tomb: Family Honour and the Law in Late Seventeenth-Century England', *Midland History*, 31 (2006), 30.
3 Clive Holmes, *The Eastern Association in the English Civil War* (Cambridge, 1974), pp. 56–7, 63.
4 Clive Holmes, 'The County Community in Stuart Historiography', *JBS*, 19 (1980), 60; restated in *idem*, 'Centre and Locality in Civil-War England', in John Adamson (ed.), *The English Civil War: Conflicts and Contexts, 1640–1649* (Basingstoke, 2009), pp. 166–70. For further discussion of a particular county's gentry, see Clive Holmes, *Seventeenth-Century Lincolnshire* (Lincoln, 1980), pp. 64–87.
5 Clive Holmes, 'Drainers and Fenmen: the Problem of Popular Political Consciousness in the Seventeenth Century', in Anthony Fletcher and John Stevenson (eds.), *Order and Disorder in Early Modern England* (Cambridge, 1985), p. 169. For further discussion in a local context, see Holmes, *Seventeenth-Century Lincolnshire*, pp. 121–30.
6 Clive Holmes, 'Parliament, Liberty, Taxation, and Property', in J.H. Hexter (ed.), *Parliament and Liberty from the Reign of Elizabeth to the English Civil War* (Stanford, CA, 1992), p. 154.
7 Jonathan Scott, *Commonwealth Principles: Republican Writing of the English Revolution* (Cambridge, 2004), pp. 20–2; Quentin Skinner, *Reason and Rhetoric in the Philosophy of Hobbes* (Cambridge, 1996), *passim*.
8 E.g., Patrick Little and David L. Smith, *Parliaments and Politics during the Cromwellian Protectorate* (Cambridge, 2007), p. 165; Beth Lynch, 'Rhetoricating and Identity in L'Estrange's Early Career, 1659–1662', in Anne Dunan-Page and Beth Lynch (eds.), *Roger L'Estrange and the Making of Restoration Culture* (Aldershot, 2008), p. 12; Roger Pooley, 'Language and Loyalty: Plain Style at the Restoration', *Literature and History*, 6 (1980), 2–18.
9 *The Letters and Speeches of Oliver Cromwell*, ed. Thomas Carlyle and S.C. Lomas (3 vols, 1904), II, 509; III, 69. For J.C. Davis's emphasis on the typicality of such anti-formalist statements amongst the godly, see his 'Cromwell's Religion', in John Morrill (ed.), *Oliver Cromwell and the English Revolution* (Harlow, 1990), p. 207.
10 *Julius Caesar*, III, ii (quote at ll. 210–11), with helpful discussion in A.D. Nuttall, *Shakespeare the Thinker* (New Haven, CT, and London, 2007), pp. 185–8. (I am grateful to George Southcombe for directing me to Nuttall's account.)

11 *Eikonoklastes* (1649), in *Complete Prose Works of John Milton, III: 1648–1649*, ed. Merritt Y. Hughes (New Haven, CT, and London, 1962), p. 361.
12 *Ibid.*, p. 393; *OED*; Thomas N. Corns, *The Development of Milton's Prose Style* (Oxford, 1982), p. 68.
13 On the broad theme, see Marcelo Dascal, 'Language and Money. A Simile and its Meaning in 17th Century Philosophy of Language', *Studia Leibnitiana*, 8 (1976), 187–218.
14 See in particular the excellent account by Sharon Achinstein, 'The Politics of Babel in the English Revolution', in James Holstun (ed.), *Pamphlet Wars: Prose in the English Revolution* (1992), pp. 14–44.
15 Quoted in Joyce Lee Malcolm, *Caesar's Due: Loyalty and King Charles, 1642–1646* (Rochester, NY, 1983), p. 149.
16 The available literature is now voluminous. See, for example, Lois Potter, *Secret Rites and Secret Writing. Royalist Literature 1641–1660* (Cambridge, 1989); James Loxley, *Royalism and Poetry in the English Civil Wars: The Drawn Sword* (Basingstoke, 1997); Robert Wilcher, *The Writing of Royalism, 1628–1660* (Cambridge, 2000); Jason McElligott, *Royalism, Print and Censorship in Revolutionary England* (Woodbridge, 2007).
17 For helpful instances of very different discourses of royalism, see Jason McElligott, 'The Politics of Sexual Libel: Royalist Propaganda in the 1640s', *HLQ*, 67 (2004), 75–99; Anthony Milton, *Laudian and Royalist Polemic in Seventeenth-Century England: The Career and Writings of Peter Heylyn* (Manchester, 2007).
18 *His Majesties Answer, To a Book, intituled, The Declaration, or Remonstrance of the Lords and Commons, The 19 of May, 1642* (Cambridge, 1642), p. 1.
19 Nath. Bernard, *ΕΣΟΠΤΡΟΝ ΤΗΣ ΑΝΤΙΜΑΧΙΑΣ, Or a Looking-Glasse for Rebellion . . .* (Oxford, 1644), esp. sigs. A2r-v.
20 Jasper Mayne, *A Sermon against False Prophets. Preached in S. Maries Church in Oxford, Shortly after the Surrender of that Garrison* (Oxford, 1646–7), p. 25.
21 For the broad theme of disillusionment, see Robert Ashton, 'From Cavalier to Roundhead Tyranny, 1642–9', in John Morrill (ed.), *Reactions to the English Civil War, 1642–1649* (1982), pp. 185–207.
22 *The Writings of William Walwyn*, ed. Jack R. McMichael and Barbara Taft (1989), pp. 296, 298.
23 *The Hunting of the Foxes* (21 March 1649), in Don M. Wolfe (ed.), *Leveller Manifestoes of the Puritan Revolution* (1944), p. 372.
24 'On the New Forcers of Conscience under the Long Parliament' (1646): John Milton, *The Complete Shorter Poems*, ed., John Carey (rev. 2nd edn., Harlow, 2007), p. 300.
25 For which, see P.R. Cavill, *The English Parliaments of Henry VII, 1485–1504* (Oxford, 2009), pp. 205–12.
26 Sir John Coke was in no doubt that '[s]overeign power is no parliamentary word': quoted in R.W.K. Hinton, 'The Decline of Parliamentary Government under Elizabeth I and the Early Stuarts', *Cambridge HJ*, 13 (1957), 124.
27 S.B. Chrimes, 'The Constitutional Ideas of Dr John Cowell', *EHR*, 64 (1949), 461–87; R.W.K. Hinton, 'Government and Liberty under James I', *Cambridge HJ*, 11 (1953), 59; Brian P. Levack, 'John Cowell', *ODNB*; idem, *The Civil Lawyers in England 1603–41: A Political Study* (Oxford, 1973), pp. 4, 81, 97–8, 100–1, 103–6; Elizabeth Read Foster (ed.), *Proceedings in Parliament 1610* (2 vols., New Haven, CT, and London, 1966), I, 25, 185–90; II, 37–9. J.P. Sommerville makes a good case for agreeing with MPs' perception that Cowell *was* an absolutist thinker: *Royalists and Patriots: Politics and Ideology in England 1603–1640* (2nd edn., 1999), pp. 113–19, 238–40.
28 Conrad Russell, *Parliament and English Politics 1621–1629* (Oxford, 1979), pp. 350–1, 357–9, 361–3, 367–8.
29 Joseph L. Black (ed.), *The Martin Marprelate Tracts: A Modernized and Annotated Edition* (Cambridge, 2008), esp. pp. xxv–xxxiv; Nye quoted in Tom Webster, *Godly Clergy in Early Stuart England: The Caroline Puritan Movement c.1620–1643* (Cambridge, 1997), pp. 259–60.

30 William P. Holden, *Anti-Puritan Satire 1572–1642* (New Haven, CT, and London, 1954), esp. pp. 41–2, 57–60; Loxley, *Royalism and Poetry*, pp. 103–10; Patrick Collinson, 'A Comment: Concerning the Name Puritan', *JEH*, 31 (1980), 486; idem, 'Antipuritanism', in John Coffey and Paul C.H. Lim (eds.), *The Cambridge Companion to Puritanism* (Cambridge, 2008), pp. 19–33, esp. 27–30.

31 Thomas Cheshire, *A True Copy of that Sermon Which Was Preached at S. Paul the Tenth Day of October Last* (1641), p. 14, quoted in modernised form in Anthony Fletcher, *The Outbreak of the English Civil War* (1981), p. 119.

32 Achinstein, 'Politics of Babel', pp. 17, 31, 33–5. For Hobbes's profound engagement with problems of language and meaning, see Skinner, *Reason and Rhetoric*.

33 Potter, *Secret Rites and Select Writing*, p. xii.

34 Blair Worden, 'The Royalism of Andrew Marvell', in Jason McElligott and David L. Smith (eds.), *Royalists and Royalism during the English Civil Wars* (Cambridge, 2007), p. 236.

35 The 'Parliament Dictionary' is now Bodl., MS Eng. hist. b. 205, fols 84–87v. All subsequent parenthetical numbers in the main text refer to folios in this document.

36 The words are academy, agitator, almighty, antichrist, army, assembly, assess or tax, associate, bishop, blaspheme, classes, committee-man, commons, compound, confide, contribution, covenant, declaration, elder, excise, gospel, militia, oath, obstruction, order, parliament-man, peerage, peers, plunder, privilege, property, and protestant. Due to damage to the manuscript, three other words are partially discussed but in terms too fragmentary confidently to reconstruct the actual object of definition.

37 After a period of relatively ineffective supervision of the press, Parliament was stimulated by the Second Civil War to devote greater attention to censorship, especially in the last months of 1648: McElligott, *Royalism, Print and Censorship*, pp. 153–63.

38 Assesse or taxe (Bodl., MS Eng. hist. b. 193, fol. 8v), militia (*ibid.*, fol. 178), plunder (*ibid.*, fol. 216).

39 Judge, justice, court of justice, lawyer (Bodl., MS Eng. hist. b. 193, fol. 215), state (*ibid.*, fol. 216).

40 De Witt T. Starnes and Gertrude E. Noyes, *The English Dictionary from Cawdrey to Johnson 1604–1755* (Chapel Hill, NC, 1946; new edn., Amsterdam and Philadelphia, 1991); Janet Bately, 'Bilingual and Multilingual Dictionaries of the Renaissance and Early Seventeenth Century', in A.P. Cowie (ed.), *The Oxford History of English Lexicography* (2 vols., Oxford, 2009), I, 41–64.

41 Loxley, *Royalism and Poetry*, p. 97; Nigel Smith, *Literature and Revolution in England 1640–1660* (New Haven, CT, and London, 1994), pp. 306–17.

42 Bately, 'Bilingual and Multilingual Dictionaries', I, 54–5, 63; Gabriele Stein, *The English Dictionary before Cawdrey* (Tübingen, 1985), Chapter 16; Starnes and Noyes, *English Dictionary from Cawdrey to Johnson*, pp. 13–19.

43 *Ibid.*, pp. 19, 23, 34; Michael Rand Hoare, 'Scientific and Technical Dictionaries', in Cowie (ed.), *Oxford History of English Lexicography*, II, 47–93, esp. 85–6 (for legal dictionaries). Cowell's *Interpreter* was republished without alteration in 1637: Sommerville, *Royalists and Patriots*, p. 119.

44 John Morrill, 'The British Problem, c.1534–1707', in Brendan Bradshaw and John Morrill (eds.), *The British Problem, c.1534–1707: State Formation in the Atlantic Archipelago* (Basingstoke, 1996), pp. 1–38; Richard Foster Jones, *The Triumph of the English Language . . .* (1953); Victor Edward Durkacz, *The Decline of the Celtic Languages . . .* (Edinburgh, 1983), esp. Chapter 1.

45 Paula Blank, *Broken English. Dialects and the Politics of Language in Renaissance Writings* (1996), p. 126; Peter Burke, *Languages and Communities in Early Modern Europe* (Cambridge, 2004), p. 152; J.G.A. Pocock, *The Ancient Constitution and the Feudal Law: A Study of English Historical Thought in the Seventeenth Century. A Reissue with a Retrospect* (Cambridge, 1987), Chapter V.

46 Lee Beier, 'Anti-Language or Jargon? Canting in the English Underworld in the Sixteenth and Seventeenth Centuries', in Peter Burke and Roy Porter (eds.), *Languages and Jargons: Contributions to a Social History of Language* (Cambridge, 1995), p. 82; Julie Coleman, 'Slang and Cant Dictionaries', in Cowie (ed.), *Oxford History of English Lexicography*, II, 314–36.
47 David Daniell, *The Bible in English: Its History and Influence* (New Haven, CT, and London, 2003), Chapters 25–6; David Norton, *A History of the Bible as Literature* (2 vols., Cambridge, 1993), I, Chapter 10.
48 BL, Add. MS 4224, fol. 76.
49 The bulk of these can be found in Bodl., MSS Eng. th. b. 4–8; Eng. th. e. 62; Eng. th. e. 176–7; Eng. hist. b. 205; Eng. misc. b. 193–5; Top. gen. c. 75.
50 Bodl., MSS Eng. th. b 6, fols 126v, 176; Eng. th. b 5, fols 14r–v, 76; Eng. misc. b 193, fols 65–8, 86–7v.
51 Edward Lee-Warner, *The Life of John Warner Bishop of Rochester 1637–1666* (1901), p. 48; Ian Green, 'John Warner', *ODNB*; D.C. Douglas, *English Scholars 1660–1730* (1939), p. 64. For a letter from Somner to Warner, see Bodl., MS Eng. misc. b. 193, fol. 11.
52 *Bibliotheca Warneriana* . . . (1685).
53 Warner inherited £16,000 from his godmother in the 1600s; his father was a successful merchant taylor. Green, 'John Warner'.
54 Kenneth Fincham, 'William Laud and the Exercise of Caroline Ecclesiastical Patronage', *JEH*, 51 (2000), 80.
55 For versions of begging letters to Sheldon in the 1660s, see Bodl., MSS Eng. hist. b. 205, fol. 25v; Tanner 49, fol. 23; Smith 22, fol. 23.
56 Kenneth Fincham, 'The Restoration of Altars in the 1630s', *HJ*, 44 (2001), 932, 939; idem, '"According to Ancient Custom": The Return of Altars in the Restoration Church of England,' *TRHS*, 6th ser., 13 (2003), 36; Julian Davies, *The Caroline Captivity of the Church: Charles I and the Remoulding of Anglicanism 1625–1641* (Oxford, 1992), pp. 218, 232–3; Kenneth Fincham, *Visitation Articles and Injunctions of the Early Stuart Church* (2 vols., Woodbridge, 1994–8), II, xx; *CSPD 1641–3*, p. 421.
57 In the second year of Charles I's reign, Warner preached a sermon at court in Passion Week on Matthew 21:38, 'When the Husbandman saw the son they sayd among themselves this is the Heir; come let us kill him, and let us seize on his inheritance', and in March 1640 he preached in Rochester Cathedral on Psalm 74:23, 'Forget not the voice of thy enemies'. The first was vigorously denounced by the House of Commons, the second by the Scots. Green, 'John Warner'.
58 Green, 'John Warner'; Davies, *Caroline Captivity of the Church*, pp. 273–4, 282–4; C.S.R. Russell, 'The Authorship of the Bishop's Diary of the House of Lords in 1641', *Bulletin of the Institute of Historical Research*, 41 (1968), 230–1.
59 [John Warner], *Church-Lands Not to be Sold* . . . (1648; though amended on Thomason's copy to 28 October 1647). On the question of dating this work, see Green, 'John Warner'.
60 Mary Anne Everett Green (comp.), *Calendar of the Proceedings of the Committee for Advance of Money, 1642–1656* (3 parts, 1888), pt. 1, 260–4; *CCC*, I, 93, 799.
61 *Calendar of the Proceedings of the Committee for Advance of Money, 1642–1656*, pt. 1, 262.
62 Kenneth Fincham and Stephen Taylor, 'Episcopalian Conformity and Nonconformity 1646–60', in Jason McElligott and David L. Smith (eds.), *Royalists and Royalism during the Interregnum* (Manchester, 2010), pp. 27–8; Ian Atherton, 'Viscount Scudamore's "Laudianism": The Religious Practices of the First Viscount Scudamore', *HJ*, 34 (1991), 576. For individual examples, see Bodl., MS Eng. hist. b. 205, fol. 3; BL, Add. MS 4224, fol. 76v.
63 Jacqueline Rose, *Godly Kingship in Restoration England: The Politics of the Royal Supremacy, 1660–1688* (Cambridge, 2011), Chapter 1.
64 Fears of the 'many-headed multitude' had troubled many in the localities immediately before the outbreak of war: Holmes, *Seventeenth-Century Lincolnshire*, pp. 151–7.

65 On this theme, see Henrik Langelüddecke, '"The Chiefest Strength and Glory of this Kingdom"': Arming and Training the "Perfect Militia" in the 1630s', *EHR*, 118 (2003), 1264–1303; Lois G. Schwoerer, '"The Fittest Subject for a King's Quarrel": An Essay on the Militia Controversy, 1641–2', *JBS*, 11 (1971), 45–76.
66 S.R. Gardiner (ed.), *The Constitutional Documents of the Puritan Revolution 1625–1660* (rev. 3rd edn., Oxford, 1906), pp. 374–6.
67 For which, see Chad van Dixhoorn (ed.), *The Minutes and Papers of the Westminster Assembly, 1643–1652* (5 vols, Oxford, 2012).
68 For Warner's memorandum of brief arguments 'Ag[ains]t roote & branch', see Bodl., MS Eng. hist. b. 193, fol. 212.
69 For a summary account of Scotophobia at this time, see Mark Stoyle, *Soldiers and Strangers: An Ethnic History of the English Civil War* (New Haven, CT, and London, 2005), Chapter 4.
70 BL, Harleian MS 6424, fols 23v–24v, 55v, 67v–68v, 70v, 99, 101v–102; Russell, 'Authorship of the Bishop's Diary', 233.
71 For the powerful hostile reactions prompted by the excise, see Michael J. Braddick, 'Popular Politics and Public Policy: The Excise Riot at Smithfield in February 1647 and its Aftermath', *HJ*, 34 (1991), 597–626.
72 Brentford was said to have been 'plundered' in 1642, and William Prynne used the term in 1643: Charles Carlton, *Going to the Wars. The Experience of the British Civil Wars, 1638–1651* (1992), p. 265.
73 David Cressy, 'Lamentable, Strange, and Wonderful: Headless Monsters in the English Revolution', in Laura Lunger Knoppers (ed.), *Monstrous Bodies/Political Monstrosities in Early Modern Europe* (Ithaca, NY, and London, 2004), pp. 40–63.
74 Christopher Hill, 'The Radical Critics of Oxford and Cambridge in the 1650s', in his *Change and Continuity in Seventeenth-Century England* (1974), pp. 127–48.
75 For the popularity of Ovid in royalist writing, see Earl Miner, *The Cavalier Mode from Jonson to Cotton* (Princeton, NJ, 1972), Chapter III, pt. iii 'The Remedies of Time'. The London petition of 11 December 1640 had included Ovid amongst the list of the authors whose works should not be published. Potter, *Secret Rites and Secret Writing*, p. 5.
76 'And your covenant with death shall be disannulled, and your agreement with hell shall not stand; when the overflowing scourge shall pass through, then ye shall be trodden down by it'.
77 For another bitter royalist's distaste for 'a thing called a Committee', see Holmes, 'Centre and Locality in Civil-War England', in Adamson (ed.), *English Civil War*, p. 153 (and pp. 155–65 for subtle discussion of anti-committee rhetoric).
78 Thomason indicates a purchase date of 11 April 1649 on his copy: BL, E.550[16]. For discussion of this sermon, see Florence Sadler, 'Icon and Iconoclast', in Michael Lieb and John T. Shawcross (eds.), *Achievements of the Left Hand: Essays on the Prose of John Milton* (Amherst, MA, 1974), pp. 178–80.
79 For Milton's view of this in 1649 – albeit, of course, from a very different perspective to Warner – see Hughes, *Complete Prose Works*, III, 348.
80 Quentin Skinner, 'Hobbes on Rhetoric and the Construction of Morality', in *idem*, *Visions of Politics* (3 vols, Cambridge, 2002), III, 89. (Skinner's interpretation of early modern English understandings of *paradiastole* has been criticised by Richard Tuck: 'Hobbes's Moral Philosophy', in Tom Sorrell (ed.), *The Cambridge Companion to Hobbes* (Cambridge, 1996), pp. 203–4 n. 25.)
81 Skinner, *Reason and Rhetoric*, pp. 176–7, 179; and, more widely, *idem*, 'Hobbes on Rhetoric', pp. 100–16.
82 See Ben Jonson's *Catiline*, in *Ben Jonson*, ed. C.H. Herford *et al*. (11 vols, Oxford, 1925–52), V, 526; Skinner, 'Hobbes on Rhetoric', pp. 93–5; Thucydides, *History of the Peloponnesian War*, trans. Rex Warner (revd. edn., 1972), bk. III, 82. I am grateful to David Sacks for first emphasizing to me the importance of this passage in Thucydides.

83 Jonathan Scott, 'The Peace of Silence: Thucydides and the English Civil War', in G.A.J. Rogers and Tom Sorrell (eds.), *Hobbes and History* (2000), pp. 118–19, 122; Skinner, 'Hobbes on Rhetoric', pp. 116–18; Richard Schlatter, 'Thomas Hobbes and Thucydides', *Journal of the History of Ideas*, 6 (1945), 350–62; Loxley, *Royalism and Poetry*, pp. 119–23.
84 For deployment of a *paradiastolic* style elsewhere in Warner's writings, see *Devilish Conspiracy*, p. 20.
85 For similar discussions, see also 'contribution' and 'declaration' (fol. 84v).
86 Martin Dzelzainis, '"Undoubted Realities": Clarendon on Sacrilege', *HJ*, 33 (1990), 515–40.
87 Loxley, *Royalism and Poetry*, pp. 111–18.
88 Jasper Mayne, *A Late Printed Sermon against False Prophets, Vindicated by Letter, from the Causeless Aspersions of Mr. Francis Cheynell* (1647).
89 Loxley, *Royalism and Poetry*, p. 115.
90 *Letters and Speeches of Oliver Cromwell*, ed. Carlyle and Lomas, III, 56–7. For Cromwell's artful manipulation of language, see Ronald Hutton, *Debates in Stuart History* (Basingstoke, 2004), pp. 97, 103–4, 108–9; Kevin Sharpe, *Image Wars: Promoting Kings and Commonwealths in England 1603–1660* (New Haven, CT, and London, 2010), pp. 470–7; *Speeches of Oliver Cromwell*, ed. Ivan Roots (1989), pp. xx–xxi. For much more on the kingship debates, see the Chapter by Jonathan Fitzgibbons in this volume.
91 *Burton*, II, 140.
92 *Ibid.*, I, 383; Austin Woolrych, 'Last Quests for a Settlement 1657–1660', in G.E. Aylmer (ed.), *The Interregnum: The Quest for Settlement 1646–1660* (1972), pp. 183–204; *Letters and Speeches*, ed. Carlyle and Lomas, III, 87.
93 Holmes, *Why Was Charles I Executed?*, pp. 171–2, 173.

6 A trader of knowledge and government
Richard Houncell and the politics of enterprise, 1648–51

Perry Gauci

In recent years, historians of national economic development have revisited the Interregnum with increased vigour to illuminate the worlds of both commerce and politics, particularly with regard to ideological change and the role of state structures.[1] Encouraged by their findings, this essay will study the thoughts and actions of an ambitious overseas merchant to highlight the obstacles and opportunities of his mid-century generation of traders as they sought to harness local networks and central authorities to their cause. In this way, it will pay ample tribute to the importance of Clive's seminal interventions into the workings of Stuart state and society. On a wider plane, it will illuminate the challenges facing individuals as they encountered difficult ideological accommodations in the course of their daily business.[2]

The businessman in question is the Alicante-based merchant Richard Houncell, whose cache of over 1,000 letters enables the reconstruction of an extensive personal network, which transcended his region, nation, and two continents.[3] In particular, this correspondence sheds valuable light on both the formal and informal methods employed by individuals to navigate the most daunting of eras. By the nature of their trade, overseas merchants always required a significant degree of state support, but the great upheavals of Britain and Europe ensured that Houncell and his contemporaries were even more hard-pressed to secure political aid. The fluidity and uncertainty of the times render the period of particular interest for the study of the resultant politics of enterprise. Revitalised scholarly interest in British responses to the economic challenges of the 1640–60 period has only underlined the continuing importance of individuals in directing commercial and imperial expansion. Richard Houncell's letters will demonstrate the enduring importance of regional communities at a supraregional level, emphasize the remarkable capacity of individuals and networks for rebirth during the hiatus of the Interregnum, and highlight the need to reconnect the economic and political development of the period in terms of both action and ideas.[4]

At first sight, Houncell presents an unpromising subject for study. Beyond the letterbook, relatively little is known about him. Unlike the dynamic 'new merchants' of Robert Brenner, whose influence has been credited with a decisive influence on the Commonwealth's foreign policy, Houncell does not rank among the stars of seventeenth-century commerce.[5] His vital dates are obscure, as is his ancestry, and he died of probable modest means in Livorno, far from kith and kin. However, he left a vibrant personal testament in the form of his letterbook, in which he minutely recorded his business as an English merchant based in Alicante between 1648 and 1651. Unlike most surviving merchant's accounts, it is far from reserved in its opinions, and its candour, gossip, and insight are particularly welcome.[6] Not only is his commentary revelatory, but its range is simply remarkable. Despite the pressing distractions of civil war and plague in Spain and huge political upheaval in England, Houncell was attempting not only to run an Anglo-Spanish trade but also to arrange deals between New England, Barbados, and the Levant. These challenges put enormous pressures on his personal skills and resources, and led him to construct strategies and networks that would enable him to turn challenging times into successful opportunities. This was the end game of his politics of enterprise, and he showed himself, in his own words, 'a trader of knowledge and government'. In order to understand how he managed this feat, this article will focus on the ways in which his regional background helped to forward his trade through the construction of supportive networks, before turning to the use of these connections amid the great political and economic challenges of 1648–51 period.[7]

Although sketchy in detail, Houncell's background demonstrates that from his early career he was placed on his mettle to refine his political skills. His family could boast a close familiarity with a range of maritime trades, but he would need skilful management to translate these foundations into a successful career as an international trader. As a sign of this, Houncell's early life remains frustratingly unclear. His immediate ancestry can be confidently identified as of Dorset origin, and he was certainly related to Andrew Houncell of Symondsbury, near the port of Bridport. Various branches of this family had been settled on the Dorset coast since at least the mid-sixteenth century, and two of Andrew Houncell's sons enjoyed successful seafaring careers in the early seventeenth century, both serving as captains of East India Company ships. The Houncells of Bridport itself were also active in the town's famous ropemaking manufacture, with at least two family members established in the trade by 1620. Thus, even if his precise parentage remains elusive, his familial and geographical background was very supportive of a commercial career abroad, although promising little in the way of start-up capital.[8]

In common with other West Country ports, Bridport's economy depended heavily on its integration with national and international markets. Fishing was the dominant maritime profession of the area, and the growth in the export market to the Iberian Peninsula was a natural development for the region, with both geography and London connections facilitating the prosperity of the likes of Dartmouth and Lyme Regis. Bridport itself suffered from a silted harbour, and thus Houncell would have had to face the prospect of relocation if he wished to become a merchant. His decision to venture abroad is entirely in keeping with mercantile practice, however, and may well have been at the behest of one of his merchant principals, either in the West Country or

London. As his letterbook shows, a steady stream of younger traders from the region were sent to Mediterranean ports to act as factors and learn their trade. There is sparse evidence for a significant English presence in Alicante before the 1630s, but the onset of peace between Spain and England, coupled with the continuing exclusion of the Dutch from Spanish markets, may well have encouraged England merchant houses to enlist agents abroad. One of England's most influential mercantile writers, Lewes Roberts, reported in 1638 that he had spent 'some years' in the city and concluded that it 'hath choice wines and good trading by its commodious situation'. Moreover, its 'commodious road' had established it in recent years as the 'scale' [or port] of Valencia, where 'the principall merchants thereof reside, and have their factors and respondents that negociate their affairs for them'. Its growing importance within regional and international commerce would thus have rendered it an attractive prospect for an ambitious merchant from the West Country.[9]

Houncell's prospects were thus not unpromising, but his family and social connections were vital both for his future progress and for the maintenance and extension of English trade in the Mediterranean. Colin Heywood has recently argued that Braudel's famed 'northern invasion' of the Mediterranean should be seen as much a regional as a national phenomenon, pointing out the importance of East Anglia for providing the products and personnel that established a direct English trade to southern waters. Houncell's experience shows that the South-West can be credited with a similar significance. He could turn not only to his nuclear family to provide support, most notably his brother William who also resided in Alicante, but also to a host of traders from the region. For instance, the letterbook opens with the death of his partner in Spain, Henry Cullamore, or Collomore (c. 1617–1648), son of William Cullamore of Swimbridge, Devon. The Cullamores had many connections in the vicinity of the port of Barnstaple, most notably the Chichester family, and Richard Chichester was also one of Houncell's correspondents. The Houncells and Cullamores clearly had a close relationship, and Houncell in fact suggested in a letter of 6 December 1649 that the loss of some £500 that Collomore owed him would 'not eaquall the greefe I receave per his death'. He also maintained direct contact with South-Western correspondents back home, such as John Lovering of Wear Gifford, Devon, who had extensive contacts with Dartmouth, Exeter, and Barnstaple.[10]

Houncell's open-hearted dealings with South-Western correspondents enable us to appreciate how these familial and social ties helped to bolster commercial networks throughout the Mediterranean. For example, perhaps mindful of his own initiation into Mediterranean trade, he wrote to James Napper (who hailed from Weymouth) to offer help in the latter's new posting at Naples, assuring him of the support of his fellow English houses there 'for wt thay owe your frends in England as that yr good behaviour and parts'. This was followed by a letter to James's father at Weymouth, in which the young merchant's 'sweete cariedge and forwardnisse' were commended, suggesting his 'suddaine cappacitie for the undergoeinge of buisnisse'. Richard's concern for the families of his contacts is a constant theme of the letters, and he clearly made great pains to accommodate them should they pass through Alicante. On 5th September 1649, he happily reported to his Genovese contact, John Lewes, that the latter's wife was enjoying their hospitality, for 'although this place is short of *regalos* [gifts/hospitality] to entertaine strangers, yet all the nations good will was much to waite on her and the rest of the ladyes'. Bad news was greeted with genuine condolence, the firm recording the death of Francis Bishoppe at Naples as the loss 'of soe good a friend and countreyman'. The correspondence also makes it clear that Houncell wrote more personalised letters to his friends and relations that do not survive, but we are fortunate that he chose to include so many personal notices in his business records.[11]

Houncell's choice of the Iberian trade may have been suggested by his familial roots and regional connections, but it is clear that his advancement in this sphere of commerce was aided by some powerful, broader connections, especially in London. Economic historians have stressed the importance of London merchants in the expansion of English trade interests in Spain and Italy, especially for their role in exploiting the Newfoundland fishery to form a triangular trade that saw Mediterranean ports import cod and export local produce to the English market. The West Country ports were critical in fitting out the fishing fleets and were also used by the Londoners to export other goods, such as tin and lead to the Mediterranean. The letterbook shines important light on the workings of this trade in detail, and Richard's whole career highlights how relations between the West Country and City were mediated by correspondents both at home and abroad.[12]

The most interesting aspect of Houncell's dealings with Londoners is his seemingly deliberate policy of liaising with City merchants who had links with the West Country. One of his closest contacts was Andrew [later Sir Andrew] Cogan, son of Richard of Dorset, who had married into the Houncells in 1600. Andrew Cogan was sufficiently prominent as a merchant to be included in the London visitation of 1633 and later caused Houncell much discomfort by becoming an active conspirator, rising to the royalist rank of admiral by May 1649.[13] City merchant Walter Elford was a less problematic contact, who hailed from Shipston in Devon and who provided vital 'incoradgment' to Houncell to join the Levant Company, of which Elford was a member. More prominent still were Francis Clarke, son of an Exeter magistrate and active in both the Levant and the East India Companies, and Samuel Mico, who had close ties with Melcombe Regis and later advanced to the rank of London alderman in 1653–6.[14]

Houncell clearly regarded these individuals as vital contacts, but it is important to recognize that he was no mere factor in Alicante, servicing the needs of his City superiors. The letters demonstrate that English merchants abroad could be active partners in international dealings, and their domestic contacts regarded their expertise and financial backing as vital to the success of their joint ventures. Far from taking every opportunity to undermine London privileges, Houncell saw the Londoners as vital cogs in boosting his region's economic prospects and worked hard to secure their respect.[15] His confidence in the agency of Londoners was most directly illustrated by his contacts with some of the most influential City merchants of all, most notably Nathan Wright and Robert Burdett. Neither Wright nor Burdett hailed from the South-West, but Houncell was able to approach them in the later 1640s once his existing circle of associates had secured him some standing within Mediterranean trading circles. Wright in particular was a formidable magnate, active in the East Indian, Levant, and Russian trades, and a major creditor of the parliamentary regimes (with advances amounting to £8,300 by 1644). Houncell paid awed testament to his influence when requesting him to intervene in the case of the seized ship [the *Providence*], reasoning that 'wee know your word will muck benifitt [us]', and he even thought that 'seeing a friend as you to desire a good issue to the business' would make rivals 'to be more timide in prosecutinge it'. Thus, over time, Houncell's commercial-political network grew organically, and encompassed both regional and metropolitan spheres. Beyond structural considerations, however, it is important to see these networks in action and to consider their agency in forwarding both individual and national interests within international commerce.[16]

The prospects for all international traders in the later 1640s and early 1650s were not good, beset as they were by political difficulties at every turn. Even though Houncell prided himself on his independence as a trader, he knew that he needed powerful connections at home to work for him if he was to survive in such desperate times. As early as July 1648, he was keen to return to England to settle his affairs, but the profound upheavals of the king's execution and the creation of the new Commonwealth counselled caution. He was clearly distressed by the execution, referring ominously to his homeland as 'that miserable countrie' on 8 March 1649, and 'the troubells' were cited as the reason for his remaining in Alicante five days later. The travails of his kinsman Sir Andrew Cogan, a merchant who did place his head above the political parapet as a royalist, and whose estate was later sequestered by Parliament, gave him all too much reason to fear the impact of prevailing ideological winds. In a letter of 29 July 1649, his political pragmatism is suggested by his willingness to recognize the authority of the consul appointed by the Rump Parliament to Algiers. Nonetheless, he remained concerned over the impact of the new regime on his commercial dealings, reporting to Nathan Wright on 19 November that a contact at Mallorca had withdrawn from a contract for oils on account of 'the troubles of England', which gave locals 'strange opinions of our Nation'.[17]

The desperate times evidently caused him and his colleagues great uncertainty but may also have brought out the best of their commercial skills, for the difficulties of war and plague forced merchants to consider new markets. As Houncell advised his contact William Rider on 17 May 1649: 'this country [i.e. Spain] being as yet fitt for noe other thinge then fish designes, . . . you may as we doe incoradge you to exsprement this yeare'.[18] An investment in Barbados was one such venture, and his readiness to integrate markets in the Mediterranean and the Atlantic suggests that many traders saw the fluidity of the international arena as a time of opportunity. In common with the initiatives set in motion by merchants faced with difficult trading conditions in the 1690s, enterprising individuals could capitalize on the fluidity of both commercial and political worlds to advance their interests. These endeavours often carried even greater risk than the usual vagaries of international trade, but the rewards for less established traders could be transformative in terms of their status as international dealers.[19]

Beyond the willingness to experiment, Houncell had to demonstrate an immense resourcefulness in keeping afloat at very trying times, and in passing the letters shine much light on the general character of relations among international merchants. With some traders he could be extremely terse and quickly move to legal process. Indeed, he was not afraid to lecture fellow merchants on the niceties of mercantile custom and exhort them 'to live like negotiants and men of repute'. Conversely, he could be extremely courteous to others and sought to develop advantageous acquaintances whenever possible, often building upon mutual contacts or incidental convergences of interest. The tone of his letters to Nathan Wright and Robert Burdett are of particular interest, for his relationship with these two eminent City merchants became more intimate across this period, and we see an initially deferential Houncell become more familiar over time. For certain, foreign-based factors knew their value, and his firm proudly boasted to one London trader to 'be assured you shall never meete with any that shall more fairely correspond, and per every good occasion that presents shall more often and largely advise you of all occurrences then ourselves'. Given his eagerness to expand his business in difficult times, in microcosm the letters illuminate the ways in which English merchants negotiated and bullied their way into a more commanding position in Mediterranean and global commerce.[20]

It was clear, however, that Houncell could not rely on correspondence alone to settle his affairs, and, having previously determined on a visit his homeland 'when we see some peace in England', he made the perilous trip there in the spring of 1650. The letters suggest that he was in two minds whether to spend his future in England or Spain, for his London contacts were advised on 23 March that he intended to return to Spain after this visit 'except he finds England in a better condition then heare reported'. Houncell's ambivalence on his future abroad is further corroborated by the fact that he took the firm's books with him, and his partners compiled an inventory of his household goods at Alicante with a view to settling payment to Richard for his effects. It soon transpired that the return home was not simply the product of commercial despair or homesickness, for his Spanish allies looked expectantly to Richard's new venture, a proposed joint partnership with Wright and Burdett, in which he had sunk 'the major part' of his estate.[21]

Richard left for England on the *Sara* in a fleet of five ships on about 20 April 1650. His predetermined objective was 'the settlement of some affaires', and (by the evidence of his later letters) he called upon on some of the leading London merchants of the day during this visit. Predictably, he paid court to Burdett, with whom he discussed the potential of the Barbados market, and later suggested that the island would be a good market for Mediterranean produce, especially if they could also ship sugar back to London. Significantly, he continued to deal with City traders with contacts to the South-West, paying a visit to Francis Clarke, who shared his thoughts on which textiles were most appropriate for the Spanish market. Thus, even if he had more ambitious trading schemes in mind, he did not miss opportunities to strengthen regional ties, which could still pay dividends in the capital. At this key juncture, the Devonian Walter Elford helped him to access important commercial and governmental agencies in London, including the Levant Company, where minutes of 21 August 1650 record:

> Richard Houncell, a merchant of Alicante, now attending, having (as was alleged by several of the company now present as well as by himself) been at much expense and suffered imprisonment there, in regard of the service and good offices he had done in the business of the Margaret, by whose means she escaped a detention at Alicante, and desiring the company to take his merits therein into consideration, it was thought fit he should be gratified with the freedom of the company in his own person only.

Houncell's decision to apply for the freedom of the company suggests that he now harboured ambitions to expand his operations into the Eastern Mediterranean, following the example of several leading London traders. His appearance before the court also demonstrated that, in the absence of a great fortune, he had a keen sense of his worth as a foreign agent. Indeed, he had attested to the value of this role to a London contact when observing, '[Y]ou know how tedious law is in Vala: [Valencia] except a man be theare in person'.[22]

Perhaps with an awareness of his true political worth, Richard had already decided to return to Spain, for the court also recorded his intention to leave England 'shortly', and a senior company official Thomas Bludworth agreed to stand surety for Houncell's taking of the freedom of the City on his next return to England. This decision to leave was probably prompted by the continuing uncertainties of the international arena and perhaps advocated by both his City contacts and his friends in Alicante. On 23 June 1650, the partners had written to London contacts to confirm news from Madrid of the royalist assassination of Anthony Ascham, the parliamentary envoy to Spain. In wonderfully guarded language, the partners simply observed to the City merchants: 'God graunt it proves good, and that it may not cause any novelty betwixt England and this Crowne'. Their letter to Richard was more desperate in tone, however, simply observing: 'God knoes what may be the event of it'.[23]

The London trip may have also convinced Houncell that it was impossible to trim his political sails any longer and that for the sake of his business, he must make more direct acknowledgement of the Commonwealth. Only a week after the audience at the Levant Company, the Council of State authorized the judges of the Admiralty Court to take the oaths of Wright, Burdett, and Houncell to complete the grant of their letters of marque. The Rump Parliament had passed an act the preceding summer to issue such licences to deter French piracy, and it is no surprise that Houncell and partners were keen to strike back at their tormentors and to make some money. However, while Houncell was grateful for the Rump's readiness to tackle the French, his decision to take the oath cannot be read as a more profound ideological shift in support for the republican regime. Indeed, on 14 September his Alicante-based partners were confident of his return to Spain because Richard was 'finding England something troublesome and dangerous'. His new London partners did him the honour of listing him as a full associate on their firm's letterhead, but it was evidently thought that he could be of most use abroad. Houncell came back via Holland and Malaga and arrived in Alicante on 25 November 1650.[24]

International affairs gave some room for optimism in the Houncell camp on Richard's return, especially with news of the Rump's more aggressive policy to secure English trade in the Mediterranean. The solicitation of Houncell and his partners may even have played some part in steeling the parliamentary regime for stern action against the French, and by the end of the year orders had been given for the first regular convoys to accompany shipping through the Straits.[25] Houncell was exultant at the arrival of the first of the convoy commanders Rear Admiral Edward Hall, assuring his Italian contacts on 30 March 1651 that Hall had taken on the commission out of 'respext to our estate and to the good of marchants'. Encouraging news of negotiations with the Turks also gave them and other Mediterranean dealers hopes that trade 'may ingoy itts former freedome'.[26]

On his return to Alicante, Richard even appeared more active in his support for the republic, if only for self-interested ends. For instance, on 1 May 1651 he was ready to aid the recovery of a ship seized by royalists, in which 'the state of England' had a stake of £2,000 for the recovery of English captives in Algiers. The firm continued in its efforts to make money out of the conflict, speculating on 7 July whether they might be able to profit from a cargo seized from a royalist ship taken by Captain Penn. They sought similar gain from Spain's civil discord, urging the speedy dispatch of fish for the Spanish army besieging Barcelona, reasoning that the twenty-thousand-strong force 'will eat aboundance of pilchards'. Businessmen to the last, they urged their poor correspondents to deliver the fish as close to the action as possible to save on carriage.[27]

Beyond the spoils of war, Houncell saw his developing relationship with Wright and Burdett as a lifeline and on 15 January 1651 promised to give 'tymely advice' of any opportunities in Alicante and 'to forbeare adviseing any other men that soe yow may be masters of the market'. The renaming of a seized ship as 'the Richard and William' also suggested that the brothers were facing the future with confidence and were eager to publicize their firm within the trade. They appeared very keen to increase their share of the Newfoundland market, Richard wishing to make 'some considerable imploiment' in the business via a Plymouth contact, once again with Wright's assistance. Emboldened by the authority of his new partnership, he pressured the contact to give them a monopoly of the first ship of pilchards to be sent and recommended the use of small vessels as a market advantage. On 30 March, the contacts made with the Levant Company were finally put to work when the Houncells approached Robert Perkett at Smyrna to start a trade in importing silk to England, using Wright as their London contact. They subsequently employed George Baker to go to Aleppo to establish a more permanent business there and urged Wright to send his own man to set up in partnership, arguing that 'it is the hopefullest factory yt is'. For certain, the letterbook ends with the Houncells in a determined mood, mindful of the challenges ahead but resolute in their trade. Both in word and action, Richard had proven himself a skilful politician, whose commercial momentum owed much to the cultivation and exploitation of a personal network connecting Alicante, London, and the South-West.[28]

Little more than four years later, both Houncell brothers were dead, and their name ceased to be a force in Mediterranean trade. From this bleak prospect, it is easy to assume that the family firm was overwhelmed by the difficulties of commerce, and there were certainly plenty of real concerns evident in their trading in 1650–1. Bad debts were a constant complaint, many of them stemming from the upheavals caused by war and plague. In one case, they were still seeking payment for Indian shirts sent to them by the rascally royalist Andrew Cogan some three years after delivery. Even local debtors were hard to discipline, and they became so frustrated by the unreliability of their contacts in Cartagena that they began to circumvent the town whenever possible. More generally, foreign competition was fierce, with the French seen as a real threat to the tobacco market. They were also let down by their suppliers at times, with regular complaints about the quality of goods they had to sell, including fish, tobacco, and soap. A deal over a New England shipping share also seems to have gone wrong, due to the deceit of the other party. Blunt speaking to the point of self-criticism, they acknowledged their own errors too, for instance when they had misunderstood orders from their correspondents. Despite all these problems, however, it would be overhasty to suggest that they were facing ruin, and the reorganisation of their business since Richard's return to Alicante suggests that others had confidence in their future.[29]

Although evidence is fragmentary, it does appear that their carefully crafted networks enabled the Houncells to continue to trade up until the time of Richard's death, which took place in Livorno at some point between April 1653 and January 1654. Valencian records duly acknowledge the re-establishment of the firm of Richard and William Houncell in 1651, and in the following year they were still paying the double tariff on their goods at Alicante. It also appears that in 1652 the title of the firm changed to William Houncell and Company. This change may well represent Richard's removal to Livorno, a move in keeping with his known plans to expand his interests into the Eastern Mediterranean. Also consistent with his readiness to recognize the Commonwealth, he had established contacts there through Charles Longland, the parliamentary agent, and he probably felt emboldened to undertake the move after his brother had managed the business during his absence in London. However, by April 1653, he was 'lying sick' at Livorno and made his will, leaving everything to brother William with the heartfelt plea that 'God forbid I should have the least thought to deprive him of any part thereof'. By that stage he was too weak to write, and he reportedly died 'shortly after' making his will, although letters of administration were not granted to his brother until 31 January 1654. There is no clue as to the size of his fortune at that time, and William's own death soon afterwards in London leaves the state of the business very uncertain. Given the connections the firm had established in the Mediterranean and in the City, there is no reason to doubt that Houncell prospects were good, especially as they were boosted by William's marriage to Robert Burdett's sister. William outlived his brother by only a few months, however, his will being proved on 29 December 1655.[30]

The Houncell name thus failed to appear alongside those of their sometime correspondents Frederick, Rider, and Mico, as leading London traders (and commercial knights) of the Restoration era. Given the commercial pedigree of this generation of Mediterranean traders, there is good reason to believe that it was only their untimely deaths that prevented them from building successful careers in England and the Mediterranean. Thus, even though their name remains obscure, their actions illuminate both the strengths and weaknesses of English traders in the region at one of the most crucial stages of English maritime expansion. As both factors and principals, they demonstrated the full range of personal qualities necessary for English success on the cusp of a commercial revolution in its global trade. In bleak economic times, they had to hone their skills and buttress their networks, schooled in such arts by a commercial culture of international dealing that was designed to overcome the vagaries of trade.[31]

The 'political' character of such enterprise has been emphasized here in order to highlight the ways in which their trading strategies were attuned to the structural and partisan opportunities open to them in difficult times, and more research is needed to understand how ordinary citizens tried to build for the future in such a fluid era. Their experience suggests that the historic rivalries between London and the provinces may obscure more productive relationships and that dynamic individuals could work simultaneously within regulated and unregulated spheres of commerce. In more formal political terms, they welcomed the support of the state and could even accommodate a new regime if it could provide effective aid, but there can be no doubt that they remained independent agents of commercial development. These findings highlight the need for further research on the interplay of economic and political forces during the republic and on the ways in which Interregnum experiences influenced the thinking and actions of traders during the more prosperous Restoration era. Houncell himself would not have seen himself as one of his generation's pioneers and would have probably rested content with acknowledgement as 'a trader of knowledge and government', a mercantile accolade he richly deserved on the evidence of his remarkable letterbook.[32]

Notes

1 For the importance of the state in the transformation of English commercial fortunes from the mid-seventeenth century, see D. Ormrod, *The Rise of Commercial Empires: England and the Netherlands in the Age of Mercantilism, 1650–1770* (Cambridge, 2003). For more specific insights concerning the role of commerce in international relations during the Interregnum, see T. Venner, *Cromwellian Foreign Policy* (Basingstoke, 1995). However, the boldest attempt to establish causative connections between domestic politics and commercial development in this era remains R. Brenner, *Merchants and Revolution: Commercial Change, Political Conflict, and London's Overseas Traders, 1550–1653* (Cambridge 1993).

2 C. Holmes, 'The County Community in Stuart Historiography', *JBS*, 19 (1980), 54–73; idem, 'Centre and Locality in Civil War England', in J. Adamson (ed.), *The English Civil War: Conflict and Contexts, 1640–9* (Basingstoke, 2009), pp. 153–74, 311–12. When seeking to reconnect commercial and political developments during the mid-century upheavals, Steve Pincus argued that contemporary outlooks were 'neither localist nor British, but European and universal', commending Clive's work for highlighting the significance of wider ideological horizons – *Protestantism and Patriotism: Ideologies and the Making of English Foreign Policy, 1650–68* (Cambridge, 1996), quote at p. 452.

3 J.I. Martinez Ruiz and P. Gauci (eds.), *Mercaderes Ingleses en Alicante en el Siglo XVII* (Alicante, 2008). I am hugely indebted to Dr. Martinez Ruiz for his leadership and scholarship throughout the course of this editorial project. The letterbook can be found amongst the Burdett papers at the Derbyshire RO, D5054/12/3. The printed edition includes full transcriptions of 415 of the 1,123 letters and provides extensive analysis of Houncell's trade and the role of other English traders in the Alicante region.

4 Studies of ideology continue to highlight the importance of the Interregnum for new approaches to economic affairs. See in particular, S. Pincus, 'Neither Machiavellian Moment nor Possessive Individualism: Commercial Society and the Defenders of the English Commonwealth', *AHR*, 103 (1998), 705–36; T. Leng, 'Commercial Conflict and Regulation in the Discourse of Trade in Seventeenth-Century England', *HJ*, 48 (2005), 933–54.

5 Brenner, *Merchants and Revolution*, esp. Chapters 10–12. For a wide-ranging study of the London merchants behind the dynamic colonial expansion of the commercial revolution, see N. Zahedieh, *The Capital and the Colonies: London and the Atlantic Economy, 1660–1700* (Cambridge, 2010), esp. Chapter 3.

6 For discussion of the self-fashioned image of the 'professional' merchant, see M. Jacob and C. Secretan (eds.), *The Self-Perception of Early Modern Capitalists* (Basingstoke, 2008); N. Glaisyer, *The Culture of Commerce in England, 1660–1720* (Woodbridge, 2006), Chapter 3; P. Gauci, *The Politics of Trade: The Overseas Merchant in State and Society, 1660–1720* (Oxford, 2001), pp. 166–75.

7 *Mercaderes Ingleses*, p. 393: Richard Houncell to Nathan Wright and Robert Burdett, 1 May 1651. For the challenges facing an Italian-based English firm in this period, see G.P. de Divitiis, 'An English Merchant in the Mediterranean: Arthur Pennington (1621–77)', in C. Vassallo and M. D'Angelo (eds.), *Anglo-Saxons in the Mediterranean: Commerce, Politics and Ideas, XVII–XX centuries* (Msida, 2007), pp. 1–16. The work of Alison Games has particular resonance here, for she has sought to connect the histories of English expansion in the Mediterranean and the New World, viewing the former as a model for the latter until the adoption of a more centralized form of imperialism from the mid-seventeenth century: *The Web of Empire: English Cosmopolitanism in an Age of Expansion, 1560–1660* (Oxford, 2008).

8 B. Short, *A Respectable Society: Bridport 1593–1835* (Bradford-on-Avon, 1976), pp. 13, 41–2; J. Hutchins, *The History and Antiquities of the County of Dorset* (2 vols, 1774), I, 237–44. His mother can also be identified as Elizabeth Houncell, who outlived both of her sons and was described as a widow of Lyme Regis at her death: TNA, C10/32/65,

bill of complaint of Lettice Houncell; PROB 11/239, will of Elizabeth Houncell, 31 December 1656.
9 L. Roberts, *The Merchants Mappe of Commerce* (1638), p. 8; R. Davis, *The Rise of the English Shipping Industry in the Seventeenth and Eighteenth Centuries* (Newton Abbot, 1962), pp. 228–55.
10 C. Heywood, 'The English in the Mediterranean, 1600–30: A Post-Braudelian Perspective on the Northern Invasion', in M. Fusaro, C. Heywood, and M. Omri (eds.), *Trade and Cultural Exchange in the Early Modern Mediterranean* (2010), pp. 23–44; *Mercaderes Ingleses*, p. 276. Heywood contests Braudel's vision of the isolation of the Mediterranean, and argues that, while important, the English navy's role in establishing English traders in the region should not obscure the draw of economic incentives (beyond plunder).
11 *Mercaderes Ingleses*, p. 225: Richard Houncell to James Napper jnr., 23 June 1649; p. 233: Richard Houncell to James Napper snr., 18 July 1649; p. 242: Richard Houncell to John Lewes and John Mead, 5 September 1649; p. 251: Richard Houncell to Hawley Bishoppe, 6 October 1649.
12 C.G.A. Clay, *Economic Expansion and Social Change: England, 1500–1700* (2 vols, Cambridge, 1984), II, 131–3. For contemporary concerns within the West Country ports regarding London's influence, see J. Thirsk and J.P. Cooper (eds.), *Seventeenth-Century Economic Documents* (Oxford, 1972), pp. 477–8.
13 J. Howard and J. Chester (eds.), 'The Visitation of London, 1633, 1634, and 1635', *Harleian Society*, 15 (1880), 179; G. Cokayne, *Complete Baronetage* (6 vols, Gloucester, 1983), III, 304. Sir Andrew (d. 1660) was the son of Richard Cogan of Dorset, who married Mary, daughter of Andrew Houncell in August 1600. Richard Houncell evidently had had many business dealings with him, and further evidence of a close relationship is suggested by the presence of John Cogan (c. 1610–58) in Alicante, where he signed the will of Houncell's partner, Henry Collamore, in April 1648. On 28 January 1649, Houncell was still in hopes that Sir Andrew might make 'his pease' with the parliamentarians, but this was a forlorn hope. Cogan's estate was sequestered by a parliamentary act of 1651, and his loyalty to the Stuarts was rewarded with a baronetcy in 1657. He died soon after the Restoration and was buried in London.
14 *Mercaderes Ingleses*, p. 379: Richard Houncell to Robert Perkett and co., 30 March 1651; F. Colby (ed.), 'The Visitation of the county of Devon in the year 1620', *Harleian Society*, 6 (1872), 105; J.R. Woodhead, *The Rulers of London, 1660–89* (1965), p. 47; G. Marshall (ed.), 'Le Neve's Pedigree of the Knights', *Harleian Society*, 8 (1873), 190.
15 Clay, *Economic Expansion*, II, 133; B. Coates, *The Impact of Civil War on the Economy of London* (Aldershot, 2004), pp. 13–14. English traders were taking advantage here of the exclusion of the Dutch from Spanish markets after the recommencement of hostilities in the Low Countries from 1621.
16 *Mercaderes Ingleses*, p. 190: Richard Houncell to Nathan Wright, 28 March 1649; M.A.E. Green (ed.), *Calendar of the Proceedings of the Committee for the Advance of Money, 1642–56* (1888), p. 343; V. Pearl, *London and the Outbreak of the Puritan Revolution: City Government and National Politics 1625–1643* (Oxford, 1961), p. 331; A. Beaven, *The Aldermen of the City of London* (2 vols, 1908–13), I, 38, 84. Both Wright and Burdett were members of the Skinners' Company, and both fined to avoid aldermanic office during the Interregnum. The network was cemented by marriages, Burdett securing a match with Wright's daughter Mary, while Burdett's sister Lettice (d. 1683) married Richard Houncell's brother William. Robert Burdett's younger brother, Leicester (b. c. 1612) passed through Alicante in late 1651 and in April 1653 was a witness to the will of Richard Houncell at Livorno.
17 Derbyshire RO, D5054/12/3, fol. 92: Richard Houncell to Edward Stephen Wright and Roger Howe, 8 March 1649; *Mercaderes Ingleses*, p. 184: Richard Houncell to Nathan Wright and Robert Burdett, 13 March 1649; p. 237: Richard Houncell to Humphrey Onesbye, 29 July 1649; p. 266: Richard Houncell to Nathan Wright, 19 November 1649.

18 *Mercaderes Ingleses*, p. 214: Richard Houncell to William Rider, 17 May 1649. Rider (d. 1669) was an experienced ship captain and trader in the Mediterranean. His career prospered after the Restoration, for he was knighted in March 1661 and became a government contractor for naval supplies, specializing in hemp. He came in regular contact with Samuel Pepys, with whom he shared his Mediterranean experiences, and he was appointed in 1662 to the commission supervising English interests in Tangier: R. Latham and W. Matthews (eds.), *The Diary of Samuel Pepys* (11 vols, 1983), III, 238; IV, 200–1. For the importance of Tangier as a sign of English imperial intent, see Games, *Web of Empire*, pp. 293–9.

19 For the commercial and political enterprise of the hard-pressed wine traders in the 1690s, see D.W. Jones, *War and Economy in the Age of William III and Marlborough* (Oxford, 1988), esp. Chapter 8.

20 Derbyshire RO, D5054/12/3, fol. 127: Richard Houncell to Augustine Kendall, 17 April 1649; *Mercaderes Ingleses*, p. 345: Houncell firm to Moses Goodyeare, 5 November 1650. Nathan Wright may have had a particularly important impact on Houncell's commercial horizons, as a Levant merchant who had also traded to New England, Virginia, and Newfoundland: Brenner, *Merchants and Revolution*, pp. 136–7. Wright's confidence in Houncell was signalled in early 1650 by the arrival of his agent Calthorp Parker in Alicante. Parker subsequently joined William Houncell as partner during Richard's absence in England and did so again in 1653. He had returned to London by 1660, when he figured among the English merchants petitioning for the recovery of goods seized by the Spanish Crown in 1655.

21 *Mercaderes Ingleses*, p. 193: Richard Houncell to Nathan Wright, 1 April 1649; p. 294: Houncell firm to John Loveringe, John Frederick, and Thomas Rouse, 23 March 1650; p. 323: Houncell firm to John Lewes and John Mead, 7 August 1650; p. 326: Houncell firm to Richard Houncell, 22 August 1650.

22 *Mercaderes Ingleses*, p. 302: Houncell firm to John Lewes and John Mead, 26 April 1650; p. 213: Richard Houncell to Nathaniel Withers, 17 May 1649; Derbyshire RO, D5054/12/3: Richard Houncell to Francis Clarke, 1 May 1651; TNA, SP105/151, pp. 74–5. Robert Brenner and others have stressed the difficulty of entering the Levant Company at this time, which is depicted as a tight oligarchy, accessible only with both wealth and connections: *Merchants and Revolution*, pp. 70–4. For the experience of Levant traders in the Mediterranean, see J. Mather, *Pashas: Traders and Travellers in the Islamic World* (New Haven, CT, 2009).

23 *Mercaderes Ingleses*, pp. 314–15: Houncell firm to Robert Burdett, 23 June 1650; p. 316: Houncell firm to Richard Houncell, 23 June 1650.

24 *CSPD 1650*, pp. 308, 545; Derbyshire RO, D5054/12/3, fol. 374: Richard Houncell to John Lewes and John Mead, 14 September 1650; *Mercaderes Ingleses*, p. 336: Houncell firm to Nathan Wright, Robert Burdett and Richard Houncell, 29 September 1650. Prior to his return, the Alicante-based partners reported that he intended to return to Spain for only one more year, and thus he might have anticipated the need for further lobbying in London.

25 Venning, *Cromwellian Foreign Policy*, Chapter 16; B. Capp, *Cromwell's Navy: The Fleet and the English Revolution 1648–1660* (Oxford, 1989), pp. 70–1. Robert Burdett's prominence as a spokesman for the Levant trade in 1651 has been noted by Robert Brenner: *Merchants and Revolution*, pp. 615–16. For the growth of suspicion towards the Rump for their rapprochement with lobbyists for sectional interests, see C. Holmes, *Why Was Charles I Executed?* (2006), pp. 142–3.

26 *Mercaderes Ingleses*, p. 381: Richard Houncell to John Lewes and John Mead, 30 March 1651. On 5 February 1651, Houncell had uttered his dismay at news of French privateers – 'god preserve us and our ffrends effects from theire insatiable clutches' – p. 363: Richard Houncell to John Lewes and John Mead.

27 *Mercaderes Ingleses*, p. 394: Richard Houncell to George Fisher, 1 May 1651; p. 410: Richard Houncell to John Lewes and John Mead, 7 July 1651; p. 423: Richard Houncell to Nathan Wright and co., 28 September 1651.

28 *Mercaderes Ingleses*, p. 359: Richard Houncell to Nathan Wright and Robert Burdett, 15 January 1651; pp. 379–80: Richard Houncell to Robert Perkett and co., 30 March 1651; pp. 428–9: Richard Houncell to Nathan Wright, 15 October 1651; Derbyshire RO, D5054/12/3, fol. 459: Richard Houncell to John Loveringe, John Frederick and Thomas Rouse, 28 February 1651.

29 *Mercaderes Ingleses*, p. 377: Richard Houncell to Sampson Love, 30 March 1651; p. 351: Richard Houncell to George Dickons and Robert Canning, 8 December 1650.

30 *Mercaderes Ingleses*, p. 27; TNA, PROB 11/239, will of Richard Houncell, proved 31 January 1654; PROB 11/246, will of William Houncell, proved 29 December 1655; TNA, C10/32/65, Houncell vs. Houncell, 1655. William Houncell had also been admitted as a freeman of the Levant Company on 14 June 1654. This suggests that he continued to harbour ambitions to expand their Mediterranean trade and that he could count on Nathan Wright to act as guarantor for the payment of his fee, indicating that the network was still strong: TNA, SP105/151, p. 214. However, in his last months, he doubtless shared the fears of other English Mediterranean traders at the deterioration of Anglo-Spanish relations: Divitiis, 'An English Merchant in the Mediterranean', pp. 12–13.

31 Houncell correspondent John Frederick (1601–85) went on to become one of the leading merchants of his generation. He specialized in the Spanish trade, and his links with West Country merchants were highlighted by his election as MP for Dartmouth in 1660. He was knighted that year, and subsequently served as MP and Lord Mayor of London: *HOP 1660–1690*, II, 363–5.

32 The most recent work of Steve Pincus has again highlighted the importance of the Interregnum and Restoration for the transformation of English attitudes towards economic affairs. He does argue that economic projects were important political issues in the 1640s and 1650s but remains cautious regarding the ideological force of 'political economic debate' before the time of the Exclusion Crisis, for these 'extremely fluid' exchanges 'did not map easily onto other political preferences': *1688: The First Modern Revolution* (New Haven, CT, 2009), Chapter 12 (quote at p. 396).

7 The uses of intelligence
The case of Lord Craven, 1650–60

Manfred Brod

The Craven case was a *cause célèbre* of the 1650s. It has at first sight a certain epic quality, involving as it does the struggle of a wealthy man and his family to preserve their patrimony from the grasp of an avaricious and arguably illegitimate state. In attempting a closer examination, this essay will take the reader on a rapid tour of the state, revealing its highways but also some less well trodden byways and some distinctly unappealing vistas. The entire story gives insight into the inner workings of the Commonwealth and later the Protectorate governments, their internal divisions, and the complex interplay within them of ideology and interest.

The number of royalist landowners expropriated by the Commonwealth government in 1651–2 was little short of eight hundred, yet only a handful of these made any serious attempt to oppose the confiscations. Most simply shrugged their shoulders, concealed what properties they could, and arranged to buy back some part of the rest on mortgage.[1] William, Lord Craven was one of the exceptions. A major proprietor, unmarried, his assets were seen as potentially family property, and he and his relatives combined in an aggressive and unprincipled campaign to make the position of the purchasers as uncertain and uncomfortable as possible.

It is the course of this campaign, from its beginning in 1650 via a low point in 1652 to its triumphant conclusion at the Restoration, that forms the matter of the first half of this work. The second part will cover the same ground but in a thematic rather than a chronological fashion. It will look in more detail at the networks of power and of money that were brought into play. It will examine the positioning of the Craven case as a point of focus for the hostility between army and civilian members in the Commonwealth parliament, and ask to what extent it demonstrates the corruption and self-interest of the civilian members that was implicitly believed in by the military at the time and is accepted by many modern scholars.[2] It will attempt to analyse the use of print publication by the two sides and its effect on outside opinion.

I

It will be as well to start by presenting the main protagonists, Lord Craven himself and his chief opponent, Captain George Bishop.

William Craven had been born in 1608. His father, also William, was a wealthy London merchant, a pillar of the Merchant Taylors and Lord Mayor in 1610–11. His mother came from a similar background. The father died in 1618, with his son and heir only ten years old. The family dealt competently with the crisis. The deceased's business affairs were gradually liquidated and the proceeds invested in land; this was divided in a ratio of roughly five to three between young William and his brother John. Like others of his class, the father had bought a country estate in Berkshire, and it was here, at Hamstead Marshall, that young William grew up.[3] He was probably the second greatest landowner in the county, after the father of Henry Marten, the future republican and regicide, but Craven's holdings extended over many counties, which Marten's did not.[4]

The young man didn't seem cut out for a business career. The family spent £7,000 in 1627 on a baronage and a suitable marriage was arranged, but it never took place.[5] He departed for the continent announcing that he wanted to make his career as a soldier. It was, after all, the time of Tilly and of Wallenstein. But, although he would distinguish himself for personal bravery, he was not cut out to be a warlord either.[6] He conceived a romantic and without doubt platonic attachment to an older woman, Elizabeth, the widowed ex-queen of Bohemia, and divided his time between campaigning in the interest of his lady and her family and keeping company with her in her small but extravagant exile court at The Hague.[7]

He was in England in 1641 but left in the following February with parliamentary approval in the entourage of Henrietta Maria.[8] His family continued to manage his affairs with their usual flair. During the war, his brother John died without issue, and he inherited the remainder of the family fortune. John had been a royalist, and his estates were under sequestration. But the total value of Craven property was now estimated as a quarter of a million pounds.[9]

George Bishop was a man of very different stamp. Originally a Bristol brewer, he had learnt the craft of military intelligence on the staff of General Philip Skippon, with whom he served at Naseby and who was military governor of Bristol in 1646.[10] He was towards the radical end of the political/religious spectrum: at the Putney debates of 1647, he brought a message from the spiritualist preacher John Saltmarsh and spoke in guarded terms of executing the king. He would finish as a Quaker.[11] After the fighting, Bishop returned to brewing but continued to carry out local tasks for the Council of State, no doubt recommended by Skippon, who was a member. In the disturbed month of May 1649, he was charged with working to prevent possible mutiny among troops passing through Bristol on their way to Ireland. He investigated abuses in the Forest of Dean, which were denying timber to the navy and in which some of the leading gentry of the region were implicated.[12] In the summer of 1650, when Cromwell took much of the Army to Scotland and Skippon was left in charge in London, he rejoined his old boss, handling the London end of the military intelligence function.[13] But a government investigator, Captain John Vernon, had recently left to accompany Henry Ireton to Ireland, and it seems that Bishop took on some of his activities.[14] After Dunbar, Bishop returned to Bristol but was almost immediately called back to continue his work.[15] He agreed to accept a full-time post in London as secretary to the Committee for Examinations, which reported to the Council of State. This made him effective head of domestic security operations while his superior, Thomas Scot, concentrated on foreign intelligence. Bishop would have a salary and whatever monies he needed from a fund operated by Gualter Frost, the Council's secretary.[16]

II

The tribulations of Lord Craven began one evening in the spring of 1650 at a castle belonging to the Prince of Orange, Willem II, at Breda. The young Charles II was there, engaged in difficult and demeaning negotiations with his less than loving Scottish subjects for an army with which to reconquer his lost southern kingdom. The prince and the princess, Charles's sister, visited frequently, and the prince was encouraging him to accept the humiliating terms and go. His presence in the Netherlands was a political embarrassment. High-ranking English exiles came and went, some hoping to be allowed to accompany the king, others offering their pessimistic farewells. Also present were the king's aunt, Elizabeth of Bohemia and, inevitably, Lord Craven.[17]

The public rooms of the castle were thronged with a motley rout of English royalist soldiers desperate for employment but whom the godly Scots would refuse to take on.[18] On at least two occasions they prepared petitions for the king. The exact wording would later be a matter of controversy, but everyone agreed that they were basically appeals for money. On that long fraught evening before Charles was to leave on his journey, one such petition was given to Craven who agreed to pass it on, via Elizabeth, to the king. It was an act that would have serious consequences.

Among the crowd there were at least two, probably more, Commonwealth spies. After the king had left, one of these decided that, after eighteen months on the continent mixing with the royalist exiles, it was time to go home. He rode to Ostend, providentially survived an encounter with pirates, and eventually reported in London to Lieutenant Colonel George Joyce who had sent him abroad in the first place.[19] Joyce is well known to history as the hero of Holdenby. In the agitated summer of 1647, a simple cornet of cavalry, he had led a force of troopers to where the king was being held as a prisoner of Parliament and transferred him bodily into the custody of the Army. His promotion thereafter had been rapid.[20] The spy was Major Richard Faulconer, a Hampshire man who had served as a cavalry officer on the Welsh Marches.[21] It was Faulconer who would be the sacrificial victim of the narrative that would develop.

The Commonwealth government in 1650, as at other times, was concerned with money. A major source of government income was the confiscation of property and its sale on the active land market that had now opened up. Bishops' lands, those of the deans and chapters, and those that had belonged to the crown had been taken over and largely disposed of without the public finances appearing much healthier for it. Royalists' estates had been sequestrated through the Commissioners for Compounding, their rents taken by the state until expensively redeemed. The next stage would obviously be the total expropriation of such royalists who had not compounded in this way or who had gone into exile as irreconcilable. In April, Parliament named a committee of thirty-one, with the indefatigable committeeman Augustine Garland as its reporter, to prepare legislation to that effect.[22]

Progress was slow, and there was obviously impatience. On 13 January 1651, Bishop's Committee for Examinations, taking a rather broad view of its remit, sent up a report to the Council of State. It proposed that the estates of those who acted against the Commonwealth should be confiscated 'without mercy' and the proceeds used in part to reward their accusers.[23] The senior body sent it back 'for further consideration', although the words used in debate may have been less polite. The report said nothing about legal process and, if implemented, might well have led to a spate of false denunciations. Furthermore, property rights were pre-eminently a matter for Parliament, not for the Council. It says little for the abilities of Lord President Bradshaw that he chaired the Committee as well as the Council.

We do not know what influence Bishop had on the abortive report, but it may have been considerable. In the previous September, Joyce had brought Faulconer to him. Bishop and Joyce probably already knew each other – they held very similar political and religious views. Faulconer brought information about a royalist rising planned for the following Christmas-tide in Norfolk, which in the event Bishop was able to crush before it became dangerous.[24] Sometime later, Faulconer also spoke to Bishop of Craven and his closeness to the king.[25] Joyce was having to keep up the appearances that went with his new rank and with the governorship of Portland, for which his military pay will hardly have sufficed. He had no money of his own. He was dabbling actively in the land market, so it seems likely that the possibility of expropriating Craven's for his own and the Commonwealth's benefit was already in his mind.[26] Be that as it may, it was certainly about the time of the report that Bishop first mentioned Craven to his superiors. A significant step was taken when on 6 February 1651 the Council instructed the Committee for Compounding to consider the evidence against Craven, which Bishop would provide.[27] The commissioners could order sequestration, not confiscation, but if they did so, Craven's name would necessarily be brought to the notice of Garland's parliamentary committee.

Faulconer, meanwhile, had been ill. Just out of his sickbed and still very groggy, he was summoned to Bishop's office, where he found himself in the intimidating presence of Bishop himself and the five members of the Compounding Committee. According to later accounts, there was some discussion, after which Bishop wrote out a statement for Faulconer to sign. Faulconer demurred, if we can trust his later protests, saying that he didn't remember saying that the petition given to Craven described the parliamentarians as 'barbarous and inhumane rebels', but Bishop said 'if you leave that out, you do nothing', and Faulconer was in no condition to refuse his signature.[28] These words brought it arguably within the purview of the 1649 Treason Act, which followed Tudor practice in making treason a matter of words rather than action. A traitor's property would automatically be forfeit.[29] Faulconer was given £20 or £30 and sent away. Some of the royalist officers who by then had trickled back to London gave partial confirmations of his story but without mentioning the opprobrious words.[30]

Bishop moved fast but not quite fast enough. The interview with Faulconer had been on 10 February, and by the 13th Bishop's men were in Berkshire, gathering information on Craven's estates there. But Craven's family were well connected and had their sources of information. Craven's bailiff in Berkshire had gone into hiding, and Bishop's agents could only report that they were searching the house of Sir George Whitmore, Craven's maternal uncle, for him.[31]

Furthermore, the Compounding Commissioners were not inclined to cooperate. They will not have been pleased to have to leave their quarters at Haberdashers' Hall in the City for the long trek to Whitehall and were probably unconvinced by Bishop's assertion that for him to be seen at their office, thronged with royalist petitioners, in company with his agent would put the latter's life at risk.[32] A cousin, Sir William Craven, had an interview, arranged through John Rushworth, with Samuel Moyer, chairman of the Commission. Sir William had married a sister of the Lord General Thomas Fairfax, and Rushworth had been Fairfax's secretary and was also *persona grata* in government circles.[33] Moyer expressed doubts whether someone outside the country could be liable to sequestration. The question was referred back to the Council of State, which by then had undergone one of its annual reorganisations. On 4 March, the Council sent it to Parliament for a ruling.[34]

The Commons obviously found the question difficult and forbore to apply the Treason Act. Instead, it disinterred a declaration of 24 August 1649, which concerned soldiers in Ireland who had deserted to the enemy. There was no reasonable way this could be applied to Craven's situation, but it was nonetheless cited on 6 March 1651 as the basis for declaring him 'an offender against the Commonwealth' and resolving on the confiscation of his estates. They were to be immediately seized by the Compounding Commissioners, whose normal inquisitorial procedures were thus bypassed.[35]

Craven's affairs had legally been placed in the hands of commissioners of his own, and two of these on 12 June 1651 submitted a petition asking for a delay until Craven, serving with a Dutch army in Germany, could be informed and could prepare a defence. The request was rejected, but when on the same day the House divided on whether Craven's name should stand in the forthcoming act, the noes had it by 28 votes to 27.[36] The act of 16 July named seventy-two major landowners among the royalist exiles, but Craven was not among them.[37]

Craven's people had won a round, but the contest had only begun. The estates remained under sequestration, and there would be further acts of expropriation.

III

As Craven's side brought their networks into play, Bishop was doing the same. His contacts were among the republicans and the radical religious sects. In the Craven heartlands of Berkshire, the sequestrators were meeting resistance, and that county had to be excluded from the initial sequestration programme.[38] Berkshire had its own three-man sub-committee for sequestrations. They had a full-time agent, Christopher Cheesman, a sometime Army mutineer, a Seeker in religion, and occasional pamphleteer.[39] They had found Cheesman unsatisfactory and sacked him. Nonetheless, when in April another of Craven's commissioners, Sir Edmund Sawyer, was arrested, orders came that Cheesman and no other was to escort him to London for questioning.[40] Cheesman found a sympathetic ear for his complaints against his erstwhile employers, and on his return to Reading published a pamphlet accusing them of undue laxness in carrying out their duties.[41] There was an inquiry that found in his favour; the subcommissioners were dismissed and replaced by three men from the local radical subculture. Their leader was the wealthy mercer Thomas Curtis, related by marriage to Bishop.[42] He was sponsored by Henry Marten, Craven's Berkshire neighbour and, incidentally, debtor. Marten was generally on Craven's side, but he owed Curtis a favour for help in financing his private republican militia in 1648.[43]

In November 1651, Parliament decided on a second round of confiscations. It was to be prepared by a committee of thirty-eight, led once more by Augustine Garland.[44] Craven meanwhile, from his posting in Germany, had been sending in further petitions. One was refused because of alleged doubts on its authenticity, one miscarried, and a third did not get a reading until 10 June 1652, seven months after its receipt, in spite of constant lobbying by Rushworth.[45] But by then the conflict was beginning to move outside the doors of Parliament.

A vote on 22 June went against Craven by thirty-three to thirty-one.[46] This prompted the Craven side to settle on a strategy.[47] They would concentrate their fire on the weakest part of Bishop's case, the document signed by Faulconer, which was the main evidence for Craven's guilt. This, and its author or authors, were to be discredited. On 12 July 1652, Faulconer was indicted at the Lord Mayor's court in the Guildhall to answer charges of perjury.[48] A number of the officers who had been present in Breda at the operative time were to be witnesses. Most of them had little of importance to say. But there was one, a Colonel Drury, whose evidence might be crucial. He claimed that it had been himself and Faulconer who had drafted one of the petitions. Faulconer had wanted to put in the opprobrious words about the Commonwealth, but the other officers had refused. They saw themselves as soldiers of fortune, who could not afford to jeopardise future employment prospects. Drury claimed to have a draft of the petition in question, without the words, written in his son's school exercise book and in Faulconer's handwriting. Bishop will have had his spies in the Craven camp and would not be taken by surprise. Drury was picked up in a London street on the morning of the hearing and brought to Bishop's office, where he was browbeaten and bullied to withhold his evidence. But he was proof against threats, so Bishop simply had him locked up in a safe house on the Strand until the weekend when the sessions were safely over and then let him go.[49]

It may have seemed to Bishop a victory, but it didn't help Faulconer. Shortly after, he found himself in the prison of Upper Bench on a writ of capias. Bail was fixed at £1,000 or £1,500, and there was no way he could raise it. Somehow, he was provided with counsel, but the notoriously corrupt keeper, Sir John Lenthall, made sure they had no chance to confer.[50]

Rushworth complained of Bishop's action to the parliamentary committee but to no avail.[51] The decisive vote on 3 August was again lost by the Craven camp, by twenty votes to twenty-three. On the following day, Sir William Craven came in with a last-ditch assertion that Combe Abbey had been granted to him as part of his marriage settlement. Combe Abbey counted for almost a fifth of the total by value. He was ignored, and the second confiscation act was passed. It contained twenty-nine names, and Craven's was in first place. A proviso instructed the treason trustees who were to sell the estates to allow George Joyce property to the extent of £100 per annum clear profit. He would use this in part payment for the Craven manors of East and West Enborne, bordering on Hamstead Marshall.[52]

There was a further appeal in October, when Craven offered money to get the confiscation lifted. Cromwell was in favour, but the petition was refused a reading by thirty-four to thirty.[53] The decree was now absolute.

The Craven properties could now be sold off, and the bulk of them would be disposed of within the next two years. Members of Parliament were prominent among the purchasers; according to contemporary sources, nine members acting in their own names took up estates amounting to over half of the total annual value, and this can be largely borne out from the Close Rolls of Chancery. There will have been others who worked through agents or attorneys.[54]

IV

It may have seemed that the cause was lost, but the Craven side persisted. Their immediate plan was once more to use Faulconer in order to strike at Bishop. On 20 May 1653, having already suffered forty weeks of incarceration, Faulconer stood in the dock at Westminster Hall, charged once more with perjury, before Lord Chief Justice Rolle and a distinguished line-up of judges.[55] The case attracted enormous attention, and the court was crowded. The prosecution's tactics were *ad hominem*. They were concerned to blacken Faulconer's character and brought witness after witness to testify to his many vices. There was something there to turn everyone against him. He was a wastrel who had gone through his family's money and had vowed to use any means available to get more. He was a winebibber who drank healths – and what is more the healths were to the Devil – and drunk on his knees. He had been in prison for a felony when he was recruited for his espionage job and had taken it only to regain his freedom. He was a sodomite, who had offered money to men for sex. He was a confidence trickster, who had got an actor to impersonate Captain Bishop and promise some favour to a petitioner, for which he had been paid. Most of this, of course, can be discounted, but what must have been true was that he had earlier been in trouble with the criminal law, accused of burglary. Bishop had written on his behalf to the Lord Chief Justice, pointing out that he was a man who had served the Commonwealth well and asking that the case be dropped. It wasn't, but when it was called the witnesses proved to be unexpectedly absent, and Faulconer had been acquitted. Now both Bishop and Joyce appeared in court to testify in Faulconer's favour, but he was convicted of perjury and sentenced to jail where he would remain until his death two years later.[56]

It was clear that Bishop, not Faulconer, had been the real guilty party. By then, Cromwell had forcibly dissolved the Rump Parliament, and Bishop was in any case out of sympathy with the new regime. It seems that Thurloe would have been happy to continue his employment in a subordinate role, but he chose to resign with a suitable financial settlement.[57] His retirement would not save him from intense questioning at a later parliamentary enquiry.[58] George Joyce was cashiered from the Army soon after, allegedly for words spoken against Cromwell.[59]

The purchasers of the Craven estates were now in a difficult situation. They were left with a dubious title, and many who had elected to pay in two instalments refused to hand over the second.[60] They lobbied and published.[61] There was some expectation that the confiscation would have to be lifted, but this proved premature.[62] Craven may have been in England in September 1653, perhaps hoping for a hearing from the Barebone's Parliament that was debating the somewhat similar case of Sir John Stawell, but nothing materialised.[63] He was certainly in contact with the Protectorate government at the time of the Dutch treaty, with hints that the then lord president, Henry Lawrence, might share in any advantage that would come to him as a result.[64] In September 1654, the Protector ordered a stop to further sales, and his first parliament set up a committee to consider the matter.[65] It had no fewer than eighty-two members, a number that would increase still further as the cases of Stawell and others were added to its remit.[66] Craven's chief counsel was Serjeant Maynard, who had a track record defending people who had been deprived of liberty or property without proper process. A resolution of the House, argued Maynard, did not amount to proper process. He was scathing about the MPs on the opposing side: '[T]here is little to be said for them that are Judges and Purchasers too'. It seemed that there would be a conclusion, which might well have been in Craven's favour, at the meeting planned for 22 January 1655.[67] Unfortunately, that was the day Cromwell chose for his dissolution.

But the issue was never dormant for long. On 26 May 1657, there was a major debate on whether Craven's counsel, Mr Finch – presumably the future Earl of Nottingham – might address the House on his behalf. But the purchasers wanted the same privilege, and there were many of them. The theme developed that honour required justice for Lord Craven. John Barkstead felt it necessary to inform the House that he was not among the purchasers of Craven property, and Samuel Highland that he had bought but had cleared his Baptist conscience by selling out again.[68] The debate was adjourned, then delayed, and was not taken up again until January 1658. But that session of Parliament had more urgent problems on its mind and was dissolved without coming to a decision.

In April 1659, the debate centred on Craven being given a safe conduct to come to England and personally argue his case.[69] Both Sir Arthur Hesilrige, a great purchaser of confiscated lands who had previously been strongly against Craven, and Carew Raleigh, one of the major purchasers of the Craven properties, spoke in favour. No doubt the purchasers would welcome a conclusion, even against them, rather than continuing uncertainty. But when Craven arrived, it was to find London in turmoil after the Army had forced a dissolution and in a panic over royalist agents arriving to foment rebellion.[70] His safe conduct now worthless, he turned tail.[71]

With the change in the political environment came a change in strategy. Intelligence reports suggest that Craven money helped to finance the revolts of the summer.[72] A Stuart restoration now seemed the best hope, and we must assume that Craven's popularity with his bankers improved as that outcome became foreseeable.

As the Protectorate collapsed and the Rump returned, the Craven camp must once again have felt worried. There was a recrudescence of pamphleteering.[73] The old executive committees were resuscitated. Purchasers who had not paid their second instalments were dunned for their money and accumulated interest. George Joyce got a bill for £2,000 in respect of East and West Enborne.[74] Now once again in favour, he applied to Parliament for a respite of payment, which was granted.[75]

But the end was nigh. Even before the king's return, Craven had taken his seat in the restored House of Lords.[76] He helped to negotiate what honours were to be bestowed on Monck and Clarges.[77] On 6 June 1660, the House declared the confiscations of his properties null and void. His was one of only three cases to be so resolved; the others were those of Sir John Stawell, discussed later in this chapter, and of the London Presbyterian Alderman Bunce.[78] Various new owners of his properties went to jail until they agreed to move out.[79] It was now George Joyce's turn to flee to the Netherlands.

It was a traditional happy ending. Craven received the benefit of his long support of the king's aunt. He got an earldom, recovered all his property and more, and built the beautiful Dutch-style hunting lodge at Ashdown for his lady, though she would not live to see it finished. He had Balthazar Gerbier build him a great house at Hamstead Marshall, which burned down in 1718. It seems that he quietly married one of Elizabeth's ladies shortly before her death, no doubt to regularise a long-term relationship.[80] He continued close to Elizabeth's family, a sort of Polonius figure, often laughed at and sometimes a bore but always helpful and reliable. He did some minor government jobs, but never anything controversial and eventually died in his bed at a ripe age.[81]

V

The Craven story has now been told, and we have had our rapid tour of the English state of the 1650s that was promised in the prologue. It is time to retrace our steps, looking rather more carefully at what was previously only glimpsed. The remainder of this essay will seek to analyse the forces at play on both sides of the conflict and evaluate their strategies and tactics.

There is room for divergent opinions on the success of Craven's campaign. It is certainly true that the lifting of the confiscation came about only as a result of the Restoration, yet it was a major achievement of Craven's supporters to have kept the issue alive over a period of almost ten years. The frequency and intensity of debate, as well as the occasional prominence of the case in the newsbooks, suggests that it came to be seen as representative of deeper political conflicts. We have seen that both sides were involved in lobbying and were using and developing networks of support. It will be convenient to start with an analysis of these networks.

The initial impetus for the expropriation came from the Committee for Examinations, certainly at the initiative of George Bishop and probably at the instigation of George Joyce. High-level support came from the Committee's chairman, Lord President Bradshaw, who in April 1651 chided the Committee for Compounding for the delays in the Craven sequestrations and added a personal postscript enjoining 'speed and privacy till the work be done'.[82] The three men were linked; when, later in the year, changes in the organisation of the Council of State threatened Bradshaw's position, Bishop took the risky step of lobbying Cromwell in his support.[83] Joyce was himself involved in intelligence work, and a satirical pamphlet of the Restoration period portrays him as a remarkably flat-footed secret policeman in Marlborough, entrapping an innocent tradesman under Bradshaw's direction.[84] The intelligence establishment seems to have had more than its fair share of radical republicans who would later oppose the protectoral regime: Bishop, Joyce, Bishop's superior Thomas Scot, and his predecessor John Vernon.[85] As we have seen in the case of the Berkshire subcommissioners, the Committee could count on help when needed from radical networks in the provinces.

Against these from the start were the men Craven had chosen as his commissioners or attorneys, overseeing the administration of his properties.[86] These were substantial and well connected individuals in the world of business and finance, and most of them had family links with Craven. They were headed by his uncle Sir George Whitmore, a former lord mayor, but perhaps the most active was a cousin, Sir Edmund Sawyer, auditor of the exchequer and of the City of London, who was resident at White Waltham, Berkshire.[87] 'Captain' James Pickering was a shipowner, and John Lightfoot and Thomas Whitmore were lawyers. William Whitmore was a merchant tailor. Later, we also find included Sir William Whitmore, brother-in-law of Thomas Fairfax. Anthony Craven, probably the cousin of that name from Sparsholt, Berkshire, seems to have been in charge of what would prove to be a successful publicity campaign.[88]

There were also family connections with Parliament. It seems probable that Sir Gilbert Pickering, a member of the Council of State, was related to the sea captain. Pickering would be a teller on the Craven side at the vote of 22 June 1652.[89] The Fairfax connection was invaluable; the petition of 12 June 1651 was brought into the House by James Chaloner, also a Fairfax by marriage and whose brother Thomas was on the Council.[90] John Rushworth, still close to Fairfax, seems to have been working almost full-time at some periods for the Craven cause.[91] Local interests could be brought into play; among the tellers for Craven in various divisions were both of the knights of the shire for Berkshire, the Earl of Pembroke, and Henry Marten.[92] Another useful parliamentary ally was Walter Strickland, who may have met Craven on his diplomatic missions to the Netherlands and was certainly given a petition on his behalf from the States General, which Parliament refused to accept. It was Strickland who brought in one of Craven's later petitions and who seconded Sir William's vain attempt to save Combe Abbey from the general disaster.[93] An unlikely supporter was Lord Grey of Groby, who was leasing Combe Abbey from the sequestrators and who, it can only be surmised, was reluctant to have to purchase it outright if it were to be confiscated.[94]

Thus, much of the force behind the Craven expropriation came from republicans like Bishop and Bradshaw who would lose their positions under the Protectorate, while the influences opposing it remained. It is this that enabled the issue to be kept alive and Maynard and Finch to present it to decision makers from time to time as an illegal act that ought to be reversed.

The main arena where the conflict was fought out, especially in the early years, and where decisions were made, was the committee rooms and the floor of the House of Commons. How did it resonate there?

The Commons votes on the Craven case in 1651–2 did not attract an unusually high level of interest. They varied in total between a bare quorum and a maximum of sixty-four, which reflected a normal daily attendance.[95] There is little to identify the members who supported Craven's expropriation. Among the tellers on that side, Sir Henry Mildmay was known as a zealous money raiser for the Commonwealth and had been associated in intelligence work with Thomas Scot.[96] None of the tellers figure among the later purchasers of Craven property (although some, of course, might have purchased through agents). Several, however, would be large-scale purchasers of other royalist lands and thus have a general interest. These included Sir John Trevor, Sir Peter Wentworth, and one of the greatest beneficiaries of the system, Sir Arthur Hesilrige.[97]

But it is the list of tellers *for* Craven and their calibre that show the significance being attributed to the matter. The House had voted on 22 June 1652 to have Craven's name on the list of delinquents, and it is remarkable that there should be another vote on 3 August, the day before the bill was to pass.

The tellers for Craven were Oliver Cromwell and Henry Marten. Marten was Craven's Berkshire neighbour and at that time was working closely with Cromwell.[98] The teller at the earlier vote, along with Sir Gilbert Pickering, was the younger Henry Vane, also then still of Cromwell's inner circle. Vane's father had had some association with Craven during his distinguished diplomatic career.[99] Nonetheless, the son's position was remarkable in that the money to be raised from the second batch of confiscations was in principle destined for the Navy, in which he had a special interest.[100] At the *post facto* vote in October, the tellers for Craven were the former ambassador Walter Strickland and Sir Richard Ingoldsby. Ingoldsby was a soldier and a Cromwell cousin.[101]

The context to the debates of early August 1652 was a decided worsening in the already strained relations between the Rump and its mainly military critics. 'Considerations' and 'propositions' for reform flowed in, to be quietly ignored or politely handed back.[102] The officers were meeting regularly, with Cromwell working to restrain their anger but unwilling to jeopardise his leadership over them.[103] An Army declaration would be brought into Parliament on 13 August. Among the points it made was that MPs could not be trusted with the control of public money and that this should be taken out of their hands. It was a remarkable feat of diplomacy on Cromwell's part that the House overlooked the insult and went through the motions of setting up a committee to consider the document.[104]

The various acts for the confiscation of royalist estates were a part of the rift. There could be little dissent on the principle of dispossessing royalist exiles of their property, yet the first name in the first expropriation act of July 1651 was not in this category. That position seems to have been allotted to the man whose inclusion was the most controversial, and to emphasize a victory of the civilian members over the military. Sir John Stawell, as a royalist commander, had surrendered to the Army on terms, and in expropriating him those terms were being defiantly ignored.[105] The Army's honour was at issue, not to mention the safety of the officers should the fortunes of war at some future time be reversed. Cromwell had been otherwise engaged in the summer of 1651, but a year later could see the case of Craven as a rerun of that of Stawell, equally provocative. The question of articles of surrender would remain an active one until the Protectorate, symbolising the authority of Parliament over the operational autonomy of the officers.[106]

There would be a third act in December 1652 affecting some hundreds of small proprietors that nagged at Cromwell's conscience. He would refer to it at some length in a speech to his first parliament, emphasizing the innocence of the victims and the Army's frustration at being outvoted. He described it as one of the 'miscarriages' that had led him to the dissolution of the Rump.[107] It was after this speech that the committee of November 1654 was set up to reconsider the Craven affair, and responsibility for Stawell's and certain other cases was soon added to its remit.

Maynard had managed to present the case as one where Craven's innocence was beyond doubt and where the only question was in what form, and at whose expense, restitution should be granted. The purchasers, he insisted, had bought in full knowledge of Faulconer's perjury and of Craven's petitions, and at their own risk. This was an endorsement of the Protector's view that the Rump politicians had been abusing their powers for personal enrichment. It met with enthusiastic agreement in the Craven camp. An anonymous Craven correspondent, whose letter was intercepted and transcribed by Thurloe's agents, described the purchasers as 'a kind of projectors, who have grown rich by the public losses' and who should not be reimbursed from public funds.[108]

To what extent were these strictures justified? Do the facts of the Craven case demonstrate corruption among the Commonwealth parliamentarians?

It is impossible to produce a complete list of the purchasers of Craven properties, since not all purchases were recorded and many were made through agents and attorneys, but easily available sources yield almost a hundred individual names. They include at least eight and possibly nine members of Parliament, although one or possibly two of these are of the Barebone's Parliament rather than the Rump. Most individuals are small purchasers, possibly tenants taking the opportunity of buying their freeholds, but sixteen can be identified as having made purchases worth over £1,000. Seven of these are members, six of them of the Rump.[109] The purchases of those seven men total almost £80,000. However, the picture is distorted by the fact that £42,000, by far the largest single sum, was paid for Combe Abbey by the unwilling Grey of Groby, who raised the money through a consortium with the establishment preacher Hugh Peters and a couple of City financiers.[110] Of the non-MPs, George Joyce, making use of his special mention in the Act of 4 August 1652, appears in the list with some £3,750 paid for East and West Enborne, and George Vaux, the Whitehall housekeeper who had somehow got into the magic circle of purchasers and speculators, raised £13,000 for Caversham Park and Lodge.[111] Among the government servants to benefit was Ralph Darnell, who had been registrar for Garland's committees. His reward was a clutch of manors in Shropshire as well as some useful rental property off the Strand to a value in excess of £4,000.[112]

If it was the case that members of the Rump Parliament had been conspiring to confiscate royalist estates for their own benefit, one might expect to find a high proportion of purchasers of such estates in Garland's committees preparing the lists. The committee formed in 1650 to work on the first act had eleven purchasers among its thirty-eight members (29 per cent), while that of 3 December 1651, which prepared the second act, was more focused with seventeen purchasers out of thirty (57 per cent).[113] These are high proportions, but need to be compared with those in the House as a whole. David Underdown suggests that roughly one hundred and eighty-five of the four hundred and seventy-one members of the Long Parliament survived Pride's Purge or returned afterwards.[114] Of these, he recorded 65 (35 per cent) as having bought royalist land. The proportion that bought other confiscated properties or leased sequestrated ones will have been higher.

The evidence therefore does not suggest that Craven was specially targeted because of specific estates coveted by individual members or their friends. The appetite for properties was a general one. What the numbers do show is that members who wanted it must have enjoyed preferential access to sales and probably expected such access as a perquisite. Joyce needed a special proviso to ensure his admission to the ranks of the purchasers. At best, there was an appearance of conflict of interest, and at worst confiscations were being decided for profit rather than policy. There does therefore seem to be a firm basis for the Army's strictures and for Maynard's rhetorical flourish.

VI

The campaign on behalf of Lord Craven was noteworthy for its sophisticated use of print. This took time to develop, and while the expropriation was being discussed in the summer of 1652, such publicity as there was went in the opposite direction. *The Faithful Scout* was a mid-market publication that showed a strong predilection for feats of arms, especially if they were English, and even when they were those of Prince Rupert or the adolescent Duke of York. With the Dutch war in progress, it became jingoistic. There do seem to have been some hesitant moves towards an alliance between the States and the King of Scots, but it was only the *Scout* that connected Lord Craven with this and described him as raising regiments of royalist exiles and taking high rank in the Dutch land army. There was even a hint that it was Craven money that financed the Dutch fleet.[115] The *Scout's* publisher, George Horton, also put out separates to the same effect.[116] The Craven camp was insisting throughout that their man was serving in Germany and not personally involved in the hostilities. Whether Horton's interest was spontaneous or prompted is now unknowable.

By the next year, Craven influence and, no doubt, money, were making themselves felt. When Faulconer was condemned at Westminster Hall, four newspapers printed lengthy reports in identical words, very much slanted to favour the prosecution, while two more had shorter edited versions of the same account.[117] They had been 'no doubt well-whispered unto', commented Bishop.[118] The parliamentary committee of late 1654 also favoured several newspapers with remarkably full accounts of its proceedings.[119] The pro-Craven impact these might have had was somewhat reduced by the later disclosure that one of Craven's legal team, 'one Read', had been smuggling guns and letters for a planned rising in London.[120]

The pamphlet war began soon after Faulconer's conviction in July 1653. It was opened by Anthony Craven with a long publication that would be used as a source and model for numerous shorter pamphlets in the following years.[121] It was dispassionate and low-key, pretending to an Olympian objectivity. It printed documents – affidavits, court proceedings, extracts from the Commons Journals that were not supposed to be publicly available. There were names and dates. It constructed the Craven case as a morality story; an innocent man cheated of his rights by Faulconer who acted from the malice of his nature, by

Bishop in his own interest (although in fact he was not a purchaser), and by a corrupt Parliament that cared nothing for natural justice. Bishop was forced to reply, a distraction he could certainly have done without in what must have been a difficult summer.[122] He fell into Craven's trap, attempting to justify both the now defunct Parliament and his own actions. The Parliament's decisions, he suggested, were not to be judged by its subjects, and nor were his when he acted under its orders. The basic fact that Craven's treason consisted of his being with the king at Breda, on serving him with bended knee, on taking responsibility for his current mistress and their bastard, on running errands in preparation for the journey to Scotland – this was lost amid the mass of peripheral detail. There was the damaging admission that the words about 'barbarous and inhumane rebels' had not been used or seen by Craven; they had allegedly come from the Breda agreement between the king and the Scots. A further pamphlet from Anthony Craven contemptuously demolished his arguments.[123]

By 1655, Bishop had returned to Bristol, become a Quaker, and plunged himself into the frenetic political conflicts that split the city. A personal enmity grew up between him and a local Presbyterian, Ralph Farmer. The Presbyterians, still dreaming of a restored monarchy under their control, had decided that Craven might be a man with whom they could do business.[124] Farmer dedicated one of his long and heavily sarcastic polemics to Craven, and gave considerable space to the confiscation and to Bishop's part in it.[125] He printed what he alleged to be Faulconer's deathbed confession, expressing remorse at his action and resentment that he had never received the reward he might have expected as 'discoverer' of Craven's treason. That reward had, of course, gone to George Joyce. Even more damaging to Bishop was Farmer's reopening of the Love case of 1651. Christopher Love had been a Presbyterian minister, executed, in spite of an intense campaign in his favour, for treasonous correspondence with the Scots. He insisted to the last that it was 'the forgeries and contrivances' of Bishop and Scot, as well as 'six or eight lines which I never said' inserted by Bishop into the report of his interrogation, that had ensured his condemnation and that of others.[126] The parallel with the Craven case was plain.

Once more, Bishop was on his back foot, and his response was unconvincing. But he does give a description of the unfortunate Faulconer's last years: friendless, penniless, mortally ill, vulnerable to attempts from both sides to get statements from him supporting their positions. He believed that even in prison he was being spied on and in danger of being murdered to ensure his silence.[127] No doubt his continued imprisonment suited both sides.

VII

The Craven case shows as under a microscope certain aspects of the political culture of Commonwealth England. The ruling establishment was split and cross-split on ideology, allegiance, and personal interest. George Joyce, a republican idealist, was venal. George Bishop, another such, was not. But George Bishop had an adequate salary and a brewery to go back to, while George

Joyce's army pay will hardly have been adequate for his immediate needs, and much less to give him and his family the social position to which they might reasonably have aspired. Many civilian MPs had given up financial opportunities elsewhere to serve the parliamentarian side in the civil war and the Commonwealth. They received no salary, but were heirs to a long-standing tradition where government servants derived their compensation from whatever opportunities their functions gave rise to.[128] Army officers might grudge, but they had their pay, however irregular.[129]

Personal honour demanded an answer in tones of injured self-righteousness to any criticism; it is this that prompted Bishop's pamphlets against Anthony Craven and Ralph Farmer and indeed Farmer's initial blast at Bishop. Corporate honour was equally motivating. The Army officers were on Craven's side because he was a fellow soldier properly loyal to the cause he served, that of Elizabeth and her family. The time might yet come when they, like the royalists at Breda, would be reduced to offering their swords for hire. The civilian members were against him because they saw him as undutiful to the Parliament and regime they felt he should be serving.

Again, the Craven case shows some of the weaknesses of a government cobbled together amid the stresses of the winter of 1648–9. One might speculate on what an able and determined man could have made of the presidency of the Council of State, especially when combined with the chairmanship of the Committee for Examinations. Perhaps fortunately, Bradshaw was not such a man. His inadequacy even in routine matters was presumably one of the reasons for the presidency becoming rotative in November 1651 and for John Thurloe being parachuted in as secretary early in 1652.

But what the case shows perhaps most clearly is the power and leverage of groups outside government. The Berkshire subcommissioners could drag their feet until the local religious radicals, prompted from the centre, mounted their coup. More important was the lobbying power of Craven's family and their allies. Money could buy newspaper space, repeated pamphlet publications, probably juries, and possibly votes in Commons divisions. Rushworth seems to have been acting for long periods as an agent for the Craven cause, and his services will not have come cheap. Nor would those of Craven's legal teams – Maynard, Finch, and their juniors.

The fact remains that the expropriation was not reversed until the Restoration. But the continuing controversy ensured that, until then, the values of the confiscated properties were reduced, and the titles to them uncertain. Had it been otherwise, their return to the rightful owner might, as in the case of many other expropriations, have been politically impossible.

Lord Craven's eventual success had little to do with his own efforts and abilities, which were limited, and much to do with the determination, the contacts, and above all the wealth of his maternal family, the Whitmores, and the influence of his paternal kin and his Fairfax in-laws in Yorkshire. But none of this would have helped him had his case not conveniently lodged in so many of the cracks that fissured the Commonwealth political world, adding to the stresses that were bursting it apart. The immoderate zeal of the republicans in the security apparatus in their defence of the Commonwealth made no distinction between royalists and Presbyterians, and prevented the latter from pursuing their peacemaking agenda. The Army saw an equally immoderate zeal on the part of many MPs for their personal enrichment, while the political agendas for which the soldiers had risked life and limb went by default. Soldiers, also – whatever the cause they served – shared a code of military honour that the civilian MPs refused to recognise. The choice of the three men whose restitution was decreed in the first days of the Restoration was not a random one: Bunce had worked in 1647 for a settlement with the king; Stawell was a soldier whose terms of surrender had been repudiated; and Craven was convincingly portrayed as a victim of greed and injustice. Craven's triumph came about by an intelligent reading of a political situation and an exploitation of the opportunities it brought.

Notes

1. H.E. Chesney, 'The Transference of Lands in England, 1640–1660', *TRHS*, 4th ser., 15 (1932), 181–210; J. Thirsk, 'The Sales of Royalist Land during the Interregnum', *EcHR*, 5 (1952), 188–207; J. Thirsk, 'The Restoration Land Settlement', *JMH*, 26 (1954), 315–28.
2. Blair Worden, *The Rump Parliament* (Cambridge, 1974), pp. 86–102; Clive Holmes, *Why Was Charles I Executed?* (2006), pp. 140–3.
3. 'Hamstead' and 'Hampstead' are alternative spellings. I follow Margaret Gelling, *Place-Names of Berkshire* (1974) II, 299, preferring the earlier usage.
4. Ian W. Archer, 'Sir William Craven', *ODNB*; Christopher Durston, 'Berkshire and Its County Gentry' (unpublished PhD thesis, University of Reading, 1977), I, 33.
5. Bodl., Craven deposit 69–70.
6. M.A. Green, rev. S.C. Lomas, *Elizabeth Queen of Bohemia* (1909), p. 286.
7. R. Malcolm Smuts, 'William Craven, earl of Craven', *ODNB*; Lisa Jardine, *Going Dutch: How England Plundered Holland's Glory* (New York, 2008), p. 191.
8. *The Correspondence of Elizabeth Stuart, Queen of Bohemia*, ed. Nadine Akkerman (2 vols, Oxford, 2011), II, 941; *CSPD*, 9 February 1642; *LJ*, 7 February 1642.
9. Anon., *To the Parliament of the Common-Wealth of England, Scotland, and Ireland. The Humble Peticion of Severall Well-Intentioned Persons Purchasers of the Estate of William Lord Craven* (1654) (Thomason 669.f.19[45]).
10. Jonathan Harlow, 'The Military Career of George Bishop', *Friends Historical Society Journal*, 61 (2009), 187–95.
11. *CP*, I, 340, 383.
12. *CSPD 1649–50*, 19 May, 19, 25, 29 December 1649; 7 January 1650.
13. *CSPD 1651*, 11 August 1651.
14. *CJ*, 1 April 1650; 12, 28 May 1652; R.L. Greaves and R. Zaller (eds.), *Biographical Dictionary of British Radicals of the Seventeenth Century* (3 vols, Brighton, 1982–4), III, 272.
15. *CJ*, 14 September 1650.
16. *CJ*, 26 November 1650; 13 January, 15 February 1651; G.E. Aylmer, *The State's Servants: The Civil Service of the English Republic 1649–1660* (1973), p. 21.
17. S.R. Gardiner (ed.), *Letters and Papers Illustrating the relations between Charles the Second and Scotland in 1650* (Scottish Historical Society, orig. ser., 17, 1894), p. 59.
18. *Ibid.*, pp. 77–80.
19. George Bishop, *A Rejoinder Consisting of Two Parts* (1658), pp. 15–26.

20 *CP*, I, xxiv–xxxi, 118–19.
21 [George Bishop], *The Lord Craven's Case* (1653), p 16 (E.1071[2]).
22 *CJ*, 6 April 1650.
23 *CSPD* 13 January 1651.
24 J. Nicholls (ed.), *Original Letters and Papers of State Addressed to Oliver Cromwell* (1743), pp. 33–4.
25 [Bishop], *The Lord Craven's Case*, pp. 13–14.
26 G.E. Aylmer, 'George Joyce', *ODNB*.
27 *CSPD* 6 February 1651.
28 Ralph Farmer, *The Imposter Dethron'd* (1658), pp. 87–91.
29 S.R. Gardiner (ed.), *The Constitutional Documents of the Puritan Revolution 1625–1660* (3rd edn, Oxford, 1906), pp. 388–91.
30 Anthony Craven, *A True and Perfect Narrative of the Several Proceedings in the Case Concerning the Lord Craven* (1653), p. 3 (E.1071[1]).
31 TNA, SP 23/14, fol. 6.
32 Farmer, *Imposter Dethron'd*, p. 92.
33 Aylmer, *The State's Servants*, p. 260.
34 *CSPD* 4 March 1651; Craven, *A True and Perfect Narrative*, p. 4.
35 *CJ*, 6 March 1651.
36 *CJ*, 12 June 1651.
37 *A&O*, II, 520–45.
38 *CCC*, II, 1617 (under 13 February 1651).
39 Manfred Brod, *The Case of Reading: Urban Governance in Troubled Times 1640–1690* (Peterborough, 2006), pp. 46–50, 60–5.
40 *CCC*, II, 1617 (under 16 April 1651).
41 Christopher Cheesman, *Berk-shires Agents Humble Address to the Honourable Commissioners for Compounding* (1651), esp. p. 1 (E.636[6]).
42 *CCC*, I, 517, 524, 527, 672, 479, 682. I thank Dr Jonathan Harlow for unpublished information on Bishop's family relationships.
43 Christopher Durston, 'Henry Marten and the High Shoon of Berkshire', *Berkshire Archaeological Journal*, 70 (1979–80), 87–95; J.M. Guilding, *Reading Records: Diary of the Corporation* (4 vols, 1892–6), IV, 300.
44 *CJ*, 26 November 1651, 3 December 1651.
45 Craven, *A True and Perfect Narrative*, pp. 7–10.
46 *CJ*, 22 June 1652.
47 Craven, *A True and Perfect Narrative*, 'To the Reader'.
48 *Ibid.*, p. 13.
49 *Ibid.*, p. 16.
50 [Bishop], *The Lord Craven's Case*, pp. 6–7, 29. On Lenthall: Aylmer, *The State's Servants*, p. 163; John Lilburne, *Englands Birth-Right Justified* (1645), p. 28 (E.304[17]).
51 Craven, *A True and Perfect Narrative*, p. 17.
52 *CJ*, 3, 4 August 1652; *A&O*, II, 591–8.
53 *CJ*, 29 October 1652; Craven, *A True and Perfect Narrative*, pp. 21–3.
54 [Anthony Craven], *A Reply to a Certain Pamphlet Written by an Unknowing and Unknown Author* (1653), pp. 22–3 (E.1071[3]); TNA, C 54, *passim*.
55 [Bishop], *The Lord Craven's Case*, pp. 6–7.
56 Craven, *A True and Perfect Narrative*, pp. 36–8.
57 *CSPD* 10, 30 June, 7, 8 July, 6, 12 September 1653.
58 *Weekly Post*, no. 205 (21–28 November 1654) p. 1652 (E.236[27]).
59 *CCSP*, II, 254, 260 (16 September, 9 October 1653).
60 Bodl., Craven deposit 152.
61 Anon., *To the Parliament of the Common-Wealth of England, Scotland, and Ireland* (1654).
62 *CCSP*, II, 212 (27 May 1653).

63 *TSP*, I, 467: Sir Robert Stone to Sir Walter Vane, The Hague, 19 September 1653 (NS); A. Woolrych, *Commonwealth to Protectorate* (Oxford, 1982), pp. 302–4.
64 *TSP*, II, 139–40: Elizabeth Queen of Bohemia to Henry Lawrence, President of the Council of State, Heidelberg, 4/14 March 1654.
65 *CCC*, p. 1618.
66 *CJ*, 3 November 1654.
67 *Mercurius Politicus*, 9–16 November 1654, pp. 4013–14 (E.817[7]); 16–23 November 1654, p. 4038 (E.817[15]); 11–18 January 1655, pp. 5056–9 (E.825[4]); 18–25 January 1655, pp. 5073–4 (E.826[7]); *Perfect Diurnall*, 6–13 November 1654, pp. 3945–6 (E.236[18]); 27 November–4 December 1654, p. 3987 (E.236[31]); 25 December 1654–1 January 1655, pp. 4053–4; *Weekly Post*, 31 October–7 November 1654, p. 1625 (E.236[14]); 14–21 November 1654, p. 1645 (E.817[12]); 21–8 November 1654, p. 1652 (E.236[27]); 26 December 1654–2 January 1655, pp. 4058–9 (E.237[14]); 2–9 January 1655, p. 1660 (E.237[21]); 9–16 January 1655, pp. 1668–9 (E.237[26]); 16–23 January 1655, pp. 1667–9 (E.479[6]); 30–1 January 1655 (sic), pp. 1674–6 (E.479[13]).
68 *Burton*, II, 26 May 1657.
69 *Ibid.*, IV, 11 April 1659.
70 Godfrey Davies, *The Restoration of Charles II 1658–1660* (Oxford, 1955), p. 127.
71 *TSP*, VII, 665: Lord Craven to Secretary Thurloe, Gravesend, 27 April 1659.
72 *CCSP*, IV, 302 (? July 1659), 314 (6 August 1659).
73 Anon., *The Lord Craven's Case: Considerations Humbly Offered* . . . (1659); Anon., *An Answer to a Printed Paper Called the Lord Craven's Case* (1659); Anon., *The Lord Craven's Case* (1660).
74 Bodl., Craven deposit 152.
75 *CJ*, 9 September 1659.
76 *LJ*, 27 April 1660.
77 *CCSP*, V, 10 (4 May 1660).
78 *LJ*, 6 June 1660. On Bunce, see Keith Lindley and David Scott (eds.), *The Journals of Thomas Juxon, 1644–1647* (Camden Society, 5th series, 13, 1999), p. 162; *CJ*, 23 October and 25 December 1649.
79 *LJ*, 23, 26 June 1660.
80 On Margaret Broughton, later Lady Craven, see *CSPD 1661–2*, 25 February 1662; *CTB 1660–7*, 5 June 1662; *CTB 1676–9*, 31 May, 6 July 1676, 23 June 1677.
81 Smuts, 'Craven', *ODNB*.
82 *CSPD 1651*, 30 April 1651.
83 Nicholls (ed.), *Original Letters*, pp. 49–51.
84 Aylmer, 'Joyce', *ODNB*; C.V. Wedgwood, *The Trial of Charles I* (1964) p. 184; William Houlbrook, *A Black-Smith and No Jesuite* (1660) (E.2138[2]); HMC, *Seventh Report*, Appendix 1, p. 109; *CCSP*, IV, 300 (30 July 1659).
85 S.R. Gardiner, *History of the Commonwealth and Protectorate 1649–1656* (4 vols, 1903), III, 228–9; on Vernon: Greaves and Zaller (eds.), *Biographical Dictionary*, III, 272.
86 TNA, SP 23/14 fol. 46v.
87 *VCH Berkshire*, III, 174.
88 *Ibid.*, IV, 312.
89 *CJ*, 22 June 1652.
90 David Scott, 'James Chaloner', *ODNB*.
91 Craven, *A True and Perfect Narrative*, p. 9.
92 *CJ*, 12 June 1651, 3 August 1652.
93 *CJ*, 29 October 1652; Craven, *A True and Perfect Narrative*, pp. 19–21; [Bishop], *The Lord Craven's Case*, pp. 2–4; [Anthony Craven], *A reply*, pp. 17–20.
94 J. Richards, *Aristocrat and Regicide: The Life and Times of Thomas, Lord Grey of Groby* (2000), pp. 366–7; TNA, C 54/3705/7; *LJ*, 4 June 1660.
95 David L. Smith, *The Stuart Parliaments 1603–1689* (1999), p. 136.
96 *CJ*, 3 August 1652; J.T. Peacey, 'Henry Mildmay', *ODNB*.

97 Wentworth on 22 June 1652, Trevor on 29 October 1652, Hesilrige on 12 June 1651 and 22 June 1652.
98 C.M. Williams, 'The Political Career of Henry Marten with Particular Relation to the Origins of Republicanism in the Long Parliament' (unpublished DPhil thesis, University of Oxford, 1954), p. 469; Sarah Barber, 'Henry Marten', *ODNB*.
99 Green, *Elizabeth of Bohemia*, p. 286.
100 Ruth E. Mayers, 'Sir Henry Vane, the younger', *ODNB*.
101 Timothy Venning, 'Sir Richard Ingoldsby', *ODNB*.
102 *The Faithful Scout*, 2–9 July 1652, p. 605 (E.795[34]); 23–30 July 1652, pp. 626–7 (E.796[8]); 6–13 August 1652, p. 641 (E.796[17]); *The Weekly Intelligencer*, 27 July–3 August 1652, pp. 541–2 (E.673[3]); *Perfect Account* 21–8 July 1652, pp. 653–4 (E.672[3]); Bulstrode Whitelocke, *Memorials of the English Affairs* (Oxford, 1682), p. 512.
103 Blair Worden, *The Rump Parliament* (Cambridge, 1974), pp. 306–8.
104 *CJ*, 13 August 1652; *Mercurius Politicus*, 12–19 August 1652, p. 1803 (E.674[6]).
105 Sean Kelsey, *Inventing a Republic: The Political Culture of the English Commonwealth 1649–1653* (Manchester, 1997), pp. 131–2.
106 Worden, *Rump Parliament*, p. 284; Woolrych, *Commonwealth to Protectorate*, p. 38.
107 *The Letters and Speeches of Oliver Cromwell*, ed. Thomas Carlyle and S.C. Lomas (3 vols, 1904), II, 368 (13 September 1654).
108 Bodl., MS Rawlinson A 7, fols 146–9.
109 From TNA, C 54: Carew Raleigh £8,800, Thomas Mackworth, £7,700, Nicholas Love £2,700, Grey of Groby, £42,000, Sir Michael Livesey £5,400, William Cawley £4,600, John Hildersley £8,100 (all to the nearest £100).
110 TNA, C 54/3705/7.
111 TNA, C 54/3747/10, 3743/33, 3702/2; *CCC*, pp. 1616–26.
112 *CJ*, 30 December 1656; TNA, SP 23/18 ff. 826v, 931v (23 and 24 March 1653, 19 November 1653); C 54/3897/27. See also TNA, C 54/3715/31.
113 I have included cases where it is unclear whether the purchaser is the committee member himself or a brother or father/son.
114 David Underdown, *Pride's Purge: Politics in the Puritan Revolution* (Oxford, 1971), Chapter VIII. The total of 185 emerges from his table on p. 220 and his statement that 'at least' 31 members categorised as 'abstainers' eventually returned to the House.
115 *The Faithful Scout*, 25 June–2 July 1652, pp. 592, 593, 597 (E.795[30]); 2–9 July 1652, p. 600 (E.795[34]).
116 Anon., *A Great and Terrible Fight in France* (1652), p. 6 (E.681[8]); Anon., *The Declaration and Message Sent from the Queen of Bohemiah, Lord Craven, Lord Goring, and Divers Other English gentlemen* (1652); Anon., *The Declaration of the States of Holland, Concerning the King of Scots* (1653), p. 5 (E.701[7]).
117 The full accounts are in *Several Proceedings of State Affaires*, 19–26 May 1653 (E.213[19]); *A Perfect Account of the Daily Intelligence*, 18–25 May 1653 (E.698[3]); *The Moderate Publisher of Every Daies Intelligence*, 20–7 May 1653 (E.213[21]); *A Perfect Diurnall of Some Passages and Proceedings*, 16–23 May 1653 (E.213[18]). The shorter articles are in *The Armies Scout*, 20–7 May 1653 (E.213[22]) and *The Weekly Intelligencer of the Commonwealth*, 24–31 May 1653 (E.698[10]).
118 [Bishop], *Lord Craven's Case*, p. 2.
119 See n. 67.
120 *Mercurius Politicus*, 1–8 February 1655, p. 5100 (E.826[23]); 8–15 February 1655, p. 5132 (E826[28]); *Perfect Diurnall*, 12–19 February 1655, p. 4157 (E.479[22]); *Weekly Post*, 6–13 February 1655, p. 1694 (E.479[23]).
121 Craven, *A True and Perfect Narrative*.
122 [Bishop], *The Lord Craven's Case*.
123 *Ibid.*, *A Reply to a Certain Pamphlet*.
124 *CCSP*, II, 211–12 (27 May 1653).
125 Farmer, *The Imposter Dethron'd*, esp. pp. 66–105.

126 Christopher Love, *A Cleare and Necessary Vindication of the Principles and Practices of me Christopher Love* (1651), p. 39; Farmer, *The Imposter Dethron'd*, pp. 111–14.
127 Bishop, *A Rejoinder*, pp. 15–23.
128 G.E. Aylmer, *The King's Servants: The Civil Service of Charles I, 1625–42* (1961), pp. 160–81.
129 Aylmer, *State's Servants*, pp. 106–11.

8 The definition of treason and the offer of the crown

Jonathan Fitzgibbons

For Clive Holmes the key question of the 'kingship crisis' of 1657 is not why did Cromwell refuse the crown, but why was he offered it in the first place? His answer – that those behind the offer believed the royal title was the 'integument' of the English constitution – is a powerful one.[1] In their conferences with Cromwell, MPs stressed repeatedly the antiquity of the kingly title; it was 'known' to the law. Yet, as Clive has also shown on numerous occasions, the nature of the English constitution was itself contested. Appeals to its timelessness veiled its evolutionary nature. As such, even if those who offered Cromwell the kingship did so to safeguard the English constitution, it is worth asking what they understood that constitution to include and how this had developed in light of the experience of the events of the 1640s? MPs urged Cromwell to be king, but what precisely did they understand that title and office to mean? These issues can be illuminated by a discussion of treason and its shifting definition in the mid-seventeenth century.

On the eve of the civil war, the law of treason was a blend of Roman law and feudal concepts: a crime against both the monarch's person and their body politic. This reflected and entrenched the early modern theory of the king's two bodies: the notion that the king's mortal person and his immortal body politic were distinct but inseparable. Any design against the king's person was, inherently, a design against the body politic and vice versa. While late Tudor and early Stuart theorists could conceive of the 'state' as a corporate entity, it remained inextricably joined or entailed to the king. Throughout the 1640s, however, as Parliament defended its actions and exactions, a fully impersonal conception of the body politic emerged in which the king was assigned the subordinate role of a chief magistrate, an officer of state elected to govern in the people's interests. This mental separation of the king's two bodies provided the juristic foundations for the trial of Charles I in 1649. Treason was defined as a crime against the 'state', whose sovereign authority derived from the people represented in Parliament by the House of Commons.[2]

This chapter assesses how far these trends continued into the Protectorate. Specifically, it examines whether the return of government with a single person marked a retreat from notions of the impersonal 'state' embodied by the people. It has become commonplace to see the protectoral judges and lawyers as monarchical cuckoos in the Cromwellian nest. Alan Cromartie has suggested that their insistence upon the common law hastened the collapse of the Interregnum and ensured that the restoration of monarchy was the ineluctable outcome. The post-regicide regimes 'appealed to law, but the law recommended monarchical rule'; they were 'loyal to standards that only a kingdom could meet'.[3] In the Restoration era there was reason enough for the former protectoral judges and lawyers to stress their preference for monarchical forms of government. More must be done, however, to recover their political outlooks as they stood in the 1650s. By studying their handling of treason trials during this period, it is possible to learn a great deal about their attitudes towards sovereignty, kingship and the law itself – and, more importantly, explain why many of those same lawyers and judges urged Cromwell to accept the crown.

I

In his 1656 critique of the Protectorate, *The Excellencie of a Free State*, Marchamont Nedham claimed it was ever the practice of kings to usurp 'the power of creating Judges . . . to create such, as would make the Laws speak in Favour of them, upon any occasion'.[4] The parallel with the Protectorate was obvious: as Lord Protector, Oliver Cromwell filled the bench with men of his choosing.[5] But even though there were some timeservers among them, such as the Lord Commissioner of the Great Seal John Lisle, not all of his choices were ciphers to the Cromwellian interest.[6] Writing after the Restoration, even Cromwell's inveterate critic James Heath conceded that he supplied the benches 'with the ablest of the Lawyers' including Matthew Hale, Hugh Wyndham and Richard Newdigate – all of whom later found employment under Charles II.[7]

Yet we must not be fooled into thinking that the only scrupulous judges were those who longed for monarchical forms of government or who, later in the (dis)comfort of the Restoration period, declared themselves closet royalists all along. Clearly some believed kingless government was incompatible with the rule of law. Of the fifteen judges serving in late 1648, only eight accepted new commissions under the post-regicide regime the following year.[8] But those who continued should not be labelled weathercocks in comparison to those 'principled' judges who did not. Even those who accepted the Rump's commissions refused to serve until that Parliament first declared its commitment to the 'Maintenance of the fundamental Laws of this Nation'.[9] Their concern for the rule of law did not mean they yearned for monarchical forms of government, however. Their thinking was exemplified by Francis Thorpe, then a serjeant at law, and soon after a baron of the Exchequer, when delivering his charge to the grand jury at the York Assizes in March 1649. Thorpe was clear that the 'People (under God)' were 'the Originall of all just Power'. They could 'let the Government run out into what Forme it will, Monarchy, Aristocracy, or Democracy, yet still the Originall Fountain thereof is from the consent and agreement of the People'. Kings were not lawgivers but officers of state, appointed by the people and accountable for their misgovernment when they transgressed those 'Lawes by which the people did agree they would be governed'.[10] Thorpe thought it better to 'keep the Crowne within its proper place' and 'to allow the Law only to King it among the people'; henceforth, the people's 'Representatives' would be 'the only Keepers of their owne Liberties by Authority derived from their owne Supreme and Soveraigne power'.[11] In short, the rule of common law did not necessitate kingly forms of government, but it made essential government grounded upon the people.

During the 1650s, however, the judges struggled to square this reverence for popular sovereignty with the realities of those regimes they served. While the Rump, purged of a significant portion of its membership, was hardly representative, its expulsion in April 1653 and the subsequent establishment of the Protectorate stretched beyond credulity claims that the government was founded upon popular consent. Not only was the *Instrument of Government* the work of a military junto, but it established government with a single person who claimed a negative voice over the people's representatives. Even more disturbing for those who believed the people should be governed by the laws that they themselves had made, the *Instrument* allowed the Protector and his Council a temporary extra-parliamentary legislative power to 'make laws and ordinances' to be 'binding and in force, until order shall be taken in Parliament concerning the same'.[12]

Little wonder many of the judges greeted the creation of the Protectorate with only qualified acceptance. A glimpse into their thinking is provided by the journal of the Lord Commissioner of the Great Seal Bulstrode Whitelocke, who was on embassy in Sweden at the time of Cromwell's inauguration. When asked by the Swedish Chancellor Axel Oxenstierna about that 'great alteration' in England, which seemed to be 'setting up another Monarchy', Whitelocke stressed that – as far as he was concerned – there had been no change at all. The 'Government remains the same still as it was before in a Commonwealth', he explained: the Protector was simply 'the Head or Chiefe Magistrate of that Commonwealth' and the 'Lawes continue the same still'. In Whitelocke's opinion, the 'limited power of a chiefe magistrate' made that office 'lawfull & tollerable'; the Protector was bound 'by the Law & by his Oath'. But he also recognised that those 'bridles of Tyranny' were worthless unless Cromwell received parliamentary approbation 'of his being Protector'.[13] Like Thorpe, Whitelocke's thinking was clear: only government founded on popular consent could secure the rule of law. Until then the Protectorate was on probation: he turned a blind eye to its origins on the expectation that the regime would, sooner rather than later, receive parliamentary assent.

The meeting of the first Protectorate Parliament in September 1654 was therefore a crucial juncture. Discussion in its opening days inevitably centred upon the Protector's powers and their origins. According to the Parliament's diarist, Guybon Goddard, it was 'agreed' by the 'judges, Commissioners of the Seal, and generally, by all the Long Robe' that properly 'the legislative power was in the House of Commons, in Parliament alone'. It was apparently not only the republican MPs who believed that failure to settle the government upon the people represented in Parliament would mean that all who served the parliamentarian cause since 1642 'were the greatest and most infamous regicides and murtherers and villains in the world'.[14] Among the most notable critics of the *Instrument* was Justice of the Common Pleas and MP for Gloucester Matthew Hale. According to Goddard, Hale moved that the single person should be placed firmly and unambiguously under Parliament's control: the government should 'be in the Parliament and a single person, limited and restrained as the Parliament should think fit'.[15] Hale was not demanding kingship: he was happy to allow Cromwell his existing title of Lord Protector, provided it was settled by Parliament.

When, despite the Protector's reprimands, MPs pressed on with their plans to rewrite the *Instrument* and settle the Protectorate upon Parliament, Cromwell dissolved them angrily on 22 January 1655. Thereafter, a number of confrontations between the Protector and the bench followed. Having relied so long on the judges' good credit, many now declared the regime legally bankrupt. Particularly contentious was the status of the extra-parliamentary ordinances. When the merchant George Cony was put on trial in May 1655 for refusing to pay customs, his counsel stressed that taxation could be collected only by parliamentary consent. Cony's lawyers were duly interrogated by the Council and sent to the Tower for 'using words tending to sedition, and the subversion of the present government'.[16] Even worse for the authorities, however, Lord Chief Justice Henry Rolle, proved sympathetic to Cony's plight and resigned his place rather than give a verdict in the case.[17] At the same time there was also confrontation between Cromwell and the officers of the Court of Chancery, who refused to execute an ordinance from the previous August for reforming the court's proceedings. Whitelocke, for one, claimed his 'judgement & conscience' would not allow him to accept that 'which he knew to be no law, butt an exorbitant power'.[18] For their continued resistance, both Whitelocke and his fellow lord commissioner Widdrington were duly 'putt out of their places'.[19]

Equally controversial was the Treason Ordinance. Passed by Cromwell and the Council in January 1654, it deemed guilty any who claimed that 'the Lord Protector and the people in Parliament assembled are not the Supreme Authority of this Commonwealth' or that 'the said Authority or Government is Tyrannical, usurped, or unlawful'. By its very nature this ordinance exuded Cromwell's personal authority and eschewed a wholly depersonalised conception of treason. It was in stark contrast to the Rump Parliament's Treason Act of 1649, which declared it treasonous to deny that 'the Commons in Parliament assembled' alone were 'not the Supreme authority of this Nation'.[20] In the protectoral ordinance, treason was once again a supra-personal crime: it was treason to 'compass or imagine the death of the Lord Protector'; also guilty were any who should 'plot, contrive or endeavour to stir up or raise force against the Protector or the present Government, or for the subversion or alteration of the same'. Other crimes that fell within the ordinance's purview were attempting to 'stir up Mutiny' in the Army, inviting a foreign invasion, and proclaiming Charles Stuart or his relations to be 'King or Chief Magistrate'. The ordinance was supposedly omnicompetent: 'no other Matter, Fact, Crime or Offence whatsover' than those 'herein mentioned' was to be adjudged High Treason, 'any Law, Statute, Act, or Ordinance to the contrary in any wise notwithstanding'.[21]

Even before the first Protectorate Parliament failed to ratify this ordinance, however, some judges showed their misgivings. When a plot to assassinate Cromwell was discovered in June 1654, the Protector and Council issued an ordinance establishing a High Court of Justice to try the accused according to the provisions of the Treason Ordinance.[22] Heading the list of commissioners were representatives of all four Westminster Courts, with John Lisle serving as the court's president.[23] But at least one of those judges, Edward Atkins, refused to serve outright, claiming it was illegal to proceed by a High Court of Justice, for 'by the lawes, noe man indicted for treason but ought to be tryed by a jury'.[24]

Procedural scruples aside, however, even those who served the High Court were reluctant to act upon the Treason Ordinance. True, the indictment was couched in terms that echoed the ordinance: the prisoners were accused of joining in a 'traiterous Design to have murdered his Highness the Lord Protector', of planning to proclaim Charles Stuart king and plotting to involve the 'Nation in a bloody war'.[25] Yet, as Protector's Serjeant-at-Law John Glynne explained, '[T]o kill the supreme magistrate was treason to the common law of England'.[26] Even if the Treason Ordinance were 'not in being', the 'Laws of old of Treason against the King' were 'of force'. Whenever those former laws named a 'King', Glynne clarified, it merely meant the 'Supream Governor' regardless of what title that individual happened to have.[27] When delivering the court's verdict, Lisle reiterated the point that to 'compasse the death of the supreme magistrate of this nation, whether called by the name of king, queene, or what name soever, is treason'. This was 'by the common law of England' and 'declared soe' not just by 'a late law' but also 'by the Sta[tute] of 25 Ed: 3d and by severall lawes made since'.[28] Far from defending the Treason Ordinance, Glynne and Lisle rendered it unnecessary. Whereas the ordinance declared that only matters contained therein were treasonous – notwithstanding any previous 'Law, Statute, Act, or Ordinance' – the officers of the High Court claimed that ordinance merely expounded previous treason legislation and general common law principles.

The dissolution of the first Protectorate Parliament only complicated matters further. Not only did it leave the status of the Treason Ordinance less certain than before, but the Protector and Council no longer had the legislative power to establish a new High Court to execute it. It was in the context of this constitutional quagmire, and partly because of it, that a series of royalist risings occurred in the spring of 1655. The most serious of these began in Salisbury in the early hours of 12 March 1655 when Lord Chief Justice Rolle and Baron of the Exchequer Robert Nicholas, then riding the western circuit, were seized in their beds and threatened with violence. This rising, known to posterity as Penruddock's Rising, subsequently saw a force of a few hundred men march in arms through Wiltshire, Somerset, and Dorset before being routed in Devon.[29]

More problematic for the government than quelling the rising was dealing with those arrested. Unable to erect a new High Court by ordinance, the Protector and Council instead issued commissions of oyer and terminer and gaol delivery to tour the western counties, thereby grounding proceedings firmly upon the common law. They also ensured that at least one judge from each of the four Westminster Courts was named a commissioner.[30]

These judges met with members of the protectoral counsel at Salisbury on 12 April to frame the indictment. Attorney-General Edmund Prideaux, tasked with leading the prosecution, brought from London a draft for their consideration.[31] Despite the failure of the first Protectorate Parliament, this proposed indictment was grounded upon the Treason Ordinance and boiled down to three main charges: levying war, compassing the death of the Lord Protector, and proclaiming Charles Stuart to be king.[32] According to Prideaux, however, the commissioners were unwilling to proceed upon these terms. Rather, after 'a pretty long debate', it was decided that the indictment should 'bee only for leavying of warre'.[33] Prideaux and Glynne were tight-lipped in their correspondence to Thurloe about the reasons for streamlining the indictment, thinking the matter too delicate to consign to a letter.[34]

As in 1654, the judges were reluctant to ground their proceedings upon the Treason Ordinance. The revised indictment charged the rebels with the 'violation and contempt of the laws of England' and acting 'against the force of the statute in such case made and provided'.[35] But what exactly was this statute? As Glynne explained to Thurloe, the decision was taken to proceed only upon the charge of 'leavyeing of warre against the lord protector and the government' because this was 'a treason by the fundamentall lawe of the land' or, as Prideaux put it, 'treason by all lawes'.[36] As in 1654, they argued that the Treason Ordinance simply embodied principles derived from previous statutes and the common law. By this logic, the proceedings were based upon the letter of the Treason Ordinance but, equally, need not derive authority from it.[37]

These arguments spiked the guns of the defendants. Among the *Thurloe State Papers* is a document, composed on behalf of the prisoners to be tried at Exeter, detailing thirty-five objections that they planned to raise in court.[38] Aside from a number of familiar tactics to frustrate proceedings, their main line of defence rested on the legality of the indictment: it was 'neither grounded on the common law, nor statute; and the judges are sworn to execute only the laws' (point 5). They clearly expected the indictment would be based upon the 1654 ordinance: legislation must have parliamentary approval, they claimed, there could 'be no treason by an ordinance' (points 22–23). If, however, the judges claimed that the prisoners were indicted upon the statute '25 Edw. III for levying war against the king', they would 'demand that statute be read' and remind the jury 'how all kingly government and authority was abolished by the act 1649' (point 35). With some irony, the royalist prisoners invoked the legality and continued applicability of the 1649 Act abolishing kingship in order to challenge the proceedings against them.

No official record of the trial at Exeter survives, but a printed account, purportedly written by Penruddock shortly before his execution, suggests that he followed the prisoners' plan meticulously. He opened by requesting that 'Councell' be assigned to 'dispute the illegality' of the indictment.[39] After being coerced into entering a plea, he then 'challenged about 24 of the 35' jurors and demanded a copy of his indictment, but to no avail.[40] With these procedural tactics exhausted, he then shifted to the crux of the prisoners' defence: that 'there can be no high Treason in this Nation, but it must be grounded upon the Common, or the Statute law'. As this indictment was based upon neither, 'ergo no treason'.[41] Looking upon the indictment, Penruddock pointed to the part that declared him guilty of 'High Treason by vertue of a Statute in that case made and provided': he demanded that 'it be read; I know none such'.[42]

According to Penruddock, Prideaux answered this objection by stating that the jury should be satisfied with 'what hath been already said', but in his account little had been said.[43] In reality, it seems the judges presiding over the trials had already provided assurances that their proceedings were not based solely upon the 1654 ordinance. When delivering the charge to the grand jury at Salisbury, for instance, Justice of the Common Pleas Hugh Wyndham emphasized that 'by the common law, and the statute laws both ancient and moderne', it 'was adjudged treason to leavy warre against the chiefe magistrate'.[44] At Exeter, the grand jury questioned the 'bills of high treason', particularly 'the statute laws, against which the offence is alleaged to bee committed' and how 'they could bee meant of his highnesse the lord protector'. In reply, Glynne, who presided over the trial, did 'very learnedly and fully' explain that 'by the statute 25 Edw. III and the common law, the levying warre against the chief officer of the commonwealth (lett the name be whatsoever) was high treason, and by the word 'king' in that statute must be meant the chief office (and the beareing of that office)'. After this eloquent defence, the jury 'were quicklie satisfied'.[45]

The prisoners' tactics failed because the judges shared their misgivings and anticipated them. Little wonder Penruddock moved quickly from criticism of the Treason Ordinance to pursue other avenues. In particular, he 'urged divers cases to make the businesse but a Riot'.[46] The prisoners' plan made clear that they would raise the question of what precisely constituted 'levying war'; they would claim their 'bearing of arms' was 'only a riot or unlawful assembly'.[47] Penruddock's recourse to such arguments, however, shows his failure to sway the court over the protectoral definition of treason. These arguments would be 'insisted on' only if the 'grand point in law be overuled by the court'; in this war of judicial attrition they must only 'lose ground by inches'.[48] But Penruddock, finding that his objections about the Treason Ordinance were failing to hit their mark, fell back quickly.

So many factors ensured these trials ended with convictions, but few were novel to the period. Most obviously, it required vigorous leadership from those presiding. As one of the commissioners at Salisbury noted, had it 'not ben for the zeale' of Lisle, Steele, and Glynne, he believed 'not a man had been condemned'.[49] The juries were also carefully appointed. At Salisbury, none were returned but those 'of the honest well-affected party to his highness and the present government'.[50] At Exeter, Prideaux commended the jurors for being 'very well affected, and willinge to dispatche the cavaliers'.[51]

As important, however, was securing sufficient evidence. It was arguably this problem, and not simply misgivings about the Treason Ordinance, that compelled the commissioners to frame the indictment around the single point of levying war. Demonstrating the rebels' warlike actions was relatively straightforward: plenty of people saw them in arms as they passed through the western counties.[52] Of course, as the rebels knew well enough, it was more difficult to prove their treasonous intentions, to show that they were guilty of more than a mere riot. As Prideaux explained to Thurloe, such considerations meant they were necessitated 'to respite proceedings against some prisoners' whose evidence was essential for proving the 'rebellious action' of 'the most active persons': they had to resort to 'plowing with theire owne heyfars'.[53]

But even if the charge of levying war was a convenient means to focus proceedings, it is still intriguing that the commissioners were unwilling to pursue the attendant charge of compassing the death of the Lord Protector. After all, the same logic that led the judges and lawyers to construct treason upon the 1352 Statute as a levying of war should have allowed them to construct it as the compassing of the Protector's death – just as a number of them previously had done when serving the High Court in 1654.

In fact, by focusing upon the charge of levying war, the judges made a clear statement about their attitude towards the single person, whether or not they happened to be called king or Lord Protector. It reflected those definitions of sovereignty offered by the Parliament's apologists during the 1640s that allowed the mental separation of the king's once inseparable two bodies. The king became a chief officer empowered by the people; his body politic was not his own but was held in trust. As the body politic was not inherently or inseparably in the single person, it was no longer logical for the levying of war *ipso facto* also to mean compassing the death of the single person: the one no longer led inexorably to the other. As such, it seems that only when there was clear evidence of direct involvement in a plot to assassinate Cromwell, as in 1654, were the judges prepared to proceed upon the point of compassing the Lord Protector's death.[54] When evidence of a direct threat to the Protector's life was wanting, however, they preferred to define treason primarily as a crime against the people or Commonwealth, the real locus of sovereign authority. Even when those presiding over the trials spoke of levying war *against the single person*, what they really meant was a crime against *those who empowered him*. As Wyndham and Glynne explained to the grand juries, treason meant levying war against the 'chiefe magistrate' or 'chief officer of the commonwealth'. Their reasoning was not dissimilar to Thorpe's claim in his charge to the York grand jury in 1649 that 'king' really meant nothing more than the 'publique Interest of the People', albeit they now substituted Lord Protector for king.[55]

The judges evaded the issue of Cromwell's personal authority and defined treason in its broadest, impersonal, sense as a crime against the people or 'state'.

It was not simply the case that the judges were 'happy to defend the Lord Protector, so long as he confined himself to acting as a king'.[56] Rather they served the regime, provided its foundations were understood to be parliamentary: governed by the laws that the people themselves had made. They argued that a 'Lord Protector' was synonymous with a 'king', but what they took to be a 'king' was shaped by their experiences of the 1640s. It meant nothing more than a chief magistrate whose powers derived from the people, the real source of sovereign power. By ignoring the Treason Ordinance and instead applying the 1352 Treason Statute to the Lord Protector, the judges were not 'hastening the moment when he took the royal crown': they were drawing conspicuous attention to the *Instrument of Government*'s lack of popular (or, more properly, parliamentary) approbation.[57]

But even though the manner of the trials in the western counties implicitly criticised the Protectorate, this did not mean the judges were unwilling to proceed against the royalists. In fact, the focused effort of the trials, grounded upon the attenuated indictment, yielded a high conviction rate. Of the ten men indicted by the Salisbury grand jury for 'Treason in levying war', one confessed the fact and a further six were found guilty.[58] At Exeter, with Glynne presiding, the figures were more impressive: of twenty-nine men indicted by the grand jury, five confessed the fact and a further twenty-one were found guilty.[59] The precise number indicted for treason at Chard is unknown, but sources suggest five or six people were convicted.[60] Even though examples were made of the most prominent offenders, however, many remained imprisoned without trial. One report claimed there were one hundred and five prisoners still languishing in Exeter gaol after the commissioners moved on.[61] But this reflected more the lack of clear evidence than any unwillingness among the judges to try the rebels. Not that such legal niceties bothered Cromwell: he subsequently commanded that all those rebels tried at Exeter – including 'those acquitted' as well as 'those not tryed, and those condemned' – should be kept in prison 'until farther order'.[62] Nine of the rebels, including Penruddock, were eventually executed; the rest remained in prison until the following year when, on Cromwell's orders, they were sent to Barbados.[63]

II

The trials of the western rebels despite, and perhaps because of, disagreements over the indictment passed relatively smoothly. The same cannot be said of the proceedings against those involved in an attempted rising in Yorkshire. On the evening of 7 March 1655, a number of royalists planned to gather on Marston Moor, of all places, before marching on York. Although several thousand were expected, only a few hundred materialised. Disheartened by the meagre turnout and mistaking the shouts of stragglers for approaching Cromwellian soldiers, the royalists dispersed quickly, scattering their weapons as they fled.[64] In the ensuing melee, many were taken prisoner by the governor of York, Colonel Robert Lilburne.

Francis Thorpe, then Baron of the Exchequer, was named alongside Justice of the Upper Bench Richard Newdigate and Serjeant-at-Law Robert Hutton to head the commission of oyer and terminer to deal with the rebels.[65] When their commission arrived in York, however, the judges perceived a number of problems. Immediately, they wrote to Solicitor General William Ellis, then making his way from London to lead the prosecution, to express their concerns. Not only did their commission fail to allow the mandatory fifteen days 'betwixt the summons and retorne' of writs 'as by law ought to be', but they also thought it 'fitt' that Ellis should 'peruse the matter of fact' before proceeding further.[66] As Lilburne reported to Thurloe, he found in the judges 'a doubtfulnes, whether in point of law, this matter of facte can, according to law, bee declared by them to be treason'. They wondered whether Whitehall had 'taken such advice as is necessary, that is to say, consulted with the judges in this weighty case'. It was imperative that there should be no 'lamenes' or 'so much knottines' in the matter 'that the naile cannot bee driven into the head'.[67]

As with the trials in the west, the commissioners not only were concerned about the status of the Treason Ordinance but feared the proceedings might fail through lack of evidence. Receiving the judges' letter in the early hours of 12 April while resting at Grantham, Ellis was unsure what to do. As he explained to Thurloe, 'the evidence will not be soe cleare and plaine, as I did apprehend it would have been'. Most problematic was the lack of witnesses. If they relied solely upon those 'that were actors in the designe and plott', Ellis believed their evidence would 'be but lame, and not to bee relied on'; he doubted that the testimony of co-conspirators would 'bee soe prevayling with a jury' as opposed to the testimony of 'persons not ingaged'.[68] While similar problems vexed those proceeding against the western rebels, the difficulty in the north was much greater because the rising had been such a damp squib. There were no witnesses beyond those present at Marston Moor and the fact those fleeing threw away their weapons meant few were taken in possession of arms. Ellis warned that the testimony must 'bee very cleare and evident of the plott, designe, and intention, of those men', otherwise the 'jury wil be hardly perswaded, that meeting together, though in such a manner as they did, and going away without effecting more, is high treason'. In Ellis's opinion the proceedings in the west were different: in that business the evidence of their treasonous intent was 'much more cleare'.[69]

The northern commissioners were caught between a rock and a hard place: reluctant to proceed for fear that the lack of evidence would lead to acquittals, their inaction became a source of embarrassment for the government. When privy councillor Walter Strickland, sent north to investigate the delay, ran into the judges at Doncaster, he claimed that he found them holding 'opinions, which differ in the foundations; I mean about the ordinance of treason'. Despite imploring the judges to consider the 'great concerne of the bussiness in hand', Strickland found the 'difficulty' to be 'incurable'; they could not 'agree in principles'.[70] On 3 May, after interrogation by the Council, Thorpe and Newdigate were duly dismissed from office.[71]

Certain aspects of this episode demand closer inspection, however, particularly Strickland's suggestion that the judges' opposition was grounded primarily upon their opposition to the Treason Ordinance and its 'foundations'. When petitioning Cromwell in June 1656 for arrears of pay still outstanding from his judicial office, Thorpe stressed that he had been prepared to 'serve yor highness so farr as . . . my Judgm[en]t & Conscience' allowed.[72] Yet it must not be assumed that the northern judges were any more principled than those in the west simply because they failed to act. Charles Cremer, then a student at Gray's Inn, believed the northern judges' inaction was because 'they only were confined to that Ordinance'. Those trying the western rebels, by contrast, 'had liberty & so tryed the sev[era]ll offenders according to the Statute of 25 Edw[ard] 3' wherein 'king they expounded to be meant (supreme) Magistrate'.[73] Yet, as their worried letters to Thurloe suggest, any 'liberty' the western commissioners had to proceed upon the 1352 statute was taken upon their own initiative. Had the evidence allowed them to do so, the northern judges would surely have followed suit.

Thorpe, for one, would have had no problem constructing the indictment in such a way as to evade the Treason Ordinance and defend proceedings upon the 1352 statute. When delivering his charge to the York grand jury in March 1649, for instance, he had stressed that it was 'High Treason' to 'levy Warre against the Supreme Authority of the Nation'. True, the 1352 Statute stated it was treason to 'levy War against the King, or adhere to the Kings enemies within the Realm'. But Thorpe clarified that the 'name and word King' in that Statute simply meant the 'chiefe Officer to be trusted with the Government' and was merely a synonym for the 'publique Interest of the People'. To levy war against the king, in effect, meant levying war 'against the Kingdome, and the Government of it, and the Supreme Power and Authority of it'.[74]

In reality, those who tried the western rebels felt just as uneasy as those in the north about the foundations of the Protectorate. By gutting the indictment, however, they were able to proceed upon the available evidence while evading the question of the extralegal status of the *Instrument*. Unfortunately for the northern judges, the lack of evidence meant they were unable to take the same line. It meant that while the scruples of the commissioners in the west towards the Treason Ordinance were overlooked as they pushed forward with the trials, those of the judges in the north were thrown into sharp relief by their inaction.

Subsequent events, however, reveal that it was the lack of evidence, not the commissioners' concerns about the Treason Ordinance, that scuppered the trials of the northern rebels. Even when the prisoners were finally tried for levying war at the summer assizes in 1655, overseen by the recently appointed (and from Cromwell's perspective, infinitely more pliable) Chief Baron of the Exchequer William Steele, the case against the rebels still collapsed, and the prisoners were ultimately fined for rioting only.[75]

III

The judges' distaste for the Treason Ordinance was never simply because of its extra-parliamentary status. Tudor and Jacobean jurists had often favoured proceeding upon the 1352 statute due to its 'rich potential for construction'; it 'proved flexible and highly adaptable to new circumstances'.[76] Equally, new treason legislation was often justified as an affirmation of custom-derived 'common law treasons', thereby giving statutory expression to 'a body of pre-existing, unwritten, customary, fundamental law'.[77] This allowed scope for new treason legislation that moved beyond the bare letter of the 1352 statute but only so far as the judges could reconcile it to the common law. The attitudes of the protectoral judges were no different: they preferred to ground proceedings upon the 1352 statute and argued that the Treason Ordinance was applicable only so far as it declared long accepted common law principles.

This also explains the judges' underwhelming response to the second Protectorate Parliament's 'Act for the security of the Lord Protector his Person'. First read on 23 September 1656, it effectively gave statutory force to the provisions of the 1654 Treason Ordinance.[78] Those guilty of High Treason were any who did 'attempt, compass or imagine the death of the Lord Protector' or 'shall levy war, or plot, contrive, or endeavour to stir up, or raise force against the Lord Protector, or the Government'. It was treason to 'proclaim, declare, publish or promote Charles Stuart' or any 'other issue or posterity' of Charles I to be 'King, Queen, or Chief Magistrate of Great Britain'; also guilty were those 'aiding, assisting, comforting, or abetting' the Stuart cause or holding 'intelligence or correspondence' with the Stuart brothers.[79] The definition of treason was even more personal than that of the 1654 ordinance: conspicuous by its absence was the clause that deemed it treasonous to claim that 'the Lord Protector and the people in Parliament assembled are not the Supreme Authority of this Commonwealth'.[80] Whereas the ordinance stressed that sovereignty was shared, the 1656 Act exalted and defended the Protector's personal authority.

What was particularly novel about the 1656 Act, however, was its provision for bodies of commissioners for England, Scotland, and Ireland, respectively, to try any offenders presented to them by the Protector and Council. The arrangement was, in effect, the same as the previous High Courts of Justice, albeit the commissioners' powers continued longer than previously, until 'the end of the last Session of the next Parliament'.[81]

The protectoral judges were named *ex officio* as commissioners for England, but there was no stipulation that any must serve as part of the quorum of seventeen. They wanted to keep it that way. When a proposed amendment to the Act suggested that the quorum should include at least three judges, it was defeated by one hundred and seventeen votes to fifty-nine, with lord commissioners Lisle and Nathaniel Fiennes acting as tellers for the noes. Similar proposals that two, and then just one, of the 'Judges of one of the Benches, or Barons of the Exchequer' should be included in the quorum were rejected without division.[82]

Intriguingly, even after the Act was passed in November 1656, the first treason trial to arise thereafter was not tried according to its provisions but was instead referred to the Court of Upper Bench.[83] The case was that of Miles Sindercombe, an ex-soldier who had attempted to assassinate Cromwell on 8 January 1657 by planting an incendiary bomb at Whitehall. When the trial opened on 9 February, Glynne, who had replaced Rolle as Lord Chief Justice, simply reprised his arguments from previous treason trials: he stressed that 'by the Common Law to compass or imagine the death of the chief Magistrate of the Land, by what name soever he was called, whether *Lord Protector* or otherwise, is High treason'. Glynne made no mention of the 1656 Act at all. Rather, he went so far as to suggest that all statutes in cases of treason were superfluous. Even the 'Statutes of Treason made 25 Ed. 3' only declared 'what the Common Law was before the making of that Statute, and was not introductive of a new Law'. Parliamentary statutes simply confirmed existing common law principles and practices.[84]

When the provisions of the 1656 Act were finally implemented following the arrest of royalist plotters in the spring of 1658, most of the judges upheld their preference for common law proceedings. Whitelocke, for one, was totally against trying the plotters by a High Court and 'advised' Cromwell 'rather to have them proceeded against in the ordinary Course of tryalls att the Common Law'.[85] It seems the judges were adamant that the 1656 Act could only be interpreted according to common law principles and could in no way alter them. As one Army newsletter reported, those judges appointed commissioners to the High Court would 'not sitt, they being of opinion that by the Act and meaning of it (as it is said) they conceive the prisoners ought to be tried by a jury'.[86] In effect, the judges would proceed only if those commissioners named in the 1656 Act were understood to be nothing more than commissioners of oyer and terminer; any verdict, they stressed, must be reached by a jury.[87] Unsurprisingly, the serpentine Lisle was the only judge willing to play a role in the High Court of 1658. Yet the unwillingness of the other judges to serve does not make them royalists: as the trials of 1655 and 1657 demonstrated, whenever they could reconcile their proceedings to the common law, the judges were not unwilling to act against royalist plotters.

IV

When handling treason trials, the protectoral judges and lawyers proceeded upon common law principles by stressing the equivalency between a king and a Lord Protector. In the spring of 1657, however, a number of those same judges and lawyers seemed to be of a different opinion as they urged Cromwell to accept the kingship. Acting as spokesmen for the committee of ninety-nine MPs, which met frequently with Cromwell in April 1657, many of them stressed the absolute legal necessity of the royal title and its superiority to that of Lord Protector. As Glynne explained on 11 April, even though Cromwell swore to govern according to the Law, it was 'almost impossible' for a Lord Protector to 'answer the expectation of the people to be governed by the Lawes': it was a 'new office not known to the Law, and made out of doores'. A king, by contrast, was 'known by the Law' and 'run thorow so many ages in this Nation'. For Glynne, the 'Law of the Nation' was 'no otherwise, then what hath been a custome to be practised as is approved by the people to be good'. Likewise, the office of king was offered to Cromwell by 'universall consent of the people'. By accepting this offer, the laws and Cromwell's office would be compatible: they would all be based upon popular consent.[88]

Here is evidence aplenty for those who claim that the rule of law demanded government with a king. And yet, as Cromwell reminded the committee, their arguments overlooked the 'experience' of the past decade. It was 'known to you all', he explained, that the 'supreme Authoritie' going in 'another name' than that of king was 'complyed with twice without it': first under the *Custodes Libertates Angliae* from 1649 to 1653 and since then under the title of Lord Protector. Both titles 'did carry on the justice of the Nation'. Cromwell admitted that when these changes occurred, 'my Lords the Judges were somewhat startled' and did 'demur a little'; but, 'upon consideration' they did 'receive satisfaction, and did act'. No doubt glancing at Glynne and other lawyers in the room, Cromwell claimed that if 'more of my Lords the Judges were here then now', they would verify what he said.[89]

Like the judges in the treason trials of the 1650s, Cromwell stressed that 'King' was a 'name of office plainly implying the Supreme Authoritie' and could not be 'stretcht to more'. Ultimately, it had its 'originall somewhere', and that was 'in consent of the whole'. As such, Cromwell believed that whatsoever 'the Parliament settles is that which will run through the law, and will lead the thread of Government through the Land' just as well as 'what hath been'. It was the parliamentary origins of the title rather than the title itself that mattered. For that reason, Cromwell 'had rather have any Name from this Parliament then any Name without it, so much doe I value the Authoritie of the Parliament'.[90]

Cromwell's attempt to turn the judges' actions and arguments against them was ultimately unconvincing, however. True, when handling treason trials, the judges equated the title of Lord Protector with that of king – but only on the understanding that both meant a chief magistrate empowered by the supreme authority: the people represented in Parliament. Yet the reality of the Protectorate failed to match the judges' expectations. Early in the Protectorate, the judges proceeded upon the assumption that the regime would receive parliamentary approbation. After the failure of the first Protectorate Parliament, however, they found themselves defending (and defining) the Protectorate in terms that bore conspicuously little resemblance to its arbitrary reality. Despite Cromwell's bold claim that 'the lawes did proceed with as much freedom' and that the judges were 'less solicited' by 'interpositions' from the single person than any time before, his handling of Thorpe, Newdigate, Rolle, Widdrington, and Whitelocke told another story.[91] Ultimately, Cromwell and the judges were in agreement: the laws would run freely under whatever title Parliament chose to christen the chief magistrate. But the fact remained that no Parliament had ever approved the Protectorate.

Glynne defended the judges' actions. He admitted that they had 'taken their Office' from Cromwell under the title of Protector and had 'taken it to be the same with that of a King and so go on'. He did 'confess that the Judges have gone very far that way' and he chose not to 'speake my owne opinion of this case'. But he also lamented how 'there hath been variety of opinions, and judgements' since; even those 'that have been Judges of the Nation' were not in complete agreement. While most judges accepted their commissions on the grounds that the Lord Protector was nothing more than a chief magistrate, the experience of three years of arbitrary rule had proven otherwise. Some, most notably Lisle, continued to serve the Protector sedulously, but many others no longer felt they could. It would not be a 'very good establishment', Glynne stressed, that 'there shall be doubtings, in those that should be best knowing'.[92]

To avoid those 'doubtings' the office of the single person had to be settled by Parliament; Cromwell should practice what he preached and not deny what Parliament offered him. As the Master of the Rolls, William Lenthall explained to Cromwell, the *Humble Petition and Advice* was 'vox populi, for it is the voice of the three Nations in one Parliament' and Cromwell was 'bound to it'.[93] According to Whitelocke, the 'original institution' of kingship was 'by common consent', and it was true that 'the same common consent might institute any other title'. But he politely reminded Cromwell that Parliament had chosen the title 'king' – a choice made not just by 'present common consent' but confirmed time and again by Parliaments over hundreds of years.[94]

It was the parliamentary foundations of the kingly title offered to Cromwell, not simply the title itself, that made it the best guarantor of the common law. According to the first clause of the *Humble Petition and Advice*, Cromwell, as king, should exercise that office 'according to the Lawes of these nations'. But were these laws really known? Had they forgotten that civil war broke out in 1642 precisely because Parliament and king could not agree upon the bounds of the prerogative powers? In reality, the committee of ninety-nine was not looking to restore a king with those same ill-defined powers that Charles I had enjoyed prior to 1640. Rather, their vision of Cromwellian kingship embodied the ideas and experiences of the parliamentarians during the 1640s, culminating in the climactic events of 1649. They defined the king in precisely the same terms as the judges defined the Lord Protector during the treason trials: a chief magistrate empowered by the people. As Lisle explained to Cromwell, the 'title of Protector is either the same thing in power with the title of king, or it is something else'. If it was the 'same thing', then there was 'nothing of difference but a name'. If, however, Cromwell refused what Parliament offered him, the people would 'think there is more than a name' in it.[95] In effect, only by taking the kingly title offered by Parliament could Cromwell prove he was the sort of chief magistrate that the judges had always claimed the Lord Protector to be.

Many of the committee emphasized that the real benefit of the kingly office was its accountability and, in doing so, endorsed those ideas used to justify the trial of Charles I. For Lenthall, the 'ground and reason of the warr' was 'not against the office' of king but Charles I's 'breach of trust in that office'.[96] Glynne scorned those who 'pretend' that 'a Kings prerogative is so large, that we know it not'. In reality, the prerogative was 'known by Law', 'under the Courts of Justice' and 'bounded as well as any Acre of Land'. If any doubted this, they need only look to the events of January 1649. Charles I did 'expatiate' the prerogative 'beyond the dutie', Glynne explained: that was 'the evil of the man but in *Westminster Hall*'.[97] Plainly, even those judges, like Glynne, who were opposed to the manner of the king's trial and execution could still look back on those events as affirmation of the basic idea that kings were empowered by and ultimately accountable to the people.

V

By focusing upon forms of government during the 1650s, too little attention has been paid to the ideas that underpinned the constitutional experiments of the period. Those who offered Cromwell kingship were not simply looking to revert to familiar forms of government; they wanted to preserve those 'commonwealth principles' advanced by the parliamentarians throughout the 1640s and given forceful expression in 1649. True, most of the judges were shocked by the regicide. But it was the manner in which the trial of the king was conducted, not the ideas upon which those proceedings were justified, with which they disagreed.

That the judges urged Cromwell to accept kingship need not mean they yearned for monarchical forms of government or believed the laws could only ever run in the king's name. When defining treason, the judges claimed that the Lord Protector was the same as a king. Yet they argued that both titles signified nothing more than a 'chief magistrate', empowered by the people to govern according to the laws the people themselves had chosen. The experience of Cromwellian rule depreciated those claims, however, particularly after the first Protectorate Parliament failed to grant the *Instrument* parliamentary approbation. From the judges' perspective, the offer of kingship to Cromwell was intended as a means not to promote him but to make him into the sort of chief magistrate that, throughout the treason trials of the period, they had claimed the Lord Protector *ought* to be.

Ultimately, the protectoral judges were less concerned with the outward form of government than its substance. Only governments founded upon parliamentary foundations, they claimed, were lawful. Few of those judges who served the Protectorate were guilty of interpreting the law in Cromwell's favour, but this did not make them crypto-royalists either. They remained parliamentarians at heart. Even after the Restoration, their principles died hard. According to one report, in July 1660 Hugh Wyndham was brought before a committee of the House of Lords investigating the Cromwellian treason trials. When asked to explain his opinion at Salisbury in 1655 that 'the taking up of arms against the supreme magistrate *de facto*, to be High Treason by the statute of 25 Edw.

III', Wyndham did not shy away from his previous judgement but 'did avow it still his opinion'. He was duly sent to the Tower.[98] It seems that, like Cromwell before them, the Restoration authorities were unwilling to accept that the single person, whether or not they happened to be called king, was really nothing more than an officer of state.

Notes

1 C. Holmes, *Why Was Charles I Executed?* (2006), pp. 148–9, 170.
2 D. Alan Orr, *Treason and the State: Law, Politics, and Ideology in the English Civil War* (Cambridge, 2002), pp. 1–5 and *passim*; idem, 'The Juristic Foundation of Regicide', in J. Peacey (ed.), *The Regicides and the Execution of Charles I* (Basingstoke, 2001), pp. 117–37.
3 A. Cromartie, *Sir Matthew Hale, 1609–1676: Law, Religion and Natural Philosophy* (Cambridge, 1995), p. 58.
4 M. Nedham, *The Excellencie of a Free-State* (1656), pp. 60–1.
5 Although article 34 of the Instrument of Government stated that appointments of senior judges should be approved by Parliament, in reality this approbation was never sought or given. S.R. Gardiner (ed.), *The Constitutional Documents of the Puritan Revolution, 1625–1660* (3rd edn., Oxford, 1906), p. 416.
6 C. Holmes, 'John Lisle, Lord Commissioner of the Great Seal, and the Last Months of the Cromwellian Protectorate', *EHR*, 122 (2007), 918–36.
7 J. Heath, *A Brief Chronicle of the Late Intestine Warr* (1663), p. 660. For more on the Protectoral bench see S. Black, 'Coram Protectore: The Judges of Westminster Hall under the Protectorate of Oliver Cromwell', *American Journal of Legal History*, 20 (1976), 32–64.
8 Black, 'Coram Protectore', p. 34.
9 *CJ*, VI, 134, 135–6; BL, Add. MS 37344, fols 259v–260r.
10 F. Thorpe, *Sergeant Thorpe Judge of Assize for the Northern Circuit His Charge* . . . (1649), pp. 2–3.
11 *Ibid.*, p. 9.
12 Gardiner (ed.), *Constitutional Documents*, p. 414.
13 BL, Add. MS 37346, fol. 186v–187v.
14 *Burton*, I, xxviii, xxxi.
15 *Ibid.*, p. xxxii.
16 *CSPD 1655*, pp. 167–8; Black, 'Coram Protectore', p. 57.
17 Black, 'Coram Protectore', pp. 57–8.
18 *The Diary of Bulstrode Whitelocke, 1605–1675*, ed. R. Spalding (Oxford, 1990), pp. 405, 407–8.
19 *Ibid.*, pp. 408–9.
20 *A&O*, II, 120–1.
21 *Ibid.*, II, 830–1. The ordinance proved flawed almost immediately, however, when it was realised that it failed to comprehend several clauses in the *Instrument*: an explanatory ordinance was passed in February 1654: *ibid.*, II, 844.
22 *Ibid.*, II, 917–18.
23 Besides Lisle (Chancery), the judges were Edward Atkins (Common Pleas), Robert Aske (Upper Bench). and Robert Nicholas (Exchequer).
24 See Lisle's notes upon the trial at TNA, SP18/72A, fols 2v–3r. Although Atkins was the only judge openly to refuse, Lisle notes ominously how Aske later asked to be excused having 'fallen sicke of a lethorgy': TNA, SP18/17A, fol. 4r.
25 *The Triall of Mr John Gerhard, Mr Peter Vowell, and Sommerset Fox, by the High Court of Justice* (1654), p. 3.
26 TNA, SP18/72A, fols 5v–6r.
27 *The Triall of Mr John Gerhard*, p. 12.

28 TNA, SP18/72A, fols 12v–13r.
29 A.H. Woolrych, *Penruddock's Rising, 1655* (1955).
30 For the Council's deliberations concerning the commissioners, see TNA, SP25/75, fol. 737; SP18/95, fols 131–2, 185. The judges who met at Salisbury were Rolle (Upper Bench), Wyndham (Common Pleas), Nicholas (Exchequer), Lisle (Chancery). A copy of the commission of oyer and terminer is at TNA, KB33/1/1/v.
31 *TSP*, III, 361, 379.
32 *Ibid.*, III, 370–1.
33 *Ibid.*, III, 371, 378. A copy of the revised indictment is at TNA, KB 33/1/1/v.
34 *Ibid.*, III, 378, 379.
35 *Ibid.*, III, 370–1; TNA, KB 33/1/1/v; *CP*, III, 33–4, 35.
36 *Ibid.*, III, 378, 379.
37 Prideaux played down the significance of the revised indictment to Thurloe in these terms by suggesting that the wording of the revised indictment still conformed to that of the ordinance. See *Ibid.*, III, 378.
38 *Ibid.*, III, 391–4.
39 *The Triall of the Honourable Colonel John Penruddock of Compton in Wiltshire . . .* (1655), pp. 1–2.
40 *Ibid.*, p. 2.
41 *Ibid.*, p. 2.
42 *Ibid.*, p. 3.
43 *Ibid.*, p. 3.
44 *TSP*, III, 372.
45 *Ibid.*, III, 398–9; *Burton*, III, 531–2.
46 *Triall of the Honourable Colonel John Penruddock*, p. 4.
47 *TSP*, III, 392–3: see points 11, 27, and 28.
48 *Ibid.*, III, 393: point 28.
49 *Ibid.*, III, 376–7: Bingham to Disbrowe, 14 April 1655.
50 *Ibid.*, III, 318, 328.
51 *Ibid.*, III, 398.
52 Even so, Prideaux had to 'carry divers persons' from Salisbury to Exeter; otherwise he would 'want evidence to prove many of the prisoners there to have beene in armes': *ibid.*, III, 377.
53 *TSP*, III, 371. See also *ibid.*, 361, 365, 372–3, 376.
54 This would also explain why, when voting upon the guilt of the accused in 1654, the High Court found Peter Vowell guilty of conspiring to levy war but, unlike the other prisoners, did not vote on whether he was also guilty of plotting to compass the death of the Protector: the two charges were not deemed synonymous. TNA, SP18/72A, fols 7v–8v.
55 Thorpe, *His Charge*, p. 11.
56 Cromartie, *Sir Matthew Hale*, p. 81.
57 *Ibid.*, p. 81.
58 *TSP*, III, 365–6; *CP*, III, 33–4.
59 *TSP*, III, 394–5.
60 *Mercurius Politicus*, 255 (26 April–3 May 1655), p. 5307; *CP*, III, 37–8. See the copy of the bill of indictment at TNA, KB 33/1/1/v.
61 *CP*, III, 35–6.
62 *TSP*, III, 442.
63 *Mercurius Politicus*, 259 (24–31 May 1655), p. 5372; *Burton*, IV, 254–73.
64 *Ibid.*, 248 (8–15 March 1655), p. 5196; *ibid.*, 249 (15–22 March 1655), pp. 5209–10.
65 TNA, SP25/75, fol. 752; TNA, SP25/76, fol. 9; *Mercurius Politicus*, 251 (29 March–5 April 1655), p. 5244; *Mercurius Politicus*, 252 (5–12 April 1655), p. 5258.
66 *TSP*, III, 359; for the Council's letter see TNA, SP18/76A, fol. 49.
67 *Ibid.*, III, 359–60.

Treason and the offer of the crown   145

68 Ibid., III, 373–4.
69 Ibid.
70 Ibid., III, 385: W. Strickland to Thurloe, 17 April 1655. According to the docquet book, Strickland carried with him a writ of *dedimus potestatem*, directed to 'Baron Thorpe & others' to take 'the oath of Walter Strickland'. What this oath contained, however, is not stated. TNA, C231/6, p. 308.
71 *Mercurius Politicus*, 256 (3–10 May 1655), p. 5323; *CP*, III, 37–8. Newdigate was subsequently reinstated in June 1657: TNA, C231/6, p. 366.
72 TNA, SP18/157A, fol. 262. Unsurprisingly, Thorpe later made political capital out of the fact that he 'refused to try' the Royalists when pleading for Charles II's pardon: see TNA, SP29/1, fol. 163.
73 Gray's Inn Library, London, MS 34, fol. 209.
74 Thorpe, *His Charge*, p. 11
75 TNA, C231/6, p. 312; HMC, *Fifth Report* (1876), p. 183: Ayloffe to Langley, 14 July 1655; *CSPD 1655*, p. 325: Nicholas to Jane, 7/17 September 1655. The following year, a number of those involved in the rising were examined by Lilburne, acting in his capacity as Deputy Major-General, but none were proceeded against for treason and only twenty-two were subjected to indefinite incarceration. See C. Durston, *Cromwell's Major-Generals: Godly Government during the English Revolution* (Manchester, 2001), pp. 127–8; *TSP*, IV, 468, 522, 614; V, 33.
76 Orr, *Treason and the State*, pp. 11, 25–6, 28–9.
77 Ibid., pp. 15–16.
78 *A&O*, II, 1038–42; *CJ*, VII, 426–7.
79 Ibid., II, 1038–42.
80 Ibid., II, 831–5, 1038–42.
81 Ibid., II, 1038–42.
82 *CJ*, VII, 436–7.
83 It is unclear why the Protectoral authorities decided to shun the provisions of the 1656 Act. It could have been judicial resistance that prompted the decision, but there were also shortcomings in the Act itself: Sindercombe's litany of botched assassination attempts stretched back to before the sitting of the second Protectorate Parliament, meaning they were technically out of the purview of the 1656 Act, which gave authority to deal only with crimes committed 'from and after the tenth day of October' 1656. See *A&O*, II, 1038–42.
84 *The Whole Business of Sindercome, From first to last* (1656), pp. 8–9.
85 *Whitelocke's Diary*, ed. Spalding, p. 488. One report claims that Cromwell had a similar dispute with Glynne, see HMC, *Fifth Report*, p. 181: Langley to Leveson, 4 May 1658.
86 *CP*, III, 151: 25 May 1658.
87 A similar point is made in *TSP*, V, 547–8.
88 *Monarchy Asserted, To be the Best, Most Ancient and Legall Form of Government* (1660), pp. 15–19.
89 Ibid., pp. 34–5.
90 Ibid., pp. 32–4.
91 Ibid., p. 35.
92 Ibid., pp. 18–19. See also ibid., p. 78.
93 Ibid., pp. 11–14.
94 Ibid., pp. 77–80.
95 Ibid., p. 24.
96 Ibid., pp. 48–9
97 Ibid., pp. 17–18.
98 HMC, *Fifth Report*, pp. 154–5: Newport to Leveson, 21 July 1660.

9 England's 'atheisticall generation'
Orthodoxy and unbelief in the revolutionary period

Leif Dixon

According to Michael Buckley, early modern accusations of atheism 'possessed all the accuracy of the newly developed musket. For all the powder poured down the barrel, the shot was wild'.[1] This certainly could be the case, especially where contemporaries used the charge as a synonym for generically sinful behaviour. However, modern historians are a little too inclined to bemoan the lack of 'accuracy' of this polemical fire because what they were shooting at and what we wish they were shooting at can often amount to different things. Early modern people meant a lot of different things by 'atheism', only one of which meshes with the definition that really interests modern scholars – that is, the philosophical assertion that God does not exist. This does not mean, though, that all other uses of the term constitute mere misfire. As Buckley himself points out, 'the term *atheist* is not hopelessly vacuous, but unless the instance to which it is applied and the meaning in which it is used are determined, its employment is profoundly misleading'.[2] This essay will seek to specify some examples of 'instance' and 'meaning', in order to show how anti-atheist discourse adapted to changing social and intellectual climates. My main focus will be on the 1640s, when a slew of radical religious ideas emerged that tested and strained orthodox attitudes to what constituted the 'religious'.

This was a time that, according to the godly minister John Rowe, spawned the 'Atheisticall generation' of this essay's title.[3] However, the phrase can also be used to introduce an additional theme. Prior to the revolutionary period, anti-atheist writers were generally rather cautious about explicitly attaching the term to named contemporary individuals or groups within England, preferring instead to hint darkly at contemporary atheism being rife or to phrase the debate through classical allusion. In the 1640s and 1650s, though, orthodox Protestant writers became increasingly inclined to label their fellow English Protestants as unbelievers. This essay will suggest that by firing the polemical gun at this particular target, further meanings and forms of 'atheism' were accidentally generated. Indeed, in some circumstances, the stigma of atheism could even be appropriated creatively and critically by those who were targeted. My investigation will fall into four parts. First, I will attempt to show how sensitive contemporary understandings of atheism were to changing contexts. In order to do this, I will take a story first recounted by Richard Greenham in the 1580s and track it through several retellings, culminating in Thomas Edwards' use of it in 1646.[4] Secondly, I will discuss why orthodox writers thought that atheism was a threat in the 1640s but also how compromised were their efforts to create an atheist 'other'. Thirdly, I will look at a text in which an 'atheist' fights back, and runs rings around a character called Christian in a dialogue. Finally, I will show how an atheist identity could be appropriated in words and action by a pair of subversives who called themselves the 'atheist-angells'. The effect of these case studies will also be to show how contemporary 'atheism' was not an opposite to religion but rather emerged from it in ways that seem so mutually connective that it might, in some circumstances, be appropriate to think in terms of a *religious atheism*.

I

The inveterate confessional warrior, William Perkins, once wrote that Catholicism 'is but a painted Atheisme'.[5] And it should hardly be surprising that 'popery' and 'atheism', two of the most freewheeling polemical labels of the era, often experienced a mutual gravitational pull in the minds of Protestant writers. 'Atheism' was a term that was constantly tugged and pulled to the point of meaningless overextension. This point was, it would seem unconsciously, acknowledged by Perkins himself: it is 'true that there are so many sorts of Atheists, that almost the world is full'.[6] Equating atheism with the Catholic religion was problematic for several reasons – not least because the highly structured nature of the Catholic Church and the religion's emphasis on good works did not correspond well with the anarchic and immoral implications associated with unbelief.[7]

Richard Greenham, an evangelical ally of Perkins, told a story that seemed to shift atheism from a Catholic to a Protestant range of meanings. First, a word of context. Most of Greenham's writings come from the 1580s, towards the end of his twenty-year stint as a godly reformer to thirty-odd stoically uninterested households in the Cambridgeshire village of Dry Drayton. Most of his writings, though, were geared towards curing the 'afflicted consciences' of people that he knew in East Anglia who were already emotionally committed to the Protestant cause but who were in some ways brittle and in need of structured guidance. That is to say, Greenham was simultaneously fighting for a Reformation that had not been won, while also dealing with the pastoral implications of success. The following story, recounted in his 'Grave Counsels and Godly Observations', can be analysed in the light of this tension.

Greenham tells his reader of a young man that he knew who was once a Catholic but who converted to Protestantism. However, in this journey, he was given no structured support and came to fall under the influence of a group of Familists. 'The first principle that they taught him', said Greenham, 'was that there is no God'. Apparently this sensational news 'boyld much within him' and led him to the view that if there is no heaven or hell, then there is no point in deferring earthly pleasures. The decline into intellectual evil thus found its natural corollary in a descent into practical immorality. He stole a horse, got caught, was convicted, and sentenced to death. Visited by 'a godly minister', he 'confessed himself an Atheist' and would not be budged from his position. Next, Greenham describes how the young man was taken to the scaffold, made to mount the ladder, and then, the noose about his neck, he finally recanted his unbelief, declaring that 'there is a God, and the same God is just for ever to his enemies, and everlastingly keepeth his mercies with his children'.[8] Having made his peace, he was executed.

This is more or less a classic providential morality tale, particularly beloved of puritan writers much fascinated by the psychological applications of last-ditch conversion stories. It also belongs to a wider Reformation-era battle to appropriate and reshape tales of the doomed for wider edificatory and confessional purposes. The shortened life and extended afterlife of Francis Spira is one famous example.[9] Greenham's anonymous pseudo-Spira made one particular observation that came to seem prophetic. The young man:

> feared rather Atheisme than Papisme in the Realme [of England]: for many having escaped out of the gulfe of superstition, are now too farre plunged and swallowed up [within] prophanenesse, thinking either that there is no God, or else that he is not so fearfull and mercifull as his threatenings and promises commend him to be.[10]

We cannot know how much of Greenham's story is invented. But it would not be unreasonable to suggest that it had some personal resonance for him. Greenham shows some sympathy for the hanged man – as we shall see, some later variations on the story do not. One of his former students was Robert Browne, whose misguided enthusiasm led him into heresy and the founding of an eponymous separatist sect. In general, furthermore, Greenham's writings show at least as much concern with how a lively faith can be stabilised and regulated as with how it could be acquired in the first place, for this latter was primarily a matter decided by divine predestination. Browne had not lacked conviction, but clearly he did not receive proper institutional guidance. This pastoral and sociological observation is hinted at within Greenham's story. His pseudo-Spira initially converts to Protestantism but becomes lost to the cause. Having escaped 'superstition', he then loses the correct balance between 'fear' in God's judgement and hope in His 'mercy' – this balance was perhaps the central theme of Greenham's writings – and so drifts off into 'prophanenesse' and, finally, atheism. For all that the hanged man deserved his punishment, his apostasy was also a comment on Protestant pastoral provision in the 1580s, and this is something that people like Greenham and Perkins – and then a whole generation of godly ministers – sought to remedy.

Greenham's story was retold, in subtly altered form, by Miles Mosse in a Paul's Cross sermon, 'Of Saving and Justifying Faith', in 1614. Mosse was a junior member of Greenham's circle and had contributed with him to the massive best-seller, *A Garden of Spiritual Flowers* (1609), a book that sought to guide the converted towards a settled life of faith. In his sermon, Mosse gives credibility to 'this historie of an *Atheist* in *England*' by stating that it was first told by a 'man whose goodnesse, and conscience I knew well to be such, as hee would commit willingly no fable unto writing'. Mosse recounts the story faithfully enough, but he leaves out the prediction at the end. In terms of Mosse's sermon theme, his truncation of the story is perfectly justifiable. Mosse's central concern is to demonstrate the crucial Reformed distinction between saving faith and forms of faith that condemn to hell. And so we have this: '*The Devils beleeve*. What? That *there is one God*'. This fact is drolly recorded as 'a notable *Item* for *Atheists*' to consider. To Mosse, what Greenham's hanged man truly reveals is the 'invincible testimonie of conscience', which can no longer be denied as he ascends the ladder to drop.[11] Mosse does not say that the former atheist is damned despite his final statement of faith, but the implication is clearly that Jacobean Protestants need to go further than merely assenting to doctrinal truths in order to be saved.

Greenham's story is retold again in 1633, in Thomas Adams' *Commentary upon . . . the Divine Second Epistle [of] St. Peter*. Adams' treatment of the story is similar to that of Mosse. Once again, the focus is on how saving faith is distinguished from faith of other sorts. Adams identifies what he calls a 'forced faith', which one can try to deny but is shared by 'reprobates and devills' and which is ultimately 'compelled' by the irrefutable evidence of God's 'signes' in nature and the conscience. At the last resort, while 'there may be Atheists on earth, there are none in hell' – the ultimate *evidentia signorum*. Greenham's atheist is guilty first of developing his own 'forged faith', which is found 'in hereticks, who will beleeve no God, but one of their owne making'. Here, Adams dovetails two conventional definitions of atheism, to explain how the young man could make a series of bad (religious) decisions that ended in his travelling to Amsterdam – a new detail – and eventually making the (anti-religious) assertion, 'there is no God'.[12] Thus, to deny the true God places one on a slippery slope that may result in outright atheism. Although there are some subtle differences between Adams' and Mosse's handling of the story, they make the same large omission: Greenham's coda, which predicts that atheism rather than Catholicism will prove the greater threat to English religion. Mosse, for his part, quite clearly thought the reverse, noting how 'our bloodie *Papists*' conspire in the 'murdering of *Kings* [and] blowing up of Parliaments'.[13] And in 1633, Adams may have felt rather strongly that something like 'popery' was taking over the Church of England itself.

In the 1640s, though, the picture changed radically. Whereas Adams had quietly deported the sectarian atheist to Amsterdam, within a decade conservative Protestant opinion became newly defined in relation to expressions of radicalism that were undeniably both Protestant and English. To understand this new threat, the notion of 'atheism' – a word that expressed horror – was deployed in different ways by commentators as they sought to make sense of a frightening and rapidly evolving present. One of the first writers of the revolutionary period who picked up Greenham's story was Thomas Fuller, who was an instinctive moderate but who eventually sided with the brand new identity of the 'royalist'. Fuller made use of the hanged man in his *Holy State and Profane State* of 1642, and here he entirely ditches the backstory about the character's experiences of conversion and apostasy – which had been important to Mosse and Adams as these helped to parse the nature of faith – in favour of the prophetic part of Greenham's tale, which had lain dormant since the 1580s. Fuller wrote of 'that speech of worthy Master Greenham, [which] deserves to be heeded, *That Atheisme in England is more to be feared than Popery*'.[14] Suddenly Greenham's coda made a lot of sense, especially for someone inclined to split for the royalists in a dilemma between godlessness and tyranny.

Fuller, it should be noted, knew his texts well. Unlike Mosse and Adams, he cites Greenham by name. He had also, almost certainly, read Adams because he turned the latter's plodding 'there may be Atheists on earth, there are none in hell', into the prettier 'On earth were Atheists many/In hell there is not any'.[15] This sentiment was hardly a recent coinage, but the proximity of the reference to the Greenham story suggests that Fuller had Adams' text in mind. As such, he made an active decision about which account to prioritise. This question of textual lineage can be pushed further forward too, as we find the same story reworking itself again in the second part of Thomas Edwards' famous heresiography, *Gangraena* (1646). Here, Edwards prints a letter, 'sent me from a worthy and godly Minister,' who provides an approving review of the first part of the book. The minister bemoans how the evil of toleration had allowed error to emerge from orthodoxy. He asks, rhetorically, 'shall vipers be suffered to eate up the very bowels of their [own] mother?' He then says that 'the danger the whole body is in' comes from nothing less than 'Atheisme, which ... the good and godly Master *Greenham* ... long since prophesied would ... overrunne this Realm, rather than Papisme'.[16] Greenham, suddenly, was the old prophet of a new madness.

Edwards – or his fan – had probably read Greenham but showed no interest in the Dry Drayton minister's empathy with the hanged man and did not record the latter's potentially soul-saving final confession. In 1646, Presbyterians were not in a forgiving mood. He had also clearly read Mosse because the reference to eating up the 'very bowels' of their 'mother' parallels the phrase 'the ripping of my mother' in Mosse's text.[17] So the choices in terms of textual direction are again significant. Mosse's allusion to matricide is situated in the context of a classical reference to Nero disobeying the advice of Seneca – Adams had also read Mosse, and copies him here – whereas the 1646 update locates this ripping apart firmly in the context of contemporary England. 'Tis sad, very sad to see our *Anglia* ... turned into *Africa*, [which gives birth to] new monsters every day'. The fault lies with 'Independents all, and Scholars, nay Ministers, yet not by Ordination'.[18] The moral of Greenham's prediction is now that all Christians must oppose the disease of 'toleration', and Edwards' implication is that Independents should both be hanged and sent to hell.

II

As we have seen, a moral story about an atheist was chopped and changed according to its apparent relevance to the present. Each moment in which the story is retold can tell us something about the concerns of orthodox divines and the challenges that they perceived. However, the concept of 'atheism' required significant adjustment for the realities of the revolutionary period. To highlight this, it is worth returning briefly to Fuller. Although he omits the sympathetic backstory of Greenham's pseudo-Spira, he does advise caution about the temptation to label atheists. He warns that such an endeavour is 'hard' because 'some Atheisticall speeches [are] not sufficient evidence to convict the speaker an Atheist'. Such an exercise is also 'dangerous' for the accuser: 'what satisfaction can I make to their memories, if I challenge any of so foul a crime wrongfully?'[19] Edwards, on the other hand, could not have been clearer that 'the Independents' are comprised of 'Atheisticall hereticall men'.[20] Caution with words was one of the first casualties of war.

Fuller was also out of step with an emerging trend when he opted for a traditional analysis of the atheist demographic. He argued that the typical atheist lives in 'wealth and prosperity' and, as an intellectual, 'delights to puzzle Divines' with 'a register of many difficult places of Scripture'.[21] Fuller's typology of the atheist is completely typical of the anti-atheist genre in England prior to the civil wars. Authors as theologically diverse as John Carpenter, Francis Bacon, Martin Fotherby, and Thomas Jackson were agreed that atheists usually fall victim to the 'penetrating and dividing nature of their firie wits' and 'abuse' their 'abundance of learning, [to] make Objections against God'.[22] Edwards and people like him, though, did not recognise this image: the Independents were not misguided intellectuals but plebeian upstarts run wild.[23] This shift in attitude is nicely encapsulated in William Towers' *Atheismus Vapulana* (1654), which operates from the premise that 'this Sin of Atheism is a Popular Sin, the Sin of those Ignorant, though Conceited Heads, who Do know as Little of *Latine* and *Greek*, as they Would know of *God*'.[24]

The irony was that these guardians of orthodoxy were being forced to deal with the unexpected permutations of unmistakably popular forms of Protestantism that evangelical ministers had worked hard to establish but now found impossible to control. When they discovered 'atheism', therefore, they were also revealing something about themselves, and condemning tendencies that existed within their own notion of religious truth. As Christopher Hill pointed out, '[U]nderlying this plebeian irreligion, there is perhaps more theory, more theology if you like, than has been supposed'.[25] Or to turn the matter on its head, one might say, with Federico Barbierato, '[W]hen a religious belief is rejected, the forms assumed by the rejection reflect the rejected religion' itself.[26] Fully to explore this issue would take much more space than I have available to me here, but a couple of general points might profitably be made.

First, it was not always obvious to heresy hunters/anti-atheists whether their targets were rejecting formal ecclesiastical controls because they simply hated religion or because they were pursuing – foolishly, even if with sincerity – their own notion of conscience. In either case, it was difficult to critique these positions without showing some awareness of how Protestantism itself had contributed some momentum to anticlerical tendencies. Puritan thinkers had always held to some notion of a priesthood of believers and had tended to deny any categorical distinction between clergy and laity, and Independents and Presbyterians in the 1640s were united in railing against the evils of episcopacy. Sarah Mortimer has suggested that defenders of orthodoxy like Thomas Edwards were primarily concerned with 'presenting heresy as a social rather than an intellectual problem'.[27] This, she argues, was because such an approach allowed them to appeal to civil authorities to quell the subversion. This is surely correct. But we might also add that such writers were inclined to focus more upon the atheist ethic than on the atheist worldview because the latter potentially represented a knot that, if untangled, could reveal 'atheism' and Protestantism belonging to the same strand of material. Equally, a religion that had founded itself upon the rejection of papal authority and that in some of its manifestations both theorised and practised tyrannicide was not necessarily best placed to urge obedience to institutional authorities with which one happened to disagree. Edward Garland, a Calvinist minister, argued in 1657 that, 'it is a great curse to have evil Magistrates or evil Ministers, and yet it is a [curse] far greater to have none at all; for then every man teacheth what he will [and] doth what he will'.[28] Whether Garland was of this view at the time of Charles I's execution is not recorded.

This problem of creating a firm separation between Protestant orthodoxy and radicalism is accidentally underlined by Ephraim Pagitt who, towards the end of his *Heresiography* (1645), sought to compare the errors of sectarian radicalism and popery. His extensive list takes the form of opposites. For instance, whereas Catholics are excessively deferential to spiritual authority, sectarians reject it entirely; where the one treats ceremony as though it were inherently divine, the other will not even participate in formal worship; as one believes that the confession of sin is essential to salvation, so the other sees no sins to confess, and so forth.[29] On one level, this looks like a masterful exercise in establishing a 'moderate' position, against which alternatives can be subjected to regulation because of their 'extreme' nature.[30] However, Pagitt's exercise in polemical positioning also reveals how difficult it was to define a discrete middleground. Was truth analogous to a stable platform or to the point of a pin? Although George Buckley may have gone a little far when he argued that the emergence of sectarianism 'was an indictment of Christianity itself', it is certainly true that a Protestant constellation of theological and psychological ideas that tended to critique authority, located potential truth within the self, and had established itself by fighting religious and political institutions, could only critique the extremes to which it gave birth to a limited extent.[31]

To draw this point back towards the theme of atheism, much of the anxiety about unbelief during the revolutionary period centred around the ways in which the God of Reformed Protestantism had been recast in a manner that was simultaneously radical and disturbingly familiar. Highly heterodox tendencies emerged from a predestinarian tradition that, prior to the civil wars, had sought to keep a deity defined in terms of absolute power and infinite possibility under close control. When ministers articulated the nature of this imperious deity, they did so with caveats attached – for instance, in allowing for types of effective causation that were distinct from God's will, in distinguishing between natural and spiritual essences, and in distancing God from sin. Like most monotheistic deities, this god was a compromised construction that was designed to meet a wide set of individual and communal needs. As such, the religious worldview of many Protestants encompassed a deity who was both personal and unknowable, completely entangled with earthly events but also separate from them, and who could work within individuals while also remaining distinct enough to damn them freely and from before the creation of the world. This was not only a delicate balance: it was a kinetic minefield, and one that required orthodox people to think quite a bit, but also, perhaps, not too much. Some radicals thought more or thought less than an orthodox position necessitated. The Ranter Lawrence Clarkson was a deep thinker and came to the view that if God is omnipotent, then He must exist in all things, and that if God is good, then all things must be good. As such, he urged: 'Consider any act, though it be the act of Swearing, Drinking, Adultery and Theft; yet these acts simply, yea nakedly be as acts nothing distinct from Prayer and Prayses'. There is no more 'puritie in one then the other'.[32] If God is all-powerful, all things must come from Him directly, and if God is morally unified, then all actions must be of equal value.

However, this sort of radical redefinition of God seemed to argue God out of existence. Contemporaries did understand 'atheism' to encompass the philosophical argument that God does not exist, but this notion was not always meaningfully separable from the belief that an 'atheist' was describing a deity that had none of the qualities that premised a meaningful and recognisable society of people. As John Tickell wrote, in 1653, 'if every thing were God, I say there were then no God'. If enough people like Clarkson would have 'God sinning, God a swearer, God a drunkard, God a blasphemer', then, shockingly, they would also have a 'God dying'.[33] The same could be said of those who denied the Christian community created by infant baptism, who refused to correlate divine with earthly authority, or who believed in a deity that did nothing but forgive. A god who was not godlike might as well be said not to exist.

This anti-atheist *reflex* was a sincere response to feeling that everything meaningful was being challenged. However, it must also have been profoundly offensive to sincere Protestants who had thought their own way through the myriad complexities, confusions, and hopes of a time in which normality no longer seemed to work for them or even to exist. They had fought hard to uncover truth from amid the ashes of old certainties. And with the breakdown of censorship, it was also possible for the 'atheist' to fight back.

III

Alleged atheists who refused to be passive victims of polemical labelling had one very important resource available to them: the conflicted and compromised nature of the accusation itself. That is, the atheism of which they were accused was inherently relational to the Protestantism of the accuser who, in turn, was able to 'other' his adversary only by artificially denying the common bonds that formed the dialectic. To demonstrate this, we can turn to a remarkable but largely overlooked text, anonymously written – by 'G. G'. – in 1646, *A Dispute betwixt a Christian and an Atheist*. In some ways this pamphlet apes the conventions of previous edificatory books, which had a guardsman of orthodoxy disputing with an atheist or heretic – usually, for some reason, while walking together along a country road, although here, to capture the spirit of the age, in a pub – in order to highlight truth and uncover error. And 'Christian' in *A Dispute* is formally announced as the winner of the debate in the usual fashion. But this is all surface. In fact, this text merits attention not only because the author identifies with 'Atheist' but because in substantial terms it is very clearly written to show that Atheist is right and Christian a blustering fool, embarrassed by his own premises. *A Dispute* is best seen not as either an anti- or pro-atheist text, and the characters do not represent narrowly defined theological positions. Rather, the text is a commentary on the nature of the accusation. It also functions as a far-reaching and shrewd critique of how atheism is falsely identified, and even where the essence of the phenomenon might truly lie.

The character labelled Atheist makes it clear from the outset that he believes in God, believes in providence, believes in the soul, and believes in heaven. It becomes apparent, though, that he is not necessarily convinced that hell exists and that he does not think that all of Scripture represents literal truth. This is enough for Christian to say, 'Well: I perceive then that you are an Atheist: but a refined one, one of the new stamp: you believe in God, but not in Christ, his Son, nor the holy Ghost,' for 'he that denyes the Son and the holy Ghost; denyes the Father, and therefore is an Atheist'.[34] It is important to note that Atheist had denied little but simply queried whether everyone born before Christ was damned just because they had no knowledge of His sacrifice. The author may be suggesting that he or people he knows have been the victim of hysterical overreaction. But this was not an isolated moment. As William Towers argued in his anti-atheist treatise a decade later: 'He that Denies Christ to be God, as well as He that Denies Any God at all, is an *Atheist* too'.[35] This is an anti-atheism moulded for the context of a time when some radicals were playing dangerous games with the Trinity. However, it also flew in the face of many equivalent treatises from the previous half-century, in which writers as diverse as Henry Smith, John Dove, and Martin Fotherby sought to muster the monotheisms – and even some polytheisms – together into an ecumenical alliance against the lonely atheist 'other'.[36] Of course, all of these earlier writers would have agreed that a theology that excluded the Trinity was, in some hazy sense, 'atheistic'; their wider purpose, though, was to argue unbelief to the margins rather than to press it into the centre of intra-Protestant debate.

The usual rule of polemic is that the party who gets their labels to stick wins the debate. The interesting thing about this text, though, is that although Christian does all of the labelling, it becomes increasingly clear that Atheist is the more sympathetic character and the more intelligent one. The implicit argument is that people need to be very careful when they try to define orthodoxy and that because many people are not, they accidentally constitute the 'fundamentals' of religious truth in a self-defeating way. The text is really structured around Atheist's nagging voice. How should one define orthodoxy? What are the grounds of truth?

Christian confidently asserts several arguments that turn out to be deeply problematic. First, he contends that the veracity of a religious position can be discerned by its antiquity and size of membership. The *Atheos*, however, responds that 'the Church of *Rome* [is] ancienter than the Church of *England*' while, as 'for multitude, there is a greater number of *Mahumetans* then of your profession: and therefore according to that Argument you should fall into that beliefe'. Indeed, Atheist makes pointed use here of the increasing awareness of diverse global religions: '[L]ook on the people of *America*, and those of *Japan*, and all the people of the South Sea, and you shall find they will tell you, that their Faith hath endured ever since the World was'.[37] With a wider world swirling around – but finding no secure place within – Protestant consciousness, the Church of *England*'s claims to unique authority were problematic, and all the more so the claims of anti-atheists who had also rejected the Church of England.

Another argument deployed by Christian is that the true God vouchsafes the power of conversion upon His chosen people. But here the atheist voice carries a sting. In some places, conversion has been a pleasant word used to obscure the squalors of conquest and intolerance. Choosing a safe example, the *Atheos* notes that 'the Spaniards' are 'inhumane with them they have overcome' and that over a million 'harmlesse Indians in *America* [were] cruelly butchered without cause or offence given by them'.[38] The parallels between this example and English dissenters who mean no 'cause or offence' but are still persecuted by those who would claim institutional authority are obvious.

Christian is also keen to argue that some religions are plainly false because they are promoted by 'barbarous simple people'. But here Renaissance traditions of subjectivity had begun to make inroads into such complacent claims. As Atheist says: 'To you they may seeme so, but not to themselves, nor to some others, and they have greater reason to condemne Christians for barbarousnesse then we to condemne them'. Indeed, 'as the Persians seemed to the Grecians to be barbarous, so the Grecians seemed no less barbarous to them ... and who shall judge this controversie? neither party but the stander by'.[39] As William Walwyn argued in a treatise published in the same year: 'If the Presbiter examine the Independent ... they are like to find the same censure that the old Presbiters found upon being examined by the Bishops; and the bishops found from the Pope. Adversaries certainly are not competent judges.... In matters disputable and controverted, every man must examine for himself'.[40]

This was a point that Christian was unwilling to concede but had no good answer to. Their debate was not really about Grecians or Persians but about the specifically intra-Protestant conflicts of contemporary England. As Christian says, '[I]t is no strange thing in our populous Nation, to find men of severall opinions: and such as are not able to judge of things themselves: therefore they depend upon the opinion of others'.[41] Here, the debate comes to centre on the notion of princely authority. Atheists were often accused of being Machiavellian, but, of course, those who sought to limit the ambition of kings could use Machiavelli to discover the political machinations undertaken in the name of religion. As Atheist put it, '[I]s not Religion the colour for the vilest proceedings that are? doe not the Princes and States of *Europe* cloke with that their . . . oppression in the vilest manner?' While Christian gamely asserts the value of conventional hierarchies, he is left defenceless against the criticism that princes are vulnerable to self-interested counsel. Here the guardsman of orthodoxy is put on the back foot by Atheist's charge that 'Spanish' influence and a '*Frenchified* tongue' have infiltrated English politics. Given the tradition that associated atheists with courtly politicking, it is remarkable that a character titled Atheist could be made to say: 'I will not be like that simple Courtier, who being in much honour and esteem with his Prince and Countrey, for a bribe and hope of preferment, sels his . . . honour'. Lamely, Christian is forced to admit that there have been 'many over-sights in State-government as you have declared' but that these errors 'in choice of Councell' belong only to 'these latter ages of *England*'. Christian later admits that 'those you have discovered, are but pretenders to Christianity'.[42] So who is the atheist now?

Christian and Atheist come, implicitly, to coalesce around their opposition to the governance of Charles I but also agree that there are serious problems with the Erastian arrangement more generally. The corrupting and essentially foreign influence of courtiers cannot be confined to the political because the system ensures that damage is always done 'in respect as well of the temporall government as the spirituall'. Here, the 'chiefe deceivers' are 'the Clergie and Priests of each Christian Sect' because they are also made politically minded by the system itself.[43] All of this leads to the 'atheist' conclusion that belief can never be compelled or enforced. Edwards' treatment of the Greenham story served to emphasize the need for intolerance of diversity. But, again, what indisputable – or at least uncompromised – standard of truth was being defended? 'G. G.' chooses an extreme and provocative example to highlight the problem. Toward the end of the treatise, Atheist, who is now clearly in the ascendancy, reports that he knows a Brownist who would rather accept Islamic dominion than that 'the Pope or English Bishops should come to be established in the Kingdom where he lived'. Christian's astonishingly heterodox response is worth quoting at length:

> And for what you say the *Brownist* said, as touching the *Turks* dominion over *England*, I suppose it was not his hatred to his Countrey, nor his King,

that caused him to say so, but his desire to keep his body (the Temple of Christ) entirely to his worship, without . . . suffering any superstition to enter thereat, which he might imagine hee could not doe so freely under the Pope or Bishops, as under the *Turk*: For may be he had heard, that hee allowed of liberty of Conscience.[44]

So confused have the characters' labels become amid the flux of debate that Christian now upholds the value of preserving a kernel of inward sincerity even if it means formally embracing 'Turks' over 'Bishops', while Atheist can be seen decrying the essentially political nature of Erastian religion. The ridiculous position of intolerant 'orthodoxy', in the face of epistemological uncertainty and sociological reality, is rammed home in the very last exchange, in which Christian oddly claims to 'checkmate' Atheist. Earlier in the text, the latter was identified as an unbeliever because he had quibbles about hell. But by the end, Christian's initial insistence upon this point is made to boil down to a Pascalian quibble over whether it is worth living badly even if the odds of hell existing are, in Christian's words, 'a million to one'.[45] When examined closely, even cherished doctrines can be reduced to probabilities.

IV

I have suggested that the early modern concept of atheism was neither absolute nor hopelessly elastic. And those who were accused of atheism were more than capable of picking up on the tensions that existed within the polemical label. Atheist could be made to defeat Christian because the latter's arguments were, in themselves, a commentary upon Protestant claims to authority. As *A Dispute* demonstrates, the orthodox labeller could show vulnerability rather than strength through the act of labelling. We have also seen that contemporaries often located atheism in religious places. The destabilised theologies of the revolutionary period created an ambiguous – and indeed incestuous – relationship between 'orthodoxy', 'radicalism', and 'atheism' that the upholders of respectability tried as much as possible to deny. But the unacceptable 'other' was altogether too recognisable – was, indeed, troublingly familial.[46] Against whose head was the polemical musket really being held? The author of *A Dispute* may have suggested that the weapon was not really a musket but rather a mirror. In our final vignette, it was both.

Regicide in England was the stimulus for a tremendous intensity of hopeful and fearful emotion. It was a moment ripe for new gods and new atheisms. It was also a moment when people who had been spat upon rose up and bit back. One of the new gods was William Franklin, who was once 'very zealous in the duties of Religion', but having suffered from a 'distemper' beginning in 1646, came to think '*that he was God, that he was Christ*'.[47] The story of Franklin and his apostolic cohort is told by Humphrey Ellis in his *Pseudochristus*, which reads like a piece of investigative 'broadsheet' journalism. Ellis deplores what he sees, but he does try to understand it.

In late 1649, Franklin came into contact with the equally devout, and temperamental, Mary Gadbury. She had acquired an inward 'voyce' that presented her with powerful visions. Shortly after she said 'that *the Lord would send his Son to raign in the person of a man*', the wandering messiah William Franklin came to her house. 'She demanded of him thus: *Hath God revealed to you, that his Son shall raign in the person of a man?* To which he replyed, *I am the man*'. Leaving their respective families behind, and travelling together through Hampshire, the Franklin-messiah and his bride eventually set up at an inn called The Starre in Andover, and this became his pulpit. Soon they are inundated with admirers, including some 'very active persons' upon whom Franklin and Gadbury decided to bestow 'severall offices and titles'. One was appointed '*John the Baptist*, sent forth to tell that *Christ was come forth upon the earth*'. Another was named the 'mercifull angel'. And '*Henry Dixons* office was to be one of the destroying Angells mentioned in the *Revelation*, sent forth to curse the earth, and the Inhabitants of it'. We are told that 'of this wicked society was also one *William Holmes* of Houghton, he seems to be a partner of *Dixons* in his office of being a destroying Angell'.[48] Here, the Ranter and the atheist appear together, melded into one by the agency of people who had learned how to be what they had been told that they were.

Dixon and Holmes were charged by the Franklin-messiah with the task of shocking people out of their complacency by offending them as much as possible. The curses that they laid could, presumably, be lifted only by Franklin, who would also prove that there was a deeper meaning to the barren existential picture painted by his 'destroying Angells'. According to a report sent by the Constable of Andover, '*Dixon* said, that there was neither God nor Devill, and that all things came by nature, and did curse me'. Meanwhile Holmes, 'a very loose and prophane young man ... now fallen into this depth of wickedness', went to even greater extremes. According to the testimony of a local minister, Holmes approached him, 'having a gun in his hand, and in his mouth many hard speeches and blasphemies against God'. When he urged Holmes to '*have God in your heart*: He answered, *What dost thou know what God is* (or to that purpose:) *God is a toad, a Snake, and a Devil*'.[49]

Soon enough, the apostolic outlaws were rounded up, and they were presented to the Winchester Assize in January 1650. Witnesses were called to attest to the frauds of Franklin and Gadbury and to the atheism of their angels. One witness 'affirmed upon Oath, this *Dixon* to say, *That there was neither God nor Devil, but all things came by nature*'.[50] The apostles initially defended themselves by arguing that Franklin was the messiah and must be obeyed. Unfortunately, though, Franklin proved rather invertebrate as messiahs go and soon folded, admitting to his imposture, and after this blow his followers soon recanted their former statements. In the March Assize, a very secular-minded verdict was delivered, with Franklin and Gadbury being found guilty of adultery and bigamy, made worse because their fraud was perpetrated 'under the cloak of Religion'.[51] Franklin was imprisoned 'till he give good security for his good behaviour', and the same sentences were delivered to his most prominent followers. Luckily for Holmes, he escaped before the trial – the guilty verdict being, he surely knew, wholly inevitable – and nothing more is known of him. Dixon was given the same sentence as Franklin but was released from jail quickly because he retained useful connections within the county community. A strange world of inversion was thus ended in the most prosaic of fashions.

What, though, can we make of this confusing and, indeed surreal, picture?[52] The first point to consider is that nobody knew quite what to make of this holy-unholy-criminal alliance. This is partly because the protagonists knew how to play their roles. One witness reported, '[T]*he said* Dixon' to have claimed that he '*was the God of Light, and the God himself*' and further 'affirmed upon Oath, this Dixon to say, *That there was neither God nor Devil*'. This gave pause to consider how 'contradiction, as well as Blasphemy, possessed these persons, as in the same breath to affirm, *That there is no God; and yet that he himself is God: That there is neither God nor the Devill*; and yet presently in his cursing to use the names of both of them'.[53] Dixon – and presumably Holmes – knew how to play the game. They had been taught the game through a process of saying what they thought and then being told what they had apparently said. By repeating back a garbled charge through their own voices, they could make conventional society listen to its own incoherence.

Some evidence for this role-play is provided by another acolyte, Henry Spradbury, who – perhaps grateful for having been granted the 'somewhat better office' of 'an healing Angell' – argued that Dixon and Holmes were not synonymous with their personas. Yes, '*Dixon* had in the discharge of his office cursed and destroyed', just as Spradbury was happily tasked 'to heale and restore againe'; but Spradbury urged that others 'should not be offended at it, that it was [Dixon's] office, and what he did therein was but the discharge of his office'.[54] This defence had one origin within anti-atheist literature itself. For instance, in the preface to his dialogue between a Christian and an atheist in 1608, Jeremy Corderoy was at pains to stress that he did not empathise with the unbeliever whose words he would voice, but he still dedicated the book to Lord Chancellor Ellesmere because he 'thought it verie necessarye to shrowd my selfe under the protection of some Honourable person', who had made it their professional business to 'daily punish the outragious dealing of Atheists'.[55] Similarly, in his *Atheomastix* of 1622, Martin Fotherby anticipated and sought to refute the potential criticism that in 'the very seeking to prove' the 'grounded Principles of Religion' he would be seen to be 'carrying with it (in shew) a secret doubting of them'.[56] The muddy distinction between atheist voice and anti-atheist intention, in other words, had a lengthy lineage within orthodoxy.

Further evidence that the atheist-angels were functioning within familial boundaries is provided by Humphrey Ellis himself, who makes a point of dissenting from the judges' verdict that these activities had about them only a 'cloak of Religion'. Instead, Ellis sees religion as providing a once nurturing shroud. He is scrupulous in reporting the one-time Christian credentials of each defendant. Dixon was initially an upstanding member of the godly community, and even the 'loose and prophane' Holmes was once 'very hopeful for Religion'.[57] These speakers of unbelief had been religious enthusiasts and, before that, perhaps just good, solid Protestants. For Ellis, the problem stemmed from the transitional point at which sincere believers come to view 'Gospel-Ordinances of Word and Sacraments' as mere 'carnal low Administrations' and 'please themselves to live without them', while starting to 'censure all the Churches of Christ, who walk in the practise of any of his Ordinances, to be Antichristian'.[58] In other words, potential atheists are made when individuals come to see the religion to which they belong as 'Antichristian'. A sort of atheism perceived begat another sort received.

On Ellis's account, therefore, embodied atheism stemmed from a complex process in which once religious men and women rejected established religion because it was not, in their view, actually religious. This was, for puritans, the dilemma of the age. But dilemmas exist only in relation to realisable possibilities. Greenham spoke for an emerging generation of 'moderate Puritans' who sought to direct the power of Protestant enthusiasm within the Church of England because they realised how precarious that settlement really was. For the next generation, the practical danger lay much more within lazy Protestant assent than in an enthusiasm that Adams even exported to the continent. And amid the strange new realities of the 1640s, Edwards, who was, in old money, a 'separatist', could also take it upon himself to uphold a conservative orthodoxy with violent language, against people that he deemed too radical. An atheist person that Greenham could pity became an atheist other that the new orthodoxy would hate. But the unbelief that these guardians would seek to exceptionalise was inherently familial, and by daubing the emotional slur of 'atheism' upon countrymen who were also theologically engaged, they gambled upon scaring people back into line but also risked making the label itself laughable.[59] Indeed, the desperate nature of the attack allowed some radicals to inspect the polemical musket that had been aimed at them, to reconfigure it to their own ends, and to fire it back. The author of *A Dispute* did this with learned cool. His weapon was a mirror. The gun-toting atheist-angels, on the other hand, did it with actions and words that were designed to intimate anger and violence. They appropriated a stigma that, I think, had hurt them and sought to throw it back upon conventional society in a manner that suited their own temperaments. They knew what moral regulation constituted because they had once been orthodox themselves, and they had learned to speak back its compromises and contradictions in creative ways. This 'atheism' was real, but it was also dependant, for it acted only through the religious beliefs that gave it a body and the polemical attack that gave it arms to fight back.

Notes

1 Michael Buckley, *At the Origins of Modern Atheism* (New Haven, CT, and London, 1987), p. 10.
2 *Ibid.*, p. 6.
3 John Rowe, *Tragi-comoedia* (1653), p. 34.

4 I am indebted here to a passing reference in Michael Hunter's excellent 'The Problem of Atheism in Early Modern England', *TRHS*, 5th ser., 35 (1985), 138.
5 William Perkins, 'A Godly and Learned Exposition upon... the Epistle of Jude', in *The Workes of William Perkins* (3 vols, 1631), III, 578.
6 Perkins, 'A Cloud of Faithfull Witnesses', in *ibid.*, p. 31.
7 For a more representative account of how Perkins thought about atheism, see Leif Dixon, 'William Perkins, "Atheisme", and the Crises of England's Long Reformation', *JBS*, 50 (2011), 790–812.
8 Richard Greenham, 'Grave Counsels and Godly Observations', in *The Workes... of Richard Greenham* (1605), p. 3.
9 See Michael MacDonald, 'The Fearefull Estate of Francis Spira: Narrative, Identity and Emotion in Early Modern England', *JBS*, 31 (1992), 32–61.
10 Greenham, 'Grave Counsels', p. 3.
11 Miles Mosse, *Justifying and Saving Faith Distinguished from the Faith of Devils* (1614), p. 18.
12 Thomas Adams, *Commentary upon... the Divine Second Epistle [of] St. Peter* (1633), p. 16.
13 Mosse, *Justifying and Saving Faith*, p. 19.
14 Thomas Fuller, *The Holy State and the Profane State* (Cambridge, 1642), p. 383.
15 *Ibid.*, p. 382; Adams, *Commentary*, p. 16.
16 Thomas Edwards, *The Second Part of Gangraena* (1646), p. 18.
17 *Ibid.*; Mosse, *Saving and Justifying Faith*, p. 18.
18 Edwards, *Gangraena*, p. 18.
19 Fuller, *Holy State*, p. 383.
20 Edwards, *Gangraena*, p. 114.
21 Fuller, *Holy State*, pp. 379, 380.
22 Martin Fotherby, *Atheomastix* (1622), sigs A2r, B3r. These sentiments are also expressed in John Carpenter, *A Preparative to Contentation* (1597), sig. A2r; Francis Bacon, *Essayes or Counsels* (1625), pp. 90–1; Thomas Jackson, *A Treatise Containing the Originall of Unbeliefe* (1625), pp. 12, 36.
23 This view is supported, with some nuancing, by Ann Hughes, *Gangraena and the Struggle for the English Revolution* (Oxford, 2004), pp. 108–17.
24 William Towers, *Atheismus Vapulana* (1654), Dedicatory Epistle.
25 Christopher Hill, 'Irreligion in the "Puritan" Revolution', in J.F. McGregor and Barry Reay (eds.), *Radical Religion in the English Revolution* (Oxford, 1986), p. 198.
26 Federico Barbierato, *The Inquisitor in the Hat Shop: Inquisition, Forbidden Books and Unbelief in Early Modern Venice* (Farnham, 2012), p. 88.
27 Sarah Mortimer, *Reason and Religion in the English Revolution: The Challenge of Socinianism* (Cambridge, 2010), p. 181.
28 Edward Garland, *An Answer to a Printed Book, Intituled A Blow at the Serpent* (1657), p. 53.
29 Ephraim Pagitt, *Heresiography* (1645), pp. 152–4.
30 Ethan Shagan, *The Rule of Moderation: Violence, Religion and the Politics of Restraint in Early Modern England* (Cambridge, 2011).
31 George Buckley, *Atheism in the English Renaissance* (Chicago, IL, 1932), p. 43.
32 Lawrence Clarkson, *A Single Eye All Light, No Darkness* (1650), p. 9.
33 John Tickell, *The Bottomles Pit Smoaking in Familisme* (1652), pp. 53, 60.
34 'G.G.', *A Dispute Betwixt an Atheist and a Christian* (1646), p. 13.
35 Towers, *Atheismus Vapulana*, Dedicatory Epistle.
36 Henry Smith, *Gods Arrow against Atheists* (1609), pp. 1–3; John Dove, *A Confutation of Atheisme* (1605), p. 24; Fotherby, *Atheomastix*, pp. 20–33. It is also worth noting that Thomas Adams brings in Bellarmine to support his point that the essentials of religious truth are also agreed by 'reprobates and devills': *Commentary*, p. 16.
37 *A Dispute*, pp. 4, 5, 6.
38 *Ibid.*, pp. 6–7.
39 *Ibid.*

40 William Walwyn, *Toleration Justified and Persecution Condemned* (1646), p. 3.
41 *A Dispute*, p. 10.
42 Ibid., pp. 46, 26, 47.
43 Ibid., p. 46.
44 Ibid., pp. 46, 48.
45 Ibid., p. 50.
46 Ann Hughes, 'Thomas Edwards' *Gangraena* and Heresiological Traditions', in David Loewenstein and John Marshall (eds.), *Heresy, Literature, and Politics in Early Modern English Culture* (Cambridge, 2006), p. 140.
47 Humphrey Ellis, *Pseudochristus: Or, a True and Faithfull Relation of the Impostures . . . [of] William Frankelin and Mary Gadbury* (1650), p. 7.
48 Ibid., pp. 11, 17, 32.
49 Ibid., pp. 32, 33.
50 Ibid., p. 37.
51 Ibid., p. 51.
52 For a wider account than the one given here, see Jerome Friedman, *Blasphemy, Immorality, and Anarchy: The Ranters and the English Revolution* (Athens, OH, 1987), pp. 161–6.
53 Ellis, *Pseudochristus*, p. 37.
54 Ibid., p. 32.
55 Jeremy Corderoy, *A Warning for Worldlings* (1608), sig. A4v.
56 Fotherby, *Atheomastix*, sig. Br.
57 Ellis, *Pseudochristus*, p. 33.
58 Ibid., p. 61.
59 By way of analogy, see Peter Elmer, '"Saints or Sorcerers": Quakerism, Demonology and the Decline of Witchcraft in Seventeenth-Century England', in Jonathan Barry et al. (eds.), *Witchcraft in Early Modern Europe* (Cambridge, 1996), pp. 145–79.

10 Thomas Ady and the politics of scepticism in Cromwellian England[1]

George Southcombe

Clive Holmes is, he insists in seminars, 'a legal historian'. The statement is on one level unexceptionable. He has never had difficulty comprehending 'legal ratiocination' and the 'professional discourse' of lawyers.[2] On another level, however, it is clear that he has a very particular notion of what defines a legal historian. He has been consistent in his critiques of the legal history conducted by lawyers and its overly internalist explanations for change. For Clive, legal history has too often been divorced from the social, cultural, and political contexts in which it was forged.[3] Clive's own work has thus concentrated on the dialogic processes by which the law was shaped and administered. This is nowhere clearer than in his work on witchcraft – five articles that taken together constitute a major contribution to the field of study.[4] Clive's concentration has primarily been on the way in which the learning of the judicial elite was exposed to, and adapted as a result of, folkloric beliefs concerning witchcraft. Here the central case – rarely discussed in depth in his substantive work but underlying his approach and conceptualisation throughout – is that of Joan Prentice and her ferret. In this case of 1589 – known from a pamphlet account based on the legal materials although no doubt further redacted – Prentice confessed to consorting with her familiar spirit, the aforementioned ferret, in order to bring about harm. In her confession the ferret has a peculiar dual identity. It is 'Bidd' and it is 'satan'.[5] In Clive's reading, the interrogatory procedure that brought about the confession is made clear. The confession, presented as a narrative, is shown to be the textual remnant of a dialogue in which the elite interrogator's belief in the Satanic origins of witchcraft was mapped on to a pre-existing folkloric belief in the relationship that witches enjoyed with animals. The 'dissonance' between the two worldviews remains clear – that Satan masqueraded as a ferret was something with which the judicial and clerical elites remained uneasy – but they were forcefully brought together in the crucible of the legal process and fused. This is most obviously apparent in the 1604 statute against witchcraft that made it a specific offence to 'feede or rewarde any evill and wicked spirit'.[6]

More recently, Clive has traced the strains that this dialogic process ultimately put the legal system under, as the judges found it increasingly difficult to maintain the conceptual doublethink necessary to conclude that those brought before them – still often engaged in close relations with those unlikely furred and unfurred manifestations of demonic power – were in fact Satan's minions on earth.[7] It is with the question of decline that this chapter is concerned. In particular, it concentrates on a period that has been little studied by historians of witchcraft – the Protectorate – and a key sceptical text produced within it, Thomas Ady's *A Candle in the Dark*.

The Interregnum has always presented something of a puzzle to historians of witchcraft. During the civil wars, England's capacity to sustain a large-scale hunt was demonstrated. From 1645 to 1647, encouraged by the *soi disant* Witchfinder General and clear pervert, Matthew Hopkins, and enabled by the breakdown in central authority, those who believed themselves to have been bewitched in East Anglia drove forward a hunt unique in England for its violence and intensity.[8] Figures are difficult to establish, but it seems clear that at least one hundred were executed.[9] However, following this fervid period, the popular will to persecute was once again contained. Figures constructed from the surviving materials for the Home Circuit provide some indication of the level of witch-hunting. From 1649 to 1653, of those thirty-six tried for witchcraft for whom the outcome is known, twenty-four were not found guilty,[10] four were imprisoned, six were hanged,[11] and two were reprieved before sentencing. From 1654 to 1658, of the fifteen tried for witchcraft, ten were not found guilty, and four or five were hanged.[12] These figures are not inconsequential – clearly the potential to prosecute witches remained higher than it had under the Caroline regime[13] – but they remain suggestive. All but one of those punished for witchcraft from 1649 to 1653 were sentenced in Kent in 1652 in what was clearly a significant but unusual hunt.[14] What is more, this hunt was met with immediate scepticism in the form of Robert Filmer's *An Advertisement to the Jury-Men of England Touching Witches*.[15] Following the Commonwealth, the opportunities to hunt witches narrowed again. This is ostensibly surprising. Oliver Cromwell's dissolution of the Rump was based in part on his disillusionment with its failure to push forward Reformation, and clearly the role of godly magistrate was central to his self-conceptualisation. As he told his second Protectorate Parliament in September 1656:

> And a man may tell as plainly as can be what becomes of us, if we grow indifferent and lukewarm 'in repressing evil,' under I know not what weak pretensions. If it lives in us, therefore; I say, if it be in the general 'heart of the Nation,' it is a thing I am confident our liberty and prosperity depends upon, – Reformation. To make it a shame to see men to be bold in sin and profaneness, – and God will bless you.[16]

And yet these sentiments did not transfer into the persecution of witches. In August 1655 the Major Generals had been enjoined to further Reformation by waging war on a series of 'abominations' including 'Drunkeness prophanes blaspheming and takeing of the Name of God in vaine by swearing and cursing'.[17] Witchcraft was notably absent from the list. A point of comparison is provided by Scotland in 1649–50 when a theocratically charged government supported a hunt that saw around one hundred and fifty executions.[18] The combination of religious zealotry and political uncertainty could provide a fertile context for would-be witch-hunters. In Cromwellian England, however, it did not.[19]

The 1640s and 1650s had also witnessed the publication of key sceptical materials. Before Robert Filmer's response to the Kent trials of 1652, the puritan John Gaule had attacked the assumptions and methods of Matthew Hopkins in 1646.[20] Perhaps most importantly, in 1651 Reginald Scot's seminal sceptical work was reprinted for the first time since its initial publication 1584.[21] Scot's *The Discoverie of Witchcraft* was an extraordinary book. Most sceptical writing shared the conceptual framework of the demonologists. It emphasized particular strands of the demonological accounts – the illusory nature of much that witches believed that they achieved, the difficulties inherent in *proving* the crime of witchcraft – but launched no fundamental challenge to the basis of belief in witches.[22] Scot, drawing attention to what he saw as the absurdities of the 'witchmongers' with coruscating wit, opened up a dichotomy between the material and spiritual worlds that made the crime of witchcraft as conceived of by his contemporaries a simple impossibility.[23] His work was reprinted again in 1654, and in certain respects its radicalism fits more easily within Interregnum religious and print culture than in its original context. It is no surprise that its first interregnal publisher was the purveyor of radical works, Giles Calvert.[24]

The composition and printing of Thomas Ady's *A Candle in the Dark* might in a general sense be located within both the development of godly scepticism towards witch persecution and the market for the (re-)publication of sceptical works. Ady explicitly vindicated Scot, and sought to place himself in a direct line of descent from the Elizabethan. Scot's work '*did for a time take great impression in the Magistracy, and also in the Clergy, but since that time* England *hath shamefully fallen from the Truth which they began to receive; wherefore here is again a necessary and illustrious discourse for the Magistracy, and other People of this Age*'.[25] As will be demonstrated, Ady accepted the radical basis of Scot's argument, but like Scot he also sought to develop a wide range of arguments against the persecution of witches. In particular, he engaged in the ridicule of popular beliefs.

The gender imbalance of the hunt had long been, and would continue to be, a significant part of the sceptical case. The assumption, apparently deeply held at a popular level, that witches were likely to be women was pointed out to be logically improbable.[26] Why would Satan raise his armies on Earth from those who, according to contemporary discourse, were necessarily its weakest members? Why did Scripture not carry a warning that witches would generally be women? Ady dealt with this point in a relatively perfunctory way: 'whereas *Moses*, in all the Law, speaketh more fully of Witches in the Masculine, than in the female Sex; it confuteth that common tradition of people that Witches are most of the female Sex'.[27] He spent considerably more space on another element of popular belief that, as has been shown, had become central to the legal process: the witches' familiar. Indeed, on the very first page of his work

Ady emphasized the irreligious nature of familiar belief by drawing attention to what he saw as the primitive beliefs of a non-Christian society:

> *It is reported by Travellers, that some People in* America *do worship, for a day, the first living Creature they see in the morning, be it but a Bird, or a Worm; this Idolatry is like the Idolatry of this part of the World, who when they are afflicted in Body, or Goods, by Gods hand, they have an eye to some Mouse, or Bugg, or Frog, or other living Creature, saying, It is some Witches Impe that is sent to afflict them, ascribing the Work of God, to a Witch, or any mean Creature rather than to God.*[28]

English folklore was presented as the moral equivalent of indigenous belief systems in the New World. It was a point that was confirmed for Ady by the absence of 'imps' from Scripture:

> Where do we finde any such thing in Scriptures, or any such description of a Witch, or that a Witch was such a one as hath made a League with the Devil, and sealed it with his bloud, or hath Imps sucking him, or Biggs, or privie Marks, or that lyeth with *Incubus*, or *Succubus*, or any such phrase or expression in all the Scriptures? What least inkling have we of these things in all the Scriptures?[29]

But perhaps most importantly Ady drew attention to the simple absurdity of witnessing to the keeping of 'imps':

> [I]f the Witnesses can swear that any person keepeth and feedeth Imps, it is not a material Oath, for it as lawful to keep a Rat, or Mouse, or Dormouse, or any Creature tame, as to keep a tame Rabbit, or Bird; and one may be an Imp as well as another, and so may a Flea or Louse by the same reason; and so the Devil need not go far for a bodily shape to appear in, or to suck mens or womens flesh in; and if these were material Oathes, who then may not be proved a Witch?[30]

The cracks that remained in the image of the English witch as the result of the assimilation of Satanic and folkloric beliefs were here reopened. The evidential weight that the witches' familiar was expected to carry was represented as wholly unjustifiable.

The point was further strengthened by Ady's consideration of a form of proof intimately related to familiar belief. The witches' familiar was conceptually linked in England with the witches' mark. The insensate brand of continental witchcraft became in the English account a teat from which the familiar could feed.[31] The search for the mark became a regular part of the legal process. Ady was scathing in his account:

> Some will object, and say, They have helped search, and have found Biggs, and privie Marks upon such as have been accused to be Witches; but

I demand of them, Where doth the Scriptures teach us that a Witch is known by Biggs, or privie Marks? I also answer, That very few people in the World are without privie Marks upon their bodies, as Moles or stains, even such as Witchmongers call *The Devils privie Marks*[32]

Many had been condemned for having piles, '*Verrucae pensiles*' ('a certain kind of long fleshie Warts'), tumours called '*Thymion*' ('which sometimes being fell, and full of pain by reason of the rankness of bloud that feedeth them, and therefore issuing forth bloud, are called of ignorant Witchmongers, *Devils Biggs*'), and 'Natural parts of the Body called by a general name *Glandulæ*, and by a particular name *Tonsillæ*, in the jaws of people'.[33] Again, though, the witchmongers' fault lay not simply in their mistaking of natural protuberances for the witches' mark but in their illogicality:

[L]et any wise man consider, what body, of whatsoever constitution, especially of poor people that commonly want food, can spare a daily exhausting of bloud to nourish Imps sucking them, without an exhausting and over-throwing of their own Natural lives? whereas few poor or old people, but through want of nourishment and weakness of nature, have rather want of bloud, than an overplus of bloud.[34]

Like Scot, Ady was thus determined to overturn what he saw as the gross superstition of popular belief and the absurd procedures of the witchmongers. Like Scot too, Ady did not see that alone as sufficient. Ady was concerned to remove the witch-hunters' most powerful weapon: their Biblical mandate. As a result he dedicated the first book of his work to a systematic exploration of the terms used for witch in Deuteronomy 18:10–11.[35] As Scot had, Ady combined philological learning with illustrative anecdotes drawn from contemporary and near contemporary events. So it is that the reader, in being instructed about the qualities of a 'Jugler' learned of the master of sleight of hand 'who called himself, *The Kings Majesties most excellent Hocus Pocus* . . . because that at the playing of every Trick, he used to say, *Hocus pocus, tontus talontus, vade celeriter jubeo*, a dark composure of words, to blinde the eyes of the beholders, to make his Trick pass the more currantly without discovery, because when the eye and the ear of the beholder are both earnestly busied, the Trick is not so easily discovered, nor the Imposture discerned'.[36] The overall effect is potent. Ady was at pains to insist that neither he nor Scot denied the existence of witches, but his claim that he wished to show '*that Witches are not such as are commonly executed for Witches*' is far from an anodyne statement that witches were simply being misidentified.[37] The crimes that witches were said to commit were impossible, the very way in which witchcraft had been defined was incorrect. As Ady summarised with peculiar force in the second book: '[t]his indeed is the only Witchcraft that can kill or hurt any man . . . seducing the people to Idolatry, whereby they do cause them to provoke God to anger, and to strike them in his displeasure'.[38] What was more, the hunting of witches as generally understood was not simply a misguided solution but central to the problem: it was an idolatrous action based on a 'darksome Idolatrous opinion of Witches power':[39]

> [T]his Doctrin of Witches power is the main strength of Antichristian policy; for whereas that *Romish* Whore knoweth, that in all Nations the Civil Magistrate will hold his power, and not resign it to her, to have absolute power to kill for Religion, she maintaineth this damnable Doctrin to this end, that under the name of Witches she may melt away all whom she feareth, or suspecteth will be opposers of her Antichristian pride, and herein she ingageth the Civil Magistrate, by her subtill Doctrin, to cut off whom she pleaseth: and how can that be said to be a Government for the defence of peoples Lives and Estates? where contrary to all Law these Villains can steal away both life and estate from whom they please (except from such as are in places of Dignity, or so well esteemed in Common-wealths, or have such friendship among the potent of the Land, that thereby they are able to withstand their Adversaries) and these poor accused people have no redress, or help at the hands of the Magistrate; but he who ought to be their Defender is bewitched, and ingaged against them; he is taught indeed not to suffer a Witch to live, but never truly taught who, and what are Witches; and that many times they that ingage him by their lying Doctrin, are the very Witches themselves, aimed at in the Scriptures, that ought not to be suffered to live.[40]

This daring redescription of witchcraft ultimately rested on the same rejection of the possibility of witchcraft – as generally understood – seen in Scot. The demonologists had come up with various ingenious ways of explaining how the devil – who is a spirit – can act corporeally. For Ady, as for Scot, this was the purest nonsense, fuelled by popish assumptions. Ady poured scorn on traditional depictions of Satan: 'that he is some ugly terrible Creature to look upon, some black man with a pair of Horns on his head, and a Cloven Foot, and a long Tayl, or some monstrous Beast that inhabiteth in Woods, and walketh about in the night to scare people'.[41] The Scripture was clear:

> Further, Christ saith, *A Spirit hath not flesh and bones*, Luke 24.39. and yet some say, the Devil can condense a body, some say he can assume a body, some say he can have an apparent body; thus do they make the Word of God of no validity by their groundless traditions; for if the Devil can have so much as an apparent body, what validity was in the words of Christ, to take away the doubt of the Disciples, when they supposed they saw a Spirit?[42]

Ady's text thus represents the fullest, radically sceptical attack focused on witch belief since Scot. In those terms alone it is historically significant. However, two interrelated questions remain concerning first its specific purpose and secondly the timing of its publication. Its purpose might be explored in relation to the religious identity of its author and the particular way in which its argument is framed.

The specific range of reference in the text to near contemporary cases of witchcraft identifies Thomas Ady as being from Wethersfield in Essex.[43] He matriculated at Emmanuel College, Cambridge in 1624, and took his BA in 1627/8 proceeding MA in 1631.[44] Emmanuel was still at this point the intellectual crucible of the 'godly mafia'.[45] Ady seems in many respects to have been a relatively typical puritan product of this environment. The preamble to his will, drawn up on 15 October 1662 and proved 20 May 1672, recorded that he was 'a professed member of the true Christian Protestant Church of England desireing to live and dye in the true Christian faith yet not knowing the time of my finall dissolution from this fraile and Transitory Life'.[46] The wording is unusual, but in its series of qualifiers on the nature of the Church of England (in contradistinction to conformists who might refer to the Church's catholicity), it points towards a godly sensibility.[47] The point is strengthened by a consideration of Ady's use of other authors.

The third book of *A Candle in the Dark* is given over to demonstrating the 'vanity of some English Writers concerning Witches'.[48] Alongside James VI's *Daemonologie*, whose authorship Ady doubted, he considered works by four clergymen: Thomas Cooper, William Perkins, John Gaule, and George Gifford. Thomas Cooper, whose *The Mystery of Witch-Craft* was published in 1617, is dealt with viciously ('instead of being himself a Minister to instruct . . . he became a bloudy Inquistor to finde out Witches, that is a bloudy Persecutor of the poor') and dismissed sardonically: 'And so I leave this *Cooper* where I found him, namely, in a Stationers shop, dear of taking up'.[49] His account of the other, unimpeachably godly authors is more circumspect. Perkins, 'such a chosen instrument of preaching Gods Word in his life . . . whom I honour in his Grave' caused him particular problems.[50] He hypothesised a series of possibilities that might remove Perkins' responsibility for the text. As Perkins did not put the text into print himself – it being published following his death 'for the benefit of his Wife' – it might be considered whether it 'was of his own writing or not'. If it was, it might 'bee questioned, whether hee wrote it, with an intent to teach it for Truth openly, or only with an intent to confute such Heresies, as had formerly been delivered by *Bodinus*, *Hiperius*, and other popish writers, if hee had lived, for if it be well considered and compared with those Authors, it is only a collection of mingled notions out of them'. It might in fact have been interpolated into his works by an enterprising 'Ignorant or Popish Heretique' seeking to obtain respectability for his views by using Perkins' name. It might have been added by those who put his works into print 'either for the bolstring of their own Errors' or 'to make the Book sell the better'.[51] It was with a heavy heart, and in a perfunctory manner, that Ady noted that all those who nonetheless believed it was Perkins' work had to do was to 'compare it with the Scriptures' in order to uncover its errors.[52] In a different way, Ady also lightened his condemnation of Hopkins' critic, John Gaule, who 'in his zeal for God, & in his Religious hatred to the barbarous cruelty of this age, in persecuting the poor and innocent' was 'inclining to the Truth'. But Gaule had given in 'to the common contagion of Error that hath defiled the World' in thinking 'that Witches in the Scripture sence, are such as have made a familier compact with the Devil, and receive power from him to kill and the like'.[53] Finally, the Elizabethan puritan George Gifford, ultimately misled into error, 'had more of the Spirit of truth in him than many of his profession'.[54]

Ady explicitly maintained that the sceptical elements in the work of Gaule and Gifford – elements that if applied would have dramatically limited the hunt – were insufficient, but he did so in a way that displayed respect towards the godly.[55] Ady's scepticism was uncompromising, but his presentation of it was intended to appeal to a broad godly audience. This impression is confirmed by what he left out of Scot's account. At the end of his work, Ady noted that he might have added 'a Treatise of Spirits, or the nature of Devils ... but for brevity' he referred 'the Reader to Mr. *Scot*, who hath excellently written in the latter end of his Discovery of Witchcraft, a Discourse called, *A Treatise of Spirits*'.[56] He then moved swiftly on. It was a careful evasion. Scot's 'A Discourse upon Divels and Spirits' was the most radical part of his treatise.[57] It is in that part of the text that David Wootton has most forcefully identified Familist influence.[58] This may be an extrapolation too far, but the account offered by Scot is scarcely orthodox. It is unsurprising that Ady's search for brevity led him to omit it.

Ady's work is thus on one level unflinching in its total scepticism but on another produced for a mainstream godly audience. It puts the most radical case about witchcraft in the least radical way. The question remains: why was it produced in 1655?[59]

Ady was clearly disgusted by Matthew Hopkins and his activities. He was 'a wicked Inquisitor pretending authority for it', and his use of sleep deprivation was a particular abuse.[60] But Hopkins was long dead, and the hunt had declined. Ady's work was not born in immediate anger in the 1640s. An alternative specific context must be sought. An investigation into the politics of the text and its publication might serve to illuminate matters.

Discerning the politics of the text is unfortunately not a straightforward affair. Ady gave various examples of regimes that had engaged in the hunting of witches and then fallen. He wrote of Charles I (a monarch whom it was difficult to portray as witch-hunter):

> When King *Charls* went last to *Scotland* before these Wars, as he came back again sayling over the River *Humber*, the Vessel in which his Plate was carried, was reported to be cast away, and then was that Atheism so great, even at the very Court of *England*, that they reported Witches had done it, instead of observing Gods supream Providence ... since which we have had bloudy Wars, and where is the Court now?[61]

He wrote too of the vanquished Scots:

> A little before the Conquest of *Scotland* ... the Presbytery of *Scotland* did, by their own pretended authority, take upon them to Summon, Convent,

Censure, and Condemn people to cruel death for Witches and . . . they caused four thousand to be executed by Fire and Halter, and had as many in prison to be tried by them, when God sent his conquering Sword to suppress them, by occasion of which Wars there were many Ministers (whereof many were Presbyters) slain; What is become of their Presbyterian Authority now?[62]

Ady's rhetorical questions were posed with savage and easily interpretable intent. His account of the implications of the Hopkins hunt lacks this clarity. He launched a bitter attack on the 'great slaughter of Men and Women called Witches, at the Assizes at *Berry*, and at *Chelmsford*' in 1645, and ended 'What troubles have followed this Slaughter, blinde men may see'.[63] Anybody in England would have identified that they lived in a time of troubles, but interpreting the nature of those troubles depended on the political perspective of the observer, and on that Ady was frustratingly opaque. However, his highlighting of the fall of the king and the Scots at least opens up the possibility that when Ady wrote, he did so with at least one eye on those at the centre of government.

Ady's framing of his argument might also point in this direction. In his prefatory address to 'the more Judicious and Wise, and Discreet part of the Clergie of ENGLAND', he drew attention to Joshua 7.11:

> THese words, *Israel hath sinned*, are not so to be understood, as if *Israel* had been free from all other sins but only that of *Achan*, and yet that sinne of *Achan* was the sinne that kindled the anger of God against *Israel* . . . Then you that should be as messengers from God, in that you cry against sinne in generall, yee do well, but in that yee seek not out this cursed *Achans* wedg that hath defiled *England* and the Christian world, look to it betimes, lest it be laid to your charge, if the Nations perish for lack of knowledg.[64]

To assert that the sin of Achan was the persecution of witches was a novel interpretation, but the providentialist rhetoric used here of a nation that had sinned was one that would be increasingly echoed by central government over the next two years.[65]

It might reasonably be objected that such providentialist language was hardly the preserve of central government. It is therefore with the aim of cementing further the connections between Ady and those at the centre that the publication of his work is considered. *A Candle in the Dark* was published by Robert Ibbitson. Ibbitson was a prolific publisher. He had been one of the printers who had produced official accounts of Charles I's trial, and in 1653 he was considered for the position as printer to the Council of State.[66] In the late 1640s he published news in *Perfect Occurrences* that was in line with Independent views, and following the licensing act of September 1649 he published one of initially two official newssheets, *Severall Proceedings*.[67] Ibbitson was therefore a publisher much used by central government, and potential purchasers of books may well have recalled this association when they saw his imprint.

A further clue to unpicking the context in which Ady wrote may be offered by the other work Ibbitson published in 1655 that referred to witchcraft. This was Ralph Gardiner's *Englands Grievance Discovered in Relation to the Coal-Trade*, which, among many other things, recounted the activities of a Scottish witch-pricker in Newcastle around 1649–50, who had been brought in by the magistrates of the town. His methods produced a large number of suspected witches, and many were executed. Gardiner was scathing in his account. The pricker, he pointed out, had been executed for his 'villanie' after he returned to Scotland. On the scaffold, 'he confessed he had been the death of above two hundred and twenty women in *England* and *Scotland*, for the gain of twenty shillings a peece'. Gardiner asked 'by what Law the Magistrates of *Newcastle* could send into another Nation for a mercinary person to try women for Witches'?[68] The incident of the witch-pricker was part of a larger indictment of the government of Newcastle's magistrates that Gardiner presented in a work dedicated to Oliver Cromwell. Gardiner implored Cromwell to act 'for the glory of God, the same of your Law, the contentment of the free people of *England*, the preservation of Trade and Navigation, and increase of your publique Revenue'.[69] That Gardiner chose to use the perversion of justice represented by the witch-pricker to appeal to Cromwell is potentially instructive. Gardiner's assumption was clearly that the Protector could be moved by such an episode.

Taken together the evidence concerning the politics and publication of Ady's text suggests that it was in part focused on central government. Its publication in 1655 was therefore not coincidental. Its specific context is provided by the early stage of protectoral government. Ady's scepticism was designed to provide a full, scripturally justified vindication for the cessation of the hunting of witches. He may have sought to shape the views of those at the centre, or his text may have been endorsed by them from the start. That is to say, his text could have been an intervention that sought to alter opinions about witchcraft at the centre, or it could have reflected opinions that were already held. It may even have reflected the views of Oliver Cromwell himself. Certainly, for whatever reason, the Protector did not seek to prove his godly credentials by acting as a witch-hunter.

Ady's text was reissued in 1656 and again under a different title in 1661.[70] His thought crossed the Atlantic in godly circles. Cotton Mather reported that the minister George Burroughs had drawn on Ady in his (unsuccessful) defence against a charge of witchcraft in Salem in 1692.[71] As Burroughs' fate suggests, Ady's arguments, however much they might have been read and discussed, were not necessarily accepted. For some, Ady's scriptural scholarship was easily dismissed. One reader noted in the margins of a copy now in the Bodleian Library, Oxford: 'it is written thou shalt not suffer a witch to live now would the almighty make a law against what could never happen. – you fooll'.[72] Nonetheless, Ady's work was clearly a significant contribution to the seventeenth-century witchcraft debate. It offered a sanitised but undiluted version of Scot's uncompromising radicalism for a godly audience. Recently, historians have sought to overturn older accounts of the 'decline of magic', but

A Candle in the Dark is a reminder of the role played by godly discourse in challenging a worldview in which witch-hunting could be sustained.[73] It is a chapter in the story of what an earlier historiography would have called the Puritan Revolution and the 'disenchantment of the world'.[74]

Notes

1. I would like to thank Clive Holmes and Grant Tapsell for commenting upon an earlier draft of this chapter.
2. These are the criticisms Clive levelled at Geoffrey Elton's work: Clive Holmes, 'G.R. Elton as a Legal Historian', *TRHS*, 6th series, 7 (1997), 267–79.
3. Even the doyen of early modern legal history, J.H. Baker, is considered too 'internalist' in his approach: see the review of J.H. Baker, *The Law's Two Bodies: Some Evidential Problems in English Legal History* (Oxford, 2002), in *EHR*, 118 (2003), 206–7.
4. Clive Holmes, 'Popular Culture? Witches, Magistrates and Divines in Early Modern England', in Steven L. Kaplan (ed.), *Understanding Popular Culture: Europe from the Middle Ages to the Nineteenth Century* (Berlin, 1984), pp. 85–111; idem, 'Women: Witnesses and Witches', *P&P*, 140 (1993), 45–78; idem, 'Witchcraft and Possession at the Accession of James I: The Publication of Samuel Harsnett's *Declaration of Egregious Popish Impostures*', in John Newton and Jo Bath (eds.), *Witchcraft and the Act of 1604* (Leiden, 2008), pp. 69–90; idem, 'The Case of Joan Peterson: Witchcraft, Family Conflict, Legal Invention and Constitutional Theory', in Matthew Dyson and David Ibbetson (eds.), *Law and Legal Process: Substantive Law and Procedure in English Legal History* (Cambridge, 2013), pp. 148–66; idem, *Why Did the Prosecution of Witches Cease in England?* (Historical Association, 2013).
5. *The Apprehension and Confession of Three Notorious Witches* (1589), in Marion Gibson (ed.), *Early Modern Witches: Witchcraft Cases in Contemporary Writing* (2000), p. 135.
6. Statute quoted in Holmes, 'Popular Culture?', p. 98. Clive includes brief comments on the Prentice case, in *ibid.*, p. 100, but his fullest exploration appears in Lady Margaret Hall's in-house magazine: 'Bid the Ferret', *The Brown Book* (2008), 24–30. Clive vindicates the use of source criticism based on searching for dissonances, and acknowledges his intellectual debt to Ginzburg and Monter, in Holmes, 'Popular Culture?', p. 94.
7. Holmes, *Why Did the Prosecution of Witches Cease?*
8. Malcolm Gaskill, *Witchfinders: A Seventeenth-Century English Tragedy* (2005).
9. James Sharpe, *Instruments of Darkness: Witchcraft in England 1550–1750* (pbk edn, 1997), p. 129. See also the more detailed discussion in Holmes, *Why Did the Prosecution of Witches Cease?*
10. This figure combines those cases thrown out by the Grand Jury and those found not guilty by the Petty Jury.
11. Of these six – all tried in Kent in 1652 – three were reprieved by parliament, but the reprieves arrived too late. See Malcolm Gaskill's headnote to H.F., *A Prodigious & Tragicall History* (1652), in James Sharpe (gen. ed.), *English Witchcraft 1560–1736* (6 vols, 2003), III, 455–6; Malcolm Gaskill, 'Witches and Witchcraft Prosecutions, 1560–1660', in Michael Zell (ed.), *Early Modern Kent, 1540–1640* (Woodbridge, 2000), pp. 245–7.
12. These figures are based on C. L'Estrange Ewen, *Witch Hunting and Witch Trials: The Indictments for Witchcraft from the Records of 1373 Assizes held for the Home Circuit A.D. 1559–1736* (New York, 1929), pp. 107–8, 235–51, supplemented by Alan Macfarlane, *Witchcraft in Tudor and Stuart England: A Regional and Comparative Study* (2nd edn, 1999), p. 270.
13. On the low level of witch-hunting under Charles I see the comments of Sharpe, *Instruments of Darkness*, pp. 126–7, and Holmes, *Why Did the Prosecution of Witches Cease?*
14. Brian P. Levack, *Witch-Hunting in Scotland: Law, Politics and Religion* (2008), p. 70.
15. Robert Filmer, *An Advertisement to the Jury-Men of England touching Witches* (1653).

16 *The Letters and Speeches of Oliver Cromwell*, ed. Thomas Carlyle and S.C. Lomas (3 vols, 1904), II, 540–1. I have omitted Carlyle's interpolations.
17 TNA, SP 18/100/42–3.
18 Levack, *Witch-Hunting in Scotland*, p. 55.
19 Explaining why Oliver Cromwell did not persecute witches is the subject of one of Clive's unpublished papers: '"The Curious Incident of the Dog in the Night-Time": Oliver Cromwell and Witchcraft'.
20 John Gaule, *Select Cases of Conscience Touching Witches and Witchcrafts* (1646).
21 Reginald Scot, *Scot's Discovery of Witchcraft* (1651). There are two 1651 imprints of this work, Wing S943 and S943A. See further the comments of Holmes, 'The Case of Joan Peterson', p. 156.
22 Stuart Clark, *Thinking with Demons: The Idea of Witchcraft in Early Modern Europe* (Oxford, 1997), Chapter 13.
23 Scot's wit is nicely brought out in Clive's (critical) review of Philip C. Almond, *England's First Demonologist: Reginald Scot and 'The Discovery of Witchcraft'*, in *EHR*, 128 (2013), 952–3.
24 A point made in Holmes, 'The Case of Joan Peterson', p. 156.
25 Thomas Ady, *A Candle in the Dark* (1655), sig. A3r.
26 Holmes, 'Popular Culture?', pp. 94–5.
27 Ady, *Candle in the Dark*, p. 36.
28 *Ibid.*, sig. A3r.
29 *Ibid.*, p. 93.
30 *Ibid.*, p. 135.
31 Holmes, 'Popular Culture?', pp. 98–9; Holmes, 'Women: Witnesses and Witches', pp. 69–75.
32 Ady, *Candle in the Dark*, p. 127.
33 *Ibid.*, pp. 127–8.
34 *Ibid.*, p. 128.
35 *Ibid.*, pp. 9–90. Cf. Scot's shorter discussion: Reginald Scot, *The Discoverie of Witchcraft* (1584), pp. 113–16.
36 Ady, *Candle in the Dark*, p. 29.
37 *Ibid.*, sig. A3r.
38 *Ibid.*, p 136.
39 *Ibid.*, p. 103.
40 *Ibid.*, p. 138.
41 *Ibid.*, p. 150.
42 *Ibid.*, pp. 109–10.
43 *Ibid.*, p. 79: the reference is to 'a Maid ... lately at *Brantree* in *Essex*'.
44 John Venn and J.A. Venn, *Alumni Cantabrigienses* (10 vols, Cambridge, 1922–54), I, s.v. 'Ady, Thomas'.
45 Sarah Bendall, Christopher Brooke and Patrick Collinson (eds.), *A History of Emmanuel College, Cambridge* (Woodbridge, 1999), Chapter 6.
46 TNA, PROB 11/339/95.
47 I am very grateful to Dr Ian Archer and, particularly, Professor Kenneth Fincham for advice on this point. Peter Elmer, *Witchcraft, Witch-Hunting, and Politics in Early Modern England* (Oxford, 2016) appeared too late for its findings to be taken fully into account. However, Elmer's careful tracing of Ady's biography confirms, and substantiates on the basis of a wealth of evidence, the reading offered here of his religious identity: see *ibid.*, pp. 164–7.
48 Ady, *Candle in the Dark*, p. 139.
49 *Ibid.*, pp. 151, 162 (mispaginated, in fact p. 154).
50 *Ibid.*, p. 162 (mispaginated, in fact p. 154). The best account of William Perkins's pastoral purposes is now Leif Dixon, *Practical Predestinarians in England, c. 1590–1640* (Farnham, 2014), Chapter 2.
51 Ady, *Candle in the Dark*, pp. 162–3 (mispaginated, in fact pp. 154–5).

52 *Ibid.*, p. 163 (mispaginated, in fact p. 155).
53 *Ibid.*, pp. 163–4 (mispaginated, in fact pp. 155–6).
54 *Ibid.*, p. 167 (mispaginated, in fact p. 159).
55 George Gifford maintained the reality of witchcraft while deriding much that constituted popular belief, and focusing particular fire on the cunning-folk – the devil's 'other sort of Witches' – whom he saw as misleading and endangering the people. See his *A Dialogue Concerning Witches and Witchcraftes* (1593), quotation at A3r. If Gifford's views had been adopted, then the numbers of those suspected of witchcraft would have dramatically declined.
56 Ady, *Candle in the Dark*, p. 169 (mispaginated, in fact p. 161).
57 Scot, *Discoverie*, pp. 351–401.
58 David Wootton, 'Reginald Scot/Abraham Fleming/The Family of Love', in Stuart Clark (ed.), *Languages of Witchcraft: Narrative, Ideology and Meaning in Early Modern Culture* (Basingstoke, 2001), pp. 119–38.
59 A similar chronological conundrum impels Clive's analysis in Holmes, 'Witchcraft and Possession at the Accession of James I'.
60 Ady, *Candle in the Dark*, p. 101; Gaskill, *Witchfinders*, pp. 276, 278.
61 Ady, *Candle in the Dark*, p. 104.
62 *Ibid.*, p. 105.
63 *Ibid.*, pp. 104–5.
64 *Ibid.*, p. 3.
65 Blair Worden, 'Cromwell and the Sin of Achan', in Blair Worden, *God's Instruments: Political Conduct in the England of Oliver Cromwell* (Oxford, 2012), pp. 13–32.
66 Amos Tubb, 'Printing the Regicide of Charles I', *History*, 89 (2004), 511; H.R. Plomer, *A Dictionary of the Booksellers and Printers Who Were at Work in England, Scotland and Ireland from 1641 to 1667* (1907), s.v. 'Ibbitson, Robert'.
67 Amos Tubb, 'Independent Presses: The Politics of Print in England during the Late 1640s', *Seventeenth Century*, 27 (2012), 297; Joad Raymond, *The Invention of the Newspaper: English Newsbooks 1641–1649* (Oxford, 1996), p. 75.
68 Ralph Gardiner, *Englands Grievance Discovered in Relation to the Coal-Trade* (1655), pp. 107–10, at 109.
69 *Ibid.*, sig. A2v.
70 Thomas Ady, *A Candle in the Dark* (1656); Thomas Ady, *A Perfect Discovery of Witches* (1661).
71 Bernard Rosenthal, *Salem Story: Reading the Witch Trials of 1692* (Cambridge, 1993), p. 150; Cotton Mather, *The Wonders of the Invisible World* (Boston, 1693), p. 104.
72 Bodl., Oxford Antiq.E.1656.7, Thomas Ady, *A Candle in the Dark* (1656), p. 8.
73 For the challenges to older models, see the historiographical review by Alexandra Walsham, 'The Reformation and the Disenchantment of the World Reassessed', *HJ*, 51 (2008), 497–528.
74 The phrase has its roots in Max Weber's use of *Entzauberung*. See e.g. Max Weber, *The Protestant Ethic and the Spirit of Capitalism*, trans. Talcott Parsons (Routledge Classics edn., 2001), pp. 61, 71, 97. For discussion of Weber's meaning and a reminder that 'disenchantment' is a poor translation of *Entzauberung*, see Peter Ghosh, *Max Weber and the Protestant Ethic: Twin Histories* (Oxford, 2014), Chapter 6, esp. pp. 249, 260–4.

11 The demand for a free parliament, 1659–60[1]

Blair Worden

The endings of revolutions can need as much explanation as their causes. Though the weaknesses and divisions of puritan rule in its late stages are obvious enough, contemporaries were astonished at the return, by peaceful means, of the monarchy in May 1660. The military and naval might of the republic was overcome without those dreaded and seemingly unavoidable means, foreign invasion and the renewal of civil war. Much of that story turned on political contingencies and on the calculations and abilities of leading political actors. Yet behind those features there lay a political movement that had swept through English politics in the preceding winter and that made a peaceful solution to the national crisis possible. The demand for 'a free parliament' persuaded General George Monck to take what proved to be the decisive steps in the overthrow of the republic. First he abandoned his commitment to the Rump and restored the full Long Parliament. Then he insisted on the elections that produced the Convention, the body, generally accepted as a 'free parliament' or as near to one as circumstances allowed, which met on 25 April and welcomed back the king the following month.

Although a number of accounts of the late Interregnum have commented helpfully on the movement for a free parliament, none of them has explored it very far. Historians have not reconstructed the movement or grasped the extent of its significance. Contemporaries knew its importance. Observer after observer agreed that the movement had the will of 'the nation' or of 'the people' behind it. The campaign flooded the press, animated riots and demonstrations, and was backed by declaration after declaration on behalf of local communities. Elsewhere I attempt to trace the origins of the campaign, to reconstruct its chronology, and to assess its place in the wider movement that produced the Restoration.[2] In this essay I examine the expressions and the extent of the appeal that it commanded. But first we need some background.

The term 'free parliament', though it had an ancestry, came into common use only during the civil wars, when parliaments acquired a huge and hitherto inconceivable place both in the running and in the political consciousness of the country – only for their deliberations to be terminated or interrupted, and their membership curtailed, by a succession of equally unprecedented military interventions and coups. The phrase 'free parliament' was widely partnered by another, a 'full parliament', which was used in protest against the rows of empty seats in the Commons left vacant by the military purges. Twice in 1659, first in May and then in December, the Army despairingly restored the regime it had evicted in 1653, the Rump, the regime created by the most extensive purge of the revolution, Pride's Purge of 1648. In its restored forms, the Rump, which often struggled to raise a quorum, represented only about a fifth of the constituencies. Though it grudgingly recognized that it would need to fill the benches, it proposed to do so through by-elections, which would enable the existing members to retain their seats and which, by the imposition of 'qualifications' on voters or candidates or of tests on MPs before they took their seats, would continue to confine political participation to people ready to support the republic.

The movement for a free parliament took wing because leaders of the two political parties that had fought each other in the 1640s but had then opposed the republic – the royalists on one side and the Presbyterians on the other, though the terms are necessary simplifications, with limitations to which we shall come – agreed to suspend their differences and, for the sake of removing their common adversaries from power, formed an alliance to promote the campaign; and because the campaign itself touched public feelings that had been inflamed by the experience of military rule. It was not an even partnership. Though royalists took every advantage of the campaign and were eventually its beneficiaries, the impetus of the movement came mostly from Presbyterians, and particularly from MPs who had been 'secluded' by Pride's Purge. The Presbyterians' chief goal was the reversal of the purge and the return of the secluded members to Westminster, where they had commanded a majority. On both occasions of the Rump's restoration in 1659, the secluded members attempted to regain their seats but were forcibly prevented. Pride's Purge had thwarted their plan to restore Charles I to the throne, on conditions that would strictly limit his power. In 1659–60 they wanted to impose similar conditions on his son. Royalists, or those of them who had the king's ear, were appalled by that prospect. They hoped for an unconditional restoration of the monarchy and saw a newly elected Parliament, without partisan restrictions on voters or candidates, as a means to its attainment. Presbyterians, though indignant at the Rump's attempts to exclude them from elections, tended to take it for granted that past and present supporters of the king's cause should be disqualified, much as royalist MPs had been 'disabled' during the civil war.

Through the campaign for a free parliament there ran questions that remained unanswered, sometimes deliberately. Would a reconstituted Long Parliament of the kind envisaged by Presbyterians, which would restore only Roundheads to Westminster, count as a 'free parliament'? The term was used often enough both by the two parties and by commentators who described their exertions to entitle us to call the movement, loosely, one for a 'free parliament'. Yet Presbyterians more often than not eschewed the term, for fear either of provoking the Rump into retaliation or of giving undue encouragement to Cavaliers, who discovered in the phrase a rhetorical potency that could be directed not only against republican but against all Roundhead and puritan rule. Again, it was commonly agreed that, if the secluded members were restored, they would need to make the Commons 'full' by holding by-elections in seats made vacant by deaths since 1648. But would they then cling to power, as the Rump tried to do, in a parliament that had been elected two decades earlier?

A 'free parliament' was a central demand of Booth's rising of the late summer of 1659, that joint royalist–Presbyterian venture. Though the failure of the rising dented the movement, it persisted. It reacquired its vigour and began its period of greatest impact, in December, when the rule of the Committee of Safety, the military regime that in October had deposed the Rump for the second time, disintegrated. When on the twenty-sixth the Rump replaced the rule of the committee, the parliament became again what it had been in Booth's rising, the target of the campaign. In January 1660 agents from the exiled court secretly met leading secluded members in London to draw up declarations to be sent for subscription to the shires.[3] There was tough bargaining. The two sides had not only to protect their own positions but to carry the support of their allies in the regions, who had minds and perspectives of their own. Though tactical compromises over phraseology, made by both sides, make simple classification impossible, we can broadly say that some of the ensuing declarations confined themselves to the Presbyterian position, that a small number implicitly favoured the royalist one, but that the largest number expressed a willingness, so long as the Rump were deposed and the House filled, to accept 'either' a new parliament 'or' the return of the secluded members (with by-elections in the seats made vacant by Presbyterian deaths).[4]

The Rump imprisoned the promoters of a number of the shire declarations, some of them in the Tower. Many people may have been locked up merely for signing the documents. Agitation for a free parliament was frequently crushed by troops, and in some counties declarations were apparently 'stifled'.[5] Some of the manifestos were held back from print until after 11 February, when the first of Monck's two decisive moves against the Rump made publication safer. But most of the documents had already been either published or else delivered to one or more recipients: to the Rump itself (a practice soon ended by the regime's retaliatory responses); to the City of London, which had issued its own declaration for a free parliament on 20 December and to which many counties looked for a lead; or most commonly to Monck himself, on whose decisions, before and after arrival in London on 3 February, the political future plainly depended. On his march from Scotland, begun at the start of the year, Monck received a succession of oral demands for a free parliament from delegations from the counties through which he passed. But only after he had reached the Midlands did counties resolve to send him the written declarations that deputation upon deputation from the shires presented to him and that are our principal source for the extent and aims of the movement.

I

We have declarations, all of them printed, on behalf of more than half the counties of England, twenty-one out of thirty-nine (as well as abandoned drafts of a declaration by a twenty-second county, Derbyshire).[6] If declarations had been submitted on behalf of other counties, we would surely know of them from the observers who monitored the campaign.[7] We look in vain for correspondences between the geographical distribution of the declarations and political sympathies or grievances in the areas that produced them – for correlations, say, with the lines of regional allegiance that had formed during the civil wars or with the extent to which the declaring counties were under-represented in the Rump (where in any case no county was well represented). Although purely local grievances were occasionally voiced in the remonstrances, the emphasis of the texts was on the afflictions that, they stated, were shared by all Englishmen. The declarations applauded one another, adopted one another's arguments and wording (though always with variations), and presented themselves as expressions of a nationwide movement. No nation ever achieves unanimity. Modern historians, who like to emphasize divisions or variations of class and region, are properly suspicious of generalizations about national feeling. Yet the movement for a free parliament illustrates the potency available to movements that believe themselves to speak for a country and are believed to do so.

Although the movement was not confined to the counties that produced declarations, there is a geographical pattern to those which did. With one exception, which is of questionable authenticity, all the declarations were submitted on behalf of counties on the East Coast, in the Central or East Midlands, in the Home Counties, or in the South-West. There is a single exception to another pattern too. With one geographical gap, every shire in whose name a declaration appeared shared a border with at least one other that did so. The gap is Somerset, where the movement was vigorous nonetheless. A belligerent declaration appeared on behalf of the apprentices of Bristol, and there was also agitation in towns close to it.[8] No declaration appeared on behalf of Somerset's neighbour, Dorset, but a 'paper' for 'a free parliament' circulated for subscription in the county,[9] and Lyme Regis supplied a manifesto on behalf of the secluded members.[10] One of the 'stifled' declarations may have belonged either to Dorset or to Sussex, whence a plan for a declaration was reported.[11]

Among shires that produced declarations there was cooperation across county boundaries – even though the demands stated by the cooperating counties often differed. The royalist–Presbyterian negotiations in London produced draft declarations for Northamptonshire and Gloucestershire, which were finalized after consultations with, or alterations by, leaders of those counties and which after subscription were hurried to the capital to be printed. The text of Northamptonshire's declaration was passed on to Leicestershire and Oxfordshire, and Gloucestershire's text was forwarded to Warwickshire, though the two documents were amended substantially before those neighbouring counties adopted them. Lines of communication down the East Coast drew Yorkshire's organizers together with Lincolnshire's (whose leading figure in the movement, the secluded member Edward Rossiter, worked with the leader of the movement in Yorkshire, his former commanding officer Thomas Fairfax),[12] and linked Norfolk's declaration with (probably) Suffolk's[13] and with Lincolnshire's.[14] Sir Horatio Townshend, a leading sponsor of the movement in his native Norfolk and a nephew of Fairfax, was in York when Yorkshire's declaration was drawn up.[15] So was Sir Thomas Wharton, a key figure in the Yorkshire declaration,[16] who had a base (of some elusive kind) in Lincolnshire.[17] There is also likely to have been collusion between Nottinghamshire and Derbyshire.[18]

The highest concentration of declarations was from counties on or close to Monck's march south from Leicester in the last week of January. Only well into February did counties through which or by which he had earlier passed – Yorkshire, Lincolnshire, Derbyshire, and Nottinghamshire – produce (or in Derbyshire's case try to produce) declarations. It was probably only then, too, that a declaration on behalf of Cheshire, Shropshire, and Staffordshire (the only one to claim to speak for more than one county) was composed.[19] Though the movement made a belated impact in the city of Durham,[20] there was no declaration from the palatinate or from the other three northernmost counties or from Lancashire. There was agitation on behalf of the movement in Cardiff and in Hereford and towns near it,[21] but no declaration emerged from Wales or on behalf of Herefordshire or of Worcestershire or Monmouthshire. Otherwise, the only counties not to have declared are Wiltshire, Hampshire, Surrey, Middlesex, Cambridgeshire,[22] Huntingdonshire, and Rutland.

Seventeenth-century political petitions and addresses have been a fruitful area of recent enquiry.[23] The county manifestos for a free parliament were not 'petitions', for in the eyes of the promoters there was no legitimate authority to petition. Even the other conventional term for a respectful communal message, 'address', was avoided by all but four counties (each of which 'addressed' General Monck). Nonetheless the documents repeat a number of the patterns of the petitioning movements of the era, especially those of early 1642, when a torrent of declarations from the counties was sent to the Long Parliament, and those that supported the uprisings against Parliament in 1648.[24] In this case as in those, promoters claimed to have vast, round numbers of subscribers or potential subscribers behind them. Supposedly the Northamptonshire declaration was signed by ten thousand people and would have been signed by twenty thousand, perhaps forty thousand, others.[25] 'More than 5000 considerable persons' signed Oxfordshire's declaration,[26] and many 'thousands' signed others. Some declarations had to be drafted and circulated for subscription, at high speed, so that they could reach Monck in time to influence him before he decided the nation's fate. We are told that numbers of signatures would have been much larger had the promoters not had to move so fast or been impeded by government agents or soldiers. The sponsors of the Essex declaration, who complained of local obstruction, were embarrassed to have attracted only three hundred thirty signatures and feared lest so 'inconsiderable a number for so great a county' might 'bespeak this document forged'. They would have raised ten thousand had they not been 'forced to do in one day the work of seven'.[27]

Airy claims about the quantity of signatures cannot be tested. Though in three counties we catch glimpses of the process of subscription – of declarations being circulated in Canterbury and Rochester and 'speeded towards Dover and into the Isle of Thanet';[28] being passed round in 'the parish of Stroud' in

Gloucestershire;[29] and, in Buckinghamshire, being sent round three hundreds and in towns near Stony Stratford[30] – we have no concrete evidence about the numbers of subscribers in those or most counties. In a small number of shires, however, we are luckier. There are two lists of subscribers, in their original forms, though in both cases we may not have all the sheets of signatures. One, from Norfolk, carries seven hundred and ninety-five names, the other, from Suffolk, one hundred and forty-one.[31] The drafts of the abortive declaration for Derbyshire survive, one with eight signatures, the other with twenty-seven (four of them to be found on both documents), but many of the twenty-seven are written in a single hand. The list as a whole, though headed by prominent figures in the shire, does not suggest a wide range of socially substantial support.[32] In print we have a much more impressive list, of fifty 'esquires' who are convincingly stated to have been among the signatories of Yorkshire's declaration. It may be incomplete, for the names are crammed, on a folio sheet, into a space too small for any more.[33] The quantity of subscribers was not everything. Yorkshire explained that in seeking signatures it had been more interested in social 'weight' than in 'number'.[34] Some counties declared only in the name of their prominent landowners or 'gentry', though it was more usual to add 'the freeholders', and a number of counties added 'the clergy' or 'the ministers'.

Defenders of the Rump challenged the authenticity of the declarations or questioned the extent of their support.[35] Though such imputations sit uneasily with the government's expressions of alarm at the extent and potency of the movement, not all the manifestos were necessarily all they seemed. In most counties we have sufficient indications that the declarations were backed by substantial local figures. Yet we should take warning from an implausible manifesto that appeared in November 1659, before the movement had got into full swing, and that claimed to be a *Remonstrance* for 'a free parliament' by 'the late *Eastern, Southern, and Western Associations*'.[36] In February 1660 a declaration appeared, ostensibly on behalf of Fairfax and Yorkshire, making the same demands as the declaration we know Fairfax to have endorsed but in far more inflammatory terms. It was plainly spurious.[37] We may wonder how many people sanctioned the document of the same month that declared on behalf of three counties on the geographical periphery of the movement, Cheshire, Staffordshire, and Shropshire, '&c'.[38] Possibly too there is a question mark against Bedfordshire's declaration, also of February, which borrowed from Yorkshire's.[39]

II

Even though most of the declarations appeared on behalf of shires, the urban dimension of the movement struck contemporaries as forcibly as its support outside the towns, sometimes more so.[40] It was in towns (or cities) that the movement was boldest and keenest, especially London, Bristol, Gloucester, Exeter, and York. In Bristol, the one town where we have the leader's name, that role was taken by the merchant Richard Ellsworth, who had fought for the king in the 1640s but who in early 1660 acquired or hid behind a Presbyterian face.[41] It is no surprise that agitation centred on towns. County capitals were the conventional meeting places of the gentry, who gathered in them to forward the movement, as, at least in some cases, did humbler rural supporters of it. Signatures were easier to obtain in towns than among the scattered rural population. And towns had borne much of the most direct and visible burden of the military presence of the Interregnum, which swelled in 1659–60[42] and which the movement was determined to lift.

The declarations of Gloucestershire, Kent, Leicestershire, Lincolnshire, Norfolk, Nottinghamshire, and Norfolk all claimed to speak for the county town as well as for the shire. Yet urban supporters of the movement were repeatedly obstructed by the rulers of their towns or by groups among them: either because the authorities had personal connections to the Rump, or, as was sometimes alleged, because leading civic worthies had invested in lands appropriated from the king's cause,[43] or perhaps most commonly because, in that chaotic time, municipal rulers whose communities faced desperate problems of order and hardship clung to obedience to the prevailing power.[44] Whereas shires regarded the calling of a free parliament, which was bound to take time and involve a further period of instability, as the necessary route to settled conditions, urban magistrates saw the movement itself as an immediate threat to civil peace. Rulers of towns were anyway normally more compliant with the regimes of the day than were leaders of shires. We notice the contrast between the manifold addresses sent by town governments to Whitehall on the accession of Richard Cromwell[45] and the resistance of those bodies to moves to depose the Rump. Urban regimes could reflect on the sad fate of Chester, which had been punished severely for allowing Booth's forces into the city.[46]

In general it was an inner ring of urban rulers who held back, in defiance of their juniors. In London, where the 'naturally very pacific' mayor told the citizens that public disturbances were 'not the way' to achieve their goal 'but the ready way to destroye the citty',[47] prolonged and intense pressure from the streets was needed before the City leadership agreed to London's nervously worded declaration of 20 December, which it hoped would at last 'allay' the 'tumultuous spirits'.[48] That was the only occasion when London's rulers committed themselves to the movement on paper. They did write soon afterwards to Monck on the same subject, but in carefully equivocal terms.[49] From December to February they repeatedly prevaricated,[50] to the exasperation of citizens, who knew how eagerly counties were looking to London for leadership. It is true that London's rulers were generally happy for counties to say on paper what they would not state in writing themselves, and that they were sometimes more forthright in oral messages. Even so, the tributes by the shires to the City government's role in the movement followed a convention of seventeenth-century praise: they were at least as much encouragements to action as recognitions of it.[51] As in the summer of 1647, as in the Second Civil War in 1648, and as in Booth's rising in 1659, the City leaders disappointed the disaffected provinces. Among the rulers of other towns, too, there was little 'disposition . . . to take any risk'.[52] Mayoral or aldermanic opposition obstructed the movement in York,[53] Gloucester,[54] Bristol,[55] Exeter,[56] Leicester,[57] Canterbury, Rochester,[58] Bury St Edmunds,[59] and probably Ipswich,[60] though a large number of Norwich's leaders signed the Norfolk declaration.[61] Once Monck had turned against the Rump, however, magistrates who had stood by it or kept quiet under it endorsed his actions.[62]

The severe economic distress of 1659–60, which many manifestos blamed on the absence of settled government and looked to a 'free parliament' to redress, spurred the urban protests and riots. 'Necessitous' townsmen demonstrated simultaneously for 'bread' and for 'a free parliament'.[63] In London and the South-Western cities, and perhaps elsewhere, apprentices and other youths were at the forefront of the agitation. Apprentices in Bristol reportedly sent emissaries to Cardiff to stir agitation.[64] They also collaborated with their own counterparts in London,[65] who themselves published remonstrances for a free parliament[66] and who were always ready to link with fellow sympathizers elsewhere in the land.[67] The young – sometimes small boys – began urban riots by provoking soldiers or magistrates, often by kicking footballs near or towards them.[68]

Yet the urban disturbances were hardly the voice of an autonomous youth culture. Apprentices and other townsmen were set on by merchants or activists or, it was said, by masters who found it convenient to conceal their own sympathies.[69] The secluded member William Prynne, a native of the region and an indefatigable champion of his fellow victims of Pride's Purge, supplied material for the declaration of the apprentices of Bristol, who were thus able to parade an imposing knowledge of medieval parliamentary history.[70] He also wrote a declaration of the watermen of London and the Thames for a free parliament.[71] Prynne's literary energy was matched by that of the royalist pamphleteer Roger L'Estrange. Anonymously, L'Estrange wrote, on behalf of the gentry of Devon, a reply to Monck's riposte to the county's declaration for a free parliament;[72] composed numerous manifestos on behalf of the citizens of London, a number of them demanding a free parliament;[73] and promoted an attempt to establish, in coordination with agents outside the capital, a network of 'commissioners' to promote the movement in coordination with Londoners.[74]

In almost every town (or city) where we know of demands for a free parliament, gentry garnered support in them and used them as bases for the movement. Often we see provincial gentry forming alliances with townsmen against civic rulers. The movement in London, where national political figures encouraged the agitation in the streets, can be interpreted in the same light.[75] Yet for Presbyterians there was always a danger that the disturbances might escape their control and, as many royalists hoped they would, assist plans for a rising on behalf of the exiled court. To royalist agents, who did their best to promote tumults in Bristol and Gloucester during the campaign, the movement for a free parliament was one among a range of strategies for the recovery of the throne. Presbyterians themselves, though not averse to civil insurrection in their own cause, had mixed feelings about it. It was claimed on behalf of the Presbyterian leaders of the Devon gentry that they had suppressed a tumult in Exeter, and that the Rump had imprisoned Presbyterians from that county and elsewhere 'only' for peacefully promoting declarations.[76] The Rump had a different view, but the 'persons of a better rank' – 'a knight, and some others of note' – who allegedly 'inflamed' the 'wilder and meaner sort of people' of Exeter to 'cry out and shout for a free parliament'[77] are unlikely to have been friends to the county's secluded members. Devon's Presbyterian manifesto was published, in what looks like the result of either a compromise or some adroit manipulation of the press by the citizens, together with 'a letter from Exeter' stating that its citizens 'in very great numbers lowdly exprest their desires for a free parliament', the term that the manifesto avoided and that the 'letter' invoked without any reference to the secluded members. Perhaps it was to assuage urban feeling that Exeter's Recorder, Thomas Bampfield, was chosen to deliver the county's declaration at Westminster.[78]

At all events, it is from townspeople that we hear the most stridently worded demands for 'a free parliament'. And it is almost always from townspeople – in London[79] and the provinces[80] – that such calls are accompanied by cries for 'a king' or even for 'Charles Stuart' or 'Charles the Second'. Even in the countryside (though the evidence is thin), it looks as if the same demands, in the same tone, came from people below the gentry.[81] There are, however, no indications of class conflict in the movement. Urban manifestos emphasized the common interest of gentry and humble townsmen.[82] Declarations by gentry took up the complaints of the poor. The London barber Thomas Rugg, approvingly observing the development of the movement, was pleased at least as much by the 'rank' and 'quality' of its supporters in the shires as by their numbers.[83]

III

It is doubtful whether any of the declarations on behalf of shires had any official standing. The organizers of the movement in Devon and Gloucestershire used the gatherings of gentry at Quarter Sessions to orchestrate support. Indeed Devon's declaration presented itself as a submission by 'the gentry of the County ... met at the General Quarter Sessions in Exeter'. But the document does not quite claim to have been formally discussed or endorsed by the Sessions,[84] as had sometimes happened in 1642.[85] Suffolk asserted that its manifesto had been sanctioned by 'severall petty juries', but the authority of no grand jury was invoked, another contrast to 1642. The high sheriffs of Yorkshire and Leicestershire formally committed themselves to their counties' declarations, and those of Buckinghamshire, Cornwall, and Northamptonshire are known to have figured prominently in the movement. Yet the military presence was too potent and daunting, the wariness about provoking the government or its soldiery too widespread, and the challenge of securing agreement, in necessarily furtive meetings, on the wording of declarations too demanding, for any county to attempt a parade of solidarity remotely comparable to the arrival in Westminster of 'handsome cavalcades' and great crowds from counties delivering petitions in early 1642. Those addresses had been signed in open meetings by ostensibly loyal subjects of the regime and delivered to a Parliament in whose authority they rejoiced. No such conditions prevailed in 1660. In the light of such difficulties, the range and eminence of the support achieved by the campaign are remarkable – enough so to explain why contemporaries judged the movement to command the nation's assent and why Monck yielded to it.

The declarations of eight of the counties that delivered documents to Monck – Hertfordshire, Leicestershire, Lincolnshire, Norfolk, Northamptonshire, Oxfordshire, Suffolk, Yorkshire – gave the names of their presenters. From other evidence we can identify thirty-seven prominent figures behind the declaration in Cornwall,[86] twenty-one in Devon (though there were reportedly double that amount),[87] and, in smaller numbers, leaders of the movement in Berkshire, Buckinghamshire, Gloucestershire, and Kent. Among the known backers of the campaign, the natural leaders of the shires – the kinds of people who became MPs – are strongly represented. The evidence comes not only from the promoters themselves but from enemies or disparagers of the movement who had no motive to invent or exaggerate the involvement of men of substance. Indeed the names we have may give too narrow an impression of the support among the nation's social leadership. For although, as we shall see, royalists can be found in some of the groups that presented declarations, adherents of the king's cause were on the whole less likely to publicize their commitment to the movement than Presbyterians. The hazards run by Presbyterians were severe enough, as the imprisonment of secluded members who promoted the movement in Berkshire and Devon attests. All royalist political activity carried the risk of prosecution for high treason. Three South-Western counties, Cornwall, Devon, and Gloucestershire, produced declarations controlled by Presbyterians whose names we know. Yet from the same counties we also have alternative or rival statements that, in demanding 'a free parliament', ignored the claims of the secluded members.[88] Whether or not those texts were drawn up by people we can properly call royalists, the documents stood, in the battle for control of the movement, on the royalist side. They were prudently shrouded in anonymity.

Presbyterians had their own inducements to keep non-Presbyterian names out. Not merely did they want to give the impression that it was the Presbyterians themselves who spoke for the nation: they knew that the taint of Cavalierism would antagonize those more lukewarm supporters of the movement whom they hoped to win over. One source stated that 'so much caution was observed' that 'no gentleman signed any of these addresses, that had ever been engag'd in his present majesties, or his royal fathers cause, nor scarce any of the sons of such'.[89] It was an overstatement, but there was some truth in it. Fairfax, eager to dispel any impression that the county's declaration, which was signed at York on 10 February, was 'the contrivance of a few', wrote to Monck that the document had behind it 'for quality, estate and calling the most interested in the county'. The list we have of Yorkshire's subscribers indeed includes a great many of the county's social leaders. Yet Fairfax revealed in the same passage that men who had 'been in arms against the parliament' had been excluded; that 'the most considerable part' of the county would have 'met in far greater numbers but for giving occasion of jealousy' to the Rump's 'soldiers' (a large presence in York, where the declaration was signed, and elsewhere in the county); and that there were 'many thousand more' supporters of the declaration whom 'we forebore for avoiding suspicion to take subscriptions of'.[90] The forbearance was prompted or reinforced by the efforts of the royalist Duke of Buckingham – a divisive figure even among royalists – to participate alongside Fairfax, his father-in-law.[91] Some royalists, at least, sensed how alienating the advertisement of their names might be and preferred to assume a Presbyterian mask. Within York, Sir Philip Monckton, who had been eager to build bridges with the county's Presbyterians in opposition to the republic, gave courageous support to the movement but warned the citizens that his 'appearing' for it 'might be a disadvantage to the service', since 'the enemy might happily say it was a Cavalier designe' that would be 'owned' once the Rump and its forces were broken.[92] That there was strong royalist support behind Yorkshire's declaration is indicated by the subscription to the document of the heirs of two prominent royalists whose fathers had been executed for royalist conspiracy, Sir John Hotham and Sir Henry Slingsby.[93] The elder Slingsby had been beheaded only in 1658.

Yet there are limits to the pertinence of the terms 'royalist' and 'Presbyterian'. Being defined by divisions of the 1640s, they explain politics after 1649 insofar as those divisions remained a determining basis of conflict or rivalry. They can be properly applied (even if at costs of simplification) to the politicians who negotiated in London in January 1660 and whose aim was still the resolution of the issues of the civil war. They likewise fit many of the movement's leading supporters in the localities. But they run into difficulties on two fronts. First, collaboration between royalists and Presbyterians could involve the concealment of the differences that the two sides were trying to overcome. From the documentary legacy of their cooperation, it can be hard to identify the preferences of a number of the participants (who consequently appear as royalists in some history books and Presbyterians in others). The second, more fundamental problem is the range of opinion that may not be accommodated by, or divisible into, the two descriptions.

During the Interregnum, and especially since the fall of the Protectorate, many regional leaders of the movement for a free parliament had been courted by royalist agents, who had attempted to lure them into military collaboration or recruit them to conspiratorial organizations. A number of such leaders were involved in the plans for the rising of 1659 and were imprisoned after it. The agents knew or learned that some of those they cultivated were firm Presbyterians, to whom royalists were never more than provisional allies: the secluded member Hugh Boscawen in Cornwall,[94] secluded members in Devon,[95] Fairfax in Yorkshire.[96] We shall come to others whom royalists viewed with warmer esteem and who, if they took sides in the tussles between the two parties over the declarations, seem likelier to have taken the royalist than the Presbyterian one. Yet we shall also encounter, among the royalists' contacts, men whose views of either royalism or Presbyterianism are uncertain and who may have felt no affinity with either party.

The same challenge is magnified when we meet promoters of the movement who had no known connections either to the court or to the secluded members. Roger L'Estrange, in seeking to establish his system of 'commissioners', urged that the movement be sponsored by people who were 'never parties in the quarrel' of king and Parliament, for 'if both parties should be taken in, there might . . . be some animosities started'.[97] Similar thinking may in some cases have played its part in the choices of sponsors of declarations. At all events we always have non-party or extra-party sentiment to bear in mind, not just because of the habitual complexity of local allegiances, which could complicate or transcend national ones, but also because there may have been higher priorities than the resolution of a conflict of the previous decade. As the readiness of so many declarers for a free parliament to leave the future to 'either' a newly elected Parliament 'or' the return of the secluded members suggests, the movement could draw its adherents together because it left the political future open. When a county did opt for either the Presbyterian or the royalist formula, it may have based its decision not on party allegiances but on calculations about the likely local outcome of the elections. Or it may have been swayed less by political allegiance or reckoning than by instincts of caution or alternatively by feelings of defiance or outrage. At all events the only common goal of the declarations was an exit, via a free parliament, from the chaos and oppression of republican and military government. What else the local promoters of the movement would have liked to see we often cannot judge.

It is especially to younger men, too young to have taken sides in the 1640s, that the application of party labels may be not only difficult but misleading. The young are well represented among the known backers of the declarations. Many civil war allegiances, it is true, were inherited by the next generation and could be felt at least as keenly by it, particularly perhaps on the royalist side. But there were also those younger men who yearned to escape, by whatever means available, the havoc that the rival parties had brought. A simple exercise can give us a sense of the passage of generations within the movement. We can trace the presence of known backers of the campaign among the names of county commissioners appointed by the parliaments and governments of the Interregnum to arrange the collection of taxation; lists to which we can conveniently add, in 1659–60, the commissioners appointed to run the county militias.[98] On its own, the exercise does not, alas, take us into the minds of the appointees, but it can reveal patterns not only of age but of political position. Not all those appointed to commissions necessarily served, and many if not most of them will have had at least some reservations about the regimes they were invited to assist. If they did take up their appointments, they are likely to have done so at least as much for the interests of their communities or families as from political preference. But the commissioners would not have been named, or at least named regularly, had they been regarded as inflexible opponents of the regimes that appointed them.

As we might expect, a high proportion of the men known to have supported the movement for a free parliament were appointed to the government commissions. Essentially the nominees form three categories, which vary in proportion from county to county but which were all well-represented overall. First there are those, most of whom (or whose families) had been parliamentarians in the civil wars, who had been named to commissions through the Interregnum, and who had thus been entrusted (if only to spare them offence or to make up the numbers) by the republic of 1649–53, as well as by the Protectorate. The second category, in which the generations mingle, is of names that begin to appear only in 1657, when the protector and parliament were reaching out to families that had earlier been mistrusted by Interregnum governments or had refused to serve them. Thirdly there are those, a high proportion of them certainly or probably young men, who appear only in 1659–60. Of those, a large number were named only in the militia ordinance passed by the secluded members in March 1660, when the movement for a free parliament had done its main work. Indeed it looks as though support for the declarations was itself a qualification for appointment to, and even for the running of, the county militias appointed by the ordinance.[99] In the county for which we have most evidence about the social leadership of the movement, Yorkshire, fourteen of the fifty 'esquires' whose names accompany the county's declaration made their first appearances in public life only on the militia commission of 1660. The same was true of all four men, again 'esquires', who presented Leicestershire's declaration. Not all the newcomers of 1660 were young. Some of them, now that Pride's Purge had been undone, were restored to a political scene that they had avoided or that had avoided them since 1648. Even so, the militia ordinance helped to bring a new generation to public prominence. One young man to whom it offered an official debut was Thomas Clifford, the future minister of Charles II, whose participation in the Devonian movement for a free parliament had been another early step in his career.[100]

IV

Now let us tour the shires, where we have enough information about the local leadership of the movement to illustrate the range of political outlook and experience, as well as the social authority, that the campaign commanded. The one county where we know it to have been controlled by royalists, though they did not disclose their involvement at the time, is Kent, where the king's followers were wont to display a degree of zeal that his advisers judged imprudent.[101] The county's declaration, which emerged from the east of the shire, was penned by the royalist John Boys of Hoad Court (who has understandably been confused with other possessors of a surname so common in the county). He and his royalist assistants, among them the antiquary William Somner who represented the Canterbury Cathedral interest, did not monopolize the county's activity, for Presbyterian clergy promoted the county's declaration and are unlikely to have done so without lay Presbyterian cooperation.[102] In one sense, a partnership between royalists and Presbyterians may have been relatively easy to achieve in the county, so profoundly alienated had both parties been by the regicide and so bitter was the memory of the Second Civil War.[103] Of the seven leaders whose names we have, all boycotted or were boycotted by all the governments of the Interregnum.[104] One of them was probably the son of a Roundhead MP, Sir Edward Master or Masters, who had died in 1648.[105] Yet the rest were of Cavalier families. The distinctiveness of the movement in Kent revealed itself in March and April 1660, when a new set of declarations from the counties appeared, this time on behalf of men who by now felt it safe to proclaim their records of loyalty to the crown. In almost every other shire where we can identify advocates of a free parliament, none of them can be found among the signatories to the explicitly royalist declarations, and in no case can more than one. Yet three leaders of the movement for a free parliament in Kent signed the county's royalist declaration.[106]

The presenters of Oxfordshire's declaration, too, included names that the exiled court would have been glad to see. Lord Falkland, son of a famous royalist statesman and himself in close contact with the crown and regarded as a friend by it,[107] headed the deputation to Monck.[108] He and another of the presenters, Sir Anthony Cope, had worked together to promote the rising of 1659 (after which Falkland was imprisoned, though he was alleged to have 'betrayed' the conspiracy[109]) and would be returned for the county in the Cavalier Parliament in 1661. During the Interregnum, Cope housed the Anglican divine and conspirator Richard Allestree,[110] who was arrested by the government early in 1660. It looks as though the county aimed to demonstrate to Monck the range of opinion behind the declaration. Of the other four subscribers, one, Edward Hungerford, was (if the likeliest identification is the correct one) the son of a royalist MP and himself a generous giver of money to the exiled court;[111] another was the secluded member James Fiennes; another, William Cope, was perhaps the man of that name who had sat on government commissions for the county through the Interregnum; the last, Henry Jones, would make his first appearance on a government body as a militia commissioner in March 1660.

A comparable balance of interests lay behind the declaration of adjoining Northamptonshire. The prominent secluded member John Crewe, MP for Brackley in the county, bargained with royalist agents in London about the wording of the document. The Presbyterian peer the Earl of Manchester also used the influence he commanded in Northamptonshire.[112] On the royalist side, John Barwick, like Richard Allestree, an Anglican divine who conspired in the exiles' cause, was prominent in the preparation of the shire's declaration. Of the 'forty or fifty of the principal gentlemen of the county' who delivered the document to Monck, only the name of the county's sheriff, Henry Benson, was disclosed in print, whether or not with his approval we cannot say.[113] But the leading figure within the shire was Sir John Norris (or Norwich), whom Viscount Mordaunt, the principal royalist figure in the national organization of the movement, had 'in particular recommended' for the task.[114] He had fought for parliament in the civil war; like Benson, he had been named to government commissions through the Interregnum; and at the end of 1659 he had supported the Rump when the alternative had seemed to be military rule.[115] Yet he was keenly cultivated by royalist agents in the later Interregnum.[116] After the return of the secluded members, when it had become safe to disclose the names of backers, Northamptonshire delivered a 'second addresse' to Monck. John Crewe's heir Thomas, who had sat on a succession of Interregnum commissions, delivered it together with young Sir Henry Yelverton,[117] the son of a royalist, an ally of Norris, and himself judged to be 'full of zeal and resolution for the king's service'.[118] He too had been arrested after Booth's rising.[119] His collaboration with Thomas Crewe may have been eased by social familiarities.[120] Yelverton, who was 'the darling of the [Anglican] clergy for his father's sake' and was 'great with them',[121] no doubt cooperated on that front with Sir Anthony Cope, whose Oxfordshire home was near Northamptonshire's boundary.

In some other counties, royalists either opted out or were squeezed out. Berkshire's declaration to Parliament was presented by Richard Fincher and the secluded MP Sir Robert Pye, whose son Robert had been a fellow Presbyterian officer of Fincher in the New Model Army. Three secluded members were among the predominantly parliamentarian group of gentry responsible for Cornwall's declaration, and five among the corresponding group in Devon.[122] A close ally of the secluded members, Edward Cooke of Gloucestershire, a firm Presbyterian, was evidently entrusted by the county's seven secluded members, whom the text named, with the drafting of the declaration produced by the shire's '[16]48 party'.[123] In Devon, the two principal figures were the secluded member Sir John Northcote and another experienced MP, Thomas Bampfield,[124] a watchful opponent of arbitrary government and a firm Presbyterian in religion, troubled by the resurgence of Anglicanism.[125] A Presbyterian religious bias is also evident in Yorkshire, where six ministers put their names to the Yorkshire declaration. Five of them had been intruded into livings by the puritans, and four would lose them again in the ejection of 1662, among them the politically prominent figure Edward Bowles, who had a principal part in the declaration.[126] Like many other Presbyterians, he had had hopes for the regime of Richard Cromwell[127] but had looked askance on Whitehall since Richard's fall. The Presbyterian interest in the county was also represented by Fairfax and by Sir Thomas Wharton, another key figure in the Yorkshire movement and the brother, as the printed version of the declaration was at pains to point out, of the parliamentarian grandee Lord Wharton.[128] Yet at the head of the county's movement there stood, alongside Fairfax, his principal partner, Lord Fauconberg,[129] in whose principles royalists found a welcome 'balance' to his.[130] Fauconberg, who was of a royalist family, had become son-in-law to Oliver Cromwell but had wearied of the puritan cause after the fall of the Protectorate. He too had been imprisoned for his support for Booth's rising. The three presenters from adjoining Lincolnshire all belonged to prominent parliamentarian families. Royalists thought the movement's leading figure in the county, Edward Rossiter, 'well devoted' or 'well fixed', though there seems to be nothing to indicate that he had dropped the Presbyterian sympathies he shared with his old commander Fairfax.[131] The leading signatories of the abortive declaration for Derbyshire were two men who had first appeared on government commissions in 1657 and the contentious politician Sir John Gell, 'the most rigid Presbyterian in the county'.[132]

Of the 795 signatories to the letter to Monck that accompanied the Norfolk declaration, we can identify, from the obvious documentary sources of central government, around eighty or ninety, a figure that could be made more precise if fewer people had shared both Christian names and surnames. Perhaps nine or ten of that number can be found among the people with royalist pasts whose names are recorded in the documentary legacy of the parliamentary machinery of sequestration and compounding,[133] which targeted royalists with estates large enough for confiscation to be permissible or worthwhile. About the same number more may have been of firmly royalist families. Yet here too such evidence may give a far from adequate impression of the extent of royalism, or of a readiness within the movement to back royalism. There was apparently royalist agitation — too late to be accommodated by the Norfolk manifesto or too distant from Norwich where it was organized — in and around King's Lynn, long a centre of royalist feeling, which royalists hoped to see taken by a powerful figure in the region, young Sir Horatio Townshend, whom royalists had assiduously cultivated and whom Mordaunt thought 'very careful of his majesty's concern'.[134] There may even — though the tiny evidence is hard to interpret — have been moves through Norfolk and Suffolk to build an armed royalist organization on the back of the declarations.[135]

Yet Townshend defies simple classification. He came of a parliamentarian family, had sat on parliamentary commissions through the Interregnum, and had even been appointed to the Rump's council of state in 1659, though he had taken no part in its proceedings.[136] There was a limit to royalists' trust in him.[137] He presented the county's declaration to the Speaker of the Rump in the company of two men:[138] Lord Richardson, whose father had supported the king but not fought for him, and whose first nomination to a government body was as a member of the county's militia commission of 1660; and Sir John Hobart, who though a critic of Oliver Cromwell's rule had been made a member of his 'Other House', the protectoral substitute for the House of Lords.[139] The secluded member Sir John Palgrave was among the signatories. So were men who, with Hobart, had represented the county in one or both of Oliver Cromwell's protectoral parliaments. They had been shocked by the forcible purge of the parliament of 1654, had worked closely together in responding to it,[140] and had been excluded by the government (as had some sponsors of the movement in other counties) from the parliament of 1656.[141] Members of that group, together with presenters of the declaration of 1660, took control of the Norfolk militia that spring.[142] Yet the county's movement for a free parliament was a coalition, not a song of harmony. Here as elsewhere the elections to the Convention would divide men who had united in favour of the movement that produced it.[143]

The two most boldly worded declarations on behalf of shires, and the ones likeliest to please uncompromising royalists, came from Suffolk and Essex,[144] even though those had been the counties of the parliamentarian and puritan heartland, and even though Roundhead gentry figure prominently among the one hundred and forty-one signatories of Suffolk's manifesto. The Suffolk manifesto demanded 'a full and free parliament' – for which 'the nation' was 'lifting up its vowes to heaven' – 'in its genuine sense' and said nothing about the return of the secluded members. We cannot tell how the document also came to speak, as its heading tells us, for the 'sea-men' of the county, whom royalist agents believed to be its militant supporters.[145] Doubtless the mariners were inspired by the equally militant 'seamen' of London,[146] to whom royalists were also looking for support – though not optimistically – at just this time.[147] Two days after the meeting at Ipswich on 19 January, when subscription to the county's missive to Monck began,[148] the government issued an order for the arrest of Sir Henry Felton,[149] one of the three men who on the twenty-eighth would deliver the county's declaration to the general at St Albans (so that he cannot have been in custody for long). In June 1659, a royalist agent had described Felton as 'of good affections and interest', though his commitment to the king's cause seems to have been limited.[150]

He delivered the document to Monck with two other Suffolk gentry, one of whom, Robert Brook, then travelled to London and submitted it to the City government alongside two more gentlemen from the county.[151] Of the five Suffolk presenters, one, Thomas Bacon, had been appointed to parliamentarian bodies through the 1640s and 1650s. The others made their first appearances on Interregnum government commissions only in 1657 (Felton among them) or 1659. One of them, Philip Parker, was the heir of a secluded member. Of the one hundred and forty-one signatories to Suffolk's covering letter to Monck, only four or so can be confidently identified as having royalist records or as belonging to hardened royalist families. Yet that figure, too, appears to conceal a broader undercurrent of anti-Roundhead or anti-puritan belligerence. The belligerence stretched down the East Coast. In Yorkshire and Lincolnshire, where the declarations were accompanied by threats of armed risings, there were emotions stronger than the manifestos on behalf of those counties could contain.[152] Feelings also ran especially high not only in royalist Kent but in its neighbour Essex.

For Essex's was by far the most provocative and risky of the county declarations, which perhaps explains not only why it did not disclose the names of its promoters but why the document was held back from publication until shortly before the king's return. Though declarations of other shires frequently assailed the coup that had brought the Rump to power in 1648 and the evils that had prospered under its rule, they were prudent enough not to attack the Rump itself. Admittedly the original version of the royalist declaration of Kent had a sentence depicting the Rump as government in the interests of a few, but the text was quickly withdrawn in favour of one which omitted the offending passage.[153] The sponsors of the Essex manifesto had no such inhibitions. The document launched a vituperative adjectival assault on the parliament, lifted from a *Remonstrance* written in the name of the citizens of London by Roger L'Estrange.[154] Perhaps his promotion of the initiative to establish regional 'commissioners' to cooperate with Londoners on behalf of the movement bore fruit in the document. Essex's declaration was also unique, or almost so, in using language with Anglican or neo-Anglican resonances in condemning the nation's ecclesiastical chaos. Except for the manifesto of Nottinghamshire – another county to conceal the sponsors' names and, again apart from Essex, the only one whose declaration was not printed until far into the spring – Essex's was alone in claiming to speak for the 'commonalty' of the shire as well as their superiors. And whereas a number of other shires stated their support for the City's rulers, Essex instead declared its backing for 'all' the 'worthy Remonstrators of the City of London'.

Neighbouring Hertfordshire produced an unusual combination in the delivery of its declaration to Monck.[155] The only man to announce his support for the movement who had fought for Charles I, the traveller Sir Henry Blount, joined with Alban Coxe, the only former parliamentarian Army officer to commit himself publicly who had undertaken military service since the clear-out of Presbyterians from the New Model Army in 1647. Neither man conformed to type. Blount, a colourful figure, departed from orthodox royalism both in his antipathy to tithes and in his readiness to serve on the Rump's commission on law reform in 1652.[156] He appears not to have attracted the interest of royalist agents. Coxe was an emollient personality, respected in Hertfordshire by people with political views and records different from his.[157] He was an officer in the Hertfordshire militia forces that served under the major generals.[158] Yet he warned against accretions of executive power, whether under Charles I or Cromwell, spoke for 'the liberties of England' against them, and stood up for the rights of the House of Commons against the Lords. In principle he favoured Parliament's proposal to make Cromwell king in 1657, but he opposed its passage at that time because there was 'not a full and free House'.[159] In next-door Buckinghamshire, the county's declaration was energetically and hurriedly organized by young Sir Richard Temple, whose first appointments to government commissions came in 1659–60, and by Sir Tobias (or Toby) Tyrell (or Turrell), who was the heir of a royalist and was appointed to no Interregnum commissions.[160] It looks as if the royalist spirit at work in Oxfordshire and Northamptonshire had extended to their neighbour Buckinghamshire. Monck, to whom Temple delivered the document, interpreted it as an affront to the parliamentarian cause of the civil wars. Temple would end his career as a kind of Tory, and yet 'was a great stickler all his life' for 'parliamentary privilege'.[161]

The four esquires who presented *The Humble Desires of . . . the County and Burrough of Leicester* were little known outside the county. The only one of them ever to become an MP was the sheriff George Faunt, or Fawnt, who took the lead and who was arrested for the part he had played. His family had avoided commitment in the civil wars.[162] Another of the presenters, Richard Halford, was of a royalist family. The document had one claim to uniqueness. Although we find occasional remonstrations in the national press against the movement for a free parliament – objecting either that the campaign was a cover for royalist conspiracy or that parliaments, like nations, can be 'free' only in republics – Leicestershire's was the only declaration to provoke a formal written riposte. The declaration itself was more cautious than its model, Northamptonshire's. It omitted the term 'free parliament', which royalists had managed to insert into the Northamptonshire document. The county's address was presented to Monck only a week after he had moved on from the county. After a further week, on 6 February, the corporation of Leicester wrote to the Rump to renounce the declaration, which had been published in its name as well as in the county's. It explained that, though Faunt had 'moved' the mayor and aldermen to sign, they had unanimously refused.[163] The town's rulers had tried to persuade Monck to bypass Leicester on his journey south, impressing on him the ill effects it had already suffered from free quarter,[164] though when he arrived the town followed other corporations in extending an effusive greeting.[165]

On 8 February the opposition to the county's declaration expanded. According to a government newsbook, 'persons of worth and interest' in the shire, 'such as had ever adhered to the parliament', held 'a great meeting' in Leicester, which agreed that 'most' of those who had presumed to declare in the county's name were at best 'neutral' and that 'many' of them had been 'in arms' for the king's party. The gathering resolved to send a 'sober petition' to the Rump, in which Leicestershire was the only shire to retain both its county members.[166] The newsbook invited readers to await publication of the petition,[167] but it never appeared, just as a reply to Yorkshire's declaration was proposed in the county but never penned.[168] No doubt the local weight of the Rump's leading grandee, the indomitable Sir Arthur Hesilrige, one of the county's MPs, who had sat for either the shire or the borough in all the parliaments of the civil wars, was a factor in the protests. Perhaps too they owed something to the reluctance of the county's Presbyterian clergy – a class that in other shires was supportive of the movement but that in Leicestershire had a reputation among the republic's enemies for political timidity – to challenge the regime.[169]

At all events the universal failure of the Rump or its followers to produce remonstrances in opposition to the counties' clamour for a free parliament is a testament of eloquent silence to the national feeling behind the movement that destroyed the republic. On 6 February, five days before Monck struck against the Rump, he warned it that on his march south he had 'observed the people in most counties in great and earnest expectations of settlement' and had learned 'the chiefest heads of their desires' from them, of which the longing for 'a free and full parliament' came first.[170] By satisfying that demand, he made an end to the civil wars possible.

Notes

1 I am most grateful for the comments of Henry Reece, David Scott, and Paul Seaward on a draft of this essay.
2 See my 'The Campaign for a Free Parliament', forthcoming in *Parliamentary History* (2017), and my '1660: Restoration and Revolution', in Janet Clare (ed.), *From Republic to Restoration: Legacies and Departures* (Manchester, forthcoming 2017). A number of points made briefly in this essay are amplified and documented in those ones.

3 The story is told in my 'The Campaign for a Free Parliament'.
4 I here confine myself to the movement in England. It had, at the same time, a comparably consequential effect in Ireland: Aidan Clarke, *Prelude to Restoration in Ireland* (Cambridge, 1999), *q.v.* 'free parliament'.
5 TNA, SP18/219, no. 44 (cal[endared] in *CSPD 1659–60*, p. 347).
6 All except Essex's and Nottinghamshire's were published on their own, as single sheets. All but four were reprinted in *A Happy Handfull* (1660) [hereafter *HH*]. A few were given publicity by their appearance in government newsbooks edited by Marchamont Nedham – to the dismay of a rival government editor (*M[ercurius] Pub[licus]* 2–9 February, pp. 81–2; cf. *[The] Parl[iamentary] Int[elligencer]* 16–23 January, p. 56). That is possibly because Nedham was preparing to jump ship (cf. Marchamont Nedham, *The Excellencie of a Free-State*, ed. Blair Worden (Indianapolis, IN, 2010), p. liv). Alternatively, or additionally, he may have been engaged in a damage-limitation exercise, for as a rule he was gentle towards the more moderate tendencies within the movement and excoriated extreme ones.
7 *The Letter-Book of John Viscount Mordaunt, 1658–1660*, ed. Mary Coate (Camden Society, 3rd series, 69, 1945: hereafter *Mordaunt*), p. 180; HMC, *Leybourne-Popham*, p. 144; Thomas Carte (ed.), *A Collection of Original Letters and Papers* (2 vols, Dublin, 1759), II, 305; *CCSP*, IV, 483; *No Droll* (1660), p. 7; *The Diurnal of Thomas Rugg, 1659–1661*, ed. William L. Sachse (Camden Society, 3rd series, 91, 1961: hereafter *Rugg*); Bulstrode Whitelocke, *Memorials of the English Affairs* (4 vols, Oxford, 1853).
8 *[The Pub]lick Int[elligencer]*, 6–13 February [1660], p. 1094; *ibid.*, 20–27 February, p. 1117.
9 *Merc[urius] Pol[iticus]*, 2–9 February, pp. 1069–70.
10 *An Exact Accompt*, 25 February–9 March, p. 748.
11 *Pub. Int.*, 30 January–6 February, pp. 1066–7.
12 Bodl., MS Clarendon 68, fol. 85; MS 69, fols 159, 164 (cal. *CCSP*, IV, 563, 564); *CCSP*, IV, 508, 589, 591, 592; *SPC*, III, 701. *An Extract of a Letter from York* (1660); Francis Maseres (ed.), *Select Tracts relating to the Civil War* (2 vols, continuously paginated, 1815), p. 748. See too *Merc. Pol.*, 16–23 February, p. 1116; *CP*, IV, 38. For Rossiter's role in the movement see too Clive Holmes, *Seventeenth-Century Lincolnshire* (Lincoln, 1980), pp. 217–18.
13 HMC, *Seventh Report*, p. 462; *Rugg*, p. 32; *Merc. Pol.*, 26 January–2 February, pp. 1064–5. The two counties adopted a distinctive tactic in (i) sending declarations both to Monck during his march south and to the capital and (ii) sending covering letters to Monck with long lists of signatures.
14 See *Merc. Pol.*, 16–23 February, p. 1116; my '1660: Restoration and Revolution'.
15 BL, Add. MS 21425, fol. 204; cf. Bodl., MS Clarendon 69, fol. 176v (cal. IV, 567).
16 *HH*, p. 36; HMC, *Leybourne-Popham*, p. 147.
17 BL, Add. MS 21425, fol. 204; *A&O*, II, 1435.
18 BL, Stowe MS 185, fols 148–50.
19 *A Declartion [sic] and Protest of the Lords, Knights and Gentlemen in the Counties of Chester Salop Stafford, &c.* (1660).
20 HMC, *Leybourne-Popham*, pp. 159–60, 161–2.
21 *Pub. Int.*, 20–27 February, p. 1117.
22 See, however, *CCSP*, IV, 549.
23 David Zaret, 'Politics and the "Invention" of Public Opinion in the English Revolution', *American Journal of Sociology*, 101 (1996), 1497–555; Mark Knights, *Representation and Misrepresentation in Later Stuart Britain* (Oxford, 2005), part iii; Derek Hirst, 'Making Contact: Petitions and the English Republic', *JBS*, 45 (2006), 26–50.
24 Anthony Fletcher, *The Outbreak of the English Civil War* (1981), Chapter 6; Robert Ashton, *Counter-Revolution. The Second Civil War and its Origins* (New Haven, CT, and London, 1994), Chapter 4.
25 *The Address of the County of Northampton* (1660); Bodl., MS Clarendon 69, fol. 20v (cal. IV, 524). The watermen of London and the Thames claimed their declaration to be 'owned by ten thousand of us': *HH*, p. 42.

196 Blair Worden

26 *The Declaration of the County of Oxon* (1660).
27 *HH*, pp. 51–2.
28 *Pub. Int.*, 30 January–6 February, pp. 1066–7; *HH*, pp. 16–19.
29 *Merc[urius] Pub[licus]* (Bodl., Wood Pamphlets 393) 2–9 February, p. 81; cf. *ibid.*, 12–19 January, p. 44.
30 Henry E. Huntington Library, Stowe Papers, SSTM/5/13. I am most grateful to the Curator, Vanessa Wilkie, for locating this previously elusive document.
31 Norfolk: Hamon Le Strange (ed.), *An Address from the Gentry of Norfolk and Norwich to General Monck in 1660: Facsimile of a Manuscript* (Norwich, 1913), p. 11; John T. Evans, *Seventeenth-Century Norwich* (Oxford, 1979), p. 224n. Cf. Ronald Hutton, *The Restoration: A Political and Religious History of England and Wales 1658–1667* (Oxford, 1985), p. 318; Rugg, p. 32. Suffolk: Suffolk RO (Ipswich branch), MS HA93/7/33; Alan Everitt, *Suffolk and the Great Rebellion 1640–1660* (Ipswich, 1960), pp. 127–9. The 'roll of parchment' sent by Warwickshire to the City government (London Metropolitan Archive, COL/CC/O1/01 [Journal of the London Common Council: hereafter *CCJ*], fol. 220; cf. *Peace to the Nation* [1660]) does not survive. The paucity of the archival legacy of the movement is in keeping with the thinness of local evidence about the politics of the Interregnum. The survival of revealing evidence may have been impeded by the unofficial character of the movement but also by the predominantly Presbyterian character of the campaign and by eagerness in local communities, amid the resurgent royalism that accompanied and followed the king's return, to forget or explain away commitments to Presbyterian positions. On the other hand, the publication of the collection of declarations, *A Happy Handfull*, was possibly an attempt to preserve a Presbyterian face. It appeared on or around 2 May (BL, Thomason Tracts, E1021[17]), but the arrangement of the document suggests (though it does not prove) that the collection was gathered at some point in February and was added to as the gatherer acquired further texts. Another edition followed, with minor changes that did not affect the texts that concern us here (compare Bodl., G. Pamph. 2276(1) with A S. 5(1) Linc.). The divine Thomas Fuller, an Anglican with Presbyterian connections who was ready to publicize his commitment to parliamentary constitutionalism after the Restoration, played a part, perhaps the leading one, in the preparation of the document: *HH*, pp. 66–73; Thomas Fuller, *An Alarum to the Counties* (1660); *idem*, *Mixt Contemplations* (1660), pp. 10–11. The tract has its puzzles, among them its dedication, in the earlier version, to 'his Highness' George Monck, to whom the later one offers a slightly less extravagant tribute than the first.
32 BL, Stowe MS 185, fols 148–9.
33 *A Declaration of the Nobility . . . of the County of York* (1660). The names of only forty-five of Norfolk's seven hundred and ninety-five signatures could be fitted onto the folio that printed the declaration that Norfolk delivered to Monck: *A Letter and Declaration of the Gentry of the County of Norfolk* (1660). The two hundred and eighty-five names of London citizens on a declaration for a free parliament similarly occupy all the available space; there may have been a number more signatories, some by people from outside the capital: *A Declaration of the People of England for a Free-Parliament* (1660); Rugg, p. 27.
34 *HH*, p. 37.
35 *Merc. Pub.*, 12–19 January, p. 53; *ibid.*, 2–9 February, pp. 81–2.
36 BL, Thomason Tracts, 669f.22[11]; *HH*, pp. 43–9. The implausibility is noticed by Henry Reece, *The Army in Cromwellian England 1649–1660* (Oxford, 2013), p. 181n.
37 Robert Latham and William Matthews (eds.), *The Diary of Samuel Pepys* (11 vols, 1970–83: hereafter *Pepys*), I, 55n.; cf. my 'The Campaign for a Free Parliament'.
38 *Declaration . . . Stafford, &c*. It may be relevant that the document, which is strongly Presbyterian in character, has resemblances of tone and argument to a much longer declaration from Dublin (*HH*, pp. 55–63), which is likely to have passed through Cheshire on its passage to London. See too (for Cheshire) *Extract of a Letter from York*, 'postscript', and *No Droll*, p. 7; and (for Shropshire) the reports of agitation in Shrewsbury given in *Pub. Int.*, 20–27 February, p. 1126; *Merc. Pub.*, 1–8 March, p. 152.

39 *The Declaration of the Gentlemen . . . of the County of Bedford* (1660). Both documents seem to have been printed only after – though very soon after – the return of the secluded members (BL, Thomason Tracts, 669f.23[55, 60]), when there was no need for local supporters of the documents to conceal their identities. Yet neither declaration named its sponsors, and neither was addressed or delivered to a recipient.
40 Bodl., MS Clarendon 68, fol. 129v (cal. IV, 515–16); F.P.G. Guizot, *History of Richard Cromwell and the Restoration*, trans. A.R. Scoble (2 vols, 1856: hereafter Guizot), II, 326, 328, 333, 346; TNA, SP77/33, fol. 10 (cal. IV, 324); *Mordaunt*, pp. 160, 167; HMC, *Leybourne-Popham*, p. 143; and see *HH*, p. 15.
41 TNA, SP29/9, fols 46–7; HMC, *Leybourne-Popham*, pp. 142–5, 160–5; *A Letter of the Apprentices of Bristoll* (1660).
42 Reece, *Army*, Chapter 9.
43 *Mordaunt*, p. 150; David Scott, 'Politics, Dissent and Quakerism in York' (unpublished PhD thesis, University of York, 1990), p. 283.
44 Reece, *Army*, p. 181. The predicament of local magistrates in the midwinter of 1659–60 emerges from *CCJ*; from Bristol RO, MS M/BCC/CCP/1/6 (Common Council Proceedings); and from BL, Add. MS 21245, fol. 204 (York).
45 *A True Catalogue, or, an Account of the Several Places* (1659); see too Guizot, II, 341–2.
46 *CP*, IV, 294; *Merc. Pub.*, 23 February–2 March, p. 137.
47 Guizot, II, 321 (cf. II, 345); *Rugg*, p. 14.
48 Bodl., MS Clarendon 67, fol. 260 (cal. IV, 489); cf. *CCSP*, III, 601.
49 *PCH*, XXII, 61.
50 For telling glimpses, see *CCJ*, fol. 220 (cf. *Peace to the Nation* [1660]); Sir Richard Baker, *A Chronicle* (1665 edn), p. 742 (cf. *SPC*, III, 666).
51 For hints of that purpose, see Bodl., MS Clarendon 68, fol. 100v (cal. IV, 511); HMC, *Fifth Report*, p. 193; *The History of Independency. The Fourth and Last Part* (1660), p. 87.
52 Guizot, II, 341–2.
53 Scott, 'Politics, Dissent and Quakerism in York', pp. 280–4. For the course of events, see BL, Add. MS 21425, fol. 204; York City Archives, H.B. 37, fol. 134; *HH*, pp. 36–8; and the slightly differing account in HMC, *Leybourne-Popham*, p. 147. It looks as if the mayor and a majority of the aldermen, having resisted the common councillors' support for the county's declaration, quickly changed their minds and endorsed it. But the statement by Phil Withington ('Views from the Bridge: Revolution and Restoration in Seventeenth-Century York', *P&P*, 170 [2001], 121–51, at p. 148) that they came round 'after military officers occupied the council chamber' appears to rest on a misreading of a council minute (which is itself misdated, under 11 February: fol. 134v).
54 *Parl. Int.*, 16–23 January, pp. 52–3; cf. *ibid.*, 9–16 January, p. 40.
55 HMC, *Leybourne-Popham*, pp. 160–1.
56 *Parl. Int.*, 16–23 January, p. 55; cf. *HH*, pp. 34–5, where endorsement of the movement by the corporation is conspicuous by its absence.
57 H. Stocks and W.H. Stevenson (eds.), *Records of the Borough of Leicester . . . 1603–88* (Cambridge, 1923), p. 459.
58 *HH*, p. 17; *Pub. Int.*, 29 January–6 February, pp. 1066–7.
59 Bodl., MS Nalson VIII, fol. 277; *Rugg*, p. 52; cf. *Merc. Pol.*, 16–23 February p. 1117.
60 *CSPD 1659–60*, p. 369.
61 Evans, *Seventeenth-Century Norwich*, pp. 224–5 (though also *ibid.*, p. 210).
62 York City Archives, H.B. 37, fol. 134; *Exact Accompt* 25 February–9 March, p. 748; Everitt, *Suffolk*, p. 126.
63 *Merc. Pub.*, 12–19 January, p. 46.
64 *Pub. Int.*, 20–7 February, p. 1117.
65 *A Letter of the Apprentices of the City of Bristoll* (1660).
66 *HH*, pp. 8–14.
67 *CSPD 1659–60*, pp. 54, 58, 61.

198   Blair Worden

68 *Rugg*, p. 13; *The Weekly Intelligencer*, 29 November–6 December 1659, p. 240; *Parl. Int.*, 16–23 January, pp. 54–5; *Merc. Pub.*, 9–16 February, p. 102; Withington, 'Views from the Bridge', 142, 146. Cf. John Latimer, *The Annals of Bristol in the Seventeenth Century* (Bristol, 1900), p. 292; Godfrey Davies, *The Restoration of Charles II 1658–1660* (Oxford, 1955), p. 104.
69 TNA, SP29/9, fol. 46; *Rugg*, p. 9; *Merc. Pol.*, 2–9 February, p. 1084; Guizot, II, 299, 302, 308.
70 Compare *Letter of the Apprentices of the City of Bristoll*, p. 6, with Prynne, *A Legal Vindication of the Liberties of England* (1660), pp. 8–9.
71 *HH*, p. 43.
72 [Roger L'Estrange,] *L'Estrange his Apology* (1660), p. 58.
73 *Ibid., passim*; George Kitchin, *Sir Roger L'Estrange* (1913), pp. 33ff.
74 *Ibid.*, pp. 50–4; *A Free Parliament Proposed by the City to the Nation* (1660). For his role, see too Mark Knights, 'Roger L'Estrange, Printed Petitions and the Problem of Intentionality', in John Morrow and Jonathan Scott (eds.), *Liberty, Authority, Formality. Political Ideas and Culture, 1600–1900* (Exeter, 2008), pp. 113–30.
75 Guizot, II, 313.
76 *CJ*, 23 February; *Merc. Pub.*, 12–19 January, p. 47; *Parl. Int.*, 16–23 January, p. 55; *Merc. Pol.*, 19–26 February, p. 1049; *L'Estrange his Apology*, p. 132; William Prynne, *The Signal Loyalty* (1680), p. 95.
77 *Merc. Pol.*, 19–26 January, p. 1049. The statement in Kent's declaration that 'the clamors and out-cries of the people' had 'enforced' the drawing up of the document (*HH*, p. 15) is belied by the evident zeal of the promoters for its cause.
78 *A Letter from Exeter* (1660); *HH*, p. 35.
79 E.g. *Rugg*, p. 34; Guizot, II, 350; BL, Add. MS 21425, fol. 208; cf. T.H. Lister (ed.), *Life and Administration of Edward. First Earl of Clarendon* (3 vols, 1937–8), III, 83.
80 E.g. *Rugg*, p. 42; HMC, *Leybourne-Popham*, pp. 159, 162; *Merc. Pol.*, 9–16 February, p. 1109; *Pub. Int.*, 20–7 February, p. 1117 (cf. *ibid.*, 6–13 February, p. 1085); cf. *A Faithfull Representation of the State of Ireland* (1660), p. 3.
81 *Merc. Pub.*, 5–12 January, p. 32; *Parl. Int.*, 23–30 January 1660, p. 72.
82 *HH*, p. 41; *L'Estrange his Apology*, pp. 45, 74.
83 *Rugg*, pp. 29, 41, 50.
84 *Merc. Pub.*, 29 December–5 January, p. 11; *ibid.*, 12–19 January, p. 44; *HH*, p. 34.
85 For the points about 1642 made here, see Fletcher, *Outbreak*, pp. 194, 196–7.
86 Mary Coate, *Cornwall in the Great Civil War and Interregnum* (Oxford, 1933), p. 309n.
87 *Pub. Int.*, 9–16 January, p. 48.
88 See my 'The Campaign for a Free Parliament', and for Devon, see p. 183–4.
89 Baker, *Chronicle*, p. 742.
90 HMC, *Leybourne-Popham*, p. 149.
91 *Merc. Pub.*, 29 December–5 January, pp. 12–13; *Pub. Int.*, 2–9 January, p. 1002. Cf. BL, Add. MS 21245, fol. 204; *SPC*), III, 660. A parallel policy was pursued to a parallel end in Ireland: Bodl., MS Nalson VIII, fol. 267.
92 E. Peacock (ed.), *The Monckton Papers* (Philobiblion Society, 1884), p. 33. We must allow for an element of self-service in Monckton's retrospective account, but he is broadly persuasive.
93 *Declaration of . . . York*.
94 Bodl., MS Clarendon 68, fols. 100v, 115 (cal. IV, 510–11, 513); *CCSP*, IV, 168, 512.
95 *Ibid.*, fol. 179 (cal. IV, 551); *CCSP*, IV, *q.v.* Northcote, Sir John.
96 *SPC*, III, 714.
97 Roger L'Estrange, *A Free Parliament proposed by the City to the Nation* (1660); *L'Estrange his Apology*, p. 53; and see Knights, 'Roger L'Estrange'.
98 The names are to be found in *A&O*, II.
99 HMC, *Leybourne-Popham*, p. 181; *Merc. Pub.*, 29 March–5 April, pp. 210–11, 214; *ibid.*, 19–26 April, pp. 255, 260.

100 *Parl. Int.*, 9–16 January, p. 48.
101 *Mordaunt*, p. 145.
102 See my 'The Campaign for a Free Parliament'.
103 Alan Everitt, *The Community of Kent and the Great Rebellion* (Leicester, 1966), pp. 271–3.
104 *Pub. Int.*, 30 January–6 February, pp. 1066–7; *CSPD 1659–60*, pp. 330, 349; John Boys, *Aeneas his Descent into Hell* (1660), pp. 218–25.
105 Everitt, *Community of Kent*, p. 307. Although my assessment of the movement in Kent is naturally indebted to Everitt's, it differs somewhat from his.
106 *HH*, pp. 79–83.
107 *SPC*, III, 483, 522, 582, 597; David Underdown, *Royalist Conspiracy in England* (New Haven, CT, 1960), *q.v.* Carey, Henry, Lord Falkland.
108 *Merc. Pol.*, 26 January–2 February, p. 1060; *Merc. Pub.*, 26 January–2 February, p. 73.
109 *CCSP*, IV, 386.
110 *HOP 1660–1690*, II, 125.
111 *Ibid.*, II, 613.
112 See my 'The Campaign for a Free Parliament'.
113 Compare *An Extract out of a Letter from a Gentleman of Quality* (1660), with *The Humble Address, and Hearty Desires of . . . the County of Northampton* (1660: printed in two slightly different versions).
114 Bodl., MS Clarendon 69, fols 7–8 (cal. IV, 532); *Merc. Pol.*, 26 January–2 February, p. 1059; *Merc. Pub.*, 26 January–2 February, p. 73.
115 Bodl., MS Nalson VIII, fol. 207; Bodl., MS Clarendon 68, fols 107–8 (cal. IV, 512).
116 *CCSP*, IV, *q.v.* Norris, Sir John, and Norwich, Sir John; *Mordaunt*, p. 66; *SPC*, III, 677.
117 *The Second Address from the Gentlemen of the County of Northampton* (1660).
118 *SPC*, III, 613. Cf. *ibid.* III, 623; *Mordaunt*, pp. 66, 73, 117; *CCSP*, IV, 476.
119 *CSPD 1658–9*, p. 83.
120 *Pepys*, I, 73; *Mordaunt*, p. 73.
121 *Carte*, II, 201; *Mordaunt*, pp. 66, 73.
122 *Merc. Pol.*, 12–19 January, p. 1036.
123 See my 'The Campaign for a Free Parliament'.
124 *Merc. Pub.*, 12–19 January, pp. 43, 47.
125 *PCH*, XXII, 421, 477; XXIII, 6, 9, 24; *SPC*, III, 747; *Calendar of the Correspondence of Richard Baxter*, ed. N.H. Keeble and Geoffrey Nuttall (2 vols, Oxford, 1991), i, 401, 428–9, 431–2, II, 104; G.R. Abernathy, *The English Presbyterians and the Stuart Restoration, 1648–1653* (Transactions of the American Philosophical Society, new series, 55, 1965), p. 45; and see my *God's Instruments. Political Conduct in the England of Oliver Cromwell* (Oxford, 2012), p. 83.
126 *HH*, p. 38; BL, Add. MS 21245, fol. 204.
127 *A True Catalogue, or an Account of the Several Places* (1659), p. 45.
128 BL, Add. MS 21245, fol. 204; *HH*, p. 39; HMC, *Leybourne-Popham*, p. 147.
129 HMC, *Leybourne-Popham*, pp. 147–50; *HH*, p. 38; BL, Add MS 21425, fol. 204.
130 *SPC*, III, 597, 714.
131 *Ibid.*, III, 583, 701, 718; Bodl., MSS Clarendon 68, fol. 85; 69, fol. 164v (cal. IV, 508, 564); *A Letter from divers of the Gentry of the County of Lincoln* (1660); *CCSP*, IV, *q.v.* Rossiter, Col. Edward; *Merc. Pol.*, 16–23 February, p. 1116; Underdown, *Royalist Conspiracy*, p. 271.
132 *HOP 1660–1690*, II, 384.
133 *CCC*.
134 Bodl., MS Clarendon 68, fol. 176v (cal. IV, 567); *CSPD 1659–60*, pp. 349, 355; *SPC*, III, 433, 486, 510, 702; *CCSP*, IV, 592; *Merc. Pub.*, 19–26 April, p. 260.
135 Bodl., MS Clarendon 72, fol. 27 (cal. IV, 676); cf. Underdown, *Royalist Conspiracy*, p. 269.
136 *CSPD 1658–9*, p. xxiv.
137 Underdown, *Royalist Conspiracy*, pp. 240, 269.
138 *Merc. Pol.*, 26 January–2 February, pp. 1659–60. See too *ibid.*, 16–23 February, p. 1116.

139 Patrick Little and David L. Smith, *Parliaments and Politics during the Cromwellian Protectorate* (Cambridge, 2007), *q.v.* Hobart, Sir John.
140 *Burton*, I, xxxv–vi.
141 Le Strange, *Address*, p. 19; Little and Smith, *Parliaments and Politics*, Appendix 1.
142 HMC, *Leybourne-Popham*, p. 181; *Merc. Pub.*, 19–26 April, p. 260; *ibid.*, 26 April–3 May, p. 275.
143 Godfrey Davies, 'The General Election of 1660', *HLQ*, 14 (1952), 211–35, at pp. 216–17. Cf. *Merc. Pub.*, 29 March–5 April, pp. 214–15 (though see also *ibid.* 5–12 April, p. 245).
144 *HH*, pp. 32, 50–2.
145 Bodl., MS Clarendon 69, fol. 39 (cal. IV, 538); cf. Underdown, *Royalist Conspiracy*, pp. 40, 269–70, 298.
146 Tim Harris, *London Crowds in the Reign of Charles II* (Cambridge, 1987), p. 42.
147 *CCSP*, IV, 533.
148 Everitt, *Suffolk and the Great Rebellion*, p. 128.
149 *CSPD 1659–60*, p. 568.
150 *SPC*, III, 485, 676; *CCSP*, IV, 225; Underdown, *Royalist Conspiracy*, *q.v.* Felton, Sir Henry.
151 *A Letter agreed unto . . . by . . . the County of Suffolk. Presented to . . . Monck* (1660); *A Letter agreed unto . . . by . . . the County of Suffolk. Presented to . . . the City of London* (1660); *Merc. Pol.*, 26 January–2 February, p. 1063; *CCJ*, fol. 219v.
152 *The Declaration of Thomas Lord Fairfax, and the rest of . . . the County and City of York* (1660; cf. *Pepys*, I, 55); *The Copy of a Letter from a Lincolne Shire Gentleman* (cf. *Three Letters of Publick Concernment* [1660], pp. 8–20); my '1660: Restoration and Revolution'.
153 Boys, *Aeneas*, p. 219; *HH*, pp. 15–16.
154 Compare *HH*, pp. 50–2 with *L'Estrange his Apology*, p. 42.
155 *To his Excellency the Lord General Monck. The Humble Addresse . . . of . . . the County of Hartford* (1660).
156 John Aubrey, *Brief Lives*, ed. Kate Bennett (2 vols, continuously paginated, Oxford, 2015), I, 336–9.
157 C.H. Firth and Godfrey Davies, *The Regimental History of Cromwell's Army* (2 vols, Oxford, 1940), II, 442 (though cf. *Merc. Pub.*, 29 March–5 April, pp. 214–15).
158 TNA, SP25/77, fols 861ff: Hertfordshire; *Writings and Speeches of Oliver Cromwell*, ed. W.C. Abbott (4 vols, Cambridge, MA, 1937–47), III, 699, IV, 256, 735.
159 *Burton*, II, 437, 442; III, 418, 512–13.
160 *To his Excellency General Monck, The Congratulation . . . of . . . the County of Bucks* (1660). It may be that the declaration, to which Monck gave a dusty answer, was modified before publication, so that a plea for 'a free and a full parliament' was omitted in print: *Parl. Int.*, 23–30 January, p. 72; Huntington Library, Stowe Papers, SSTM/5/13; *Rugg*, p. 32. Conceivably declarations from other counties were likewise adjusted before being printed, but there is enough evidence to indicate that this was not a normal practice.
161 Godfrey Davies, 'The Political Career of Sir Richard Temple (1634–1697) and Buckinghamshire Politics', *HLQ*, 4 (1940), 47–83, at p. 47.
162 *HOP 1660–1690*, II, 304.
163 Stocks and Stevenson, *Records of the Borough of Leicester*, p. 459.
164 *Ibid.*, p. 458; Reece, *Army*, p. 184.
165 *Merc. Pol.*, 19–26 January, p. 1052.
166 D. Brunton and D.H. Pennington, *Members of the Long Parliament* (1954), p. 208.
167 *Merc. Pol.*, 9–16 February, pp. 1095–6.
168 HMC, *Leybourne-Popham*, p. 149.
169 *A Lively Pourtraict of our New-Cavaliers* (1661), p. 9; and compare *Merc. Pol.*, 24 August–1 September 1659, p. 691 with *ibid.*, 8–15 September 1659, pp. 721–3, 731.
170 *PCH*, XXII, 88–9.

12 The revolution of memory

The monuments of Westminster Abbey

Peter Sherlock

If there is any constant feature in the history of Westminster Abbey, it is the church's remarkable capacity to appear timeless and unchanging despite the reality of continuous alteration, accretion, and, occasionally, revolution.[1]

Perhaps there is no better example of this than the Abbey's handling of the English revolution. The Abbey itself managed to survive the upheavals of the mid-seventeenth century relatively intact. Moreover, until relatively recently, the building contained almost no sign that anything had ever happened. It is as if the collective memory bypassed the 1640s and 1650s altogether. This is despite the Abbey's central place as a site of national memory, whether for politicians, royal-watchers, or tourists, and despite the innumerable wars and battles celebrated in the Abbey's many tombs, from the Hundred Years War to the Second World War, from Agincourt to Dunkirk.[2]

As is always the case with sites of memory, the seeming absence of monuments from the 1640s and 1650s was no accident. For in 1661, Charles II ordered the removal of the bodies of the regicides and their families from Westminster Abbey. Some bodies were reburied in a common grave at St Margaret's Westminster, while others – including Cromwell, Ireton, and Bradshaw – were ritually humiliated in an attempt to compensate for the execution of Charles I over a decade earlier. Their funeral hearses and monuments were destroyed and their graves reused.[3]

It was not until the nineteenth century and the renovating enthusiasm of the famous Dean, A.P. Stanley, that the names of the disinterred reappeared in the Abbey precinct. Stanley – ever keen to promote his own, more comprehensive, version of English history – thoroughly explored the vaults and graves underneath the Abbey's many chapels, then caused plaques to be placed over the graves of famous persons who had no memorial. This included the creation of memorials not only for seventeenth- and eighteenth-century sovereigns and members of the royal family but also for Cromwell, Ireton, and Bradshaw in the Henry VII Chapel. Later, in 1880, Stanley wrote to the *Daily Telegraph* to express his support for the erection of a monument to Napoleon III's son in Westminster Abbey, following a negative vote in the House of Commons. Stanley compared the 'party passions' and 'ungenerous spirit' of the present Parliament to that of 1661 and offered his own act of seemingly unpartisan tribute to the leaders of the 1650s as a better way forward for the British Empire.[4]

Then in 1898 a statue of Cromwell was erected outside the Houses of Parliament, not in the Abbey grounds but nonetheless gazing perpetually towards the 'house of kings' that was briefly his tomb.[5] Finally, in 1966 the Abbey's companion church of St Margaret, Westminster, became host to what was intended to be a permanent acknowledgement of the leaders of the English revolution. The Cromwell Society held a ceremony to honour the memory of the twenty-one men and women whose mortal remains had been removed from the Abbey in 1661. A record of their names was inscribed in the tower of St Margaret's in an attempt to restore to them some of the honour and dignity that had been stripped by the most extreme act of disinterment (Figure 12.1).

Despite the absence of contemporary references to the 1640s and 1650s in the Abbey, this period was nevertheless a highly influential one in the history of monumental commemoration at Westminster. For, as John Physick points out, arguably it was under Cromwell that the Abbey became a 'national Valhalla'. During the mid-seventeenth century, the Abbey was the place of carefully orchestrated funerals for military leaders such as Essex, Ireton, Popham, and Blake, many of whom then had monuments erected at the cost of the state.[6]

Very little scholarly attention has been given to the practice of monumental commemoration in England in the 1640s and 1650s.[7] There are now excellent studies of the impact of iconoclasm on monuments in this period, whether through the activities of parliamentary soldiers or of special commissioners like William Dowsing.[8] Isolated studies of individual examples, such as the famous Verney tomb at Middle Claydon or the St John monument at Lydiard Tregoze, are suggestive of a deep need to address the familial grief and national divisions that resulted from the civil wars.[9] Yet there remains a need to understand how the dead were commemorated to posterity in the mid-seventeenth century.

Figure 12.1 Memorial at St Margaret's Westminster erected by the Cromwell Association. © Dean and Chapter of Westminster.

As Edward Parry points out in his 2011 study of mid-seventeenth-century monuments in Wales and the Borders, 'while most of the recent scholarly work on monuments concentrates on their cultural background and on identifying craftsmen and patrons, little has been written about the political messages – implicit and explicit – they bear'.[10] What was the impact of the English revolution on monuments to the dead? Memorialisation may have slowed but certainly did not cease in this period, so what were the political and religious messages delivered in images and inscriptions, and what if any change occurred in the aesthetics of commemoration?

This essay begins to address this deficit through analysis of monuments erected at Westminster Abbey in the 1640s and 1650s. Interpretation of monuments such as these requires the interrogation of material culture on the one hand, and reconstructive textual work on print and manuscript sources on the other, as in many cases the actual monuments have not survived or have been moved or reshaped by subsequent generations. Printed sources for Westminster Abbey are plentiful, the main ones being the catalogues of monuments published by Henry Keepe in 1682 and John Dart in 1723.[11] My interpretative approach relies on a mix of archaeology, visual interpretation and cultural history, drawing in particular on the work of Jonathan Finch, Nigel Llewellyn, and Adam White.[12] This methodology was developed during my doctoral work in the late 1990s under the supervision of Clive Holmes and draws on his collaborative work with Felicity Heal on the gentry and their monuments.[13]

I

Monuments were, as Heal and Holmes have noted, a major form of 'material display' for the gentry and nobility in parish churches and cathedrals across England.[14] Whatever their religious or political content, monuments ensured that the gentry occupied a disproportionate share of physical space in that communal space – the church – long after death. The monuments of the 1640s and 1650s, just as much as those of the 1630s and 1660s, were testimony to the honour and piety displayed by their subjects. Monuments bore witness to the notion that this honour and piety were inherited from their ancestors and passed to their descendants. Their images and inscriptions stressed the contribution and service of their subjects to the government and well-being of the country through political service and charitable acts.

But burials, graves, and monuments are not merely signs of their times. As suggested in the introduction to this essay, they have an ongoing life, whether revered or neglected, restored or destroyed. To understand the shape of monumental commemoration is to understand how history itself is represented. Such understanding requires both attention to the dynamic contest that determines such representation and recognition that there is always potential for the unnoticed to be celebrated or for this generation's victor to be the next generation's victim. Part of the challenge in writing about the monuments of Westminster

Abbey in the mid-seventeenth century is that they themselves have been agents in this contest for representation, whether in their own time or in more recent centuries. Many have not survived, and others have been altered in content or context.

Recent studies of political propaganda and image-making in the 1640s and 1650s have highlighted the role of poetry and polemic and, increasingly, of images, rituals, and material display. Thus the little evidence that survives about the funeral rites and monuments of figures such as Cromwell, Ireton, or Thomas May has been used to illustrate the attempts of the republican regime to promote itself in words and practices drawn from classical antiquity.[15] Similarly, their disinterment and ritual humiliation in 1660 and 1661 have also been widely studied to understand how restoration of the monarchy was performed and to assess the merits of Charles II in the process. Yet little has been said about what the monuments to Ireton, May, and others at Westminster Abbey have to tell us about monumental culture itself. This site is especially significant given that by the mid-seventeenth century the Abbey was already a church celebrated for the tombs of royalty and aristocracy that half-filled its many chapels and aisles.

Kevin Sharpe has claimed with reference to events such as the burning of Cromwell's effigy in London in 1660, the disinterment and humiliation of the bodies of the regicides, and the reinterment of royalists executed by the republican regime, that these transactions of denigration and affirmation were necessary to the restoration of a culture of honour.[16] Yet the culture of honour had never really gone away; it had simply been redirected. While this redirection was awkward to achieve at the highest level of authority of king or Protector, it was not so difficult to manage for other political and aristocratic leaders. Thus, in the 1640s and 1650s, monuments continued to be built in imitation of antique or contemporary European styles, deploying heraldry and other insignia of honour, and displaying learned inscriptions that told of the lineage, valour, and piety of their subjects.

By the time the Wars of the Three Kingdoms broke out, Westminster Abbey was already established as the major site of monumental commemoration in early modern England, regularly visited by tourists.[17] Virtually no monuments were erected at the Abbey during the uncertain transformation of the building in the mid-sixteenth century from a monastery to a cathedral, back to an abbey, and finally into a collegiate church. But once the regime had settled in the 1580s, members of the court, especially those with residences in Westminster, began to bury their dead under splendid monuments in the Abbey's many chapels, now disused. When James VI and I ascended the throne, many of the best positions had already been occupied by tombs built by the Southwark School of Masons, bearing triumphal arches, effigies, and lavish heraldic displays. James himself drew on this tradition to bury his predecessor and his mother in Henry VII's Chapel, reviving royal commemoration. During his reign and into the 1630s, the pace of monument building only increased and diversified, including monuments in new styles to soldiers and poets, philosophers and judges, royal favourites and relations, as well as English aristocrats.[18] Perhaps no monument was more surprising than that of Thomas Parr, alleged to be one hundred and fifty-two years old at his death in 1635 following a trip to London to meet the king.[19]

The pace and shape of commemoration changed markedly after 1640. Although the number of tombs erected did not drop dramatically, the quality of the genre changed. Gone were the multi-storied monuments of the nobility and the tributes to service of the king.[20] The last of these sumptuous tributes for the time being was Nicholas Stone's monument for the ambassador Dudley Carleton, Viscount Dorchester (d. 1632), erected in 1640 complete with reclining effigy, grand inscription panels, large heraldic shields, and an elegant classical frame (Figure 12.2).

Instead, the monuments of the 1640s were mostly ledger stones or modest wall plaques for members of the House of Commons and their relations. Some of these survived the disinterments of 1661, when tombs outside Henry VII's Chapel and monuments for women (such as the grave of Cromwell's daughter Elizabeth) appear to have been overlooked by Charles II's officers. One remarkable survival typical of the period is the mural tablet of Grace Scot (d. 1646), even though it records that she was daughter of Sir Thomas Mauleverer and wife of Colonel Thomas Scot, both judges at the trial of Charles I, and displays their coats of arms (Figure 12.3.). Her simple epitaph concludes with a statement of marital affection: 'He that will give my Grace but what is hers, must say her death hath not made only her deare Scot But vertue, worth and sweetness Widowers'.[21] George Wild (d. 1650), a Member of Parliament, was typical of those buried in the Abbey in this era, with his epitaph (now lost) referring to his honest life, knowledge of the law, and his fortitude and piety in death ('*In vita honest. in lege & literis erudit. in morte fortis & pius*').[22]

The apparent modesty of the monuments of this decade was not reflected in the commemoration of the dead displayed at major funerals. The most notable of these by far was that of the Earl of Essex in 1646 when Parliament was said to have spent over £5,000 on the funeral ritual, including a hearse and effigy to rival those of royal funerals.[23] Nevertheless, the turmoil of the 1640s and the associated uncertainty about the future of ecclesiastical space and commemorative culture clearly took their toll on the Abbey. These concerns were dramatically expressed in a manuscript account of the state of the Abbey's furnishings written in 1645 and updated to 1647. Now among the treasures of the Westminster Abbey Library, it was formerly housed at Mostyn Hall, Flintshire, and is referred to here as the Mostyn manuscript.[24]

The manuscript's observations were copied at least in part from printed sources, for as the title page reported, the record was 'Colected and gathered from Sunderye Authors as well as from the Monnuments them selves, with the inscriptions as on them exprest'.[25] Nonetheless, the Mostyn manuscript record is invaluable. Not only does it record in detail burials and tombs from the first

Figure 12.2 Monument of Dudley Carleton, Viscount Dorchester (d. 1632), Westminster Abbey.

© Dean and Chapter of Westminster.

Figure 12.3 Monument of Grace Scot (d. 1645), Westminster Abbey.
© Dean and Chapter of Westminster.

half of the seventeenth century for which very little other information survives, but it also includes commentary on the state of the Abbey in the midst of the great revolution unfolding in the 1640s.

The manuscript's author was almost certainly in the service of the controversial Dean of Westminster and Archbishop of York, Dr John Williams, as it devotes considerable space in its first few pages to his career. This section of the manuscript ends with Williams' fate in the 1640s when 'he once more got out of his former habitation to a place of Libertie Travellinge Towards Yorke and from thence to his own Country wher he abides peaceabley and quiete, haveinge rune through almost as much Varietye of fortunes as the Church had suffer'd from its begininge'. The Mostyn manuscript made a point of contrasting the repairs to the Abbey overseen by Williams with the destruction authorised by the Parliament: 'In ye yeare 1645 were ye Rich Windowes (Contayeninge ye history of ye new Testament) and ye Brassen Alter of Henry the 7th demolished by ye Parliament as Types of superstition, as also many of ye carved Statues in ye Chappell and Church'. Here and elsewhere, the manuscript attempted to make the point that the parliamentarians, in the destruction of supposed 'Types of superstition', were also attacking the scriptures and, in the case of the altar in Henry VII's Chapel, the monument of the most Protestant of England's monarchs, Edward VI. Finally, the author directly addresses an imagined future reader to lament the uncertainty that hung over the Abbey, 'being in this pressent yeare 1647 without goverment and unsettled, I canot but referr you to the futter wherin you may be your owne Judges what it hath bine and what it may in yor tymes contynew'.[26]

Despite its pessimism, the Mostyn manuscript contained signs that the Abbey was capable of absorbing the peculiar contradictions of the 1640s. It recorded two recent burials from opposite ends of the political spectrum. Under the central crossing of the Abbey, at the foot of the steps leading up to the Lord's Table, was the grave of John Broxholme (d. 1647).[27] Broxholme was elected to represent Lincoln in the Long Parliament in 1640 and supported the parliamentarian party throughout this period.[28] Just to the south in St Benedict's Chapel was the monument of Dr John Spottiswoode, Archbishop of St Andrews, who died in exile in England in 1639. As the manuscript recorded, Spottiswoode 'was by ye persecution of the Natives of that country driven out of itt, they haveing Rayesd an Army and entered the kingdome of England in oposition to ye Government of Bishopps'. The epitaph (perhaps on a plate on the coffin or a table hanging at the grave, for there is no record of a permanent monument) included the claim that Spottiswood 'stood To ye Last gaspe for holy Churches good, For ye King alsoe, and for ye faith true, Gainst Church Robbers a false trayterous Crew'.[29] Spottiswoode's inscription thereby functioned for the Mostyn manuscript as a kind of meta-epitaph, standing in for the iconoclastic and sacrilegious destruction the author envisaged would continue to take place at Westminster.

II

Despite the context of authorised iconoclasm and the allegation of sacrilege, the moderation of the scale of monuments at Westminster in the 1640s was only temporary. In the 1650s, the leaders of the Commonwealth and Protectorate and their families were frequently buried at the Abbey, and the monuments erected to them returned to the more lavish standards possible in a time of relative peace. The funeral business saw no downturn in trade as a result of the changed state of government, especially after the conclusion of civil war. The account book of an unknown heraldic painter in the British Library records a great deal of work completed around London and the home counties in the 1650s, including a fee of 12 shillings for a day's work at the Abbey 'For Helping Mr. Smith on the funerall of Adm[ira]l Deane who was buryed June ye 24 1653 ... in ye Chappell of Hen: the 7th'.[30]

What can be reconstructed of the tombs at Westminster erected in the 1650s suggests that what was true of the funeral business was also true for monumental masons. Preachers, propagandists, and admirals are recorded among those buried at Westminster Abbey in this decade, with a reasonable number appearing to have had a monument of some kind. An intriguing development is the survival of several wall tablets or ledger stones from the 1650s in the Abbey cloisters, most little more than a name or a date recording the lives of men and women who were perhaps residents of Westminster. These include the epitaph of Richard Gouland (d. 1659), commemorated as 'the first keeper of the Library of this College' and 'a man truly Orthodox, of an undissembled piety and uprightness'[31] (Figure 12.4). Unfortunately, it is not clear from the available evidence how many of the people disinterred in 1661 also had monuments that were destroyed. There is enough surviving evidence to provide a reading of three tombs, those of Thomas May, Henry Ireton, and Edward Popham. The monuments of May and Ireton were torn down, and while we have a record of the inscriptions, there is only a general indication of their appearance. Remarkably, Popham's tomb survives but has no inscription.

Thomas May was a poet, translator of Lucan, and author of the official history of Parliament. When he died in November 1650, the Council of State arranged for a state funeral, burial, and monument in Westminster Abbey, with instructions for the total cost not to exceed £100.[32] His grave was placed in the west side of the south transept, opposite the area now known as Poets' Corner. His monument was erected on the west wall, probably as an attempt to align him with the nearby monuments of earlier historians such as William Camden. The monument was removed in 1661 when May's body was disinterred, and its place was later taken by the memorial to Thomas Triplet (d. 1670). John Aubrey recorded that May's monument could for a time be found 'upside downe in the chapell where the earle of Middlesex tombe is', that is, in St Benedict's Chapel on the east side of the south transept. No further record of the monument has been found, and it is likely that not only was it turned 'upside down' but also that its materials were reused. Fortuitously, Aubrey was able to find a record of the Latin inscription on the memorial, while Anthony Wood later claimed it was written by Marchamont Nedham.[33]

The monument was probably in the form of a large marble slab against the wall, displaying the Latin inscription. The text emphasized May's republican credentials in effusive language, drawing attention to his scholarship and his parliamentary commissions: 'Champion of the English Republic, ornament of letters, most renowned poet of his age, delight of posterity, another Lucan, more than Roman, loyal historian' ('*Quem Anglicana respublica habuit vindicem, ornamentum literaria, secli sui vatum celeberrimus, deliciae futuri, Lucanus alter plusquam Romanus, historicus fidus*').[34] Yet May's honour did not flow solely from

210 Peter Sherlock

Figure 12.4 Monument of Richard Gouland (d. 1659), cloister, Westminster Abbey.
© Dean and Chapter of Westminster.

his personal achievements. The epitaph went on to point out that he was 'first-born son of a knight' even as he 'added his own glory and fame to his father's titles' ('*equitis aurati filius primogenitus . . . qui paternis titulis claritatis suae specimen usque adeo superaddidit*'). The epitaph concluded with the information that Parliament itself had caused the monument to be erected, a habit that was common in the eighteenth century but one not seen before in the Abbey.

The high-minded republican sentiments of this monument did not go unchallenged in the 1650s and at some point a wag pinned another inscription to the tomb, claiming that May was indeed just like Lucan, 'for each was an ungrateful traitor to his Prince, the one to the tyrant Nero, the other to Charles, best of kings', and proceeding to call May a 'lying poet'. The author of this counter-monument went on to cast the erection of the tomb as a kind of treason against the building itself: 'Because these unworthy ashes are buried amongst so many heroic poets and noblemen, the marbles seem to weep. Nor did the rebels regret placing him here, they who have turned so many churches and sanctuaries of God into stables for horses'.[35] Although Westminster Abbey had not been used for stables, this was the case at several cathedrals including St Paul's London. The counter-monument used this illustration and the denigration of May's life and character to link rebellion, treason, and sacrilege.[36]

Henry Ireton died in 1651 in Ireland, and the regime took the trouble to transport his body back to England for burial in Henry VII's Chapel.[37] On 5 February 1652, John Evelyn witnessed what he described as 'the Magnificent Funeral of that arch-Rebell Ireton'. This included all the military grandeur of a state funeral including four heralds 'carrying the arms of the State (as they cald it)', emblems designed to replace the royal arms.[38] Colonel Rich commissioned one of the leading masons in England, William Wright, to provide a monument at a cost of £120. By February 1654, Wright had not been paid and so petitioned Cromwell for his costs, reporting that the 'Tombe of same' was complete in a form that was 'hee hopeth to the good contentment of yo:r Highnesse, and the most skilfull beholders, and to the well deserving same of the said late Ld Deputy'. He advised that he would 'bee enabled to make Erection of the said Tombe' on payment of the money owed to him. The Lord Protector approved payment, and Wright's account was settled by the end of March.[39]

It is noteworthy that Ireton had a substantial tomb in the Abbey's most prestigious space, commissioned by the government and completed by a prominent London mason. The whole idea of such a grand tomb and the pomp and ceremony of a state funeral was likely at odds with Ireton's austerity and his views on how the dead should be commemorated. The *Memoirs of Edmund Ludlow* recorded in 1698 that Ireton:

> if he could have foreseen what was done by them, would certainly have made it his desire that his Body might have found a Grave where his Soul left it, so much did he despise those pompous and expensive Vanities; having erected for himself a more glorious Monument in the hearts of good Men, by his affection to his Country, his abilities of Mind, his impartial Justice, his diligence in the Publick Service, and his other Vertues, which were a far greater Honour to his Memory, than a Dormitory amongst the Ashes of Kings, who, for the most part, as they had governed others by their Passions, so were they themselves as much governed by them.[40]

The shape of monumental commemoration had barely changed from the process used half a century earlier to erect the monuments of Elizabeth Tudor and Mary Stuart in the same part of the Abbey. The ruling power decreed that there would be a monument complete with architecture, effigies, heraldry, and epitaph; the responsibility was entrusted to an officer of the state or crown, and a mason was commissioned to deliver the same. The content of Ireton's monument, however, did reflect the new republican order of things.

A variety of evidence points towards the possible inscription. Hugh Peters published a single sheet of Latin verses eulogising Ireton that concluded, 'Hugh Peters inscribed this epigram at his own expense'.[41] This may indicate Peters' verses were in fact those inscribed on the monument, although it is perhaps simply an indication that he paid the costs of printing his own tribute to Ireton. Jonathan Scott notes that Ireton's inscription was reported elsewhere as, '*Ireto regali tumulo jacet + Dorylaus/Rex Carlus nullo. Credimus esse Deos*'. This text imitated Pompey's famous epitaph – '*Pompeius nullo. Credimus esse Deos*' – and was a means of comparing Ireton to Pompey and, by implication, Cromwell to Caesar.[42] Thus a simple epitaph, whether actually engraved on a tomb or circulated in manuscript or print, could be the agent of sensitive political comparisons.

These forms of commemoration were not uncontested. Anthony Wood recorded that a hatchment was hung at Somerset House while Ireton's body was lying in state, 'with this motto under his arms depicted thereon, *Dulce est pro patria mori*, which was englished by an honest cavalier thus, *It is good for his country that he is dead*'.[43] Other epitaphs and elegies circulated in print. David Norbrook records one prominent republican example that described Ireton 'as fit/For th'Camp as *Julius*: yet abhorred it./He for the Pallace also was as fit,/As wise *Augustus*: yet disdained it'.[44]

Ireton's tomb was destroyed after his remains were disinterred in January 1661, along with those of Cromwell and Bradshaw.[45] Evelyn described how their 'Carkasses' were 'draged out of their superbe Tombs (in Westminster among the Kings)'.[46] Anthony Wood wrote that 'Ireton's tomb was broken down, and what remained over the graves of Cromwell and Bradshaw were clean swept away, and no footstep left of their remembrances in that royal and stately burial place of our English kings'.[47]

In stark contrast to the monuments of May or Ireton, the appearance of which can only be surmised, the monument of Edward Popham (d. 1651) remains intact in the Abbey but without any epitaph. Popham was the first of the three admirals to be buried in the Abbey, the others being Richard Deane (d. 1653) and Robert Blake (d. 1657). In his 1683 book on the Westminster monuments, Henry Keepe described the Popham tomb 'of curious wrought Alabaster, but there is no Inscription of Epitaph, which was ordered to be defaced upon the restauration of his *Sacred Majesty*'. Originally it had been intended to destroy the whole monument when the regicides were disinterred. Keepe claimed, however, that 'by the intercession of some of his Ladies Friends, who had eminently served his Majesty, the stone was only turned whereon the Epitaph was insculpt, and the Monument permitted to remain'.[48]

The stone facing on the central table was investigated by the Abbey for signs of any inscription on its reverse, and no evidence was found. It may be that the story was wrong and that there never was an inscription on the monument. In the eighteenth century, John Dart repeatedly tried to track down a copy of the inscription for his *magnum opus* on the Abbey tombs, without success.

The Popham monument is a most unusual survival from the 1650s, the only contemporary monument to a regicide that remains within the Abbey walls. The attribution of its survival to the widow Popham's family is probably correct. Having remained a widow throughout the 1650s, Anne Popham remarried Philip, Lord Wharton, on 26 August 1661. Although he had been a parliament man and one of the peers summoned by Cromwell to the Other House in 1657, he had played an instrumental role in the return of Charles II in 1660. It was most likely his intervention, just a month or two after his marriage, that was responsible for saving the monument and its image of his new wife.[49]

The monument portrays Popham standing, leaning on a table, his wife Anne opposite in a posture mirroring his. In between them on the table sits a helmet and gloves, positioned below Popham's coat of arms (Figure 12.5). Under Popham's foot is a ship's chart box, a typically English, playful means of making reference to his admiralty. While these items represent Popham's military career and fame, their positioning also shows that he can now rest from his labours. Having conquered the seas under his feet, his head and hands are now bare. Freed from the constraint and protection of helmet and gloves, he is serenely contemplative as he awaits the resurrection to eternal life. In the absence of an inscription saying who he was and when he lived, and surrounded by heraldic shields and military accoutrements and tributes of honour, it is nigh impossible to distinguish Popham's tomb from those of the royalists nearby.

III

With the return of the king and the expulsion of the regicides from the Abbey, monuments were again erected to courtiers, soldiers, bishops, and their families, many triumphantly proclaiming the restoration of honour. The memorial of Colonel Thomas Blagge (d. 1660), now lost, spoke of his service to the king as 'an extraordinary example of obstinate fidelity, for which merits, after the King's happy Restoration, he was made colonel of a troop of guards and Governor of Yarmouth' ('*fidei suae obstinationem ubique singulari exemplo app. ob hoc sub Regis felicissimo reditu cohortis stipartorum Tribunatu, & Praefectum Yarmuthe . . . donatus*').[50] Thus the epitaph on the monument of Sir Thomas Ingram (d. 1671) proudly told of 'his eminent loyalty, sufferings, and services to and for their Majesties King Charles I. and II' and how his death was a 'loss to his Prince and the Publick'.[51]

England's sixteenth-century Protestant reformers had been willing for the most part to turn a blind eye to the reminders that their ancestors had once

214 *Peter Sherlock*

Figure 12.5 Monument of Edward Popham (d. 1651), Westminster Abbey.
© Dean and Chapter of Westminster.

believed in purgatory and, through epitaphs and images, continued still to seek the prayers of the living. In the same way, the revolutionary leaders of the mid-seventeenth century were for the most part able to view the tombs and thrones of the kings and queens of England and the statues of the saints that surrounded them at Westminster Abbey as reminders of a history that needed only to be surpassed, not suppressed. History had taken a different, providential turn, and only a few, truly offensive elements needed to be removed, most notably the elaborate altar in Henry VII's Chapel under which Edward VI was buried, and the stained glass that adorned the Abbey's windows. The greater disruption to the Abbey's commemorative culture came not with the sixteenth-century reformation of religion, the meeting of the Westminster Assembly, or the death of Charles I, but with the restoration of the monarchy in 1660. For it was in January 1661 that bodies were disinterred, graves destroyed, and tombs removed or defaced.

The ultimate act of restitution for the royalist party would have been a monument for Charles I. Yet his body still lies where it was placed after his execution, in the grave of Henry VIII and Jane Seymour at St George's Windsor. In the late 1670s, the Parliament did indeed consider an extravagant proposal to commission a monument and reinter the royal remains. One version of this project, designed by Christopher Wren, was estimated to cost the vast sum of £70,000. This took the form of a rotunda containing an effigy of the late king standing on a shield borne by the virtues Prudence, Temperance, Justice, and Fortitude.[52] Like other monumental projects, such as the unfinished tomb for Henry VIII, the project never came to fruition as insufficient will existed to overcome the financial – and political – barriers.

In mid-seventeenth-century England, the desire to grieve for the honourable dead, to proclaim their virtues, to acknowledge their practice of true religion (whatever that might be) continued to find expression in funeral monuments, for both royalist supporter and republican visionary. Honour endured the English revolution unscathed, and was reinforced time and again through funerals and through monuments. If anything, the military achievements of the revolutionaries reinvigorated the culture of honour, as funerary tributes and epitaphs could point to actual deeds in battle whether on land or at sea. Not even the execution of the monarch or the disinterment of the revolutionary leaders could replace the cult of honour, which drew readily on the language and symbols of classical republicanism to replace divine kingship and feudal power.

While a monument to Charles I was conceivable by the 1670s, though never built, little changed in this period for the ordinary men, women, and children of England. Despite the aspirations of some revolutionaries, most of the population remained wholly unrecorded and unrepresented in the stones, plaques, and sculptures at Westminster Abbey. The idea that a monument in the Abbey could signify the labour, lives, and sacrifices of the ordinary man or woman would remain beyond the national imagination for another two hundred and fifty years until the arrival of an even more violent war to end all wars.

Notes

1 The best modern account of the Abbey is Richard Jenkyns, *Westminster Abbey* (Cambridge, MA, 2005).
2 I draw the concept of a 'site of memory' from Pierre Nora's influential work. See Pierre Nora, 'Between Memory and History: *Les Lieux de Mémoire*' [1984], trans. Marc Roudebush, *Representations*, 26 (1989), 7–24.
3 For a full account of the disinterment, see Jonathan Fitzgibbons, *Cromwell's Head* (2008).

4 John Physick, 'The History of the Later Monuments', in Tim Tatton-Brown and Richard Mortimer (eds.), *Westminster Abbey: The Lady Chapel of Henry VII* (Woodbridge, 2003), pp. 300–1.
5 Nicola Smith, *The Royal Image and the English People* (Aldershot, 2001), pp. 187–205.
6 Physick, 'History of the Later Monuments', p. 308. See also Julia F. Merritt, *Westminster 1640–60: A Royal City in a Time of Revolution* (Manchester, 2013), pp. 97–103; and A.P. Stanley, *Historical Memorials of Westminster Abbey* (8th edn., 1896), pp. 204–10.
7 The best study remains Hugh Collinson, *Country Monuments: Their Families and Houses* (Newton Abbot, 1975), pp. 59–74, which demonstrates neatly how the flight of Charles II from the Battle of Worcester was recorded in funeral monuments in churches along the route long after the event.
8 Philip Lindley, *Tomb Destruction and Scholarship: Medieval Monuments in Early Modern England* (Donington, 2007); *The Journal of William Dowsing: Iconoclasm in East Anglia during the English Civil War*, ed. Trevor Cooper (Woodbridge, 2001).
9 Lawrence Stone, 'The Verney Tomb at Middle Claydon', *Records of Buckinghamshire*, 16 (1955–56), 67–82; Nigel Llewellyn, *Funeral Monuments in Post-Reformation England* (Cambridge, 2000), pp. 300–1; Peter Sherlock, 'Patriarchal Memory: Monuments in Early Modern England', in Megan Cassidy-Welch and Peter Sherlock (eds.), *Practices of Gender in Late Medieval and Early Modern Europe* (Turnhout, 2009), pp. 279–99.
10 Edward Parry, 'Monumental History: Funerary Monuments and Public Memory', *Archaeologia Cambrensis*, 160 (2011), 219–34.
11 Henry Keepe, *Monumenta Westmonasteriensia* (1682); John Dart, *Westmonasterium, or the History and Antiquities of the Abbey Church of St Peters Westminster* (2 vols, 1723; 2nd ed. 1742).
12 Jonathan Finch, *Church Monuments in Norfolk before 1850: An Archaeology of Commemoration* (Oxford, 2000); Llewellyn, *Funeral Monuments*; Adam White, 'A Biographical Dictionary of London Tomb Sculptors c.1560–c.1660', *Walpole Society*, 61 (1999), 1–162.
13 See for example their reading of the monument of Jane Bacon (d. 1659): Felicity Heal and Clive Holmes, '"*Prudentia ultra sexum*": Lady Jane Bacon and the Management of Her Families', in Muriel C. McClendon, Joseph P. Ward, and Michael MacDonald (eds.), *Protestant Identities: Religion, Society and Self-Fashioning in Post-Reformation England* (Stanford, CA, 1999), pp. 100–24.
14 Felicity Heal and Clive Holmes, *The Gentry in England and Wales, 1500–1700* (Basingstoke, 1994), pp. 338–40.
15 For example, David Norbrook, *Writing the English Republic: Poetry, Rhetoric and Politics, 1627–1660* (Cambridge, 1999), pp. 235–6; Kevin Sharpe, *Image Wars: Promoting Kings and Commonwealths in England 1603–1660* (New Haven, CT, 2010), pp. 433, 520–2.
16 Kevin Sharpe, *Rebranding Rule: The Restoration and Revolution Monarchy 1660–1714* (New Haven, CT, 2013), pp. 152–3.
17 Peter Sherlock, 'The Art of Making Memory: Epitaphs, Tables and Adages at Westminster Abbey', in Jennifer Spinks and Dagmar Eichberger (eds.), *Religion, the Supernatural and Visual Culture in Early Modern Europe: Essays in Honour of Charles Zika* (Leiden, 2015), pp. 354–69.
18 Peter Sherlock, 'The Monuments of Elizabeth Tudor and Mary Stuart: King James and the Manipulation of Memory', *JBS*, 46 (2007), 263–89; idem, 'Militant Masculinity and the Monuments of Westminster Abbey', in Susan Broomhall and Jacqueline van Gent (eds.), *Governing Masculinities in the Early Modern Period: Regulating Selves and Others* (Aldershot, 2011), pp. 131–52; Adam White, 'Westminster Abbey in the Early Seventeenth Century: A Powerhouse of Ideas', *Church Monuments*, 4 (1989), 16–53.
19 Keepe, *Monumenta Westmonasteriensia*, p. 220.
20 The surviving evidence suggests around thirteen monuments were erected in the 1630s, compared to eleven in the 1640s.
21 Keepe, *Monumenta Westmonasteriensia*, pp. 184–5.

22 Keepe, *Monumenta Westmonasteriensia*, p. 344.
23 John Adamson, 'Chivalry and Political Culture in Caroline England', in Kevin Sharpe and Peter Lake (eds.), *Culture and Politics in Early Stuart England* (Stanford, CA, 1993), pp. 191–3.
24 Westminster Abbey MS 44.
25 *Ibid.*, title page.
26 *Ibid.*, pp. 5–6.
27 *Ibid.*, p. 41.
28 For Broxholme, see Clive Holmes, *Seventeenth-Century Lincolnshire* (Lincoln, 1980), pp. 140, 143, 180.
29 Westminster Abbey MS 44, pp. 101–2.
30 BL, Harley MS 1050, fol. 24.
31 Keepe, *Monumenta Westmonasteriensia*, p. 356.
32 TNA, SP 25/13, fol. 25: Council of State Day's Proceedings, 18 November 1650.
33 John Aubrey, *Brief Lives*, ed. A. Clark (2 vols, Oxford, 1898), II, 56–7. See also David Norbrook, 'Thomas May', *ODNB*.
34 Aubrey, *Brief Lives*, II, 57. The English translation is available at 'Thomas May', Westminster Abbey, http://westminster-abbey.org/our-history/people/thomas-may (accessed 10 July 2015).
35 For the counter-monument, see *ibid.*
36 David Crankshaw, 'Community, City and Nation, 1540–1714', in Derek Keene *et al.* (eds.), *St Paul's: The Cathedral Church of London* (2004), p. 63. On sacrilege, see Martin Dzelzainis, '"Undoubted Realities": Clarendon on Sacrilege', *HJ*, 33 (1990), 515–40.
37 H.F. McMains, *The Death of Oliver Cromwell* (Lexington, KY, 2000), pp. 58–9.
38 *The Diary of John Evelyn*, ed. E.S. de Beer (6 vols, Oxford, 1955), III, 57–8.
39 TNA, SP 18/67, fol. 24: Petition of William Wright to Oliver Cromwell, 20 February 1653/4.
40 *Memoirs of Edmund Ludlow* (3 vols, Vivay, 1698), I, 384.
41 Hugh Peters, *Aeternitati sacrum Terrenum quod habuit sub hoc pulvere deposuit Henricus Ireton* (1651).
42 Jonathan Scott, *Algernon Sidney and the English Republic, 1623–1677* (Cambridge, 1988), p. 105 n. 44.
43 Anthony Wood, *Athenae Oxonienses* (5 vols, Oxford, 1817), III, col. 300.
44 Norbrook, *Writing the English Republic*, p. 236.
45 On Ireton's burial, funeral, and disinterment, see David Farr, *Henry Ireton and the English Revolution* (Woodbridge, 2006), pp. 1–14.
46 *Diary of John Evelyn*, ed. de Beer, III, 269.
47 Wood, *Athenae Oxonienses*, III, col. 301.
48 Keepe, *Monumenta Westmonasteriensia*, pp. 126–7.
49 J. Kent Clark, *Whig's Progress: Tom Wharton between Revolutions* (Madison, WI, 2004), p. 18.
50 Keepe, *Monumenta Westmonasteriensia*, pp. 186–7, and for the translation, see 'Thomas Blagge', Westminster Abbey, http://westminster-abbey.org/our-history/people/thomas-blagge (accessed 10 July 2015).
51 Keepe, *Monumenta Westmonasteriensia*, pp. 339–40.
52 Robert Beddard, 'Wren's Mausoleum for Charles I and the Cult of the Royal Martyr', *Architectural History*, 27 (1984), 36–45; David Howarth, *Images of Rule: Art and Politics in the English Renaissance 1485–1649* (Basingstoke, 1999), pp. 183–90.

13 'A pair of *Garters*'
Heralds and heraldry at the Restoration[1]

Adrian Ailes

In the spring of 1660, not one but two kings were restored to these islands. They were Charles Stuart, now truly *King* of England, Scotland, France, and Ireland, and Sir Edward Walker, his Garter Principal *King* of Arms. One result was that the new sovereign found himself sporting, to repeat a contemporary broadsheet, 'a pair of Garters' since the one intruded by Parliament, Edward Bysshe MP, still technically presided over the heralds' home, the College of Arms, albeit for not much longer. The broadsheet, now in the Bodleian Library, Oxford, consists of a dozen sarcastic and cryptic questions offered by a bemused and bitter onlooker as he or she watched a *parliamentarian* king of arms in a *royal* tabard proclaim the 'new' king. (See the Appendix to this chapter on pages 230–1.) This work – a piece of political and heraldic propaganda – merits careful examination since it provides a unique snapshot of how the Restoration heralds in their 'turncoat' tabards were perceived by some at this confusing time of yet another regime change.

For the heralds and heraldry, the Restoration was the best of times and the worst of times. It was the best of times for numerous reasons. The civil wars between king and Parliament that had taken place intermittently between 1642 and 1651, the execution in 1649 of the king's father, Charles I, 'that icon of Stuart monarchical pretension' (to quote Clive Holmes), and the Interregnum that followed, first under a republican Commonwealth and then from 1653 under a Protectorate directly headed by Oliver Cromwell and briefly by his son and successor, Richard, had not levelled society; in 1660, the bulk of the gentry reclaimed much of their wealth and power, returning to their traditional roles in local government. Indeed, as Clive Homes has pointed out, the 1650s witnessed a gradual strengthening of the old order.[2] In 1657 and 1658 Cromwell, who had already told his MPs he would keep up the nobility and gentry, created two new hereditary peers. These men were expected to take up their places in the newly constituted Upper House restored to replace the House of Lords swiftly abolished after Charles I's death. At the same time he conferred about a dozen baronetcies.[3] Concepts of social hierarchy, ancient codes of honour, and traditional notions of dignity – all so dear to the heralds – had survived surprisingly well, though, it is true to say, they were coming under increasing pressure.

It is perhaps not surprising, therefore, that early on, Parliament had seen fit to continue with the College of Arms, even appointing its own heralds. The College had first been incorporated in 1484 and consisted (and still consists) of three kings of arms (the senior of whom is Garter), six heralds and four pursuivants. They are all often generically styled as simply 'heralds', or 'officers of arms', and in normal times are members of the royal household. The corporation held heraldic jurisdiction over England and Wales and is still headed by the earl marshal, described by Charles II as 'the next and immediate Officer under Us for determining and ordering all matters touching Arms, Ensigns of Nobility and Chivalry'.[4] The principal duties of the College at the time consisted of organising and marshalling state ceremonies as well as the private heraldic funerals of the nobility and gentry, making important proclamations, granting arms, and recording pedigrees. Despite the defection of a number of heralds to the king, Parliament issued an ordinance in 1646 not abolishing but simply regulating the office of arms. Later that year it hurriedly appointed three new kings of arms (including the confirmation of Bysshe as Garter) so that they could officiate at the splendid public funeral of the Earl of Essex, the late general of the parliamentary army.[5] In 1652 new tabards emblazoned with the Commonwealth arms were produced for the parliamentary heralds, and sometime after March 1655 these were replaced by coats bearing the new quarterly arms of Cromwell's Protectorate.[6] In late 1657 the Protectorate even decided to revive visitations, whereby itinerant heralds recorded the arms and pedigrees of the local gentry and could publicly disclaim those usurping arms or (in their eyes) wrongly styling themselves 'gentleman' or 'esquire'. In the event, Cromwell's death in September 1658 and his son's abdication the following May resulted in the commission never being sealed, and, instead, the parliamentarian heralds had to stay put in the capital wondering who their next master was going to be.[7]

Thus, even during the Great Rebellion the officers of arms, whomsoever's rich coat they bore upon their backs, still had a role to play, not least at the grand funeral of Oliver himself, an occasion replete with state and Cromwellian heraldry.[8] The Interregnum might well have resulted in heraldry and genealogy dropping in the gentry's list of priorities, but so deeply engrained were they amongst the middling and upper sorts that they never entirely disappeared – far from it. At the Restoration, Edward Waterhouse's *Discourse and Defence of Arms and Armory* re-emphasized God's hierarchically ordered society and the need for 'distinctions' between men such as esquires, gentlemen, and others. It was just one of a number of important heraldic works published in 1660 and 1661.[9]

Not surprisingly, the return of the king resulted in the old royalist order at the College of Arms being restored. The leading antiquarian and historian, William Dugdale, for example, who had been Rouge Croix Pursuivant and Chester Herald under Charles I, was promoted to Norroy King of Arms. His learning was much admired by Sir Edward Hyde, later earl of Clarendon and Lord Chancellor to Charles II, and the Restoration allowed him to re-enter the mainstream of public life, bringing him new responsibilities and new opportunities.[10] A grateful Charles II appointed his loyal supporter, Elias Ashmole, as Windsor Herald with special precedence immediately after the pre–civil war heralds, George Owen, now York Herald, and William Ryley, now Lancaster. In conciliatory fashion, the king allowed the parliamentary appointees, Henry Dethick, Rouge Croix Pursuivant, and Edward Bysshe to remain in the College. The latter was demoted from Garter to Clarenceux, but his new position allowed him to go on visitation and grant arms within his heraldic province south of the Trent. The scholarly calibre of the officers of arms in 1660 was exceptionally high. William Ryley, was also keeper of the public records, and Dugdale was perhaps our finest ever herald. Ashmole's visitation of Berkshire in 1665–6 was both well organised and particularly thorough, and he went on to produce a definitive history of the Order of the Garter.[11] Even Bysshe, despite harsh criticism from his colleagues, produced short but accurate visitational pedigrees, as well as scholarly editions of medieval treatises on heraldry.[12] Normal heraldic order was, it seems, being restored.

The Restoration was also the best of times in terms of heraldic activity. The first part of the decade proved to be halcyon days for the new Garter Walker and his heralds. In September 1660, the king gave Walker full power to grant augmentations 'of any of Our Royall badges' to be added to the arms of loyalist supporters as a reward for services rendered; the royal warrant followed similar lines to one given by Charles I to Walker fifteen years earlier. This gave him power to make grants to a wide variety of men without the control of the earl marshal and without reference to the provincial kings of arms. In total, he made about fifty grants of augmentations under the terms of these warrants.[13] Moreover, the heralds had to make a quantity of new grants to replace those of the usurping parliamentary heralds that were now annulled by the king. The result was three hundred and forty grants of arms produced in the 1660s, over twice that of the preceding two decades combined.[14]

There was also the small matter of a coronation to organise and run. It took place on St George's Day 1661 and proved to be the single most expensive and elaborate ceremony of the king's life. The last such occasion had taken place in 1626, and there had been no state entry since 1604 and no coronation feast since 1559. To add to the confusion, the crown jewels and royal regalia needed to be recreated, the old ones having been sold or destroyed in the civil wars and Interregnum. All the heralds participated in the coronation, but the organisation was principally a monument to one man, Sir Edward Walker, Garter.[15] Elsewhere, the trappings of monarchy and the rituals of royalty were generally restored and court ceremonial resumed. Just before the coronation, the officers of arms were involved in the Garter celebrations held at Windsor (15–17 April) to install those knights created during the exile and since Charles' return, and a fortnight after the coronation they were back in Westminster (8 May) to take part in the state opening of Parliament.[16]

In the same year the heralds attempted to put through a bill in Parliament to ensure the proper recording of the matches and descents of the gentry and nobility.[17] Not surprisingly, then, the marquess (and future duke) of Newcastle urged the new king to look to his heralds to set down in writing the ceremony and order for all degrees of the nobility and for all the great officers of state to ensure their proper place and put the clock back to the old hierarchical structure following the socially disruptive and democratic tendencies of the Interregnum.[18] In 1662 two new visitation commissions were issued, the first to pass the great seal for over a quarter of a century, and this time the heralds went, visiting over twenty counties before the end of the decade.[19] The men at the College were back in business as busy servants of the restored crown and were fast lining their pockets from the fees charged.[20] It was, it seems, the best of times.

Sadly, as so often the case in its half millennium of existence, division within the College and popular misconceptions of its role from outside meant that for the heralds and heraldry, it was also the worst of times. Even before the war there was animosity towards the office of arms. In 1640 the newly elected MP for Wootton Bassett, Edward Hyde, twice raised the matter of the heralds and their fees in the House. He described the College and the Court of Chivalry 'as grievous to the gentry, as the Court [of Charles I] was to the people'.[21] Only the outbreak of war saved the heralds from facing Parliament. In the years that followed, the property of a number of heralds was sequestered, and those who remained in London continued to fight among themselves, especially over promotion and the profits of grants and visitations.

Internal discontent continued after Charles II's return. Bysshe may well have harboured a long-standing enmity to George Owen, Norroy King of Arms under Parliament and now York Herald.[22] Garter Walker believed that the parliamentarian Bysshe did not deserve to stay in the College and later accused him of various visitational malpractices. He was particularly angry that, as the newly created Clarenceux, Bysshe now had rights to grant arms and go on visitation, and he did his best to hinder the granting of a new visitation commission. Many of the heralds believed Bysshe to be in league with their business rivals, the Painter-Stainers, who poached much of their heraldic and funerary artwork. Outside the College, men thought Bysshe dishonest and supercilious and his visitations a trick to get money.[23]

Walker was not squeaky clean either, but arrogant and truculent. He is said to have had a great personal dislike of Dugdale, and he may well have jeopardised the heralds' bill going through Parliament by raising the age-old dispute between Garter and the provisional kings of arms over who could grant arms and go on visitation.[24] Edward Hyde and Sir Edward Nicholas, secretary of state, were certainly not impressed by Walker. The latter considered him 'a very importunate, ambitious, and foolish man, that studies nothing but his own ends.' Hyde responded, 'Why should you wonder that a herald who is naturally made up of embroidery, should adorn his own services?'[25]

On top of all this, the heraldic infrastructure, on which so much depended, was unstable. In 1660 there was no lord high constable and no earl marshal.[26] When commissioners for the earl marshal were appointed in 1662, they were, according to Dugdale, weak and divided.[27] The Court of Chivalry was not sitting and would not do so again until 1687. Whilst after the Restoration, the commissioners, deputy earl marshal, and earl marshal continued to deal in a formal manner with armorial disputes, there was no machinery to enforce their orders so that their quasi-judicial proceedings lacked any effective sanction.[28] In a similar vein, although visitations were revived in 1662, they were often met with scorn or, even worse, indifference by the local gentry, and the heralds' ultimate threat of having one's arms and gentry status publicly disclaimed was increasingly ignored. Moreover, the distinction between gentry and those beneath was becoming increasingly ill-defined and more difficult to police.[29] The heralds' bill for registering descents and arms failed to get through Parliament.

In 1660 the heralds' dispute with the Painter-Stainers of London seems to have reached a crisis. In October, Walker put forward proposals to regulate what he saw as the painters' encroachment upon the heralds' rights. The Painter-Stainers replied with a petition to the earl marshal, and the dispute rumbled on unresolved for many more years.[30] Heraldic funerals, a lucrative trade for the heralds, were threatened, and the College was forced to lower its fees for such occasions; it also discontinued funeral certificates.[31] Occasionally the heralds' high-handed manner in policing such funerals caused serious offence to the bereaved.[32]

The upsurge in grants of arms proved to be a blip, and new grants slumped in the 1670s down to one hundred and to only sixty in the 1680s.[33] To cap it all, in 1666 the very fabric of the College, old Derby House, given to the heralds a century beforehand, went up in flames during the Great Fire of London, though mercifully the records (as well as the officers of arms) were saved. For the heralds and heraldry, it was also the worst of times.

We must not, however, look too far into the future. All this – the best of times and the worst of times – was still largely to come and therefore unknown to the anonymous author of our broadsheet as he or she witnessed the heralds' proclamation on that eventful day in May 1660. A copy of the broadsheet is bound into a large folio volume of eight hundred and fifteen papers and tracts, now catalogued as Ashmole MS 840 in the Bodleian Library, Oxford. It is printed on one side only and is perhaps typical of the ephemeral broadsheets of the day intended 'to instruct, exhort, entertain, and, perhaps above all, to persuade an audience, even if only to part with a penny'.[34] Indeed, 1660 proved something of a boom year for such works, those in the early months often cryptic or employing anagrams. The broadsheet is more technically a satirical 'Query', in which scandalous and hypocritical behaviour was exposed by offering a series of cryptic and rhetorical questions.[35] Like others of its day, its ultimate aim was to drum up loyalty for the returning monarch and to castigate the losers, in this case the parliamentarian heralds still enjoying their rooms at the College of Arms.

Ashmole clearly thought the sheet worth preserving, presumably as a lamentable sign of the heralds' standing at the time, although he may just have kept it as a useful reminder of the disquiet felt towards his parliamentary colleagues in the Restoration College. Maybe, as a loyal royalist himself, he quietly agreed with much of what it said. The sheet is entitled 'upon sight of the heralds coat xii Occasional Queries at the proclaiming of the king, May 8, 1660'. Both houses of the specially convened Convention Parliament had voted for the restoration of the Stuart monarchy on 1 May. Although Charles was yet to return from exile in Holland, there was a universal sense of euphoria as festivities and celebrations were held up and down the land. Feelings were running high, and the outward symbols of the old republican regime came in for special treatment. On 11 May in Boston, Lincolnshire, the proclamation of the new king resulted in the old state arms being taken down by the young men of the town who then proceeded to drag them up and down the streets. They then got the local beadles to whip the arms before they in turn defaced them. Finally, the soiled shield was ignominiously thrown onto the bonfire that 'for joy' had been erected at the recalling of the king.[36]

London likewise celebrated with bells and bonfires. The heralds' solemn proclamation in the capital on 8 May was conducted with due pomp and pageantry. Pride of place went to William Ryley, the parliamentarian Clarenceux, to make the announcements. He was entitled to wear the royal arms for the occasion since he had been appointed Bluemantle Pursuivant and Lancaster Herald under Charles I. His only problem was that he had no royal tabard to wear since it had been plundered during the wars, and for the past eight years he had worn the Commonwealth and Protectorate coats. He, therefore, hurriedly gained the permission of the earl of Manchester, the speaker of the House of Lords, to wear the tabard emblazoned with the Stuart arms that had hung amongst the funeral achievements of James I for thirty-five years in Henry VII's chapel in Westminster Abbey.[37]

Ryley was accompanied by two other officers of arms on the day, Garter Bysshe and his brother, Henry, Somerset Herald. Both were parliamentary creations and both, therefore, now not technically entitled to wear a Stuart tabard.[38] Surrounded by members of the Lords and Commons, trumpeters and troops, and later by the Lord Mayor and aldermen of London, Ryley repeated his proclamation four times, being careful to note that the *new* king had been reigning since the death of Charles I eleven years ago. The following day he slipped the tabard back into the Abbey. Elsewhere on 9 May, ex-Lord Protector Richard Cromwell, in a final gesture of renunciation, hung up his equally impressive embroidered robes as Chancellor of Oxford University and quietly slipped away. England's republican experiment was over, but for the compiler of our broadsheet questions still had to be answered.

The first query on the sheet asks how it is there were three kings of arms in England and no king in England? This refers to the fact that during the Interregnum, when Charles was in exile in Scotland or on the continent, Parliament had appointed its own kings of arms. Indeed, on the day that the heralds proclaimed Charles II as the new king, he was still not in England whilst three parliamentary kings of arms sat in their rooms in London.[39]

The second query is complex and asks what means Garter, Clarenceux, and Norroy seeing it was never known for kings of England to have a pair of Garters? It goes on to say that neither can Clarenceux agree with Norroy seeing they are of two contrary houses, York and Lancaster, as witnessed by Haberdashers' Hall and the records in the Tower.

The 'pair of Garters', as already mentioned, refers to Bysshe, the parliamentary Garter, and Walker, the royalist Garter, both men having held the same office consecutively for several years. As for the clash between Norroy and Clarenceux, the two parliamentary kings of arms, this alludes to their prolonged arguments over who should be Clarenceux, the senior of the two provincial posts.[40] The two men were of the rival houses York and Lancaster, since Norroy Owen had originally been York Herald under Charles I and would soon revert to the same position under Charles II, and Clarenceux Ryley, as we have seen, had previously been Lancaster Herald, a post to which he too would soon revert. The two houses also refer to that other internecine struggle, the Wars of the Roses between the House of Lancaster and the House of York. Norroy's and Clarenceux's previous incarnations as York and Lancaster could be confirmed by the civil servants at Haberdashers' Hall (a building much used by the parliamentary government) and from the public records then partly housed in the Tower of London.

The third query asks how it was that Derby House, the heralds' home in 1660, has got three arms to their three legs, having left the good old coat as being too cold for Oxford and too hot for Westminster, forsaking their royal master and donning instead a cross and grid iron. The reference to the three arms is perplexing. Maybe it refers to the three kings of arms then ensconced in the College whose arms might have somehow decorated Derby House; we know that in the early seventeenth century, shields of the then reigning kings of arms adorned the fabric of the building. The three legs might refer to the three legs of Man, a lordship of the Stanley family, earls of Derby, and original owners of the house. It is possible they too could be seen on the pre–Great Fire building. Or perhaps the three legs refer to Sir Thomas Fairfax, given the lordship of Man by a grateful Parliament – it is difficult to say.[41]

The good old coat (the phrase is perhaps a deliberate play on the 'Good Old Cause' of the late republican movement) presumably refers to the king's rich coat emblazoned with the Stuart arms as once borne by the pre–civil war heralds and again worn by Ryley on 8 May 1660. It appears that, for some officers of arms at the outset of the war, to wear such royalist sympathies literally on their sleeves and so close to Westminster was too hot to handle, and they fled the capital to join the king at his new headquarters in Oxford. Having got there, however, some found the exile too cold and distant, and gradually they drifted back to London and the parliamentary College. The exodus began with Ryley, who as Lancaster Herald, returned to the College in July 1643, albeit with the king's permission. In June the next year, Robert Browne, Bluemantle, followed, and in August they were joined by William Crowne, Rouge Dragon Pursuivant.[42]

Following the execution of the king in 1649, these new servants of the state donned tabards bearing the new arms of the Commonwealth. These consisted of the cross of St George for England and the Irish harp, or, as the printed broadsheet contemptuously puts it, the cross and the gridiron. The new republican iconography had been invented by the Rump Parliament to replace the trappings of the ousted regal polity.[43] The Stuart monarchy had been abolished in England and Ireland but not in Scotland; the northern kingdom, at least for the time being, was allowed to pursue its own historical (and heraldic) path. With the union of the crowns severed, there was no need to incorporate the Scots quarter into the state insignia. The parliamentary heralds first wore the Commonwealth arms in February 1652 at the 'Magnificent Funeral of that arch-Rebell [Henry] Ireton'.[44] They carried them again when Cromwell was formally proclaimed as Lord Protector in December 1653, though the herald making the proclamation on that occasion was mocked by the crowd.[45] At the City of London's formal public recognition of the country's new ruler in February 1654, we are told that 'his Highness's heralds with rich coats adorn'd with the Commonwealth arms' went before Cromwell's coach.[46] They wore the same tabards the following April when they made the proclamation of peace between England and the Netherlands, as can be seen in a rough contemporary print.[47]

As the old Commonwealth gave way to new Protectorate, so the old cross and gridiron gave way to a new republican iconography. The answer to the fourth query thus lies in the new tabards worn by the parliamentary heralds of Cromwell's personal polity. It asks how the heralds came to wear a quarterly coat with a great beast in the middle unless it was to make the crosses of England more conspicuous and to put the sceptre in the paw of a lion and allow them to dance in the streets (without music?) at the funeral of the notorious . . .

The quarterly coat referred to is that of Cromwell and his new Protectorate. It was formally adopted on 6 March 1655 when Cromwell gave his approbation for the inclusion of the arms on the new great seal of the Protectorate. The full achievement is a curious mixture of royal, republican, and personal heraldry. Its shield bears the crosses of St George and St Andrew, patron saints of England and Scotland respectively, effectively replacing the royal arms of the late king. The Stuart unicorn supporter has been ousted by the Welsh dragon.[48] Unlike the arms of the Commonwealth, St George's cross is shown twice and, as stated by the broadsheet, is therefore more prominent. Another innovation is the Scottish quarter. Following the Scots' coronation of Charles II as king of Britain in 1651, the Edinburgh Parliament was abolished and the country absorbed into an enhanced English state; Cromwell was addressed from the beginning as His Highness Oliver, Lord Protector of the Commonwealth of England, *Scotland*, and Ireland.[49] At the centre of the new state arms were those of Cromwell himself – sable a lion argent – symbolizing his pivotal role as Lord Protector. Here, then, was the great beast in the middle spoken of by the broadsheet (Figure 13.1).

Figure 13.1 Seal of the Protectorate.
From A. and A.B. Wyon's *Great Seals of England*, 1887.

The reference to putting the sceptre in the lion's paw alludes to the heralds' role in the recent investiture of Cromwell as Lord Protector on 26 June 1657. This was the second time he had been so invested, though on this occasion it was more like a kingmaking ceremony. Amongst the numerous outward displays of royal dignity exhibited that day were the coronation chair, a canopy of state, a purple robe, and a 10-pound solid gold sceptre.[50] Whilst there is no evidence that officers of arms had taken part in the first investiture in December 1653, Garter, Norroy, and two heralds participated in the second, when they very probably wore the new state arms of the Protectorate. On 1 June 1657, a few weeks before the investiture, the same arms were included on new coinage, again a design as regal as the previous was republican.[51] And, as already noted, heralds were again very much in evidence at Cromwell's quasi-royal funeral, an event again alluded to in the broadsheet. Banners bearing the arms of the Protectorate and those of Cromwell's family were carried in the funeral procession.

The fifth query asks whether the heralds should be allowed so near to the king as to touch his coat, seeing they have turned it so often. In other words, should those officers of arms, who were literally turncoats, be allowed in

1660 to swap sides yet again, or should they pay the price for their armorial cross-dressing? This barb was almost certainly aimed at Ryley and Owen, though it could have applied to William Crowne, Rouge Dragon Pursuivant under Charles I. He had become a colonel of the parliamentary militia and in 1654 one of its MPs. Crowne was in America at the Restoration, having resigned from the College, but in 1661, despite the doubts raised by the broadsheet, was allowed to don again a royalist tabard at the king's coronation.[52]

The sixth query asks whether it was the sign of a fool or a knave that was republican one day and for Charles II the next. In other words, were those heralds who swapped tabards in 1660 simply foolish or, worse still, turncoat rogues who, like Owen, had 'miserably swerved from his loyalty'.[53]

The next riddle is especially baffling. It asks whether the petition of the heralds was for '*Honi soit qui mal y pense*', and if so, if they had their due, whether a threefold cord could be easily broken? Could this be the three parliamentary kings of arms desperately sticking together (despite their rivalries) in a threefold cord and petitioning to hang on to their old posts following the Restoration? Or would they now at last be shamed for their usurpation and receive their due reward so that the ties that once bound them together in a threefold cord would be finally severed?

The Garter motto quoted could refer to either Bysshe or Walker. If the latter, then it might refer to his petition, possibly dated April 1660, to exercise the office of Clarenceux (in addition to his role as Garter). The present royalist incumbent, Sir William Le Neve, had been found insane in 1658. As Walker pointed out, no herald (technically junior to a king of arms) could also act as a senior king of arms, and Clarenceux and Norroy had no jurisdiction in each other's province, whereas Garter could act in both. Charles acceded to Walker's request before their return to England, and from 20 July 1660 Walker temporarily executed Le Neve's office as Clarenceux – an unprecedented heraldic situation that would undoubtedly have broken the threefold cord traditionally binding the three kings of arms together. Maybe the author of the broadsheet was concerned that Walker was aiming for complete domination; he was not universally liked and had already tried to unite the office of Garter with those of Clarenceux and Norroy whilst in exile.[54]

Alternatively, the petition might be that of a frustrated George Owen, Norroy, who had recently sought to become Clarenceux.[55] In the spring of 1658, he had petitioned Cromwell stating that his appointment as Clarenceux had already passed the signet and privy seal but had been obstructed by the notary public, John Watson, Parliament's Bluemantle Pursuivant and Registrar and Treasurer at the College. Owen's petition was referred in April 1658 to five commissioners for enquiry and report. They met the following month to consider affidavits made in December 1657 from Turbeville Morgan, Watson's cousin and onetime servant to Bysshe, and a John Blethin, who had since died. At the enquiry, Morgan stated that Watson had told him that the 'rogue Owen' had betrayed the late king at Gloucester (either during or shortly after its siege in 1643) and that Owen wished to ruin both him (Watson) and Bysshe. Bysshe was very probably behind Watson's machinations; the two held great malice towards Owen. A lot of 'shame unto him who evil thinks of it' was clearly floating around the corridors of old Derby House in the late 1650s, and presumably Owen was determined to break the threefold cord that bound together his accusers, Bysshe, Morgan, and Watson. In the event, Owen was not made Clarenceux, and Bysshe was able to impose his own terms on the new Clarenceux (Ryley) and the new Norroy (Owen) regarding the profits of visitations and grants. Whatever the case, it is difficult to know exactly what this question is trying to ask or prove.

The eighth query is, thankfully, more straightforward and asks whether G.O. will 'go' over to the king and, if so, whether he will not have a whip and GO. Presumably 'GO' refers to George Owen, York. Owen, as we have seen, was a turncoat who was very active for the cause of Parliament. He was also unpopular with the gentry and with his colleagues. Before the civil war, he had been accused of going 'upp and downe the Countrey sharkeing and cheating' while on visitation in Worcestershire and Herefordshire as deputy to Richard St George, Clarenceux.[56] In the end, Owen did decide, or rather was permitted, in 1660 to 'go' back over to the king, and he resumed his old post of York as initially granted to him by Charles I. The whip is perhaps a not so subtle hint as to the hastening of his departure? Owen eventually resigned in 1665 in favour of his son-in-law, John Wingfield.

The ninth query again refers to Owen, this time specifically in his capacity as Norroy King of Arms. It asks whether No Roy (i.e. Owen) be a king (i.e. Norroy) or no king (i.e. no *roy*), since he had never been granted this kingly position by a king (i.e. Charles I or Charles II). Owen had only ever been appointed a king of arms by Parliament and, like his colleague Clarenceux Ryley, was uncrowned at the Restoration, reverting in Owen's case to his pre–civil war office of York. Unlike Ryley, however, he had been especially supportive of the parliamentary cause, whereas Ryley had steered a middle course between the two factions, thus escaping being singled out by our broadsheet. Ryley was, as Sir Anthony Wagner succinctly put it, 'more attached to the College and the Records than to either King or Parliament'.[57]

The last three queries in effect merge into one long statement (or rather doggerel) of intense disapproval and questioning as to the legality of those that now wear the king's coat and proclaim his restoration. Does the royal tabard befit these individuals, seeing that these same men, now the king's servants, once served another master? Indeed, whose coats were they wearing, the king's or old Nol's, namely Cromwell, whose body was shortly to be dug up and defaced? Perhaps only Ryley on that day in May 1660 wore a royal tabard, the other officers of arms having to do without. And, whilst such men did wear these coats, were they not indelibly stained by duplicity and treason?

Our anonymous author is clearly not impressed by the overnight change in allegiance shown by certain individuals in the College of Arms. But who was he (or possibly she)? The eighth and ninth queries in particular suggest an intense dislike of George Owen, Norroy, and may refer to the disputes that possibly lie behind the petition referred to in the seventh and most enigmatic query. This would point to John Watson. He had been appointed Bluemantle Pursuivant by the parliamentary commissioners in October 1646 in order to supply the place of Robert Browne at the funeral of Lord Essex, and in December the same year, following Browne's death, was appointed Bluemantle for life.[58] Down to June 1658, he played a prominent part in the College of Arms acting as a kind of general factotum. He did not, however, take part in Cromwell's funeral in September 1658. Maybe the fallout from the Owen dispute had forced him to resign, or he had been sacked. This would explain the vituperative nature of the broadsheet. Although himself a parliamentarian intruder into the College, Watson was a royalist and had possibly served as commissary and treasurer to Major Legg and Colonel Washington in the king's army at Evesham.[59] Again this would account for his antipathy towards those parliamentarian creations still in office, yet now proclaiming a regal master.

The broadsheet thus ends on a bitter note, heavy with sarcasm and imbued with ill feeling, despite the fact that it owed its existence to the good news that the king was about to return. These were clearly turbulent times. Maybe the sense of universal jubilation and almost hysterical excitement added to the confusion and fear felt by many. Here were Parliament's heralds proclaiming a new king, with at least one of them dressed in a royal tabard, a rich coat very probably not seen in public since (somewhat ironically) the proclamation of Charles I's dreadful trial.[60] Well might our document ask whose side were these men on, and how could such turncoats behave in so hypocritical a manner? Who amongst them would now forfeit their position, who would be restored, who would be reappointed? Both within and without the College, there was a natural and inevitable reaction against those who had been disloyal to the king and who had held a monopoly of power. How were the heralds' new masters, the two 'new' kings, Charles II and Garter Walker, going to deal with this unique heraldic situation? The Restoration was truly a time of joyous celebration, but it was also a time of retribution. The author of our broadsheet provides us with not just a clever set of riddles but a rare heraldic glimpse of the mixed feelings of joy and fear, revenge and reconciliation, hope and hurt that must have overwhelmed many a citizen after nearly twenty years of turmoil.

No full study exists of the way in which the heralds as a corporate body reacted to the non-monarchical situation they faced between the outbreak of war and the Restoration. Such a work would have to examine the mixed motives and actions of all those individual officers of arms who followed Charles I to Oxford or his son on to the Continent, or of those who stayed put in London, or of those whom Parliament imposed upon the College, as well as take into account the unprecedented political, physical, financial, and military pressures they and so many others were under. Apart from a desire to maintain social norms and hierarchy upon which so much of their raison d'être and financial resources depended and, in the case of a few worthy exceptions, to preserve the College records, there appears to be little overall agreement; indeed, as we have seen, civil war sometimes raged inside as well as outside the

College walls, a response heavily exploited by the broadsheet. Further research might, of course, prove otherwise.

The Restoration settlement represented a more or less acceptable compromise and the new regime at the College, following some judicious appointments in June 1660, was to reflect the broad base of power sharing on which Charles set out to build his regime. But on 8 May 1660, all that was yet to come. In the meantime, for the heralds who found themselves the butt of our broadsheet, it was the best of times and the worst of times, and no one that spring day could have known just how this tale of two Garters was going to end.

Appendix

Bodl., MS Ashmole 840, p. 753

VPON SIGHT OF THE HERALDS COAT
XII Occasional Queries and the proclaiming of the KING, May 8. 1660.

1. Quere, How comes it there was three Kings of Arms when there was no King in *England*?
2. What means *Garter, Clareniceulx* and *Norroy*, seeing it was never known the Kings of *England* had a pair of *Garters*? neither can *Clarencieulx* agree with *Norroy*, seeing they are of two contrary houses, *York* and *Lancaster*, witness both *Haberdashers* Hall, and the *Records* in the *Tower*.
3. How came it that *Derby* house, otherwise the *Heralds Office*, hath got three *Arms* to their three *Legs*, having left the *good old* **Coat** as being too cold for *Oxford*, & too hot for *Westminster*, and took up a *Cross* and *Gridiron* to forsake their Master and follow many to proclaim against Kingly Government?
4. How came they by a *Quadriparted Coat* with a great *Beast* in the middle, except it were to make the Crosses of *England* more conspicuous, and to put the Scepter in the paw of the *Lion*, and that you might not want musick to it, went dancing about the streets, at the Obsequies of the most *Notorious* –
5. Whether they ought to come so neer his Majestie as to touch his *Coat*, seeing they have turned it so often?
6. Whether it were not a **Signe** of a Fool or a K – that was (*Republica*) one day, and *Charles* the *Second* the next?
7. Whether the Petition of the *Heralds* was not for HONY SOIT QUI MAL Y PENSE? and if so, if they had their due, whether a threefold Cord would be easily broken.
8. Whether G.O. do go over to the King, and if so, whether he may not have a whip, and GO?
9. Whether *No Roy* be a King, or no King, seeing he never had it by his Majesties Gift?

10 Whether his Majesties Coat doth not better become his Majesties Servants, seeing the Wearers made me doubt of the true *Owner*, [space] and ask this Quere also,
11 Whose Coat is this? the Kings? or is't old *Nol/His Servants* were it oh! *Pol aedopol*, /Oh pluck it off, the Kings Coat hath a Blot,
12 (While such do were it,) Quere, Hath it not?

Notes

1 I am very grateful to Dr Andrew Hopper for reading a draft of my talk before its presentation and to Thomas Woodcock, Garter King of Arms, and Dr Angela McShane for further comments and helpful suggestions prior to publication.
2 Clive Holmes, *Why Was Charles I Executed?* (2006), pp. 93, 179–87. See also Felicity Heal and Clive Holmes, *The Gentry in England and Wales 1500–1700* (Basingstoke, 1994), pp. 226–34; John Morrill, 'The Impact on Society', in John Morrill (ed.), *Revolution and Restoration: England in the 1650s* (North Pomfret, VT, 1992), pp. 91–111; Barry Coward, 'The Experience of the Gentry 1640–1660' in R.C. Richardson (ed.), *Town and Countryside in the English Revolution* (Manchester, 1992), pp. 198–223; G.E. Mingay, *The Gentry: The Rise and Fall of a Ruling Class* (1976), pp. 63–6; and Joan Thirsk, *The Restoration* (1976), pp. xv, xx.
3 *The Letters and Speeches of Oliver Cromwell*, ed. Thomas Carlyle and S.C. Lomas (3 vols, 1904), II, 342; III, 540; Holmes, *Why Was Charles I Executed?*, p. 180. Roy Sherwood, *The Court of Oliver Cromwell* (1977), pp. 81, 164; idem, *Oliver Cromwell: A King in All but Name 1653–1658* (Stroud, 1977), pp. 105–6.
4 Quoted in *The Heralds' Commemorative Exhibition 1484–1935* (1936, reprinted 1934), p. 19.
5 *A&O*, I, 838–9. The three kings were Edward Bysshe as Garter, Arthur Squibb as Clarenceux, and William Ryley (Lancaster Herald under Charles) as Norroy. Sir Anthony Wagner, *Heralds of England: A History of the Office and College of Arms* (1967), pp. 257–8. Wagner provides the best record of the College during this period.
6 H.S. London, 'The Heralds' Tabards under the Commonwealth', *Notes and Queries*, 198 (July 1953), pp. 276–8.
7 TNA, SP 18/20, pp. 490–506; *CSPD 1658–59*, p. 291; Wagner, *Heralds of England*, pp. 261–2; H.S. London, 'George Owen, York Herald', *Transactions of the Honourable Society of Cymmrodorion* (1947 for 1943 and 1944), pp. 78–107 (86–9, 104–5). The commission was drafted sometime between 25 February and 25 March 1659.
8 Sir John Prestwich, *Respublica* (1787), pp. 178, 189; *CSPD 1658–59*, p. 143; BL, Harleian MS 1438, fols 74vff; London, 'George Owen', p. 89 n. 4; Sherwood, *Oliver Cromwell: A King in All but Name*, pp. 158, 159.
9 Edward Waterhouse, *A Discourse and Defence of Arms and Armory* . . . (1660); see Andrew Sharp, 'Edward Waterhouse's View of Social Change in Seventeenth-Century England', *P&P*, 62 (1974), 27–46.
10 Graham Parry, 'Sir William Dugdale', *ODNB*; Ann Hughes, 'William Dugdale and the Civil War', pp. 51–65 (esp. 65); and Stephen K. Roberts, '"Ordering and Methodizing": William Dugdale in Restoration England', pp. 66–88 (esp. 66–73), both in C. Dyer and R.C. Richardson (eds), *William Dugdale, Historian 1605–1686: His Life, His Writings and His County* (Woodbridge, 2009).
11 Adrian Ailes, 'Elias Ashmole's "Heraldicall Visitacion" of Berkshire 1665–66' (unpublished DPhil thesis, University of Oxford, 2008); Elias Ashmole, *The Institution, Laws and Ceremonies of the Most Noble Order of the Garter* (1672).

12 Wagner, *Heralds of England*, pp. 259, 273.
13 Wagner, *Heralds of England*, p. 275; Thomas Woodcock and John Martin Robinson, *The Oxford Guide to Heraldry* (Oxford, 1989), pp. 70–1; and see also J.F. Huxford, *Honour and Arms: The Story of Some Augmentations of Honour* (1984).
14 Edward Elmhirst, 'The Fashion for Heraldry', *Coat of Arms*, 4 (1956–8), 47–50 (48).
15 Sir Roy Strong, *Coronation: A History of Kingship and the British Monarchy* (2005), pp. 287–309; Lorraine Madway, '"The Most Conspicuous Solemnity": The Coronation of Charles II' in Eveline Cruickshanks (ed.), *The Stuart Courts* (Stroud, 2000), pp. 141–57; Anna Keay, *The Magnificent Monarch: Charles II and the Ceremonies of Power* (2008), pp. 3–8.
16 Ronald Hutton, *The Restoration: A Political and Religious History of England and Wales 1658–1667* (Oxford, 1985), p. 128; Keay, *Magnificent Monarch*, pp. 8, 180; Tim Harris, *Restoration: Charles II and His Kingdoms 1660–1685* (2006), pp. 68–9. For the revival of the Garter at this time, see Antti Matikkala, *The Orders of Knighthood and the Formation of the British Honours System, 1660–1760* (Woodbridge, 2008), pp. 62–6, 277–8.
17 Wagner, *Heralds of England*, p. 266.
18 Bodl., MS Clarendon 109, fols 52–4 quoted in Thirsk, *Restoration*, pp. 153, 157; Matikkala, *Orders of Knighthood and the Formation of the British Honours System*, p. 41 (and references cited there).
19 Sir Anthony Wagner, *The Records and Collections of the College of Arms* (1952), pp. 74–5, 83–4 (where the commissions are incorrectly dated 1663).
20 Dugdale seems to have done particularly well financially (Roberts, '"Ordering and Methodizing": William Dugdale in Restoration England', in Dyer and Richardson (eds.), *William Dugdale, Historian 1606–1686*, p. 67).
21 G.D. Squibb, *High Court of Chivalry* (Oxford, 1959), pp. 62–7; Bodl., MSS Ashmole 840, fol. 69–71; Ashmole 857, fols 545–56; Wagner, *Heralds of England*, pp. 235, 252–3.
22 College of Arms, MS Heralds VI, fols 157b, 181; London, 'George Owen, York Herald', p. 88 n. 2; Wagner, *Heralds of England*, p. 261.
23 *The Life and Times of Anthony Wood, Antiquary, of Oxford, 1632–1695, described by himself*, ed. Andrew Clark (5 vols, Oxford: Oxford Historical Society, 19, 21, 26, 30, 40, 1891–95), II, 152, 453 n. 1; BL, Add. MS 38140, fols 137, 139, and see also Bodl., MS Ashmole 840, fol. 811; *CSPD 1660–61*, pp. 399–400; Wagner, *Heralds of England*, pp. 270, 273–5. For the heralds' dispute with the Painter-Stainers, see W.A.D. Englefield, *The History of the Painter-Stainers Company* (1923, reprinted 1996), pp. 125ff.
24 Wagner, *Heralds of England*, p. 275.
25 *CCSP*, II, 346, quoted in Madway, '"The Most Conspicuous Solemnity": The Coronation of Charles II', pp. 143–4.
26 See Squibb, *High Court of Chivalry*, p. 73.
27 Bodl., MS Top.Yorks c. 36, fol. 27. The commissioners are listed in Squibb, *High Court of Chivalry*, pp. 232–3.
28 Squibb, *High Court of Chivalry*, pp. 83–4, 87.
29 Ailes, 'Elias Ashmole's "Heraldicall Visitacion" of Berkshire 1665–66', pp. 13–18, 70, 202–5.
30 Englefield, *History of the Painter-Stainers*, pp. 125–9.
31 Julian Litten, *The English Way of Death: The Common Funeral since 1450* (1992), p. 189; G.W. Marshall, 'Memoranda relating to the Heralds' College', *Genealogist*, new series, 13 (n.d.), 137–40.
32 Squibb, *High Court of Chivalry*, pp. 75–7; *CSPD 1664–65*, p. 272.
33 Elmhirst, 'Fashion for Heraldry', p. 48.
34 Angela McShane, 'Ballads and Broadsides' in Joad Raymond (ed.), *The Oxford History of Popular Print Culture, vol. 1: Cheap Print in Britain and Ireland to 1660* (Oxford, 2011), pp. 339–62 (quotation at 341).
35 Gerald Maclean, '1660' in Joad Raymond (ed.), *Oxford History of Popular Print Culture, vol. 1* (Oxford, 2011), pp. 619–28 (esp. 620, 622, 624).

36 *The Diurnal of Thomas Rugg, 1659–1661*, ed. William L. Sachse (Camden Society, 3rd series, 91, 1961), p. 84 (and cf. p. 90), quoted in Harris, *Restoration*, p. 44; Patrick Morrah, *1660: The Year of Restoration* (1960), p. 130.
37 *CSPD 1668–69*, p. 135.
38 BL, Harleian MS 1438, fol. 83; *Diurnal of Thomas Rugg*, ed. Sachse, pp. 79–80; Morrah, *1660*, pp. 125–8; Mark Noble, *A History of the College of Arms, and the Lives of all the Kings, Heralds and Pursuivants from the Reign of Richard III* ([1804]), p. 267. When formally asked who they were, Ryley replied they were the heralds appointed by the Lords and Commons (*Diurnal of Thomas Rugg*, ed. Sachse, p. 80).
39 The three were Edward Bysshe, Garter, William Ryley, Clarenceux, and George Owen, Norroy.
40 For this rivalry, see London, 'George Owen, York Herald', pp. 86–7, and Wagner, *Heralds of England*, p. 261.
41 John Campbell-Kease, 'Some Seventeenth-Century Decorations at Derby Place' in John Campbell-Kease, *Aspects of Heraldry: Selected Essays* (2001), pp. 79–92; the shields are drawn in National Library of Scotland, MS 2515, fols 182–3. See also W.H. Godfrey and Sir Anthony Wagner, *College of Arms Monograph* (1963), pp. 3, 7, and E. Kandell, 'The Trie Cassyn: An Account of the Arms of the Kingdom of the Isle of Man', *Coat of Arms*, 9 (1967), 218–23.
42 Wagner, *Heralds of England*, p. 256.
43 Soon after Charles' decapitation, orders were given to expunge his arms from Westminster and throughout the land: Sean Kelsey, *Inventing a Republic: The Political Culture of the English Commonwealth 1649–1653* (Stanford, 1997), pp. 40, 86, 88). The broadsheet was not the first to deride the arms. Some had said the conjoined shields (the two arms were usually shown side by side) resembled a pair of breeches – very suitable for the Rump, whilst others proclaimed the cross superstitious idolatry and the harp a papist relic (Kelsey *Inventing a Republic*, p. 102). Flags sometimes depicted the arms impaled (London, 'Heralds' Tabards under the Commonwealth', p. 277).
44 E.S. de Beer (ed.), *The Diary of John Evelyn* (6 vols, Oxford, 1955), III, 57–8; *CSPD 1651–52*, pp. 586, 595; London, 'The Heralds' Tabards under the Commonwealth', p. 276; *Life, Diary and Correspondence of Sir William Dugdale*, ed. William Hamper (1827), p. 98.
45 Sherwood, *Oliver Cromwell: A King in All but Name*, pp. 12–13; Noble, *History of the College of Arms*, p. 256.
46 Sherwood, *Oliver Cromwell: A King in All but Name*, p. 17.
47 *The Names of the Members of Parliament Called to take upon them the Trust of the Government of this Commonwealth, which Began on Monday the Fourth of June 1653 . . . with the Several Transactions since that time* (1654), p. 35; illustrated in Sherwood, *Oliver Cromwell: A King in All but Name*, p. 35.
48 For the arms see Sir Anthony Wagner, *Historic Heraldry of Britain* (London and Chichester, 1972), pp. 74–5, and Sherwood, *Oliver Cromwell: A King in All but Name*, pp. 45–8.
49 The formal ordnance uniting Scotland with England was not promulgated till April 1654, after which it was decreed the Scots arms should be borne with those of the Commonwealth (*A&O*, II, 873).
50 For the investiture, see Sherwood, *Oliver Cromwell: A King in All but Name*, pp. 95–104.
51 Sherwood, *Oliver Cromwell: A King in All but Name*, p. 94.
52 Wagner, *Heralds of England*, p. 256.
53 Anthony Wood, *Athenae Oxoniensis . . . to which are added the Fasti Oxoniensis*, ed. P. Bliss (4 vols, 1820), IV, column 61 of *Fasti*.
54 Wagner, *Heralds of England*, p. 263; Hubert Chesshyre, 'Sir Edward Walker', *ODNB*. Bysshe had held the post of Garter and Clarenceux simultaneously from 1650 to 1658.
55 For what follows, see London, 'George Owen, York Herald', pp. 87–8, based on College of Arms, MS Heralds VI, fols 154–200.

56 G.D. Squibb (ed.), *Reports of Heraldic Cases in the Court of Chivalry, 1623–1732* (Harleian Society, 107, 1956), p. 23.
57 Wagner, *Heralds of England*, p. 263.
58 Squibb, *High Court of Chivalry*, pp. 69, 70.
59 Mary Anne Everett Green (comp.), *Calendar of the Committee for the Advance of Money, 1642–56* (3 vols, 1888), p. 1103, where it refers to a John Watson of St Benet's, Paul's Wharf, the address of the College and where Watson was probably buried and his son baptised (Noble, *History of the College of Arms*, p. 254; Godfrey and Wagner, *College of Arms Monograph*, p. 198).
60 Noble, *History of the College of Arms*, p. 229.

14 Remembering regicides in America, 1660–1800

Matthew Jenkinson

In Boston in 1793, Ezra Stiles, under the pseudonym Philagathos, published his *Poem, Commemorative of Goffe, Whaley, & Dixwell*. In it he noted that figures like Nathanael Greene and Richard Montgomery, major generals in the Revolutionary War, had been given memorials, while other American heroes had their names given to garrisons: Hamilton, Knox, Franklin, Jefferson. 'Yet scarce are mention'd in the historic page', Stiles lamented, 'Thy mother Britain's best-deserving sons'. These sons, who fled from the 'second Charles's rage', were the regicides William Goffe, Edward Whalley, and John Dixwell.[1] Stiles was not the only one to perceive this neglect. Aedanus Burke, Chief Justice of South Carolina, wrote to Stiles suggesting that subscriptions be requested for the erection of a monument to Whalley, Goffe, and Dixwell. This could be placed in front of Yale, he suggested, to provide 'the youth a good lesson, and conspicuous example, that the fame of great men, who undergo hazards and suffer in the cause of public freedom, is not to perish utterly'.[2] The implication was that the absence of such a monument would expedite the perishing of the regicides' fame and indeed that the names of Whalley, Goffe, and Dixwell were not readily on the tongues of the American Revolutionaries.

For Stiles and Burke, the English regicides who fled to America represented not only the successful fight against Charles I's 'tyranny' in the 1640s but also the effective evasion of Charles II's renewed 'tyrannical' efforts after 1660. Whalley and Goffe, in particular, were perceived as defenders of liberty on both sides of the Atlantic. At the Restoration of the monarchy, the full list of who was going to be punished for their complicity in the regicide was not totally clear. Charles II's pre-Restoration negotiations and declarations, followed by the Act of Indemnity and Oblivion, allowed for a significant number of former Stuart enemies to be pardoned. Yet there was always a core group of regicides who were not going to be forgiven and their crimes forgotten. Whalley and Goffe clearly knew they were part of this core, as within a fortnight of Charles II setting sail to return to England, they were on the *Prudent Mary* sailing across the Atlantic towards New England. Whalley was a cousin of Oliver Cromwell and a veteran of the battles of Marston Moor and Naseby, who had personally guarded the captured Charles I. Goffe had contributed to the Putney Debates and the Windsor Prayer Meeting, at the latter of which Charles was declared to be a 'man of blood', a significant step on the road to his execution on 30 January 1649. Crucially, Whalley was the fourth signatory, and Goffe the fourteenth, of Charles I's death warrant.

Whalley and Goffe arrived in New England on 27 July 1660. They were initially entertained generously and openly by significant members of the colonial government, not least Governor John Endecott and the President of Harvard Rev. Charles Chauncey. Within five to six months, however, it became known within New England that Whalley and Goffe were fugitives exempt from the Act of Indemnity and Oblivion, so this level of entertainment put at risk the personal safety and freedom of those doing the entertaining, while potentially provoking the ire of the Restoration government against the colonies who were protecting England's most wanted men. It was considered politic for Whalley and Goffe to move inland, away from the first port of call of any royal commission arriving from England. Whalley spent the next thirteen years on the run in America; Goffe survived for eighteen years; both died in the American colonies without being caught by Charles II's agents. During these years, they were protected in New Haven, Milford, and Hadley; Goffe travelled to Hartford after Whalley's death.[3] While it would be inappropriate to claim that, over the course of two decades, the Restoration authorities made a sustained attempt to capture the regicides,[4] there were crucial flashpoints at which attempts were made to find them and return them to England. On one occasion, in 1661, Whalley and Goffe were very close to being captured. But their preserved freedom, through individual bravery and the wily complicity of their colonial protectors, made Whalley, Goffe, and their hosts some of the earliest colonial heroes. And they were heroes, many interpreted, of liberty against the tyranny of British kings – hence the renewed interest in their story in the years surrounding the American Revolution and hence the call from Stiles and Burke that a permanent and prominent memorial be erected in their memory.

We can garner from the biography of Ezra Stiles, the first man to write a full book on the regicides in America, some reasons why Whalley, Goffe, and (to a lesser extent) Dixwell lacked much particular attention in the first half of the eighteenth century. When the regicides were still alive in the seventeenth century, many colonists judged it prudent not to advertise knowledge of their existence, so as not to implicate themselves in illegally protecting fugitives – or at least not informing Charles II's agents of their location. This clandestine culture continued into the eighteenth century, observed Stiles's biographer, because the regicides' 'ashes [were] liable to violation' if they were discovered. Any thorough and open research into the regicides was described as 'impracticable'. Very little was handed down on paper; 'The select few, to whom the secret was originally entrusted, handed it down with singular care, by verbal tradition'. It was a little odd, then, for Stiles to complain under the pseudonym Philagathos that the regicides had not yet been commemorated publicly; few people would have known, or would have overtly admitted to knowing, who Whalley, Goffe, and Dixwell were. This was not a simple case of neglect; it was a combination of ignorance, feigned ignorance, and covertness. In the aftermath of the American Revolution, though, 'the graves of the enemies of tyrants were sure of protection, if not of veneration', so 'the difficulty of obtaining the history of these Judges became sensibly diminished'.[5]

The argument went, then, that a full and open account of the regicides in America could not safely be written until after the American Revolution. This is not to suggest, however, that regicide and the regicides were absent from American culture and rhetoric in the decades preceding and including the Revolution, just because there were not yet grand monuments to the English regicides; nor should we assume that no one publicly conveyed any information about the regicides before the Revolution, just because Stiles's biographer (who had a hagiographical interest in promoting his subject's originality) implied such.

When Whalley, Goffe, and Dixwell were invoked – before, during, and after the Revolutionary years – interest in the regicides focused on two key episodes. The first was the period in 1661 when the regicides were first pursued in America by Charles II's government and when colonial authorities, for the first time, had to decide whether they were going to protect the regicides. The second was the 1664 commission from England, which was ostensibly concerned with advancing claims over New Netherland but whose mission could be interpreted, in part, as a renewed attempt to capture the regicides. Both the 1661 and 1664 episodes concerned attempted direct interference by the British government in colonial affairs; both were seen to culminate in colonists resisting this interference, either subtly or overtly. In sum, both episodes were seen as miniature precursors to the American Revolutionary years, and – in combining colonial American history with the relationship between local elites and central government – their study is an appropriate tribute to Clive Holmes and two of his interests.

I

Thomas Kellond and Thomas Kirke (1661)

In 1661, when it became clear that Whalley and Goffe could no longer be safely protected in Cambridge or Boston, the regicides travelled to New Haven. There were at least five advantages to this relocation. Firstly, New Haven was the puritan colony furthest from Boston, which would be one of the first places to be searched by the Restoration authorities. Secondly, New Haven had proved itself to be the colony most resistant to the Restoration of Charles II: news of the king's return to England had arrived there on 27 July 1660 and rejection of the move was considered as a real possibility. Thirdly, because of this open hostility, New Haven harboured little hope of gaining a charter from the king, so it was barely worth cooperating with him against Whalley and Goffe.[6] Fourthly, one of the leading figures in New Haven was William Jones, with whom the regicides had crossed the Atlantic. Fifthly, New Haven was the home of John Davenport, the preacher who had delivered a sermon encouraging his congregation to 'hide the out-casts'.[7]

Davenport was friend and correspondent of Whalley's brother-in-law, William Hooke, who had spent time in New Haven during the 1640s, and it was at Davenport's house in New Haven that Whalley and Goffe arrived on 7 March 1661, just one day before the authorities of the Massachusetts Colony issued a warrant for the regicides' arrest. This was a half-hearted attempt to catch them. Governor Endecott would have known that Whalley and Goffe had left his jurisdiction and that few, if any, Bostonians would be inclined to chase them through the New England woods in the depths of winter. By issuing the warrant, Endecott could give the impression to the English authorities that he was following orders and attempting to arrest the regicides. Yet by delaying the warrant until the regicides were safely out of his colony, he could be sure for the time being that this warrant would have no practical effect. Whalley and Goffe stayed with Davenport until the end of April, with just one diversion. They visited Milford on 27 March, perhaps to give the impression that they were travelling south to join the Dutch at the colony of New Netherland, which was just over seventy miles away.

On 28 April 1661, another mandate for the apprehension of the regicides arrived in Boston. It was dated 5 March, signed by Edward Nicholas, and it noted that Whalley and Goffe were 'lately arrived at New England, where they hope to shroud themselves securely from the justice of our lawes'. Colonial authorities were instructed to 'cause both the said persons to be apprehended, and with the first opportunity sent over hither under a strict care'.[8] This mandate was addressed 'To our trusty and well-beloved the present Governour, or other Magistrate or Magistrates of our Plantation of New England'. The colonial authorities may have been mistaken or mischievous in how they interpreted this, and they were aided by Nicholas's questionable syntax. The colonial authorities read the address as if it included an extra comma: 'to ... the present Governour, or other Magistrate or Magistrates[,] of our Plantation of New England'. This way, the mandate could read as if it were addressed to 'the present Governour ... of New England'. However, Nicholas may have intended the address to refer to a 'Governour' of any such colony in which the mandate was read, while only the 'Magistrate or Magistrates' had to pertain to New England. Whatever Nicholas's intentions, once it was in America, the mandate was read as if it were addressed to 'the present Governour ... of New England', leading to anxiety, consternation, and delay. This was perceived as a threat to the autonomy of the individual colony; there were fears that there was going to be an overall Governor of New England.

As such a figure as the 'Governour ... of New England' did not exist, the ensuing deferral of the mandate's execution could be disguised under the cloak of bureaucratic confusion and hesitation. Governor Endecott of the Massachusetts Bay Colony dithered for over a week, long enough for the news of the renewed danger to reach Whalley and Goffe and for them to begin preparations for their journey towards another safe haven. This move was expedited on 28 April when the Massachusetts arrest warrant arrived in New Haven. Whalley and Goffe left Davenport's house on 30 April and moved to the safer residence of William Jones, their companion during their Atlantic crossing the previous year, and whose father was a regicide executed in London six months previously. Jones's attitude towards Charles II and loyalty to the Stuart monarchy can be gleaned from the oath of fidelity to the king he swore when he was chosen magistrate for New Haven in 1662. He took the oath 'with subordination' to the king, but he hoped that Charles would 'confirme the ... government for the advancem[en]t of Christs gospel, kingdom & ends in this colony, vpon the foundations already laid'. More controversially he added that 'in case of alteration of the gouernm[en]t in the fundamentals thereof', he would be free from 'the said oath'.[9] Jones was willing to go through the motions of declaring loyalty to the king (who had, through Parliament, ordered the execution of Jones's father), but clearly his primary loyalty was to the godly government and community of New Haven. If Charles encroached on that government, then Jones would free himself from the bonds of fidelity to the king. His loyalty to Charles II was conditional and limited. It was so limited, in fact, that he enthusiastically protected those who had signed the king's father's death warrant.

After receiving Nicholas's 5 March mandate, Governor Endecott appointed two royalists, a merchant named Thomas Kellond and a sea captain named Thomas Kirke, to search for Whalley and Goffe and to carry letters (dated 7 May) to the Deputy Governor of New Haven, the Governor of Connecticut, and the Governor of 'Manhatoes', or New Netherland, to aid in that project.[10] Endecott made all the right noises to suggest that he was keen that the regicides be apprehended. Whalley and Goffe were, he wrote, 'guilty of so execrable a murther', the Boston officials had 'not beene wanting' in their efforts to capture the regicides, and he was confident that his fellow governors (or deputy governors) would carry out their duty to Charles II in a 'faithfull', 'effectuall', and 'speedy' manner.[11] Endecott acted, though, as if Whalley and Goffe had fled to the Dutch jurisdiction of New Netherland, under the protection of Governor Peter Stuyvesant. On paper at least, Endecott gave the impression that the regicides had run from English justice by hiding away in the 'remote parts' of the Dutch colony far to the west of where they actually were. Endecott asked, then, that Stuyvesant apprehend Whalley and Goffe and return them to an area of English jurisdiction, so they could be conveyed back to Boston.[12] It is possible that Endecott was playing the old game of appearing diligent in the pursuit of the regicides, while expending his energies in a direction that he knew would come to nothing. Perhaps that is an uncharitable assessment. Endecott may genuinely have thought that Whalley and Goffe had decided they would be safer in a colony outside English jurisdiction. Whalley and Goffe had indeed briefly travelled to Milford, in the direction of New Netherland, and Endecott may have heard about this.

Kellond and Kirke began to travel westwards, likely following Endecott's tip-off, but their route was soon determined by new intelligence. Accompanied by a guide called John Chapin, they left Boston on the evening of 7 May and arrived in Hartford (through which Whalley and Goffe had travelled) on 10 May, when they met with Governor Winthrop. The following day, the search in

Hartford began, though Winthrop assured Kellond and Kirke that the regicides had already left in the direction of New Haven.[13] With Winthrop's assurance that a thorough search of Hartford would still be made, Kellond and Kirke wasted no time in moving on to Guilford, where they met with Deputy Governor William Leete on 11 May. Governor Francis Newman of New Haven had died the previous November, so Leete was at the time the Chief Magistrate of New Haven. Leete claimed to Kellond and Kirke that he had not seen Whalley and Goffe for nine weeks, around the time they had first arrived in New Haven. It is quite possible that Leete had not seen them in person, but this did not mean that the regicides had already moved on.

Indeed, Kellond and Kirke believed reports that Whalley and Goffe had been seen in New Haven more recently. Kellond and Kirke encountered a man named Dennis Crampton, who openly told them not only that John Davenport was housing the regicides but also that Deputy Governor Leete was in on the secret. Davenport had allegedly recently acquired a suspiciously large quantity of provisions – enough, say, to provide for an extra two men. Other rumours suggested that the regicides had been spotted travelling between Davenport's and William Jones's residences and that Whalley and Goffe had recently been spotted in nearby Milford, inflammatorily suggesting that 'if they had but two hundred friends to stand by them, they would not care for Old or New England'.[14] As it would be on other occasions, the royalists' progress was hampered by delay. They requested horses to transport them on their search from Guilford to New Haven. The horses duly arrived but not until the colonial authorities had stalled for a little more time.[15] 11 May 1661 was a Saturday. The evening was drawing in. Deputy Governor Leete could not countenance, he claimed, anyone travelling within his jurisdiction during the approaching Sabbath. Furthermore, the government in London and their royalist agents had undermined their cause through a mistaken use of language. Their commission was addressed to the 'Governor of New England'. New Haven Colony usually had a governor; Connecticut Colony had a governor. There was no such individual as the Governor of New England. So Leete insisted – stalling for time – that he would have to consult his fellow magistrates before recognising Kellond and Kirke's commission and then assembling a search party. Leete would, however, give the king's commissioners a letter to hand to the magistrate in New Haven, their next destination.[16]

But that next destination would have to wait for at least another thirty-six hours or so – the time between the commissioners' meeting with Leete and sunrise on the following Monday, after their enforced extra Sabbath day in Guilford. This was, of course, plenty of time for word to get to the regicides of the impending danger and for them to make provisions to depart from William Jones's house. Word would certainly get out because Leete had been careful to read Kellond and Kirke's letter out loud, so the exact nature of their business was known to anyone present in the room, and the regicides could be forewarned. There were reports that a local Indian left the town in the direction of New Haven; John Meigs was accused of preparing to leave for New Haven, but

Leete refused a request from Kellond and Kirke that Meigs be brought in and interrogated. Never again would the regicides be so closely pursued by those men who wished to play their part in retribution for the execution of Charles I. Kellond and Kirke's intelligence was good, but it was verging on useless if they could not physically get near their fugitives. Hearing of the royalists' impending arrival, Whalley and Goffe moved once again, on the Saturday night when Kellond and Kirke sat frustrated in their Guilford inn – this time to Westville and then to a cave two to three miles north-west of New Haven.

The delay in Guilford over the weekend of 11–12 May 1661 did not just allow word to get to the regicides about Kellond and Kirke. Leete may have given the commissioners a letter to hand to a New Haven magistrate on their arrival, but it appears that he also sent a note to Matthew Gilbert, New Haven magistrate, to make sure that Gilbert would not be around when Kellond and Kirke arrived. To delay matters even further, Leete assured Kellond and Kirke that he would follow them from Guilford to New Haven. This he did but not without the requisite couple of hours' delay to frustrate Kellond and Kirke even further. Then, to add to the farce, when Leete appeared in the court chamber, he notified Kellond and Kirke that he did not think Whalley and Goffe were in New Haven after all. He would, Leete claimed, arrange a search of Davenport's and Jones's respective houses – but only once the local freemen had assembled. The royalist agents told Leete that the king's honour was being 'despised and trampled upon', and they believed Leete was 'willing' that Whalley and Goffe should abscond. We can imagine the commissioners' blood pressure rising as Leete met the deputies and magistrates of New Haven for almost six hours, before Leete appeared to make the same statement he had made before the meeting began. Again, Kellond and Kirke told Leete that Charles II 'would resent such horrid and detestable concealments and abettings of such traitors', insisting that Leete honour the warrants they presented from Governors Endecott and Winthrop.[17]

The tense and comical proceedings in New Haven suggest that the point of contention was not just whether the colonial authorities resented the commissioners' attempts to arrest Whalley and Goffe. A discussion at the court chamber in New Haven on the evening of Monday 13 May 1661 points to a broader source of resentment on behalf of the New Haven colonists to the royal commissioners and the government they represented. The term 'Governor of New England' was a useful excuse to dither in their proceedings with Kellond and Kirke; the colonial authorities could understandably act confused about the use of a term to denote a body that did not actually exist. But beneath this bureaucratic hesitancy, there was a very real fear that the use of a term like 'Governor of New England' denoted a desire on behalf of Charles II's government to introduce such a figure, thereby significantly reducing the independence of the existing colonies. On that tense May evening, Kellond and Kirke asked the New Haven magistrates 'whether they would own his Majesty or no' – that is, would they respect his authority and yield in their resistance by giving up the regicides? This depended, the colonial authorities replied, on 'whether his

Majesty would own them'. In short, would Charles not work to reduce their independence by introducing a sinister overbearing figure like a 'Governor of New England'?

The New Haven magistrates did convene the General Court four days later, and this did in turn issue warrants to search for Whalley and Goffe in each plantation. Perhaps this was just lip service to the royal commissioners; perhaps they knew the regicides were only two miles away all along, so a search of somewhere like Virginia was not going to reap many rewards; perhaps they were genuinely interested in helping find the regicides once their protest about a 'Governor of New England' had been lodged. There is certainly a tone of earnestness in the account of the search of Milford, in which Thomas Sanford, Nicholas Campe, James Tapping, and Lawrence Ward investigated all 'dwelling houses, barnes or other buildings'.[18] It does not really matter. On 14 May, Kellond and Kirke had given up their dealings with the comically and efficiently recalcitrant New Haven authorities. They had carried out a cursory search of New Haven and offered a financial reward for help in finding Whalley and Goffe. But they returned to Boston via New Netherland, where Stuyvesant commanded a search of private boats, but he found nothing and refused any more direct assistance. Kellond and Kirke had got within two miles of the two men they were after, but the colonists of New Haven ensured they would not get any further.[19] Kellond and Kirke retired to their new estates, each of 250 acres: a sizeable reward for an ineffectual mission.

Reading Ezra Stiles's biography, we might be tempted to think that Stiles in the 1790s was the first to 'rediscover' the regicides in America after their fading from public memory. Yet there was, in fact, interest in the regicides decades before the publication of Stiles's *History of Three of the Judges of Charles I* (1794). The loyalist Governor Thomas Hutchinson included the story of Whalley, Goffe, and Dixwell in the first volume of his *History of the Colony of Massachusetts-Bay* (1764).[20] In response, a wag contributor to the *Boston Gazette and Country Journal* (20 November 1769) wrote a letter from the long dead Whalley and Goffe, on 'the 30th of . . . October. We had almost said the 30th of January': 'We mean soon to send a letter to a late Historian, to set him Right, *if he inclines to be set Right*, in Regard to some Transactions in our Day, which have been greatly misrepresented to the World'. The letter left blanks instead of naming Hutchinson outright, but readers knew the figure in question and annotated their copies accordingly.[21] It is clear, then, that in the years running up to the American Revolution, material concerning the regicides on the run in New England was collected and printed. It is important to note that much of it focused on the series of events in 1661. In 1769, for example, came the publication of the report made to Governor Endecott by the royalist agents Kellond and Kirke. Their account of the pursuit of the fugitive regicides in the summer of 1661 was rendered in precise detail. Readers in the late 1760s would learn of Kellond and Kirke's departure from Boston on 7 May 1661, their arrival in Hartford on 10 May, their meeting with Governor Winthrop, their first encounter with Deputy Governor Leete on 11 May, the reports concerning the protection of the regicides in New Haven by Davenport and Jones, and the humiliating runaround given by Leete.

Also printed in 1769 was the letter from Secretary Rawson to Leete on 4 July 1661, informing him that 'the non attendance with diligence to execute the Kings majestys warrant for the apprehending of Colonel Whaley and Goffe will much hazard the present state of these colonies', as well as Rawson's follow-up concerning the public appearance in New Haven of Whalley and Goffe. In addition, you could have learnt in 1769 about the Declaration of the Commissioners of the United Colonies concerning Whalley and Goffe, signed at Hartford on 5 September 1661, when they publicly (if insincerely) stated that 'all such person or persons, that since the publication of his Majesties order have wittingly and willingly entertained or harboured ... Whalley and Goffe, or hereafter shall doe the like, have and will incurre his Majesties highest displeasure'.[22]

We should be careful, however, not to overplay the presence of Whalley, Goffe and Dixwell in the American mind between their deaths and the American Revolution. Much has been made of the visit to John Dixwell's grave in 1774 by the Massachusetts delegation to the First Continental Congress in Philadelphia – John Adams, Samuel Adams, Thomas Cushing, and Robert Treat Payne.[23] Yet John Adams's diary for 17 August 1774 suggests that this was just one brief stop on a more extensive tour of New Haven, which also took in three congregational meeting houses, as well as the library and chapel at Yale. No ink is spilt lauding Dixwell as one of Adams's heroes. He was more concerned with contemporary debates about whether the Parliament of Great Britain had any right to legislate in the colonies.[24]

In the decades following the American Revolution, there was a boom of interest in the regicides in America. Once independence from Great Britain ensured there would be no retribution for the protection of men who had committed treason on British soil, the story of the regicides appeared in all manner of different places – not just in traditional histories or collections of historical documents. Jedidiah Morse's *American Universal Geography* in 1796, for example, featured Whalley and Goffe alongside a discussion of turnpike roads. He noted the cave north-west of New Haven in which the regicides resided when they were hiding from Charles II's agents. But Morse also knew about and conveyed the wider story.[25] In 1797, Benjamin Trumball published the first volume of his *Complete History of Connecticut*. This history, 'published in conformity to act of congress', included the story of the regicides. It referred to 'the spirit of republicanism' present in many of the New Haven magistrates. Whalley and Goffe were described as 'gentlemen of singular abilities' who had 'moved in an exalted sphere'; '[t]heir manners were elegant, and their appearance grave and dignified, commanding universal respect'.[26] They were 'universally esteemed, by all men of character, both civil and religious' in Boston and Cambridge. Yet, Trumball noted, when it became clear that Whalley and Goffe were wanted men and Governor Endecott assembled his magistrates to discuss their apprehension, 'their friends were so numerous, that a vote could not ...

be obtained to arrest them'. Some of these 'friends' continued to stand by the regicides; some advised Whalley and Goffe that they should abscond.

Upon their arrival in New Haven, Trumbull continued, the regicides continued to enjoy unstinting hospitality: 'the more the people became acquainted with them, the more they esteemed them, not only as men of great minds, but of unfeigned piety and religion'. When news arrived in New England about the execution of Thomas Harrison and other co-regicides in 1660, though, Trumbull notes that the affair of harbouring Whalley and Goffe was viewed 'in a more serious point of light'. The colonists' personal safety was at risk, as were the 'liberties and peace' of their country. This did not stop Leete in New Haven deliberately obstructing the efforts of Kellond and Kirke to find the regicides. Leete and his supporters viewed Whalley and Goffe as 'the excellent in the earth, and were afraid to betray them, lest they should be instrumental in shedding innocent blood'.[27] Trumbull's knowledge of the dates of the regicides' travels and reference to the regicide myths present in Stiles's *History of Three of the Judges of King Charles I*, which had been published three years previously, suggest that Stiles was Trumbull's principal source for his history of the regicides. As with Stiles, Trumbull's tone and focus on how highly esteemed the regicides were in New England are suggestive of sympathy towards Whalley and Goffe.

II

Richard Nichols, Robert Carr, George Cartwright, and Samuel Maverick (1664)

Others in support of the American Revolution looked back to the history of the Stuart kings and the regicides. They celebrated the principles evident in seventeenth-century New Englanders that fed into the events of the 1770s, but the story of Kellond and Kirke in 1661 was not the only regicides-related incident worthy of note and celebration. Hannah Adams's *Summary History of New-England, from the First Settlement at Plymouth* (Dedham, 1799) was 'published according to Act of Congress'. Her history included the story of Whalley and Goffe, describing them in terms very similar to Trumbull's: 'gentlemen of distinguished abilities' who had 'moved in an exalted sphere'.[28] Adams, a distant cousin of President John Adams, retold the story of the regicides' arrival in Boston, their time concealed in the cave just outside New Haven, their journey to Milford, return to New Haven, and their later time in Hadley. But their time in hiding was placed in the context of the colonies' fear of having their privileges removed by Charles II. Adams was convinced that Charles was determined to rule like his father. The colonists' enemies in England apparently 'gave exaggerated accounts of every interesting occurrence, and the king was prejudiced by their representations'.[29] Presumably one such 'interesting occurrence' would have been the case study of Whalley and Goffe and their protection, through a variety of means, by colonial authorities.

Despite the intransigence and obstructionism of the likes of William Leete, the Court in London did not totally give up hope of capturing Whalley and Goffe. On 25 April 1664, instructions were given to four royal commissioners – Richard Nichols, Robert Carr, George Cartwright, and Samuel Maverick – to travel to the New England colonies and to New York. Their visit had a number of purposes. One was to advance Charles II's claims over New Netherland. Also, the king was less than content about the reluctance among the puritan authorities in Massachusetts to allow the use of the Anglican Book of Common Prayer in their colony. They feared that such an allowance would undermine Massachusetts's religious purity, also potentially auguring the kind of Anglican dominance and persecution that had expedited the colonists' flight from England in the early seventeenth century and that had contributed to the outbreak of civil war in the 1640s. The commission was also charged with hearing and passing judgement on territorial disputes in New England. Both king and colonists were attempting a balancing act; they expressed gratitude at the respect apparently afforded each other, yet they were suspicious of conceding jurisdiction to the other side. The king had guaranteed 'all the privileges and liberties' of the Massachusetts charter, yet he still insisted on sending commissioners to enquire after issues over which his government had jurisdiction. The Massachusetts authorities were relieved that their charter had been upheld, yet they were conceding sovereignty if they allowed the king's commissioners to investigate in the way they wanted.[30]

Charles II now offered an iron fist in a velvet glove. The iron fist came in the form of the four warships and four hundred soldiers that arrived in Boston and Portsmouth in June and July 1664. This show of strength was ostensibly targeted at New Netherland, but it could quite easily be – and was – interpreted as a threat to the New England colonies themselves. The velvet glove was the way in which the commission was worded, especially with reference to Whalley and Goffe. The commissioners were to make 'due inquiry' whether any regicides had travelled to and resided in these areas. If any such regicides were discovered, they were to be put on a ship and returned straight to London, where due legal process would, no doubt, result in the termination of the regicides' lives. There is a sense, though, that these instructions were not so much designed actually to capture Whalley and Goffe – it had not happened yet; the longer they remained in New England, the more embedded they would have become and the greater knowledge of the terrain and hiding places they would have developed. Instead, almost half of the commissioners' instructions were aimed at those who had offered or who might in the future offer sanctuary to the regicides. There was a sinister detachment and passive aggression to these instructions. The commissioners were to find out by whom the regicides had been 'received and entertayned'. But they were not to arrest them, for that would violate the Act of Indemnity and Oblivion. Instead, these people may just 'be taken the more notice of and may hold themselves to take the more care for their future behaviour'.[31] The threat of retribution lingered behind a carefully worded and judiciously friendly warning.

It has been suggested that the commission had 'secret instructions from Charles [II] to tread gently with the Massachusetts puritans'. The logic goes that the king was attempting to 'woo' the colonial authorities, to entice them to loyalty towards him, after their lukewarm reticence in recognising Charles as their king. They had not proclaimed him king until August 1661, over a year after his return to England. If Charles and his courtiers had taken a tough line against those who had harboured the regicides, they would have further alienated many notable figures in colonial governance. Then any hopes at imposing a new charter on Massachusetts would have been lost.[32] This is possible, but there was also a growing sense that the chances of capturing Whalley and Goffe were diminishing; another failed attempt at their capture was less humiliating if it was subtle and measured than if it was overtly aggressive and intrusive.

For Hannah Adams in 1799, when Charles II sent the commission of Nichols (Adams called him 'Nevils'), Carr, Cartwright, and Maverick, the king's primary intention was not to advance British claims over Dutch colonies but to reduce the British colonies to 'the plan of twelve royal provinces, according to the ideas adopted by his father in 1635, and to have a viceroy over the whole'.[33] We have seen that the reality was a little subtler than this. The question of jurisdiction was present; neither king nor colonists were prepared to concede sovereignty, yet each side was careful to ensure they did not significantly rile the other. The warships and soldiers that arrived in the summer of 1664 were ostensibly targeted at New Netherland. New Englanders might fear that Charles's intention was to use this military force against them, but the king could always argue that this was a paranoid and wilful misinterpretation. After all, his pursuit of the regicides at the time was careful and measured. Nichols, Carr, Cartwright, and Maverick were to find out who had protected the regicides, but they were not to arrest them. The 'protectors' were just to be encouraged to 'take the more care for their future behaviour'. This was indeed a sinister threat, but it was not an overtly aggressive and encroaching one.

But Adams in 1799 allowed no such subtlety. The 1664 commission was just another example, she suggested, of the British government threatening the independent sovereignty and jurisdiction of New England. The colonies 'disrelished' this threat, due to their 'strong aversion to arbitrary power'. Further, Adams argued, 'The inhabitants of New-England may emphatically be said to be born free. They were settled originally upon the principle expressed at this day in all their forms of government, that "all men are born free, equal and independent"'. The 1664 commission, according to Adams, 'excited the irritability natural to a people jealous for their liberty'.[34] There can have been few more overt claims to an innate connection between the European settlement of New England and the American Revolution.

III

In December 1692, Gershom Bulkeley looked back at the recent history of New England. The rebellion against Charles I had, he noted, excited 'an anti-monarchical spirit' in America, which had become so 'strongly rooted ... as not to be easily or speedily, if ever, totally eradicated'. That spirit had led to the 'admiration' towards, and the 'entertainment' of, some of the king's 'murderers here and there in the country'.[35] Bulkeley's words were prescient. The deaths of the regicides clearly did not lead to their disappearance from American culture and thought. While we should not be so unsubtle as to join the teleological dots between the English and American Revolutions, it is important to identify the role played by the memory of regicide and the regicides in late-seventeenth and eighteenth-century America. Bernard Bailyn, among others, has shown how American colonists 'identified themselves with ... seventeenth-century heroes of liberty' like John Milton and Algernon Sidney, and how 'the ultimate origins of [colonists'] distinctive ideological strain lay in the radical social and political thought of the civil war and commonwealth period'. For example, the 'penman' of the American Revolution, John Dickinson, could not fully explain the events of the 1770s without looking back to the reign of Charles I.[36]

Commentators after 1776 were not so crass as to suggest that the English Revolution directly caused the American Revolution. They did, however, follow in the spirit of Bulkeley and spot in the seventeenth century certain principles that would be adopted by those who challenged British governance in the eighteenth century. The minister Jonathan Boucher offered his view of the causes and effects of the American Revolution in 'thirteen discourses', which he preached in America between 1763 and 1775, then published after the Revolution when he had returned to his home country of England. He was 'avowedly hostile' to that Revolution, and he noted a number of parallels between the 1640s in England and the 1760s–1770s in America. Boucher noted that 'the history of the last century, and what then passed among ourselves, is a perpetual lesson, at least to British subjects, to *leave off contention before it be meddled with*'. The English civil war had begun, as the American Revolution had, 'about matters which, comparatively speaking, were but of little moment'; the English civil war had occurred due to the interference of 'persons unknown to the laws, who began their reformation by overturning the Established Church'. That is, once puritans had meddled with the church in England, it was not long before they meddled with the state. The implication was that the same thing had happened in America.[37] Benjamin Franklin's admirers defended him, Boucher observed, in just the same way that the regicides were defended.[38]

John Locke's views on civil liberty, adopted by American Revolutionaries, were for Boucher just 'new-dressed principles', principles that had been 'industriously revived and brought forward with great zeal' in the reign of Charles I. Indeed, Boucher argued, 'there is hardly a principle or project or any moment in Mr Locke's Treatise, of which the rudiments may not be traced in some of the many political pieces which were then produced'.[39] The contribution of John Locke to the thought of the American Revolution has been well documented elsewhere. It must be remembered that Locke began writing in the reign of Charles II, a reign almost obsessively preoccupied with the sinister shadow of the English civil war – a mix of determination that 1641 would not come again but also recognition that the nature of government had changed fundamentally. Kings could lose their crowns, they could lose their heads, by the judicial will of (some of) their subjects. The political philosophy that developed in this environment crossed the Atlantic. It did not cause the American Revolution, it did not make it inevitable, but it offered a framework of thought and a language for that Revolution.

As Brendan McConville puts it, 'the English civil wars once had as strong a hold on colonials as Vietnam and World War II do on contemporary Americans'. Eighteenth-century writers looked back to the English civil wars for lessons and guidance, though these lessons depended upon different authors' perspectives and political loyalties. By the middle of that century, in the American colonies Cromwell was celebrated more than he was vilified, and Charles I vice versa. This was, in part, a puritan reaction to the rise of the Church of England in the colonies. But by the late 1770s, the civil wars and the characters therein were invoked in the context of the American Revolution. Cromwell was celebrated by the Boston Sons of Liberty as a 'glorious fellow'; Samuel Sherwood observed 'tyranny and oppression' being exercised by the British government, just as it had been during 'the reign of the stuart family'.[40]

The 'rediscovery' of the story of Whalley and Goffe, which predated Stiles's book-length account and poem, also provided an interpretative framework for the events of the 1770s. The regicides may not have had the architectural monument that Aedenus Burke desired, but as the eighteenth century progressed, they were increasingly memorialized in print. Of central interest to late-eighteenth-century authors looking back to the late seventeenth century were those points at which the independent sovereignty of New England colonies was threatened by the British government in their hunt for the fugitive regicides: the search by Kellond and Kirke in 1661 and the Nicholls/Carr/Cartwright/Maverick commission in 1664. But both cases went beyond the immediate issues and implications of capturing men who were protected by significant individuals in the New England colonies. The events of 1661 brought forth the sinister spectre of a 'Governor of New England', further perpetuating New Haven authorities' propensity to give Charles II's government the runaround. The commission of 1664 was concerned not just with Whalley and Goffe but with who held jurisdiction over territorial disputes in New England. It was not so dramatic an interpretative leap, even if it was inappropriately unsubtle, later to posit this case study as a precursor to the struggle between 'liberty' and 'arbitrary power' in the American Revolutionary years.

Notes

1 Philagathos [Ezra Stiles], *A Poem, Commemorative of Goffe, Whaley, & Dixwell* (Boston, MA, 1793), p. 16.
2 *Ibid.*, p. 15.
3 A more detailed account can be found in Christopher Pagliuco, *The Great Escape of Edward Whalley and William Goffe* (Charleston, SC, 2012); Don Jordan and Michael Walsh, *The King's Revenge: Charles II and the Greatest Manhunt in British History* (2012);

Frederick Hull Cogswell, 'The Regicides in New England', *New England Magazine* (1893), 188–200; Mark L. Sargeant, 'Thomas Hutchinson, Ezra Stiles and the Legend of the Regicides', *WMQ*, 3rd series, 49 (1992), 431–48; Mary Peale Schofield, 'The Three Judges of New Haven', *History Today*, 12 (1962), 346–53; Lemuel Aiken Welles, *History of the Regicides in New England* (New York, 1927); Lemuel Aiken Welles, *The Regicides in Connecticut* (New Haven, CT, 1935); George Sheldon, *Whalley and Goffe in New England, 1660–1680* (Springfield, MA, 1905); Jason Peacey, '"The Good Old Cause for Which I Suffer": The Life of a Regicide in Exile', in Philip Major (ed.), *Literatures of Exile in the English Revolution and its Aftermath, 1640–1690* (Farnham, 2010), pp. 167–80; Philip Major, *Writings of Exile in the English Revolution and Restoration* (Farnham, 2013), Chapter 4.

4 Charles Spencer, *Killers of the King: The Men Who Dared to Execute Charles I* (New York, 2014), Chapters 13 and 14.
5 Abiel Holmes, *The Life of Ezra Stiles* (Boston, MA, 1798), pp. 322–3.
6 Pagliuco, *The Great Escape*, p. 66.
7 Ezra Stiles, *A History of Three of the Judges of Charles I* (Hartford, CT, 1794), p. 32; Francis J. Bremer, *The Puritan Experiment* (Lebanon, NH, 1995), p. 187.
8 *Collections of the Massachusetts Historical Society*, 3rd series, VII (Boston, MA 1838), 123.
9 Charles J. Hoadly (ed.), *Records of the Colony or Jurisdiction of New Haven, 1653–1665* (Hartford, CT, 1858), p. 451.
10 *Documents Relative to the Colonial History of the State of New York* (15 vols, Albany, NY, 1856–87), III, 41.
11 Ibid., III, 41.
12 Ibid., III, 42.
13 Franklin B. Dexter, 'Memoranda Respecting Edward Whalley and William Goffe', *Papers of the New Haven Colony Historical Society* 2 (1877), 117–46.
14 Ibid., 129.
15 Ibid.
16 Ibid.
17 Ibid., 129–30; Pagliuco, *The Great Escape*, p. 72.
18 Hoadly (ed.), *Records of the Colony or Jurisdiction of New Haven*, p. 380.
19 Dexter, 'Memoranda', 130.
20 Thomas Hutchinson, *History of the Colony of Massachusetts-Bay* (Boston, MA, 1764), pp. 213–19.
21 Cf. the copy annotated by the merchant and Son of Liberty, Harbottle Dorr, in the Massachusetts Historical Society. *Boston Gazette and Country Journal* (20 November 1769), available online at http://www.masshist.org/dorr/volume/2/sequence/794.
22 [Thomas Hutchinson], *A Collection of Original Papers Relative to the History of the Colony of Massachusetts-Bay* (Boston, MA, 1769), pp. 334–45.
23 Pagliuco, *The Great Escape*, p. 107.
24 John Adams diary entry 17 August 1774, available online at http://www.masshist.org/digitaladams/aea/cfm/doc.cfm?id=D21.
25 Jedidiah Morse, *The American Universal Geography* . . . (3rd edn, Boston, MA, 1796), p. 457.
26 Benjamin Trumbull, *A Complete History of Connecticut* (Hartford, CT, 1797), p. 251.
27 Ibid., pp. 251–4.
28 Hannah Adams, *A Summary History of New-England, from the First Settlement at Plymouth* (Dedham, MA, 1799), p. 110.
29 Ibid., p. 113.
30 Douglas C. Wilson, 'Web of Secrecy: Goffe, Whalley, and the Legend of Hadley', *New England Quarterly*, 60 (1987), 532–3; Paul R. Lucas, 'Colony or Commonwealth: Massachusetts Bay, 1661–1666', *WMQ*, 3rd series, 24 (1967), 105; Pagliuco, *The Great Escape*, pp. 83–4.
31 *Collections of the Massachusetts Historical Society*, 3rd series, 7 (Boston, MA, 1838), p. 127.

32 Jordan and Walsh, *The King's Revenge*, p. 308.
33 Adams, *Summary History of New-England*, p. 113.
34 *Ibid.*, p. 114.
35 Gershom Bulkeley, *Bulkeley's Will and Doom, or the Miseries of Connecticut by and under an Usurped and Arbitrary Power* (1692) in *Connecticut Historical Society Collections*, 3 (Hartford, CT, 1895), pp. 91–2.
36 Bernard Bailyn, *The Ideological Origins of the American Revolution* (Cambridge, MA, 1992), pp. 34–5, 145, and *passim*; cf. Blair Worden, *Roundhead Reputations: The English Civil Wars and the Passions of Posterity* (2001), pp. 32, 121, 127, 174, 210, 227, 334–6, 350–1, 353.
37 Jonathan Boucher, *A View of the Causes and Consequences of the American Revolution* (1797), 'Dedication', pp. 353–4.
38 *Ibid.*, p. 448.
39 *Ibid.*, p. 532.
40 Brendan McConville, *The King's Three Faces: The Rise and Fall of Royal America, 1688–1776* (Chapel Hill, NC, 2006), pp. 92–100, 166–74.

Bibliography of the writings of Clive Holmes, 1967–2016

Books, editions, and pamphlets

(edited) *The Suffolk Committees for Scandalous Ministers, 1644–1646* (Suffolk Records Society, 13, Ipswich, 1970)
The Eastern Association in the English Civil War (Cambridge, 1974)
Seventeenth-Century Lincolnshire (History of Lincolnshire, 7, Lincoln, 1980)
(with Felicity Heal) *The Gentry in England and Wales, 1500–1700* (Basingstoke, 1994)
Why Was Charles I Executed? (2006)
Why Did the Prosecution of Witches Cease in England? (Historical Association, 2013)

Essays

'The Affair of Colonel Long: Relations between Parliament, the Lord General and the County of Essex in 1643', *Transactions of the Essex Archaeological Society*, 3rd ser., 2 (1970), 210–15
'Colonel King and Lincolnshire Politics, 1642–6', *HJ*, 16 (1973), 451–84
'The County Community in Stuart Historiography', *JBS*, 19 (1980), 54–73
'Popular Culture? Witches, Magistrates, and Divines in Early Modern England', in Steven L. Kaplan (ed.), *Understanding Popular Culture: Europe from the Middle Ages to the Nineteenth Century* (Berlin, 1984), pp. 85–111
'Statutory Interpretation in the Early Seventeenth Century: The Courts, the Council, and the Commissioners of Sewers', in J.A. Guy and H.G. Beale (eds), *Law and Social Change in British History: Papers Presented to the Bristol Legal History Conference, 14–17 July 1981* (1984), pp. 107–17
'Drainers and Fenmen: The Problem of Popular Political Consciousness in the Seventeenth Century', in Anthony Fletcher and John Stevenson (eds.), *Order and Disorder in Early Modern England* (Cambridge, 1985), pp. 166–95
'Parliament, Liberty, Taxation, and Property', in J.H. Hexter (ed.), *Parliament and Liberty from the Reign of Elizabeth to the English Civil War* (Stanford, CA, 1992), pp. 122–54
'Women: Witnesses and Witches', *P&P*, 140 (1993), 45–78
'G.R. Elton as a Legal Historian', *TRHS*, 6th ser., 7 (1997), 267–79
'The Legal Instruments of Power and the State in Early Modern England', in Antonio Padoa Schioppa (ed.), *Legislation and Justice* (Oxford, 1997), pp. 269–90
(with Felicity Heal) '"*Prudentia ultra Sexum*": Lady Jane Bacon and the Management of her Families', in Muriel C. McClendon, Joseph P. Ward, and Michael MacDonald (eds.), *Protestant Identities: Religion, Society, and Self-Fashioning in Post-Reformation England* (Stanford, CA, 1999), pp. 100–24

(with Felicity Heal) 'The Economic Patronage of William Cecil', in Pauline Croft (ed.), *Patronage, Culture and Power: The Early Cecils* (Studies in British Art, 8, New Haven, CT, and London, 2002), pp. 199–229

'Drainage Projects in Elizabethan England: The European Dimension', in Salvatore Ciriacono (ed.), *Eau et Développement dans L'Europe Moderne* (Paris, 2004), pp. 87–102

'The Strange Case of a Misplaced Tomb: Family Honour and the Law in Late Seventeenth-Century England', *Midland History*, 31 (2006), 18–36

'John Lisle, Lord Commissioner of the Great Seal, and the Last Months of the Cromwellian Protectorate', *EHR*, 122 (2007), 918–36

'Law and Politics in the Reign of Charles I: The Case of John Prigeon', *Journal of Legal History*, 28 (2007), 161–82

'Witchcraft and Possession at the Accession of James I: The Publication of Samuel Harsnett's *Declaration of Egregious Popish Impostures*', in John Newton and Jo Bath (eds.), *Witchcraft and the Act of 1604* (Leiden, 2008), pp. 69–90

'Centre and Locality in Civil-War England', in John Adamson (ed.), *The English Civil War: Conflict and Contexts, 1640–1649* (Basingstoke, 2009), pp. 153–74

'Charles I: A Case of Mistaken Identity – Debate on Kishlansky', *P&P*, 205 (2009), 175–88

'The Trial and Execution of Charles I', *HJ*, 53 (2010), 289–316

'The Case of Joan Peterson: Witchcraft, Family Conflict, Legal Invention and Constitutional Theory', in Matthew Dyson and David Ibbetson (eds.), *Law and Legal Process: Substantive Law and Procedure in English Legal History* (Cambridge, 2013), pp. 148–66

'The Identity of the Author of the "Statement by an Opponent of Cromwell"', *EHR*, 129 (2014), 1371–82

Reviews

Menna Prestwich, *Cranfield: Politics and Profits under the Early Stuarts. The Career of Lionel Cranfield Earl of Middlesex*, in *Cambridge Review*, 89, no. 2146 (29 April 1967), 314

A.P. McGowan, *The Jacobean Commissions of Enquiry, 1608 and 1618*, in *AHR*, 80 (1975), 402–3

Anthony Fletcher, *A County Community in Peace and War: Sussex, 1600–1660*, in *AHR*, 82 (1977), 632–3

Brian Manning, *The English People and the English Revolution, 1640–1649*, in *AHR*, 82 (1977), 96–7

Joel Samaha, *Law and Order in Historical Perspective: The Case of Elizabethan Essex*; A. Hassell Smith, *County and Court: Government and Politics in Norfolk, 1558–1603*, in *JMH*, 49 (1977), 495–500

J. S. Cockburn, *Crime in England, 1550–1800*, in *Journal of Interdisciplinary History*, 9 (1979), 534–7

Kevin Sharpe, *Sir Robert Cotton 1586–1631: History and Politics in Early Modern England*, in *HJ*, 24 (1981), 1026–8

'New Light on the New Model' [Patricia Crawford, *Denzil, First Lord Holles*; Mark Kishlansky, *The Rise of the New Model Army*], in *HJ*, 24 (1981), 505–8

Stephen Saunders Webb, *The Governors-General: The English Army and the Definition of the Empire, 1569–1681*, in *AHR*, 86 (1981), 589–90

Keith Lindley, *Fenland Riots and the English Revolution*, in *AHR*, 88 (1983), 388–9

William Hunt, *The Puritan Moment: The Coming of Revolution in an English County*, in *Albion*, 15 (1983), 353–5

DeLloyd J. Guth and John W. McKenna (eds.), *Tudor Rule and Revolution: Essays for G.R. Elton from his American Friends*, in *Law and History Review*, 2 (1984), 153–6

Richard Weisman, *Witchcraft, Magic and Religion in Seventeenth-Century Massachusetts*, in *Law and History Review*, 3 (1985), 209–11

Ronald Hutton, *The Restoration: A Political and Religious History of England and Wales, 1658–1667*, in *Albion*, 18 (1986), 282–4

G. E. Aylmer, *Rebellion or Revolution? England, 1640–1660*, in *AHR*, 92 (1987), 656–7

Barry Reay (ed.), *Popular Culture in Seventeenth-Century England*, and David Underdown, *Revel, Riot and Rebellion: Popular Politics and Culture in England 1603–1660*, in *Social History*, 12 (1987), 243–7

Stephen Foster, *The Long Argument: English Puritanism and the Shaping of New England Culture, 1570–1700*, in *EHR*, 107 (1992), 964–6

Jerome Friedman, *Miracles and the Pulp Press during the English Revolution*, in *Social History*, 19 (1994), 427

Victor L. Stater, *Noble Government: The Stuart Lord Lieutenancy and the Transformation of English Politics*, in *Albion*, 28 (1996), 99–101

Mark Kishlansky, *A Monarchy Transformed. Britain, 1603–1714*, in *EHR*, 113 (1998), 119–21

Anne Duffin, *Faction and Faith. Politics and Religion of the Cornish Gentry before the Civil War*; John Gwynfor Jones, *Law, Order and Government in Caernarfonshire, 1558–1640. Justices of the Peace and the Gentry*, in *EHR*, 113 (1998), 177–9

Mary Wolffe, *Gentry Leaders in Peace and War. The Gentry Governors of Devon in the Early Seventeenth Century*, in *EHR*, 114 (1999), 979–80

(with Anna Bayman) Marion Gibson, *Reading Witchcraft: Stories of Early English Witches*, online in H-Albion (February 2000)

James Sharpe, *The Bewitching of Anne Gunter. A Horrible and True Story of Football, Witchcraft, Murder and the King of England*, in *Times Literary Supplement*, 5078 (28 July 2000), 23

Jonathan Scott, *England's Troubles. Seventeenth-Century English Political Instability in European Context*, in *JEH*, 53 (2002), 175–8

Brian Manning, *Contemporary Histories of the English Civil War*, in *EHR*, 117 (2002), 1342–3

Frederick Valletta, *Witchcraft, Magic and Superstition in England, 1640–70*, in *EHR*, 117 (2002), 183–4

J.H. Baker, *The Law's Two Bodies: Some Evidential Problems in English Legal History*, in *EHR*, 118 (2003), 206–7

Trevor Cooper (ed.), *The Journal of William Dowsing: Iconoclasm in East Anglia during the English Civil War*, in *EHR*, 118 (2003), 222–3

Robert Poole (ed.), *The Lancashire Witches: Histories and Stories*, in *Social History*, 30 (2005), 128–9

Malcolm Gaskill, *Witchfinders: A Seventeenth-Century English Tragedy*, in *Times Literary Supplement*, 5341 (12 August 2005), 24

Antony Whitaker, *The Regicide's Widow: Lady Alice Lisle and the Bloody Assize*, in *Times Literary Supplement*, 5420 (16 February 2007), 12

Dennis R. Klinck, *Conscience, Equity and the Court of Chancery in Early Modern England,*, in *EHR*, 127 (2012), 997–8

Philip C. Almond, *England's First Demonologist: Reginald Scot and 'The Discovery of Witchcraft'*, in *EHR*, 128 (2013), 952–3

Charles W.A. Prior, *A Confusion of Tongues: Britain's Wars of Reformation, 1625–1642*, in *EHR*, 128 (2013), 1572–4

Richard Cust, *Charles I and the Aristocracy, 1625–1642*, in *EHR*, 129 (2014), 455–7

David Cressy, *Charles I and the People of England*, in *EHR*, 131 (2016), 449–50
Nigel Ramsay (ed.), *Heralds and Heraldry in Shakespeare's England*, in *EHR*, 131 (2016), 660–1
Michael J. Braddick (ed.), *The Oxford Handbook of the English Revolution*, in *EHR*, 131 (2016), 670–2

Other works

Foreword to C.V. Wedgwood, *A King Condemned: The Trial and Execution of Charles I* (2011)
(Exhibition Review) 'The Lost Prince: The Life & Death of Henry Stuart', in *Renaissance Studies*, 28 (2014), 469–74

Compiled by George Southcombe and Grant Tapsell

Index

Abbot, George 80
Act of Indemnity and Oblivion 235, 236, 245
Adams, Hannah 244, 246; *Summary History of New-England, from the First Settlement at Plymouth* 244
Adams, John 243, 244
Adams, Samuel 243
Adams, Thomas 149–50, 160, 161; *Commentary upon . . . the Divine Second Epistle [of] St. Peter* 149
Adamson, John (historian) 32
Admiralty Committee 45
Admiralty Court 98
Advertisement to the Jury-Men of England Touching Witches, An see Filmer, Robert
Ady, Thomas 164, 165–73, 174; *A Candle in the Dark* 164, 165–73, 174
Agincourt, Battle of 201
Agreement of the People 63–4, 68–9, 70
Aleppo 100
Algarkirk (Lincs) 17
Algiers 96, 99
Alicante 92, 94, 95, 96, 97, 98, 99, 100, 104
Allestree, Richard 189
America 155, 166, 227; colonies and colonists 236–48; revolutionaries and the Revolutionary War 235, 237, 242–3, 246–8
American Universal Geography see Morse, Jedidiah
Amicable Grant (1524–5) 20
Amsterdam 82, 149
Andover 158
Anglo-Scottish Treaty (1641) 35
Appeal to the Degenerate Representative, An see Overton, Richard
apprentices 179, 183

army: Essex's 32, 35–6, 37–9, 41–3, 52; expeditionary 10, 12; New Model Army 32, 43, 44, 46, 47–8, 52, 55–64, 66–7, 69, 70, 85, 106, 107, 108, 114, 117, 119, 121, 122, 130, 135, 139, 177, 190, 193
Armyne, Sir William 44
An Arrow against all Tyrants see Overton, Richard
Ascham, Anthony 98
Ashdown lodge 114
Ashhurst, William 47, 48
Ashmole, Elias 220, 222–3
Aske, Robert 143
atheism and atheists 146–60; attitudes in the 1640s 149–50; critique of orthodox positions on 154–7; and orthodoxy 157–60; pre-Civil War understandings 147–9; and religious radicalism 151–3
Atheismus Vapulana see Towers, William
Atheomastix see Fotherby, Martin
Atkins, Edward 131, 143
Aubrey, John 209

Bacon, Francis 73, 76, 151
Bacon, Thomas 192
Bailyn, Bernard (historian) 247
Baker, George 100
Baker, Phil (historian) 65
Bampfield, Thomas 184, 190
Bancroft, Richard 76, 79; *Rules to be observed in the Translation of the Bible* 79
Barbados 93, 96, 98, 135
Barbierato, Federico (historian) 151
Barcelona 99
Barkstead, John 114
Barnes, Thomas (historian) 10, 14
Barnstaple 94
Barwick, John 189

256　Index

Bassett, William 20
Bayntun, Edward 47
Bedfordshire 19, 20, 181, 197
Belasyse, Thomas *see* Fauconberg, Lord
Benson, Henry 189
Berkshire 15, 107, 110, 111, 115, 116, 121, 185, 190, 220
Bible: translation project (1611) 79
Biddenden (Kent) 17
Bidd the Ferret 163
Bishop, George 106, 107–8, 109–10, 111–13, 115, 116, 119, 120–1
Bishoppe, Francis 95
Bishop's Tawton (Devon) 15
Blagge, Thomas 213
Blake, Robert 212
Blethin, John 227
Bloody Project, The see Walwyn, William
Blount, Sir Henry 193
Bludworth, Thomas 98
Book of Common Prayer 246
Book of Orders (1631) 9, 10, 13–18, 23
Booth's rising (1659) 178, 182, 186, 189, 190
Boscawen, Hugh 186
Boston (Lincs) 223
Boston (Mass.) and Bostonians 235, 237, 238, 239, 242, 243, 245
Boston Gazette and Country Journal 242
Boston Sons of Liberty 248
Boteler, William 22
Boucher, Jonathan 247
Bower, Richard 12
Bowles, Edward 190
Boys, John (MP) 47
Boys, John (royalist) 188
Brackley (Northants) 189
Bradshaw, Lord President John 109, 115, 116, 121, 201, 212
Bramhall, John 58, 60
Branston (Leics) 15
Braudel, Fernand (historian) 94
Breda 108, 111, 120, 121
Brenner, Robert (historian) 92
Bridport (Dorset) 93
Bristol 107, 120, 179, 181, 183; All Saints parish 17
Brooke, Lord (Robert Greville) 38
Browne, Robert (herald) 224, 229
Browne, Robert (sectarian) 148
Browne, Samuel 44, 52
Broxholme, John 208
Buchanan, David 45
Buckingham, Duke of (George Villiers) 186

Buckinghamshire 19, 180, 184, 185, 193, 200
Buckley, George (historian) 152
Buckley, Michael (historian) 146
Bulkeley, Gershom 246–7
Bunce, James 114, 122
Burdett, Robert 96, 97, 98, 99–100, 103, 104
Burke, Aedanus 235, 236, 248
Burroughs, George 172
Burton Latimer (Northants) 12, 17
Bury St Edmunds 171, 183
Bysshe, Edward 218, 219, 220, 221, 223, 224, 227–8, 231
Bysshe, Henry 223

Cadiz 10
Calvert, Giles 165
Cambridge (Mass.) 237, 243
Cambridgeshire 14, 180
Camden, William: monument 209
Campe, Nicholas 242
Candle in the Dark, A see Ady, Thomas
Canterbury 180, 183; Canterbury Cathedral 188
Cardiff 180, 183
Carleton, Dudley *see* Dorchester, Viscount
Carpenter, John 151
Carr, Robert 245–6, 248
Cartagena 100
Carter, D.P. (historian) 10
Cartwright, George 245–6, 248
Cary, Henry *see* Falkland, Lord
Case of the Army Truly Stated, The 60–1, 61–2, 63
Catholicism and Catholics 34, 147, 149, 152, 155; 'Papisme' 140, 148
Cavaliers *see* royalists
Cavendish, William *see* Newcastle, Marquess of
Caversham Park and Lodge 118
Cawdrey, Robert: *A Table Alphabeticall* (1604) 79
Cecil, Robert *see* Salisbury, 1st Earl of
Cecil, William *see* Salisbury, 2nd Earl of
Chaloner, James 116
Chaloner, Thomas 47, 116
Chapin, John 239
Chard 135
Charles I 9, 18, 23, 24, 32, 33, 35, 37–9, 40, 41–2, 43, 44, 45, 46, 47, 48, 49, 58, 61–3, 65, 66–9, 70, 74, 77, 78, 80, 81, 82, 142, 156, 170–1, 177, 193, 211, 213, 215, 221, 224, 227, 228, 247, 248; *Eikon Basilike* 74; engagement with the Scots (1648) 66;

execution 56, 66, 96, 152, 201, 218, 236, 241; negotiations with the Army (1647) 61–3; personal rule 9–10, 35; trial 127, 205, 209, 235
Charles II 128, 131, 132, 177, 184, 188, 201, 204, 205, 212, 213, 218, 219, 221, 223, 224, 227, 228, 229, 230, 235, 236, 237, 239, 241–2, 244–6, 248; coronation 220; in exile 108, 120, 223; as King of Scots 119, 225; as Prince of Wales 47; proclamation as king 223, 229
Charlton Marshall (Dorset) 11, 24
Chauncey, Charles 236
Cheesman, Christopher 111
Chelmsford 171
Cheshire 10, 15, 22, 180, 181, 196
Chester 182
Chichester, Richard 94
Cholmley, Sir Henry 41
Chulmleigh (Devon) 15
Church of England 81–2, 84, 149, 155, 160, 169; in America 245, 248; 'Anglican resonances' 193; post-Reformation 190; see also Westminster Assembly
Clarendon, Earl of (Edward Hyde) 34, 36, 38, 69, 85, 219, 221
Clarges, Thomas 114
Clarke, Francis 95, 98
Clarkson, Lawrence 153
Claypole, Elizabeth 205
Cleveland, John 78
Clifford, Lord (Thomas Clifford) 49, 188
Clotworthy, Sir John 42, 52
Cogan, Sir Andrew 95, 96, 100, 103
Cogan, John 103
Cogan, Richard 95, 103
Coke, Sir John 87
College of Arms 218–30; internal divisions 221, 224, 227–9; see also heralds; London: Derby House
Combe Abbey 112, 116, 118
commemoration 203–4, 211, 212, 215, 235, 236–7, 248
Commentary upon . . . the Divine Second Epistle [of] St. Peter see Adams, Thomas
commission to America (1664) 237, 245–6, 248
Committee for Advance of Money 45
Committee for Compounding 109, 115; Commissioners for Compounding 109, 110
Committee for Examinations 115, 121
Committee for Irish Affairs 45
Committee for Plundered Ministers 44
Committee for the Army 45, 49

Committee for the Revenue 45–6
Committee of Both Kingdoms 42, 43, 45, 49
Committee of Safety 35–8, 40, 45, 49, 178
Committee of the West 44
Commonwealth 77, 92, 96, 98, 100, 106, 108–9, 110, 111, 112, 113, 116, 118, 120–2, 129, 130, 134, 208, 218, 223, 225; declaration of 69
Complete History of Connecticut see Trumball, Benjamin
confiscations *see* expropriations
Congdon, Gregory 11
Congregationalism 44
Coningsby, sheriff of Hertfordshire 19
Connecticut Colony 239, 240
Cony, George 130
Cook, John 58, 60, 65; *Redintegratio Amoris* 58–9
Cooke, Edward 190
Cooper, Thomas 169; *The Mystery of Witch-Craft* 169
Cope, Sir Anthony 189, 190
Cope, Esther (historian) 19
Cope, William 189
Corderoy, Jeremy 159
Cornwall 15, 184, 185, 186, 190; West Hundred 15
Council of State 98, 107–8, 109–10, 115, 116, 121, 191, 209; Protectorate Council 69, 129, 130–2, 137, 138, 171
Court of Chivalry 221
Covenanters 13, 33, 35, 36, 39, 42; Engagers 48
Cowell, Dr John 76, 87; *The Interpreter* (1607) 76
Cowley, Abraham 78
Coxe, Alban 193
Crampton, Dennis 240
Cratfield (Suffolk) 11
Craven, Anthony 116, 119–20, 121
Craven, John 107
Craven, Lord (William Craven) 106–22
Craven, Sir William 110, 112, 116
Craven, William 107
Craven Case *see* Craven, Lord
Crediton 12
Cremer, Charles 137
Crewe, John 189, 190
Crewe, Thomas 189
Croft (Lincs) 11, 15, 17
Cromartie, Alan (historian) 128
Cromwell, Oliver 36, 43, 44, 46, 47, 48, 62–3, 70, 107, 112, 113, 115, 117, 118, 164, 172, 174, 190, 191, 193, 201–2,

258 Index

204, 205, 211, 212, 213, 218, 219, 227, 228, 229, 235, 248; *Custodes Libertates Angliae* 140; and the kingship 85–6, 127–8, 139–42, 143, 193; Protector 69, 74, 129–32, 134–5, 137, 138–9, 143, 172, 211, 225–6
Cromwell, Richard 182, 190, 218, 219, 223
Crowne, William 224, 227
Cullamore, William 94
Cullamore or Collamore, Henry 94, 103
Curtis, Thomas 111
Cushing, Thomas 243

Dacres, Sir Thomas 54
Daemonologie see James VI and I
Danby, Earl of (Henry Danvers) 49
Danvers, Henry *see* Danby, Earl of
Darnell, Ralph 118
Dart, John 203, 213
Dartington (Devon) 11, 12, 17
Dartmouth 93, 94
Davenport, John 237, 238, 240, 241
Deane, Richard 209, 212
De Corpore see Hobbes, Thomas
Delves, Sir Thomas 22
Derby, earls of (Stanley family) 224
Derbyshire 15, 19, 179, 180, 181, 190
Dethick, Henry 220
Devereux, Robert *see* Essex, Earl of
Devilish Conspiracy, The see Warner, John
Devon 15, 19, 20, 131, 183, 184, 185, 186, 188, 190; Coleridge hundred 14; Ermington hundred 14; Lifton hundred 14; Plympton hundred 14; Roborough hundred 14; Stanborough hundred 14; Tavistock h14
D'Ewes, Sir Simonds 32, 35, 36, 38, 40, 42, 52
Dewning, Richard 11
Dickens, A.G. (historian) 2–3
Dickinson, John 247
dictionaries 76; satirical 79; *see also* Warner, John
Dictionarum Saxonico-Latino-Anglicum see Somner, William
Discourse and Defence of Arms and Armory see Waterhouse, Edward
Discoverie of Witchcraft, The see Scot, Reginald
Dispute betwixt a Christian and an Atheist, A (1646) 154–7, 160
Dixon, Henry 158–9
Dixwell, John 235, 236, 237, 242, 243

Doncaster 136
Dorchester, Viscount (Dudley Carleton): monument 205, 206
Dorset 15, 20, 93, 95, 131, 179
Dove, John 154
Dover 180
Dowsing, William 202
Drake, Francis (MP) 54
Droitwich 63
Drury, Colonel 111–12
Dry Drayton (Cambs) 147, 150
Dublin 196
Dugdale, William 219–20, 221
Dunbar, battle of 107
Durham 180

East Anglia 94, 147, 164; Fens 73
East Budleigh (Devon) 12
Eastern Association 39, 43; Committee of the Eastern Association 44
East Harling (Norfolk) 12, 17
East India Company 93, 95
Edgehill, battle of 36, 37, 38, 39
Edinburgh parliament 225
Edward VI: monument 208, 215
Edwards, Thomas 147, 150, 151, 152, 156, 160; *Gangraena* 150
Egerton, Thomas *see* Ellesmere, Lord
Egloskerry (Cornwall) 11
Eikon Basilike see Charles I
Elford, Walter 95, 98
Elizabeth I 212
Elizabeth (Stuart) of Bohemia 107, 108, 114, 121
Ellesmere, Lord (Thomas Egerton) 159
Ellis, Humphrey 157, 159–60; *Pseudochristus* 157
Ellis, William 136
Ellsworth, Richard 181–2
Ellys, William 44
Enborne, East and West 112, 114, 118
Endecott, John 236, 238–9, 241, 242, 243
Engagers *see* Covenanters
Erle, Sir Walter 54
Essex 10, 14, 15, 20, 22, 180, 191, 192, 193; Hinckford hundred 15
Essex, Earl of (Robert Devereux) 32, 33, 35, 38, 39–40, 41–3, 44, 47, 52, 202, 205, 219, 229
Evelyn, John (diarist) 211, 212
Evelyn, Sir John, of Surrey (MP) 54
Evelyn, Sir John, of Wiltshire (MP) 38–9, 42, 47, 52, 53

Evesham, battle of 229
Excellencie of a Free State, The see Nedham, Marchamont
Exeter 12, 94, 95, 132, 133, 134, 135, 181, 183, 184
expropriations 106, 108–12, 113–15, 116, 117, 118–19, 121

Fairfax, Sir Thomas (Lord General) 48, 58, 110, 116, 179, 180, 181, 185–6, 190, 224
Faithful Scout, The 119
Falkland, Lord (Henry Cary) 189
Farmer, Ralph 120, 121
Farr, David (historian) 56
Fauconberg, Lord (Thomas Belasyse) 190
Faulconer, Richard 108, 109–10, 111–12, 118, 119–20
Faunt or Fawnt, George 193–4
Felton, Sir Henry 192
Fiennes, James 189
Fiennes, Nathaniel 47, 52, 53, 138
Fiennes, William *see* Saye and Sele, Viscount
Fillongley (Warks) 11
Filmer, Robert 164, 165; *An Advertisement to the Jury-Men of England Touching Witches* 164
Finch, Heneage (later Earl of Nottingham) 113, 116, 121
Finch, Jonathan (historian) 203
Fincher, Richard 190
Finley, Sir Moses 4
First Continental Congress (1774) 243
Fletcher, Anthony (historian) 10
Forced Loan (1626–8) 20
Forest of Dean 107
Fotherby, Martin 151, 154, 159; *Atheomastix* (1622) 159
Foxley, Rachel (historian) 60, 65
France and the French 33, 99, 100, 104; 'Frenchified tongue' 156
Franklin, Benjamin 235, 248
Franklin, William 157–9
Frederick, John 101, 105
Free Parliament 176–94; county declarations 178–81, 195, 196, 197, 200; supporters 184–94; urban declarations 181–4, 195
Freke, John 31
Frost, Gualter 108
Fuller, Thomas 150, 151, 196; *Holy State and Profane State* (1642) 150
funerals 202, 204, 207–8, 211, 219, 222, 225, 226, 229

Gadbury, Mary 158
Gangraena see Edwards, Thomas
Garden of Spiritual Flowers, A (1609) 149
Gardiner, Ralph 172; *Englands Grievance Discovered in Relation to the Coal-Trade* (1655) 172
Gardiner, S.R. 39, 40
Garland, Augustine 109, 111, 118
Garland, Edward 152
Gaule, John 165, 169–70
Gell, Sir John 191
Geneva 82
Genoa 95
Gerard, Sir Gilbert 48, 51, 52
Gerbier, Balthazar 114
Germany 110, 111, 119
Gifford, George 169, 170, 175
Gilbert, Matthew 241
Gislingham (Suffolk) 11
Gloucester 181, 183, 227
Gloucestershire 20, 22, 179, 181, 182, 184, 185, 190; Kiftsgate hundred 22
Glynne, John (Lord Chief Justice) 52, 131–5, 139–42
Goddard, Guybon 129–30
Goffe, William 235–46, 248
Goodwin, Arthur 41
Gouland, Richard: epitaph 209, 210
Grantham 136
'Grave Counsels and Godly Observations' *see* Greenham, Richard
Greene, Nathanael 235
Greenham, Richard 146–50, 151, 156, 160; 'Grave Counsels and Godly Observations' 147–8
Greville, Robert *see* Brooke, Lord
Grey, Lord, of Groby (Thomas Grey) 47, 53, 116, 118
Grierson, Philip 4
Guilford (Conn.) 240–1
Gurdon, John 37, 44

Hadley (Mass.) 236, 244
Hague, The 107
Hagworthingham (Lincs) 15
Halberton (Devon) 11
Hale, Matthew 128, 130
Halford, Richard 193
Hall, Edward 99
Hamilton, Alexander 235
Hamilton, Duke of (James Hamilton) 48
Hampden, John 34–5, 38, 40, 51
Hampden's case 18, 19, 22

Hampshire 10, 14, 15, 20, 108, 158, 180
Hamstead Marshall (Berks) 107, 112, 114
Harrison, Thomas 244
Hartford (Conn.) 236, 239–40, 242, 243
Harvard University 236
Haskell, Patricia (historian) 10
Heads of Proposals 46, 66
Heal, Felicity (historian) 3, 203
Heath, James 128
Heavitree (Devon) 12
Henrietta Maria 107
Henry VIII 215
heralds 209, 211, 212; animosity towards 221, 229; under Parliament 219, 225, 227, 228, 229; at the Restoration 220–3; satire upon 222–8; *see also* College of Arms
Herbert, Philip *see* Pembroke, Earl of
Hereford 180
Herefordshire 20, 180, 228
Heresiography see Pagitt, Ephraim
Hertfordshire 14, 15, 185, 193
Hesilrige, Sir Arthur 46, 47, 48, 52, 114, 116, 194
Hexter, J.H. (historian) 39–40
Heywood, Colin (historian) 94
High Bray (Devon) 11, 12
High Courts of Justice 138; High Court of Justice (1649) 78, 81; High Court of Justice (1654) 131, 134, 144; High Court of Justice (1658) 139
Highland, Samuel 114
Hill, Christopher (historian) 3, 151
History of the Colony of Massachusetts-Bay see Hutchinson, Thomas
History of the Peloponnesian War see Thucydides
History of Three of the Judges of Charles I see Stiles, Ezra
Hoad Court (Kent) 188
Hobart, Sir John 191
Hobbes, Thomas 74, 77, 84; *De Corpore* 77; translation of Thucydides 84
Holdenby 108
Holland *see* Netherlands, the
Holland, Earl of (Henry Rich) 35, 38, 41, 52
Holland, Sir John 73
Holles, Denzell 37, 38–9, 41, 46, 47, 48, 52
Holmes, Clive 1–7, 32, 55, 73–4, 86, 92, 102, 127, 163–4, 203, 218, 237; *The Eastern Association in the English Civil War* 2, 32; *Seventeenth-Century Lincolnshire* 2; *Why was Charles I Executed?* 1–2, 9

Holmes, William 158–9
Holy Roman Empire 82
Holy State and Profane State see Fuller, Thomas
Hooke, William 238
Hopkins, Matthew 164, 165, 170, 171
Horham (Suffolk) 11
Horton, George 119
Hotham, Sir John 186
Houghton (Hants?) 158
Houncell, Andrew 93, 103
Houncell, Richard 92–101, 103, 104
Houncell, William 94, 99, 100, 101, 103, 104, 105
Humble Desires of . . . the County and Burrough of Leicester, The 193
Humble Petition and Advice 141
Hungerford, Edward 189
Huntingdonshire 180
Hutchinson, Thomas: *History of the Colony of Massachusetts-Bay* (1764) 242
Hutton, Robert 136
Hyde, Edward *see* Clarendon, Earl of

Ibbitson, Robert 171–2
Ilminster (Somerset) 17
Independents 33–4, 42–9, 52, 150, 151, 152, 155
Ingoldsby, Sir Richard 117
Ingram, Sir Thomas: monument 213
Instrument of Government 129–30, 135, 137, 141, 143
Interpreter, The see Cowell, Dr John
Ipswich 183, 192
Irby, Sir Anthony 47
Ireland and the Irish 33, 41, 42, 44, 69, 107, 211
Ireton, Henry 47, 55–70, 107, 201, 202, 204, 209, 211, 212, 225
Islam 156; 'Mahumetans' 155
Isle of Man 224
Isle of Rhé 10
Isle of Thanet 180
Italy 95

Jackson, Thomas 151
James VI and I 66, 76, 169, 204, 223; *Daemonologie* 169
James VII and II, as Duke of York 119
Japan 155
Jefferson, Thomas 235
Jephson, William 85–6
Jones, Henry 189

Jones, William 237, 239, 240, 241
Joyce, George 108–9, 112, 113, 114, 115, 118, 119, 120–1
judges 128–43
Julius Caesar see Shakespeare, William
Justices of the Peace 10, 13–18, 20, 23

Keepe, Henry 203, 212
Kellond, Thomas 239–44, 248
Kent 16, 20, 164, 165, 182, 185, 188–9, 192, 198
King's Lynn 191
Kirke, Thomas 239–44, 248
Kishlansky, Mark (historian) 56
Knox, Henry 235
Kyneton, Henry 17

Lancashire 10, 180
Latham, Sir Thomas 20
Laud, William 80; Laudian tyranny 59
Launceston 11
law courts 131–2; Court of Chancery 112, 130; Court of Common Pleas 133; Court of Exchequer 128, 131, 136, 137, 138; Court of Upper Bench 136, 139
Lawrence, Henry (Lord President) 113
Lee, John 78
Leete, William 240, 241, 242, 243, 244
Legg, Robert 229
Leicester 183, 193, 194
Leicestershire 14, 179, 182, 184, 185, 188, 193, 194
Le Neve, Sir William 227
Lenthall, Sir John 112
Lenthall, William 141–2
L'Estrange, Roger 80, 183, 187, 192
Levant, the 93
Levant Company 95, 98, 100, 105
Levellers 56, 60, 61, 65, 68, 76
Lewannick 11
Lewes, John 95
Lewis, Sir William 52
Licensing Act (1649) 171
Lightfoot, John 115
Lilburne, Robert 135–6, 145
Lincoln 208
Lincolnshire 10, 15, 179, 180, 182, 185, 190, 192
linguistic instability 75–7
Lisle, John 128, 131, 133, 138, 139, 141, 143, 144
Littleton, Sir Edward 19, 20
Livorno 93, 100

Llewellyn, Nigel (historian) 203
Locke, John 247
London and the City of London 32, 35, 37, 39, 41, 42, 43, 45, 47, 61, 77, 93, 95, 97, 98, 101, 111, 114, 115, 118, 119, 136, 178, 179, 181, 182, 183, 184, 186, 189, 192, 193, 196, 205, 209, 223, 225, 239, 240, 245; Derby House 45, 48, 222, 224, 228 (*see also* College of Arms); Gray's Inn 137; Great Fire 222; Guildhall 111; Haberdashers' Hall 110, 224; Inns of Court 64, 73; Lord Mayor's Court 111; St Paul's Cathedral 77, 211; Somerset House 212; Strand 112, 118; Tower 130, 143, 178, 223; Upper Bench prison 112; Whitehall 110
Long Buckby (Northants) 20
Longland, Charles 100
Long Melford (Suffolk) 18
Love, Christopher 120
Lovering, John 94
Low Countries 82; *see also* Netherlands, the
Loxley, James (historian) 85
Lucan 209, 211
Lydiard Tregoze 202
Lyme Regis 93, 179

Machiavelli 156
Madrid 98
Mahoney, Michael (historian) 32
Malaga 99
Mallorca 96
Manchester, Earl of (Edward Montagu) 38, 42, 43, 47, 48, 52, 189, 223
Marlborough (Wilts) 115
Marston Moor 135–6
Marston Moor, battle of 235
Marston Trussell (Northants) 11, 12, 15
Marten, Henry 39–40, 47, 53, 62, 69, 107, 111, 116, 117
Martin Marprelate tracts 77
Mary, Princess Royal and Princess of Orange 108
Mary, Queen of Scots 212
Masham, Sir William 44
Massachusetts Bay Colony 238, 243, 245, 246
Massie, Edward 48
Master or Masters, Sir Edward 189
Mather, Cotton 172
Mauleverer, Sir Thomas 205
Maverick, Samuel 245–6, 248
May, Thomas 204, 209–11

Maynard, John 38, 113, 116, 117, 119, 121
Mayne, Jasper 75, 85
McConville, Brendan (historian) 248
Meigs, John 240–1
Melcombe Regis 95
Melksham (Wilts) 17
Melton 12
Memoirs of Edmund Ludlow (1698) 211
Mendlesham (Suffolk) 11
merchants 92–101
Merchant Taylors Company 107
Mercurius Britanicus 77
Metamorphoses see Ovid
Mico, Samuel 95, 101
Middle Claydon: Verney tomb 202
Middlesex 180
Mildmay, Sir Henry 116
Milford, Conn. 236, 238, 239, 240, 242, 244
militia 10–13; Perfect Militia 9, 10–13, 23
Militia Ordinance (1642) 58
Millington, Gilbert 44
Milton, John 74, 76, 247
Monck, George 114, 176, 178, 180, 182, 183, 185, 189–94, 195
Monckton, Sir Philip 186, 198
Monmouthshire 180
Montagu, Edward *see* Manchester, Earl of
Montgomery, Richard 235
monuments 201–13
Moore, John 44
Mordaunt, John (1600–1643) *see* Peterborough, Earl of
Mordaunt, Viscount (John Mordaunt) (1626–75) 189, 191
Morgan, Turbeville 227, 228
Morrill, John (historian) 10
Morse, Jedidiah: *American Universal Geography* (1796) 243
Mortimer, Sarah (historian) 152
Mosse, Miles 148–9, 150
Mostyn Hall, Flintshire 205
Mostyn Manuscript 205–6, 207–8
Moyer, Samuel 110
MPs 32–49, 57, 59, 60, 62, 67–8, 76, 81, 113–14, 117–19, 121–2, 127, 130, 139, 141, 177, 185, 212, 218; and the kingship 139, 141; secluded 177–8, 179, 183, 184, 185–8, 189, 190, 191, 192
Mystery of Witch-Craft, The see Cooper, Thomas

Naples 94, 95
Napoleon III, son of 201
Napper, James 94
Naseby, battle of 46, 77, 107, 235

Nedham, Marchamont 128, 209, 195; *The Excellencie of a Free State* (1656) 128
Nero 150, 211
Nether Whitacre (Warks) 11
Netherlands, the, and the Dutch 94, 113, 114, 119, 115, 225; Dutch army 110, 119; Dutch fleet 119; Holland 99; States General 116, 119; *see also* New Netherland
Newcastle, Marquess of (William Cavendish) 220–1
Newcastle Propositions 33
Newcastle upon Tyne 172
Newdigate, Richard 128, 136, 137, 140, 145
New England 82, 93, 100, 235–48
Newfoundland 94
New Haven Colony 236, 237–44
Newman, Francis 240
New Model Army *see* army
New Netherland 237, 238, 239, 242, 245, 246
New York 245
Nicholas, Robert 131, 143, 144
Nicholas, Sir Edward 221, 238, 239
Nichols, Richard 245, 246, 248
Norbrook, David (historian) 212
Norfolk 10, 14, 16, 109, 179, 181, 182, 183, 185, 191, 196
Norris or Norwich, Sir John 189, 190
Northamptonshire 14, 19, 20, 179, 180, 184, 185, 189, 190, 193, 194
Northcote, Sir John 190
Northumberland, Earl of (Algernon Percy) 35, 37–8, 41–2, 47, 52
Norwich 183, 191
Nottingham, Earl of *see* Finch, Heneage
Nottinghamshire 19, 180, 182, 193; Bassetlaw hundred 16; North and South Clay hundred 15–16
Nye, Philip 77

Order of the Garter 220
Ostend 108
Overton, Richard 59–61; *An Appeal to the Degenerate Representative* 60–1; *An Arrow against all Tyrants* 59–60
Ovid 90; *Metamorphoses* 83
Owen, George 220, 221, 224, 227–9
Oxenstierna, Axel 129
Oxford 41, 42, 75, 224, 229; Bodleian Library 172, 218, 222
Oxford Parliament 75
Oxfordshire 15, 20, 22, 179, 180, 185, 189, 193; Bloxham hundred 22

Pagitt, Ephraim: *Heresiography* (1645) 152
Painter, William 21
Painter-Stainers Company 221, 222
Palgrave, Sir John 191
Parker, Calthorp 104
Parker, Henry 58, 60; Parkerian position 61
Parker, Philip 192
Parliament 9, 55–7, 77–80, 82–5, 88, 127, 129, 130, 140–1, 177, 178, 185, 193, 201–2, 208, 215, 218, 219, 220, 221; in 1610 73, 76; Barebone's Parliament 113, 118; Cavalier Parliament 189; Convention Parliament 176, 191, 223; House of Lords 37, 38, 40, 41, 47, 48, 63, 66, 76, 80, 83, 142, 191, 193, 218, 223; Long Parliament 9, 32–49, 56–69, 80; 'Other House' 191, 213; Protectorate Parliaments 74, 113, 114, 117, 129, 130, 132, 138, 140, 141, 145, 164, 191, 193; Restored Long Parliament 176, 177; Rump Parliament 76, 96, 98, 99, 106, 109–11, 114, 116–17, 119–21, 128, 129, 164, 176–4, 186, 189, 191–2, 194, 210, 225; *see also* Free Parliament; parliamentary parties; Pride's Purge
parliamentary parties 33–49, 50; Junto 34–8; 'middle group' 39; peace party 38–42; war party 38–42; *see also* Independents; Presbyterians
Parr, Thomas 205
Parry, Edward (historian) 203
Partney (Lincs) 15
Pattingham (Staffs) 11
Payne, Robert Treat 243
Peerson, Edward 11
Pembroke, 4th Earl of (Philip Herbert) 35, 38, 41, 42, 47
Pembroke, 5th Earl of (Philip Herbert) 116
Penington, Isaac (Lord Mayor) 35, 44
Penn, William (?) (Captain) 99
Penruddock, John 133, 135
Penruddock's Rising 131–5
Percy, Algernon *see* Northumberland, Earl of
Perfect Militia *see* militia
Perfect Occurrences 171
Perkett, Robert 100
Perkins, William 147, 148, 169
Peterborough, Earl of (John Mordaunt) 21
Peters, Hugh 118, 212
Philadelphia 243
Physick, John (historian) 202
Pickering, James 115
Pickering, Sir Gilbert 116, 117
Pierrepont, William 37–9, 42, 47, 52

Plumb, Sir Jack 4
Plymouth 99
Poem, Commemorative of Goffe, Whaley, & Dixwell see Stiles, Ezra
Pompey 212
Poor Laws 13
poor relief 15–16, 27
Popham, Anne 213
Popham, Edward 202; monument 209, 212–13, 214
Portsmouth (NH) 245
Prentice, Joan 163
Presbyterians: 1640s 33, 34, 42–8, 52, 54, 119, 122, 150, 152, 155; 1659–60 177, 178, 183–7, 189, 190, 194
Prideaux, Edmund 44, 47, 49, 52, 132–4, 144
Pride's Purge 32, 47, 49, 69, 118, 177, 183, 188
Protectorate 117, 127, 129, 130, 137, 139–42, 164, 186, 190, 219, 225–6; *see also* Cromwell, Oliver
Protestantism and Protestants 82, 146, 147, 148; critiques of 155, 156; orthodox (1640s) 149–150, 151; popular 151; problems of definition 152, 153, 154–5
Prynne, William 183
Pseudochristus see Ellis, Humphrey
Purefoy, William 44
puritans 77, 152, 160; in Massachusetts 245, 246
Putney debates 56, 66, 68, 63, 107, 235
Putney Projects see Wildman, John
Pye, Robert (the younger) 190
Pye, Sir Robert 190
Pym, John 34–40, 73

Quintrell, Brian (historian) 10

Rainborowe, Thomas 47, 62–3, 64, 65, 68
Raleigh, Carew 114
Rawson, Edward 243
Read, a lawyer 119
Reading (Berks) 111
Redintegratio Amoris see Cook, John
regicides: 1664 237, 245–6; disinterment 201, 204; efforts to capture (1661) 235–42; remembered during American Revolutionary War 235–7, 242–3, 247–8
Restoration 86, 101, 115, 121, 122, 128, 142–3, 176, 204, 213, 215, 218, 219–20, 222, 223, 227, 228, 229–30, 235, 236, 237–40, 245
Reynolds, Robert 42

rhetoric and rhetoricians 73–5; English suspicion of 84
Rich, Henry *see* Holland, Earl of
Rich, Nathaniel(?) (Colonel) 211
Rich, Robert *see* Warwick, Earl of
Richard III see Shakespeare, William
Richardson, Lord (Thomas Richardson, 2nd Baron Cramond) 191
Rider, William 96, 101, 104
Rigby, Alexander 37, 39–40
Robert, Lewes 94
Rochester 180, 183
Roe, Sir Thomas 40
Roger, John 11
Rolle, Henry (Lord Chief Justice) 112, 113, 130, 131, 139, 140, 144
Rossiter, Edward 179, 190
Roundheads 75, 77, 177, 192
Rowe, John 146
royalists 33, 36, 37, 74–8, 99, 108, 114, 117, 119, 139, 150, 178, 183, 186–93, 195; 'Cavaliers' 177, 189; risings (1655) in West Country 131–5; and in Yorkshire 135–7
Rugg, Thomas 184
Rules to be observed in the Translation of the Bible see Bancroft, Richard
Rupert, Prince 119
Rushworth, John 110, 111–12, 116, 121
Russell, Conrad (historian) 3
Russell, sheriff of Cambridgeshire 19
Russell, Sir William 20
Rutland 19, 180
Ryley, William 220, 223, 224, 227, 228, 231

St Albans 192
St George, Richard 228
St John, Oliver 35, 38, 39–40, 43, 47, 52
St John family monument 202
Salem (Mass.) 172
Salisbury 131, 133, 135, 142
Salisbury, 1st Earl of (Robert Cecil) 76
Salisbury, 2nd Earl of (William Cecil) 38, 42
Salwey, Humphrey 44
Sanford, Thomas 242
satire 77–8, 79; *see also* heralds
Sawyer, Sir Edmund 111, 115
Saye and Sele, Viscount (William Fiennes) 34, 35, 38, 52
Scawen, Robert 52
Scot, Grace: memorial 205, 207
Scot, Reginald 165, 167–8, 170, 172; 'A Discourse upon Divels and Spirits' 170; *The Discoverie of Witchcraft* 165

Scot, Thomas 47, 53, 108, 115, 116, 120, 205
Scotland and the Scots 38, 39, 41–2, 43, 44, 45, 66, 78, 79, 81–2, 120, 165, 170–1, 172, 178, 223, 224; Anglo-Scottish Presbyterian alliance (1644) 33, 34; army 25, 42, 45, 46, 47, 66; Highlands 79; Scots Commissioners 34, 53; Scots' Wars 12, 19, 22; *see also* Covenanters
Scott, Jonathan (historian) 212
sectarians 148–53
Selden, John 56
Seneca 150
sequestrations 108–9, 110, 111, 115; *see also* expropriations
Severall Proceedings 171
Sexby, Edward 65, 71
Seymour, Jane 215
Shakespeare, William: *Julius Caesar* 74; *Richard III* 74
Sharpe, Kevin (historian) 204
Shelton (Norfolk) 12
Sherwood, Samuel 248
Ship Money 9, 10, 18–23, 29, 30
Shipston (Devon) 95
Shropshire 19, 20, 118, 180, 181, 196
Sidney, Algernon 247
Sindercombe, Miles 139, 145
Skippon, Philip 107
Slingsby, Sir Henry 186
Smith, Henry 154
Smith, Mr 209
Smyrna 100
Solemn League and Covenant (1643) 41, 42
Somerset 10, 15, 131, 179
Somerset House *see* London
Somner, William 188; *Dictionarum Saxonico-Latino-Anglicum* (1659) 80
South Carolina 235
South Molton (Devon) 15
South Newington (Oxon) 21
Southwark school of masons 204
Spain and the Spanish 93, 94, 95, 98, 99, 155, 156
Sparsholt (Berks) 116
Spilsby (Lincs) 15
Spira, Francis 148
Spottiswoode, Dr John 208
Spradbury, Henry 159
Squibb, Arthur 231
Staffordshire 180, 181, 196
Stanley, A.P. (Dean of Westminster) 201
Stapilton, Sir Philip 38, 40, 41, 47, 48, 51, 52

Stathern (Lincs) 11, 17, 24
statute against witchcraft (1604) 163
Stawell, Sir John 113, 114, 117, 122
Steele, William (Chief Baron of the Exchequer) 133, 137
Stephens, Edward 22
Stiles, Ezra 235, 236–7, 242, 248; *History of Three of the Judges of Charles I* (1794) 242, 244; *Poem, Commemorative of Goffe, Whaley, & Dixwell* 235
Stockton (Salop) 12, 15
Stone, Lawrence (historian) 2, 3
Stone, Nicholas 205
Stony Stratford (Bucks) 181
Strickland, Walter 116, 117, 136–7, 145
Stroud (Glos) 180
Stuyvesant, Peter 239, 242
Suffolk 10, 15, 19, 20, 179, 181, 184, 185, 191, 192
Summary History of New-England, from the First Settlement at Plymouth see Adams, Hannah
Surrey 20, 180
Sussex 14, 179
Swimbridge (Devon) 94
Swynfen, John 47, 48, 54
Symondsbury (Dorset) 93

Table Alphabeticall, A see Cawdrey, Robert
Taft, Barbara (historian) 56
Tapping, James 242
Tate, Zouche 47
Temple, Sir Richard 193
Thaxted (Essex) 17
Thirty Years War 10, 11, 82
Thornhaugh, Francis 20
Thorpe, Francis 128–9, 134, 136, 137, 140, 145
Thucydides: *History of the Peloponnesian War* 84
Thurloe, John 113, 117, 121, 132, 134, 136, 144
Tickell, John 153
Tilsworth (Beds) 22
Tompson, Giles 17
Towers, William 151, 154; *Atheismus Vapulana* (1654) 151
Townshend, Sir Horatio 179, 191
trade: overseas 93–101, 103, 104, 105; of the West Country 93–4, 95
treason 110, 112, 120, 127–8, 130–9, 142, 185; Act for the security of the Lord Protector his Person (1656) 138–9, 145; Statute of 25 Edw. III 131, 132, 133, 134, 135, 137, 138, 139, 148; Treason Act (1649) 110, 130; Treason Ordinance (1654) 130–8
Treaty of Newport 49
Trevor, Sir John 54, 116
Triplet, Thomas 209
Trumball, Benjamin 243; *Complete History of Connecticut* (1797) 243–4
Tuck, Richard (historian) 56
Turks 99, 156, 157
Tyrell or Turrell, Sir Tobias or Toby 193

Underdown, David (historian) 47, 50, 118
universities: Emmanuel College, Cambridge 169; 'Oxbridge' 73, 79; Oxford 223

vagrancy 16–18, 28
Valencia 94, 98
Vane, Sir Henry (the elder) 45, 49, 52, 117
Vane, Sir Henry (the younger) 38, 39–40, 42, 43, 44, 47, 48, 49, 52, 117
Vaux, George 118
Verney family tomb 202
Vernon, John (Captain) 107, 115
Villiers, George *see* Buckingham, Duke of
Virginia 242
Vote of No Addresses (1648) 47, 66
Vowell, Peter 144

Wagner, Sir Anthony (historian) 228
Wales 180, 203
Walker, Clement 46
Waller, Edmund 37, 38
Walker, Sir Edward 218, 220, 221, 222, 224, 227, 229
Waller, Sir William 41, 42, 43, 48, 52
Waltham (Leics) 17
Walwyn, William 33, 76, 155; *The Bloody Project* 76
Ward, Lawrence 242
Warner, John 74, 78–86, 89; *The Devilish Conspiracy* 83–4; 'Parliament dictionary' 74, 75, 77–9, 80, 81–6, 88
Wars of the Roses 224
Warwick, Earl of (Robert Rich) 34, 38, 43, 45, 47, 52
Warwickshire 20, 22, 179
Washington, Henry(?) (Colonel) 229
Waterhouse, Edward: *Discourse and Defence of Arms and Armory* 219
Watson, John 227–9, 234
Wear Gifford (Devon) 94
Welsh Marches 108
Wentworth, Sir Peter 21, 22, 39, 40, 47, 63, 116

266 Index

Westminster 40, 41, 209, 220, 224; cloisters 209; Henry VII Chapel 201, 204, 205, 208, 209, 211, 215, 223; Houses of Parliament 202; monuments in 202, 205, 208–15; Palace of 34; Poets' Corner 209; St Benedict's Chapel 208, 209; St Margaret's 201, 202; in sense of 'Parliament' 32–48, 58, 177, 184; in sense of 'regime' 10, 20, 23; Westminster Abbey 201–15
Westminster Assembly 81, 83, 215
Westminster Hall 112, 119, 141, 142
Westville (New Haven) 241
Wethersfield (Essex) 169
Weymouth 94
Whalley, Edward 235–48
Wharton, Lord (Philip Wharton) 38, 52, 75, 190, 213
Wharton, Sir Thomas 180, 190
White, Adam (historian) 203
Whitehall 110, 118, 139; in sense of 'regime' 136, 182, 190
Whitehall debates 68
Whitelocke, Bulstrode 37, 129, 130, 139, 140, 141
White Waltham (Berks) 115
Whitmore, Sir George 110, 115
Whitmore, Sir William 116
Whitmore, Thomas 115
Whitmore, William 115
Whitmore family 121
Widdrington, Sir Thomas 52, 130, 140
Wild, George 205
Wildman, John 62, 71; *Putney Projects* 62
Willem II, Prince of Orange 108
Williams, Dr John 207–8

Wiltshire 19, 20, 22, 131, 180
Wimborne (Dorset) 17
Winchester 158
Windsor Castle 220; St George's Chapel 215
Windsor Prayer Meeting 235
Wingfield, John 228
Winthrop, John 239–40, 241, 242
witchcraft and witches 163–73; familiars 163, 165–6; scepticism 164–170; witch-hunts and prosecutions 164, 165, 170, 171, 172, 173; witch-marks 166–7; witch-pricker 172
Wood, Anthony 209, 212
Woodbury (Devon) 17
Woolrych, Austin (historian) 56
Wootton, David (historian) 170
Wootton Bassett 221
Worcestershire 19, 20, 180, 228
Worden, Blair (historian) 77
Worfield (Salop) 17
Wren, Christopher 215
Wright, Nathan 96, 97, 98–100, 103, 104, 105
Wright, William 211
Wyndham, Hugh 128, 133, 134, 142–3, 144

Yale University 235, 243
Yarmouth 213
Yelverton, Sir Henry 190
Yonge, Walter 40
York 128, 134, 135, 136, 137, 180, 181, 183, 185, 186, 197, 208
Yorkshire 121, 135, 179, 180, 181, 184, 185, 186, 188, 190, 192, 194
Youngs, Frederic (historian) 14